First Edition

Leading on Purpose:

Emotionally Intelligent Early Childhood Administration

Holly Elissa Bruno, MA, JD

 **Higher Education**

Boston Burr Ridge, IL Dubuque, IA New York San Francisco St. Louis
Bangkok Bogotá Caracas Kuala Lumpur Lisbon London Madrid Mexico City
Milan Montreal New Delhi Santiago Seoul Singapore Sydney Taipei Toronto

Published by McGraw-Hill, an imprint of The McGraw-Hill Companies, Inc., 1221 Avenue of the Americas, New York, NY 10020. Copyright © 2009. All rights reserved. No part of this publication may be reproduced or distributed in any form or by any means, or stored in a database or retrieval system, without the prior written consent of The McGraw-Hill Companies, Inc., including, but not limited to, in any network or other electronic storage or transmission, or broadcast for distance learning.

This book is printed on acid-free paper.

1 2 3 4 5 6 7 8 9 0 QPD/QPD 0 9 8

ISBN: 978-0-07-337842-8
MHID: 0-07-337842-9

Editor in Chief: *Michael Ryan*
Publisher: *David Patterson*
Sponsoring Editor: *Allison McNamara*
Marketing Manager: *James Headley*
Developmental Editor: *Emily Pecora*
Production Editor: *Regina Ernst*
Manuscript Editor: *Leslie Ann Weber*
Cover Designer: *Carole Lawson*
Photo Research: *Brian Pecko*
Production Supervisor: *Louis Swaim*
Composition: *10/12 Minion by Aptara, Inc.*
Printing: *45# New Era Matte Plus, Quebecor World, Inc.*

Cover: © IT Stock Free

Photo Credits: CO-1, © SuperStock; CO-2, © prettyfoto/Alamy; CO-3, © Goodshoot/Punch-Stock; CO-4, Brand X Pictures; CO-5, © Digital Vision/Getty Images; CO-6, Brand X Pictures; CO-7, © 2005 image100 Ltd. All Rights Reserved.; CO-8, © Digital Vision/Getty Images; CO-9, © Greatstock Photographic Library/Alamy; CO-10, CO-11, Brand X Pictures; CO-12, © Digital Vision/PunchStock; CO-13, © Ingram Publishing/SuperStock; CO-14, Doug Menuez/Getty Images; CO-15, Brand X Pictures/PunchStock; CO-16, © Digital Vision/Getty Images

Library of Congress Cataloging-in-Publication Data

Bruno, Holly Elissa.
   Leading on purpose : emotionally intelligent early childhood administration / Holly Elissa Bruno. — 1st ed.
         p. cm.
   Includes bibliographical references and index.
   ISBN-13: 978-0-07-337842-8 (alk. paper)
   ISBN-10: 0-07-337842-9 (alk. paper)
1. Early childhood education—Administration. 2. Educational leadership—Psychological aspects. 3. Emotional intelligence. I. Title.
   LB2822.6.B78 2009
   372.12—dc22

                              2008039642

The Internet addresses listed in the text were accurate at the time of publication. The inclusion of a Web site does not indicate an endorsement by the authors or McGraw-Hill, and McGraw-Hill does not guarantee the accuracy of the information presented at these sites.

www.mhhe.com

*To Dr. Nelle Smither, Professor Emerita at
Douglass College of Rutgers University,
thank you for clearing my path with
your incisive emotional intelligence.*

About the Author

Holly Elissa Bruno, author, teacher, and keynote speaker in early childhood education leadership, describes herself as a "recovering" attorney. Having worked as Assistant Attorney General for the state of Maine, Holly Elissa was selected "outstanding professor" at the University of Maine–Augusta, where she also served as Dean of Faculty. An alumna of Harvard University's Institute for Educational Management, Holly Elissa teaches leadership and management courses for Wheelock College across the country. Her articles have been published in *Child Care Exchange* and NAEYC's *Young Children* journal. Her keynotes have delighted audiences from Budapest to Minneapolis, Tulsa to Tampa, as have her featured presentations at NAEYC, Smart Start, and regional Head Start annual conferences. For Holly Elissa, working with adults is as inspirational as working with children.

Contents in Brief

Contents

Preface

Early childhood directors manage through relationships. Even the most thoughtfully conceived, accurate, and efficient budget requires working with the board for approval. A director can mindfully create and compile her program's portfolio for accreditation. Without equally well-documented and artful classroom portfolios, cooperatively created by each teaching team, the director's work is incomplete. All the "book learning" in the world about diverse cultural practices and beliefs matters little if the director cannot build respectful, dynamic, and welcoming relationships with each family in her program. Book learning, essential as it may be to management, falls short unless communicated effectively to others in a way that they can fully appreciate. In the early childhood profession, people skills of management are as necessary as breathing.

For years, we have used the term "people skills" to describe what we now know is emotional intelligence. Emotional intelligence, the ability to read people as well as we read books, matters as much to the early childhood administrator as it does to each teacher in the classroom. With emotional intelligence (EQ), a leader is skilled at:

- Understanding her motivation, purpose, and vision;
- Embracing her strengths and addressing her blind spots;
- Knowing what inspires and motivates her staff;
- Building upon each employee's strengths, to help the employee grow professionally.

Leading on Purpose: Emotionally Intelligent Early Childhood Administration is the first early childhood textbook based soundly in the principles and practice of EQ.

Emotional intelligence theory builds on Howard Gardner's identification of multiple intelligences in *Frames of Mind* (1985). When Dr. Gardner described social and emotional intelligences, early childhood professionals were quick to translate his theories into our classrooms. Interestingly, however, Gardner's ideas were applied primarily to children, not adults.

Thanks to Dr. Peter Salovey of Yale University, the term "emotional intelligence" was not only coined, but also identified as an essential adult capacity and competency. Dr. Daniel Goleman translated the myriad scientific studies on EQ into a series of best-selling books including *Emotional Intelligence: Why It Can Matter More Than IQ* (1995) and *Social Intelligence: The New Science of Human Relationships* (2006). This textbook builds upon the burgeoning literature on emotional intelligence and leadership, now a crucial topic in both the business and academic worlds.

Do you recall the excitement about brain development research and its application to the early years of a child's development? In *Leading on Purpose,* research on adult brain development, thanks to the new field of neuroscience, proves equally fascinating. Finally, we can get to the root of how relationships work, from a neurological standpoint. For example, 65 to 90 percent of human emotion is communicated directly through our neurons, person to person, without words. We have always assumed that moods are catching like the flu. Thanks to recent advancements with *f*MRI (functional magnetic resonance imaging), scientists have confirmed that our "mirror neurons" actually reflect and mimic the neurons of the people around us.

Spindle cells, our largest neurons, make judgments about other people in a nanosecond, even faster than these cells reach "snap judgments" about things. Dr. Malcolm Gladwell's best-selling book *Blink: The Power of Thinking without Thinking* (2006) describes this "thin-slicing" process our brains carry on to make decisions "in the blink of an eye." Imagine how useful this research can be to the early childhood administrator who strives to build a highly functional team, supervise wisely, and help each family and child feel at home.

My goal has been to translate scientific research and theory on emotional intelligence into the context of actual early childhood practice in a reader-friendly style. In this way, the reader will see direct application to her everyday experiences. In much the same manner, *Leading on Purpose* translates and embeds crucial technical information about legal topics, budgets, and regulations into engaging real-world case studies.

As a "recovering attorney," I have learned over the years to bring case law and legislative regulations to life. When preschooler Cole's dad arrives under the influence of alcohol, demanding to drive Cole home, what are an administrator's responsibilities under the law? If a director is asked to give a reference on a former employee who resigned just before the employee was fired, what can the director say legally? Can a job description actually be written to include "maintain a gossip free work environment" as a functional requirement of the job? You will find answers to these real-life questions in *Leading on Purpose.*

I wrote this book after teaching the Early Childhood Administration course for Wheelock College over forty times in delightfully diverse locations across the country, from the Cherokee Nation in Muskogee, Oklahoma, to Boston's inner city, to the dairy land of upstate New York. My students have taught me so many things about how to make the study of early childhood administration come to life for them.

This book speaks directly to community college and university students in the early stages of their careers, as well as to teachers in the field, seasoned administrators seeking director credentialing, and people from other disciplines and professions hoping to found their own early childhood education programs. *Leading on Purpose* is the first early childhood administration textbook based in the research that 98 percent of administrators served as teachers before moving into program leadership. Here is a sampling of the book's features, which reinforce emotional intelligence principles and aim to build a relationship with each reader.

⚔ Features

- *Learning Goals,* at the onset of each chapter, provide readers with an overview of main points covered in each chapter.
- A thought-provoking *Case Study* opens each chapter and presents an issue that early childhood professionals commonly face. Case studies invite readers to consider how they would resolve the issues and utilize EQ skills.
- *Try This* 🎛 and *Exercise Your EQ* 🎤 icons are provided throughout each chapter and invite readers to immediately apply textbook theory to an engaging case study or to their own experience.
- *Practical Checklists* and *Guidelines* provide helpful, user-friendly, straightforward guidance about key concepts in early childhood leadership. Readers will find tips for designing a start-up budget, stopping gossip and whining, ensuring the safety of physical environments, and much more.

- *Marginal Quotes* provide inspiration and original perspectives on chapter topics.
- End-of-chapter *Reflection Questions* invite students to engage more deeply in the chapter concepts.
- *Team Projects* at each chapter's end offer a variety of collaborative assignments for students to express themselves and communicate their growing knowledge. The projects engage each student's multiple intelligences and diverse learning styles. One team project may culminate in a PowerPoint presentation, another in a video chronicle, and still another in a written "Guide to Local Resources for Opening Your Own Center."
- *Practical and Useable Forms* provide readers with ready-to-use models for supervision, health and safety assessment, budget formulation, and many other topics. Forms are integrated within the pages of the text and are available for downloading on the accompanying website at *www.mhhe.com/bruno1e.* Forms have been streamlined and written in user-friendly language, directly translatable to the actual work environment. Thanks to my colleague William Amaya, a businessman who founded his own center, you will find forms that are immediately useful both for study and in practice.
- *Websites* provide online resources for students to explore chapter topics of interest. Links to the sites are also available in the Online Learning Center at *www.mhhe.com/bruno1e.*
- The *References* section presents bibliography citations and resources for further reading.

Leading on Purpose covers all traditional early childhood administration topics, from financial management to marketing and development. The important difference is that *Leading on Purpose* recognizes and explores in depth the human side of management and the critical role of emotional intelligence in effective leadership.

⚓ Acknowledgments

I have written this textbook in gratitude not only to each of my students over the years, but also to the authors of all the other textbooks who have so well summarized the knowledge base essential for early childhood administration students. I have learned much from them all. The "value added" in this new textbook, *Leading on Purpose,* is EQ. With EQ as an additional knowledge base, students can learn to accomplish all the other competencies from budgeting to enrollment even more gracefully, effectively, and meaningfully.

Janet Gonzalez-Mena's work is my inspiration for this textbook. Her honest, substantive, and innovative approach to textbook writing is my model. Without Janet's encouragement and kindhearted prodding, this book would not be in your hands today. Other colleagues whose expertise and encouragement were instrumental to the writing of this book include Dr. Paula Jorde Bloom, Dr. Kay Albrecht, Gwen Morgan and Bess Emanual, Dr. Debra Ren-Etta Sullivan, Luis Hernandez, Dr. Cathy Jones, attorneys Arthur B. LaFrance and Linda J. Robinson, poet Barbara Poti Crooker, and Directors Larry and Julie Thorner.

My team at McGraw-Hill knew just how to push for excellence while understanding my considerable foibles and eccentricities. Ronni Rowland painstakingly read, revised, and graciously offered insight into every chapter. Emily Pecora's generous manner and compassionate note "Anything I can do to help?" was planted directly beside my PC. David Patterson's guidance and optimism early on gave me confidence that a textbook on emotional intelligence was not only useful but also needed in our field.

My family, both biological and by choice, have made long hours hunkered down at the computer not only possible, but memorable. To Nick and Lily Bruno-Hymoff, Richard Harrison, Wendy Dunning Carter, Marina Colonas, Hooray Childers, Diane Cecilia Alberti Gallo, Shirley Hamel, Johanna Booth-Miner, Ann Terrell of Milwaukee's "Embracing Diversity" effort, Kim Tice and her Ohio AEYC team, Lori Harris, Jo-Anne Spence, Liz Kendall, Jane Gottko Marcozzi, Eileen Bisson and the Boston Innercity Directors Network, Jan Patten, Cheri Boegemann, Susan Twombly, Evette McCarthy and her mom, Reverend Andrea McDonald, Nancy Witherill, Dr. Anne Arsenault, West Charlotte Senior High School, Marcia Farris, Joyce Hollman, Dr. Robin Fox, Mary and Skip Cecchinato, Dr. Ruth Marie Adams, Michael Gonta, Ruby Martin, Region IV Head Start's Champion for Excellence, Mary Budrawich and Jenn Woods, P. Gail Wilson and Buzzy Martin, Xavier Butler, Dr. Bruce Hull and family, Donna Rafanello, Toby and Walla, my love and my thanks. To my Mother, Louise Riggs Bruner, who left school in the tenth grade to support her family during the Great Depression, thank you for welcoming spring every year with a cartwheel across the back yard performed just for me.

To you, my reader, may your time with this book affirm your strengths, challenge you in new ways, and offer you support on your journey as a professional and as an individual with much to give back to the world, and especially to children and families.

The Pasture

I'm going out to clean the pasture spring;
I'll only stop to rake the leaves away
(And wait to watch the water clear, I may):
I sha'n't be gone long.—You come too.

I'm going out to fetch the little calf
That's standing by the mother. It's so young,
It totters when she licks it with her tongue.
I sha'n't be gone long.—You come too.

–Robert Frost (1874–1963)

Forming

Setting the Program and Yourself Up for Success

Leading with Emotional Intelligence

Learning Goals

As you study this chapter, you can look forward to reaching these learning goals:

1. Define emotional intelligence (EQ).
2. Apply the four essential EQ competencies for leaders.
3. Compare and contrast EQ and IQ.
4. Identify an "emotion blind" decision.
5. Discuss ways in which EQ can be measured.
6. Examine whether intelligence is inborn or able to be enhanced and learned.
7. Identify a "combination feeling."
8. Explain why EQ is especially important for childcare administrators.

What concerns me most these days are those people who think we must (or even can) bypass feelings in order to develop the great national resource called children.

—Fred Rogers

The function of education is to teach one to think intensively and to think critically. Intelligence plus character—that is the goal of true education.

—Dr. Martin Luther King, Jr.

Case Study: Transition Trouble

Amy and Jane have successfully team taught in the toddler classroom for five years. Together, Amy and Jane have shared a roomful of happy memories with children and families. Now that Amy has been named director, Amy finds Jane turns a cold shoulder. Amy counted on Jane's support in the transition from teacher to administrator. Other teachers also appear resentful that Amy was named director instead of them.

Amy wishes everyone could just stay friends, as they were before she became director. She yearns to make everyone happy. Amy is reluctant to say "good-bye" to the way things were.

Amy leaves the center with a headache, wondering if she made the right decision. "Is being director worth all the trouble?" she frets.

Before budgets, curriculum, and program operations, there is emotional intelligence. Perhaps one of the most overlooked, yet most important, skills for leaders in all fields, emotional intelligence is what guides us forward. In this chapter, we will explore how early childhood leaders can recognize and use emotional intelligence in everyday relationships and decision making.

❧ What Is EQ?

Emotional intelligence, also called EQ or EI, is the ability to read people as well as we read books. EQ is having the capability to acknowledge and understand feelings and to use these feelings as informational guides for thinking and action. We can not only "read" our own feelings, but also observe and read emotional messages from others. If you were given "the look" as a child, you know how powerful nonverbal communication can be.

Sixty-five to ninety percent of human emotion is communicated nonverbally. That means we need to become proficient at perceiving others' emotional messages through their facial expressions, gestures, and postures. In the same way, we need to become competent in perceiving our own emotional messages.

To lead "from the inside out," directors need to first understand themselves. Emotionally intelligent leaders willingly explore personal blind spots in order to approach others with humility, humor, and flexibility. Individuals with sharpened self-awareness are better able to read and understand others. Steadfast work at self-discovery will reward directors with sensitivity and patience in supervising staff and communicating with families.

The first three steps in the practice of being emotionally intelligent are:

1. Listen to and acknowledge your feelings. Ask: "*What am I feeling?*"
2. Accept that your feelings offer useful data. Ask: "*What useful information are my feelings telling me?*"
3. Identify your options. Rather than feeling blindsided by your emotions, step back. Ask: "*What are my choices?*"

Consider how Amy, the new director in the chapter case study, can apply these steps to her situation.

Amy's feelings about her new position, when acknowledged and identified, can help Amy sort out what to do. Rather than suffering from a stress headache, Amy can step back and ask herself, "What am I feeling?" "What are my feelings toward Jane?" "How do I feel about my new position?" By recalling and acknowledging Jane's rejection, Amy notices how angry and sad she feels. She also recognizes her own anxiety about taking on the new position. By listening to her feelings, rather than denying them, Amy takes her first step in practicing emotional intelligence.

> What lies behind us and what lies before us are tiny matters compared to what lies within us.
>
> **—Oliver Wendell Holmes**

> The heart has reasons that reason does not know.
>
> **—Blaise Pascal**

Amy's second step toward emotional intelligence is to learn from her emotional messages and recognize them as useful data. Acknowledging our feelings as data means we have feelings, but those feelings do not have to define us. In this way, Amy asks, "What does feeling sad and angry tell me?" "Why am I feeling nervous and anxious?" Amy lets her sadness and anger inform her that she is grieving over changed relationships. Her role has changed, and she has lost the comfortable feeling she had with Jane and her fellow teachers. Amy's nervousness can help her realize that she is uncomfortable with her new authority. The third step in practicing EQ will help Amy to prevent these feelings from defining her.

Identifying our options in response to emotional data is the third step in the practice of EQ. What are Amy's options once she recognizes she is angry, sad, and nervous? Anger is one of the most difficult emotions for service professionals to acknowledge. Eighty percent of childcare administrators deny their anger and avoid conflict, hoping that the problem will just go away. Amy can choose to ignore the problem and hope it resolves on its own. But most likely, it won't.

Alternatively, Amy chooses to invite Jane for a heart-to heart conversation. After a number of fits and starts, they "get it out on the table" and begin to share how they feel about the change. Amy and Jane can then begin an ongoing conversation about how to build and maintain personal and professional boundaries. Such honest conversations are not always comfortable, but directors need to develop the EQ skill of respectful honesty.

Amy, having stepped back from her emotions, is now freer to make objective and fair choices. She is no longer at the mercy of her emotions. She has made a choice to utilize a rich source of information. She has practiced EQ.

EQ and IQ Compared

Too little emotion can thwart or paralyze reasoning.

—Antonio DiMasio, *Descartes' Error*

Everyone has come in contact with the term "intelligence quotient," or IQ. Most schools test students for IQ in high school, and sometimes earlier. IQ is the traditional measurement of our capacity to think rationally. IQ measures our abilities to:

1. Combine and separate concepts;
2. Judge and reason;
3. Engage in abstract thought.

For years, IQ testing was the accepted way of measuring human intelligence. "The old paradigm held an ideal of reason freed of the pull of emotion," notes Dr. Daniel Goleman (1995, 28–29). This paradigm led to the stereotype that those who listened to their emotions were "bleeding hearts," "wishy-washy," "soft," and "overly sensitive." They were deemed to have "egg shell skulls," because they were seen as breaking down too easily.

By comparison, EQ is intelligence that takes feelings into account. "The new paradigm urges us to harmonize head and heart. To do that, . . . we must first understand more exactly what it means to use emotion intelligently," Goleman says (1995, 28–29). As an effective administrator, you will call upon all of your EQ and IQ capacities. Neither capacity is superior to the other. Historically, however, many individuals have been labeled as intelligent or not based solely on IQ scores. Researchers estimate that IQ works for only 20 percent of the decisions we make. The vast majority of daily decisions and interactions require us to use our EQ.

EQ is a much newer term than IQ. When people are asked: "Have you heard of IQ?" most respond, "Yes, I have." Far fewer people will say they have heard of EQ.

Not everyone has the same degree of emotional intelligence, just as not everyone has the same IQ scores. Some people with high IQ scores do not do well when their EQ is measured, and vice versa. Successful administrators need to use a healthy balance of IQ and EQ. Rational analyses need to be balanced with an understanding of the personal and interpersonal dynamics involved.

Emotion Blind Decisions

When decision makers fail to take emotional data into account, they make "emotion blind" decisions. Instead, only rational pros and cons are considered. Emotion blind decisions often make intellectual sense, but do not "feel right" to the people involved. Walls are swiftly built when employees feel they are being treated unfairly. Some of those walls take longer than the Berlin Wall to tear down.

Here is an example of an emotion blind decision. Recall Amy from the chapter case study. As one of her first actions, she may establish a policy for the parent and staff handbooks that forbids teachers from babysitting for children in the program. Amy's decision is rational, based on legal advice that the center may be liable if the teacher, while babysitting, unexpectedly abuses a child. After all, the parents hired the teacher because they relied on the fact that the center employed the teacher.

Teachers who have relied on babysitting income may feel Amy's emotionally blind decision to prevent staff from babysitting is unfair. Taking these feelings (anger, sadness, resentment) into account, Amy can work with her board and attorney to develop a "hold harmless" form for parents to sign that may release the center from liability. She also learns that effective directors give staff an opportunity to talk through their feelings about unpopular policies before implementing the policies. Emotional intelligence predicts how well directors will be able to manage others and themselves, and to foresee the impact of their decisions on other people.

EQ researcher Dr. Peter Salovey and colleagues (2004, 17) note:

> The emotionally intelligent person is often a pleasure to be around and leaves others feeling better. The emotionally intelligent person, however, does not mindlessly seek pleasure but rather attends to emotion in the path toward growth. EQ involves self-regulation appreciative of the fact that temporarily hurt feelings or emotional restraint is often necessary in the service of a greater objective. Emotionally intelligent individuals accurately perceive their emotions and use integrated, sophisticated approaches to regulate them as they proceed toward the important goals.

There's no way to be an effective leader or successful professional today without a clear understanding of the diverse network of people around you.

—Robert Cooper and Ayman Sawaf, *Executive EQ*

EQ is essential for childcare administrators, who "manage through relationships." Imagine the multiple ways that you could use EQ every day as an administrator:

- You comfort parents who fret over leaving their children at your program for the first time. Research tells us that parents most often feel guilty and anxious when they leave their children for the first time.
- You discover that you are unfamiliar with the cultural backgrounds of several families at your center and are worried about making a misstep. By "owning" your fear, you can identify steps to take to become more culturally informed.
- You acknowledge your embarrassment about not knowing enough about budgets and financial management. You ask appropriate people for help.

EQ Abilities and Competencies

Salovey, who coined the term "emotional intelligence" in 1985, now defines EQ as the ability to:

1. Perceive emotions accurately;
2. Appraise and express emotion;
3. Access and generate feelings when feelings facilitate thought;
4. Understand emotion and emotional knowledge; and,
5. Regulate emotions to promote emotional and intellectual growth.

Dr. Salovey promotes the theory that emotional intelligence consists of a number of capabilities, such as the ability to listen to our own emotions.

Given that one of every six persons experiences *alexithymia*, the condition of being cut off from our emotions, EQ is a needed ability in managing people. When we cut ourselves off from emotional messages, we not only lose valuable data, but also can put our health at risk. Studies show people who acknowledge and express their emotions appropriately suffer from fewer physical illnesses. Denying our emotions and their data blocks an essential process and places stressors on our body.

Dr. Daniel Goleman raised public awareness of EQ when his book *Emotional Intelligence* became a best seller in 1995. Goleman gave us language for what many have known all along: people skills are essential to good management. Whereas Salovey sees EQ as capacities (e.g., the honed ability to read nonverbal cues), Goleman defines EQ more as the characteristics exhibited by emotionally intelligent people, for example, honesty, integrity, intuitiveness, and accountability. Goleman (1995, 28) explains:

> In a sense, we have two brains, two minds, and two different kinds of intelligence: rational and emotional. How we do in life is determined by both—it is not just IQ, but emotional intelligence that matters. Indeed, intellect cannot work at its best without emotional intelligence.

EQ and Social Emotional Intelligence

The early care and education field has a history of studying and promoting social and emotional intelligence (SEL) in children. Dr. Howard Gardner's *Frames of Mind* (1983) identified "personal intelligences" such as self-awareness, sociability, and compassion. Children best develop these intelligences to listen, share, and establish personal boundaries when they are in safe, comfortable, supportive relationships. Early childhood centers work hard to create classroom environments and atmospheres that are conducive to all the ways children learn, making sure that children's feelings are heard and their relationships with others are healthy. Personal intelligences are as important to learning as the ability to identify the letters of the alphabet.

EQ confirms that adult relationships also require attention to emotional, often nonverbal communication, and the intelligence required to read those messages. This suggests that childcare administrators need to work just as diligently to create emotionally intelligent adult work environments, as they do to create SEL classrooms for children. In the next chapter, we will examine social emotional intelligence, the ability to "read" and relate to other people, in more depth.

For example, how can directors facilitate staff meetings in a way to bring out the best in each staff member? Women particularly can be adept at reading nonverbal language. Remember the message Amy got when Jane distanced herself from Amy? What message did the teachers get when they first read Amy's policy against babysitting?

When we ruminate or second guess ourselves, it cripples our ability to use EQ effectively. If Amy had called upon her social EQ, she could have created a more supportive work environment by inviting each classroom teacher to individually meet and share her concerns and hopes about the changes at the center. Once Amy has listened to each staff member and problem solved as a team, she most likely will ease the transition into her new position.

Measuring EQ

Just as IQ is measured by standardized tests, EQ can be measured by a variety of assessment tools. The most reliable EQ measurement instrument is called the MSCEIT, which was named after its developers, Drs. *Mayer, Salovey,* and *Caruso's Emotional Intelligence Test.* The MSCEIT is based on the theory that EQ consists of a number of measurable abilities, such as reading our emotions and those of others. The MSCEIT consists of scenarios that call for test takers to decide what they would do in those situations.

Great leaders put words to the formless longings and deeply felt needs of others.

—Robert Cooper & Ayman Sawaf, *Executive EQ*

"Bar-on" is an alternative instrument that measures EQ. Unlike MSCEIT, Bar-on relies on self-reporting. The Bar-on instrument assumes EQ is comprised of traits such as honesty, compassion, and accountability. Bar-on asks test takers to assess themselves, whereas MSCEIT asks them to solve problems and demonstrate their EQ. Both instruments are useful tools that can be helpful in assessing EQ. You and your instructor can decide whether your class will learn more about your EQ scores by taking one of these tests.

Assess your EQ using the test in the appendix of Goleman's *Emotional Intelligence,* or go online using the end-of-chapter websites.

Intelligence: Does It Result from Nature or Nurture?

Scientists often debate nature versus nurture. Were we born with certain capacities or do we develop those abilities? More often than not, our capacities are a result of both hereditary (nature) and life experience (nurture). For example, one out of every five children is born with a "shy, fearful" temperament. Studies demonstrate that compassionate encouragement by caregivers can help the majority of reticent children become more confident and outgoing by age three. In this study, nature was enhanced, and in fact altered, by nurture.

Assumptions are often made that IQ is an inborn trait. A child's IQ does not necessarily match that of his or her parent. Parents who conceive by use of sperm donors often request that the donor be college educated. These parents may hope to "stack the deck" in favor of having an intelligent child. IQ, in fact, can be raised by nurture.

In much the same way, EQ can be enhanced. In fact, learning takes place more rapidly and effectively in the context of supportive relationships. Simply being born to emotionally intelligent parents does not ensure that the child will be born innately emotionally intelligent. Again, nurture helps both children and adults develop their EQ.

Consider students who perform well on standardized tests. Does that capacity/skill come naturally or have they perhaps learned the art of test taking? Both are possible. One problem with IQ is that many people have been unfairly labeled early on by their IQ scores. My older sister, Karen, was told her IQ was not outstanding. She surprised herself and others when she not only completed her PhD but also went on later to complete her law degree. Was that nature or nurture, or possibly both? People who are like "bulls in the china shop" when it comes to emotional intelligence can also be labeled negatively. Sooner than later, bulls in the china shop will be labeled as lacking in EQ. With caring attention, a "bull" can become more adept and knock fewer things over.

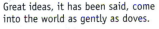

Great ideas, it has been said, come into the world as gently as doves.

—Albert Camus

Learning EQ Skills

Fortunately, EQ is learnable. We can study how to sense, identify, and work with our emotional messages. Imagine a world where everyone has this skill! Consider how your life would change today if you and your peers and family members regularly "checked in" to recognize your feelings. More of us would take responsibility for our part in making necessary changes.

As discussed earlier, the first step in using EQ is to acknowledge our emotional signals, rather than run away from them. Many early childhood classrooms have an aid to this learning right on the walls, a display of "emotional primary colors" that include joy, anger, sadness, guilt, fear, and love. *Self-Science* (1998) is a particularly helpful resource book on how to help children sense, identify, and manage their emotions. The self-science practice assumes:

1. There is no thinking without feeling, and no feeling without thinking;
2. The more conscious we are to what we are experiencing, the more learning is possible; and,
3. Self-knowledge is integral to learning.

As adults, we often have educated ourselves not to experience our feelings. Maintaining a "stiff upper lip" has been seen as more mature than crying. In childcare, in particular, many administrators attempt to be all things to all people. They focus so much on meeting others' needs that they leave little or no time to be aware of their own needs. How many of us do not take time for nutritious lunches or bathroom breaks, for example? Amy, the new director in the chapter case study, may feel she needs to put on a happy face, rather than allow herself to acknowledge the less comfortable feelings of anger and sadness.

Many of us learned to hide our fears, so as to appear less vulnerable to criticism. Some of us, for example, have a fear of looking foolish in public. I recall acting as if I knew how to solve a math problem in front of my high school classmates when I was clueless, and felt embarrassed. The shame of being publicly exposed is a painful emotion to acknowledge. Denying our emotions not only puts us out of touch with ourselves, but also causes other people to doubt our authenticity. Authenticity, being true to who we are, is an essential trait of successful administrators. This is why "leading on purpose" requires us to know ourselves first. Many leaders report that they still feel like imposters.

How Do We Identify Emotions?

Our bodily sensations alert us to our feelings. By paying attention to these bodily cues, we can identify the emotion we are feeling. For example, sweaty palms often indicate the feeling of fear. Some of us even experience feeling fear as if the hairs on the back of our necks were standing up. Adults and children alike benefit from revisiting the "primary color" chart of emotions and the bodily cues that accompany these emotions.

Every minute of every day, the gift of emotional data is available to us for the asking.

You can practice recognizing the physical signs of your emotions. Ask yourself, "What am I feeling in this moment?" Scan your body for clues. Are you tired, weary? These are often a cover over sadness or anger. Check the list of bodily sensations in Table 1.1. If you are experiencing sadness, what information does that emotion offer you? If you are angry, what bodily sensations are you avoiding or attempting to quash?

When we feel bored, we often have an underlying emotion of anger. After all, shouldn't this experience be more engaging? We might be angry that our time is being wasted. Acknowledging the anger is the first step to using our EQ. The next step is to open ourselves to the message our feelings deliver to us. "If I am bored and angry, what can I do to get connected to what I am doing right now?"

What we need more than anything else is facts about feelings.

—Don Robinson

Combination Feelings

Feelings often come in combination. For example, have you ever felt happy and sad at the same time? We often experience combination feelings at weddings. We may feel happy for the couple's optimism, while sad about some of the challenges we expect will lie ahead. The more accustomed we become to listening to our emotions, the more cognizant we can be of the complex messages our feelings deliver.

Another example of combination emotion involves jealousy and compassion. Think about the faces of beauty queen contestants when they do not win the crown. Part of their smile may be genuine excitement for the winner, while the lack of radiance in the smile reveals jealousy or sadness at having lost. What is an example of a combination feeling you have felt?

T A B L E   1 . 1

How Do We Identify Emotions?

Emotion	How to Recognize This Emotion in Our Body
Fear	Dry mouth, sweaty palms, and difficulty swallowing; tense muscles, especially at the back of the neck. Picture a cat arched with its back up.
Anger	Heat in the face, pounding heart, and surge of adrenalin energy; pressure to act immediately ("fight or flight").
Sadness	Lump in our throat, tightness in our chests, "misting" or "filling up" (tears forming behind our eyes), loss of energy, pain around the heart. Scientists have recently documented the broken heart syndrome, consisting of physiological changes that squeeze the heart muscles.
Loneliness	Coldness, yearning for touch/connection, aching heart. Isolation from others, feeling abandoned, rejected, left out.
Guilt	Need to look downward, away from people, to shield or defend your body.
Shame	Intense pressure to disappear or, alternately, the need to strike out against what/who caused you to feel shamed. Feeling unworthy, useless, undeserving. Like guilt, but harder to shake.
Joy	Light-hearted, carefree, uplifted confidence, head high, "walking tall," breathing freely, ebullient "bubbling" energy, sense that all's right with the world, "attitude of gratitude."

❈ The Value of EQ in Childcare Administration

Childcare is a service profession. Service professions are based in interpersonal relationships rather than producing end products. In a way, in early care and education, people are our product. Director Susan Twombly says, "We can help each child unfold to become who she or he was meant to become." As you can imagine, successful service professions depend on emotional intelligence. Health care providers, such as nurses, doctors, acupuncturists, and nutritionists, are all service providers. They provide a service of healing to their clients. Without emotional intelligence, even the most competent provider will not meet the client's needs. This is why doctors with a good "bedside manner" are appreciated. They utilize the best of EQ and IQ.

Childcare administrators work with several constituencies: children, parents, board members, teachers, custodians, bus drivers, vendors, volunteers, and community members. The product they sell is quality care and education. As you will see in future chapters, the best administrators utilize their emotional intelligence in every facet of their work.

EQ is free. There is no cost for the assistance it offers. However, the cost of denying EQ is high. When it comes to emotional intelligence, the wise administrator knows (as the advertisement advises), "Don't leave home without it." With EQ as part

When I dare to be powerful—to use my strength in the service to my vision, then it becomes less and less important whether I am afraid.

—Audre Lorde

of your director's tool kit, you will always have choices. This will be especially helpful during the down times when directors can feel they have too much to do and precious little time.

In the next chapters, we will build on our knowledge of EQ as we examine social emotional intelligence.

Reflection Questions

1. Looking back on your teachers and/or mentors, describe the ones who demonstrated the greatest degree of emotional intelligence. In what ways did they exhibit EQ? Give examples. What knowledge, or life lessons, have stayed with you as a result of your time with this teacher/mentor?
2. Keep a log for one-half day on how many times you practice "reading" your emotions. Record (a) the feeling; (b) the bodily sensations that alerted you to the feeling; (c) the information that emotion presented to you; and (d) the choices you made, having paid attention to your feelings. How different is this from your usual way of getting through the day? Which do you prefer?
3. List five skills you believe a successful childcare administrator must have. Once you have written your list, go back over it and describe how emotional intelligence is or is not an important part of that skill.

Team Projects

1. Read Portia's case study that follows and answer the questions: Portia has a "soft spot in her heart" for children with special needs. Portia served as special needs teacher for eight years before she transitioned to the directorship. Portia sometimes "takes over" in Inez's classroom, which has a number of children with ADHD (attention deficit hyperactivity disorder). Although Portia thinks she is helping Inez, Inez seethes from being "put down" and "edged out" by Portia. Portia often procrastinates about her other administrative responsibilities like placing orders for supplies and working on the budget. She says she "just loves those children."

   a. Describe the steps Inez can take to use her EQ to work through this challenge with Portia.
   b. What are the possible emotional clues Portia is denying, both from Inez and within herself?
   c. If Portia, feeling something might be wrong, turns to you for advice, what would you say to her? How do you think Portia can use her feelings as data? What steps do you recommend for Portia to take?

2. Imagine you are in Amy's position as the new director. How could you use emotional intelligence to prevent the problems that developed with peers like Jane and others? With a small group of your classmates, create a list of strategies about how to prevent unnecessary power struggles with colleagues.
3. Interview a childcare director about her or his successful experience dealing with challenging people (parents, staff, community). First, create with your classmates a list of three to five questions you would like the directors to answer. Interview the director (each classmate will choose a different director). Discuss with your classmates what each of you learned, specifically, how did the directors use EQ to deal with these dilemmas.

Bibliography

Cooper, R., and A. Sawaf. 1997. *Executive EQ: EQ in leadership and organizations.* New York: Grosset/Putnam.

DiMasio, A. 1994. *Descartes' error: Emotion, reason, and the human brain.* New York: Putnam Publishing.

Gardner, H. 1993. *Frames of mind* (10th ed.). New York: Basic Books.

Goleman, D. 1995. *Emotional intelligence.* New York: Bantam Books.

Rogers, F. 2005. *Life's journeys according to Mr. Rogers.* New York: Hyperion Books.

Salovey, P., M.A. Brackett, and J. Mayer. (Eds.). 2004. *Emotional intelligence: Key readings in the Mayer and Salovey model.* Port Chester, NY: National Professional Resources.

Shapiro, L.E. 1997. *How to raise a child with high EQ: A parents' guide to emotional intelligence.* New York: HarperCollins Publishers.

Stone-McCown, K. 1998. *Self-science: The EQ curriculum* (2nd ed.). San Mateo, CA: Six Seconds.

Web Resources

EQ Online Test
http://www.queendom.com/tests/access_page/index.htm?idRegTest=1121

Society for Neuroscience
http://apu.sfn.org

Consortium for Research on EQ in Organizations
http://eiconsortium.org

Directory of EQ Websites
http://eq.org

Emotional Intelligence
http://WIKIPEDIA.org/wiki/emotional_intelligence

Emotional Intelligence and MSCEIT Test Information
http://www.unh.edu/emotional_intelligence/

Comparison of EQ Tests with Critical Reviews
http://eqi.org/eitests.htm

Social Intelligence: The Neuroscience of Relationships

Learning Goals

As you study this chapter, you can look forward to reaching these learning goals:

1. Define social intelligence.
2. Discuss the history of our understanding of social intelligence.
3. Examine the neuroscience of social intelligence.
4. Summarize the neuroscience of group dynamics.
5. Explain the effects of being connected or disconnected in relationships.
6. List ways to disengage from "toxic" feelings and people.
7. Understand the danger in locking people into roles and out of authenticity.
8. Articulate how to lead with social intelligence.

I don't believe there's any such thing as meaningless communication between a caregiver and a child—not from the first touch or coo. Each, no matter how seemingly insignificant, adds to the stored experiences of all messages that have gone before. All this stored experience affects how each new communication is understood.

—*Fred Rogers*

How far you go in life depends on your being tender with the young, compassionate with the aged, sympathetic with the striving and tolerant of the weak and the strong: because someday you will have been all of these.

—*George Washington Carver*

Case Study: Who's in Charge Here?

Marvella knows she has a "short fuse." When she was in the classroom, she relied on her team teachers to remind her to back off when her buttons got pushed. Marvella has little patience for "high maintenance" parents. Now that Marvella has taken over as director at Count Your Blessings Early Childhood Center, a faith-based preschool, she finds that a lot of people push her buttons. Without a team teacher to help her cool down, Marvella slips easily into scolding parents about their "permissive ways."

A contingent of parents now depends on Marvella to instruct them in how to raise their children. Another group of parents tells Reverend Matthew that his director is getting out of hand. Matthew avoids conflict. He values Marvella's years of experience as a teacher and appreciates the "tight ship" Marvella runs. Her documentation, budget updates, and reports to the state are always on time and crisply efficient. His son, Ezra, is a toddler at Count Your Blessings.

Reverend Matthew, now aware he needs to counsel Marvella on overstepping her boundaries with parents, finds he is afraid that Marvella will lecture him! Matthew shares this problem with your directors' support group and asks you for help. He asks, "What would you do if you were me?"

Successful problem solving and conflict resolution require emotional and social intelligence. In Chapter 1, we focused on ourselves as individuals and discussed developing and using emotional intelligence. In this chapter, we will extend emotional intelligence to our relationships and identify social intelligence competencies important to leadership.

> Look honestly within, and you will see more clearly when you look into another's eyes.

❖ When EQ Goes to the Party

Directors need emotional intelligence in abundance in order to skillfully listen to their emotions and use that data to make informed decisions. "Director, know thyself" is the first gentle commandment in our profession. Building an honest relationship with yourself comes before building authentic relationships with others.

How can you have a relationship with your self? Shakespeare's Hamlet and Ralph Ellison's "invisible man" struggled to forge relationships with themselves. Hamlet's famous question, "To be or not to be?" illuminated his internal struggle with the external world. Ellison's character, a black man, suffered from being unseen and unappreciated by those around him. Both characters carried on rich inner dialogues, which carried them through perilous times and helped forge their identities. When the world outside grows inhospitable and contradictory, you can find peace in your inner world.

Do you carry on "conversations" inside? Those internal conversations can be fun, soothing, and enlightening. They also can be difficult. You can try to silence the voice inside, but denying it shuts down honest internal dialogue in a heartbeat. Early childhood leaders, like the leaders in Shakespearean plays, carry on soliloquies, internal dialogues with ourselves to find out what matters most to us. Clarity about how to act often results from being honest with ourselves in our soliloquies. Yes. You heard it here: talking with yourself is OK.

Leaders hone the ability to be progressively more honest with themselves. Honesty flashes light on our blind spots. Our internal conversation about those blind spots can free us from them. The more we accept ourselves, the better able we are to appreciate others. The only requirement for membership in the twelve-step recovery group, Codependents Anonymous (CODA), is the desire to have a healthy and fulfilling relationship with yourself and others.

> Keep a green tree in your heart and perhaps a songbird will come
>
> —**Chinese proverb**

> The appearance of things changes according to the emotions and thus we see magic and beauty in them, while the magic and beauty are really in ourselves.
>
> —**Kahlil Gibran**

✄ Social Intelligence Is Using Our Emotional Intelligence in Relationships with Others

> I've learned that people will forget what you said, people will forget what you've done, but people will never forget how you made them feel.
>
> **—Maya Angelou**

When we strip tthe veneer away, most of us simply want to be seen, loved, and appreciated for who we are, "warts and all." Walls fall down and resistance melts if we honestly and curiously listen to another person, especially if our first take on the other person was negative. In the space between my EQ and your EQ comes, we hope, social EQ (social intelligence).

Recall from Chapter 1 the EQ proficiencies a leader needs. As a leader, you will need to know:

- Your motivation and purpose;
- Your strengths and areas for growth;
- What motivates other people;
- Their strengths and blind spots.

Leadership begins with self-awareness. Awareness of others follows. By developing an honest relationship with your self, you will become better able to build authentic relationships with others.

> I cannot give you the formula for success, but I can give you the formula for failure—which is: try to please everybody.
>
> **—Herbert B. Swope**

The thorniest challenge for most leaders is how to work effectively with others while not losing a sense of self. The desire to make everyone else happy is akin to a bottomless pit. If you fail to look out for yourself, how can you look out for others? Emotional intelligence starts with self-understanding and self-care. The better we care for ourselves, the better we model for others how to care for themselves. *Emotional intelligence becomes social intelligence in the bridge we build to other people.*

Reflect on all the things that bring joy into your life. List at least three of them.

Chances are, relationships with special people are on your list. Being content with yourself frees you to be at ease with others. When you, as a leader, face your blind spots, you will have more empathy when helping your staff face theirs. With social intelligence, you can be curious, reflective, and nondefensive in relationships that might otherwise have been your downfall.

You may be thinking: "I knew that!" So many things we have intuited to be true are now confirmed by neuroscience research. Come with me to learn what our cells already know.

Social Intelligence Defined

> *Social intelligence* is a shorthand term for being intelligent not just *about* our relationships but also *in* them.
>
> **—Daniel Goleman**

Daniel Goleman defines social intelligence by comparing it to emotional intelligence. Whereas emotional intelligence is the art and science of managing one's emotions, *social intelligence is the art and science of relating to others.* Social intelligence is not only *insight about* our relationships, but *being adept in* our relationships. Social intelligence combines awareness with action. Directors need to be able to step back to gain insight into how to work with the entire team. They also need to be spontaneously effective in the very moment they work with another person. Neuroscience, the study of emotion as communicated through our cells, is a new field burgeoning daily with useful information on social intelligence.

"Neuroscience has discovered that our brain's very design makes it *sociable*, inexorably drawn into an intimate brain-to-brain link-up whenever we engage with another person. The neural bridge lets us affect the brain—and so the body—of everyone we interact with, just as they do us" (Goleman 2006, 4).

Margaret Wheatley (2002, 24) reminds us that technological advances do not need to take us away from the joy of sitting beside each other, drinking cups of tea,

TABLE 2.1

A Comparison of Emotional and Social Intelligence

Emotional Intelligence	Social Intelligence	Terminology Defined
Self-Awareness	Social Awareness	
	• Primal empathy	Being able to feel deeply for others; sensing nonverbal cues from others
	• Empathic accuracy	"Reading" the thoughts and feelings of others; correctly understanding others
	• Attunement	Listening with full receptivity; "deep" listening
	• Social cognition	Adeptness at understanding how the social world works
Self-Management	Social Facility (Relationship Management)	
	• Synchrony	Being in tune with the people around us
	• Self-presentation	Being able to manage our outward expression of emotions; "walking the talk"
	• Influence	Shaping the outcome of social situations; skillful and subtle use of one's power
	• Concern	Showing a desire to help others and acting on it

Source: Adapted from Goleman, D. 2006. *Social Intelligence.* New York: Bantam Dell, p. 331.

talking and sharing about our lives. The sweetness of kindhearted human-to-human sharing, Wheatley proposes, does not have to be lost to cyberspace. Our exercise of social intelligence has been around for a long time. "When we think about beginning a conversation, we can take courage from the fact that this is a process we all know how to do. We are reawakening an ancient practice, a way of being together that all humans remember. A colleague in Denmark stated it perfectly: 'It [reminds] me what it is to be human'" (17). Let's begin our investigation into the relational anatomy of our neurons by first clarifying the difference between social intelligence and emotional intelligence.

It is my personal approach that creates the climate. It is my daily mood that makes the weather.

—Haim Ginott, teacher

A Brief History of Social Intelligence: "Acting Wisely in Our Relationships"

Social intelligence, as Margaret Wheatley has reminded us, has long been a human attribute, but the terminology is relatively new. When soldiers in vast numbers were drafted to fight in World War I, the U.S. government needed a quick and efficient way to assign recruits to jobs for which they were best suited. The IQ test was formulated to measure soldiers' aptitudes, and the rest is history. The IQ test is commonly used to define intelligence.

In 1920, Edward Thorndike, scientist, proposed a parallel intelligence: social intelligence. In Thorndike's view, social intelligence is the ability to "act wisely in our relationships" (228). Attempts to test for social intelligence, in the way IQ was tested, failed. Without an EQ test like the IQ test, social intelligence died on Thorndike's vine. Soldiers were not tested for their ability to relate to each other, a crucial capacity then and now.

In the 1950s, David Wechsler formulated a new form of IQ test, called simply, the Wechsler. This test offered little to further our understanding of social intelligence, and Wechsler undermined the importance of social intelligence, declaring it to be no more than IQ applied to social situations. Rational assessment of others was sufficient, Wechsler shrugged. Try telling that to a couples counselor!

Later in the 1960s, psychologist J.P. Guilford crafted an intricate model of 120 forms of intelligence, which quickly fell off the radar screen. IQ, not social or emotional intelligence, continued to be the standard of intelligence.

Thanks to Howard Gardner (1985), multiple intelligences were identified and honored. Early childhood educators were quick to incorporate multiple intelligence theory into their programs and curriculum. In a field where each child is precious, no child's intelligence takes the exact shape of another's.

Originally, Gardner identified seven intelligence domains, including:

- Linguistic
- Logical-Mathematical
- Bodily-Kinesthetic
- Spatial
- Musical
- Interpersonal
- Intrapersonal

He later included two additional intelligences: naturalist and existential (spiritual).

Among the nine types of multiple intelligences Gardner described is interpersonal intelligence. This social-emotional intelligence entered our professional vocabulary and standards. Gardner's theory provides us with terminology for children's differing strengths and ideas for developing growth in all areas. Curiously, little notice was taken that adults, like children, exhibit and need a multiplicity of intelligences.

As of the writing of this text, research is under way to produce a valid test for measuring emotional and social intelligence in adults. Some day such a test may be as well known and broadly used as IQ tests like the Wechsler. The Profile of Non-Verbal Sensitivity (PONS) test and the Facial Action Coding System (FACS) were developed in the late 1970s to provide feedback and information on how to accurately read facial expressions.

No comprehensive EQ or social intelligence test to date, however, has been formulated, validated, and widely accepted although new options are coming available (Chapter 1). With or without the benefit of a comprehensive, valid EQ/social intelligence test, our job is to make sense out of the burgeoning neuroscience research on social intelligence so that information can serve us in our work.

> The prime source of nourishing interaction is authentic, intimate relating. Genuine relating is responding to the other and to his needs.
>
> —**Dr. Jerry Greenwald,** *Lessons from the Heart of American Business*

✗ Social Neuroscience

Research in neuroscience, a new discipline, is under way all around the world. Neuroscience is the study of our brain's connection with our relationships. It examines our cellular responsiveness to one another. Every encounter between one human being and another triggers complex cellular reactions in each person. Our cells compute how safe the other person is long before we offer a handshake, a hug, or neither.

Neuroscience is evolving quicker than you can say "social intelligence." If you have ever found yourself flat on your back inside a medical device called the MRI (magnetic resonance imaging), you have experienced the technology for this science first-hand. MRIs measure our response to stimulation at a cellular level.

In the beginning, MRIs were used to detect changes in our bodies that had already taken place. Since then, a new use for the MRI, called the functional or fMRI (f = functional), has become available. This functional MRI registers and measures our physiological response to stimuli in the moment. Lying flat and still in an fMRI machine, your instantaneous, complex response to the whisper of another's voice will light up the computer screen.

Your neurons' reactions spread like fireworks across the screen, indicating activated parts of your brain. Will your amygdala, the "fight or flight" region of the brain, register fear—or will your prefrontal cortex indicate intellectual distancing? (See "Amygdala Hijacks," p 18.)

Our neurons "know" things before we can speak them. For example, giving someone "the look" triggers entire systems of bodily reactions. We may have a sense that something is happening in our bodies. Our bodies, however, are way ahead of our thinking. Apply this concept to the work of an early childhood director, and we are in business!

Spindle Cells and Door Bells

Our brains vigilantly scan emotions of the people around us. In each nanosecond—in some people, less than two hundredths of a second—our neurons pick up signals from the neurons of the person beside us (Wraga, et al. 2006). The slightest tipping of the chin can speak volumes. Our words may have nothing to do with what is transpiring under our skin. This is the biological equivalent of giving mixed messages. A director may smile when greeting a parent at the end of a difficult day. However, every cell in her body screams: "Don't stay long. I need a break!" As Goleman points out (2006, 43), "At an unconscious level, we are in constant dialogue with anyone we interact with, our every feeling and very way of moving attuned to theirs." Social intelligence is the art of reading that subtext and acting appropriately.

Recently discovered, *spindle cells* are the most rapid neurons responding to our environment. Human brains have more spindle cells than any other species, about 1000 times more spindle cells than apes. Spindle cells are *big*, approximately four times bigger than other brain cells (Goleman 2006, 66). In their largeness, spindle cells are "rich in receptors for serotonin, dopamine, and vasopressin," the brain chemicals key to bonding with others. Quick to read stimuli and dominant in size, spindle cells "put the snap in snap judgment." When we examine decision making in Chapter 3, we will see spindle cells in action as we make decisions "in the blink of an eye."

Spindle cells ring doorbells inside of us. A ringing bell tips us off to danger or invites us to open wide the door. Our spindle cells ring in judgments about the people in our environment more quickly than about objects around us. We are about 1/10 of a second quicker to make snap judgments about people than we are about things. Spindle cells signal who is safe and who is not.

Mirror, Mirror in Our Cells

Partnering with spindle cells are mirror neurons. Mirror neurons sense "both the move another person is about to make and their feelings, and instantaneously prepare us to imitate that movement and feel with them" (Goleman 2006, 9). Mirror neurons do what their name implies: reflect the emotional cues of the people around us. Mirror neurons

We used to think that we were born with all the neurons we were ever going to get and that it would be hard, if not impossible, to change them beyond a certain age. But it's been quite clear for a while now that the physical changes neurons undergo when learning something happen to anybody's brain at any age. The brain remains quite plastic until we die. We are lifelong learners.

—**John J. Medina,** "The science of thinking smarter: Neuroscience can show managers ways to improve productivity"

When a good man is hurt, all who would be called good must suffer with him.

—**Euripides**

lead us to literally mirror the emotions of the person nearby. When someone is lonely, we feel her isolation with her. A person's laughter causes us to smile or laugh, too. Mirror neurons are especially useful in the practice of reflective supervision (Chapter 9) in which empathy plays an important part.

Have you watched a school of fish darting swiftly and harmoniously as one through the water? Maybe you have observed geese above honking and flapping in the chevron of autumn and spring migration. Perhaps at some primitive time, humans in groups needed to quickly fall into cellular harmony to survive together. Mirror neurons allow us to mimic the emotional movements and moods of others.

Our brains harbor a number of mirror neuron systems, not just for mimicking actions, but also for reading intentions, for extracting the social implications from what someone does, and for reading emotions. Italian neuroscientist Giacomo Rizzolatti discovered mirror neurons. Rizzolatti explains that mirror neuron systems "allow us to grasp the minds of others not through conceptual reasoning but through direct simulation. By feeling, not by thinking" (Blakeslee 2006, F1, F4). Daniel Stern (2004, 76), scientist in the Piaget tradition (Chapter 12), adds that our nervous systems "are constructed to be captured by the nervous systems of others so that we can experience others as if from within their skin."

We dance, by conscious choice or unconscious invitation, with every person we meet. Our dance can be graceful as a waltz, sensual as a tango, pulsating as hip-hop, or staid as the box step. We are neurologically wired to live in interconnection with others. Our spindle neurons guide us, while the mirror neurons align us.

Amygdala Hijacks

I call her Amy G. Dala. She's that small powerful gland in the middle of our head that can spike our hearts to pounding and our palms to sweating before we can say her name. Amy G. Dala (I find it easier to remember how to spell amygdala this way) has the power to supersede other neurological pathways. When the amygdala registers a threat, a surge of adrenalin or cortisol is set free to course through our bodies. In this heightened state, we lose perspective. Our attention is riveted on the present danger. Will we put up a fight or run away (fight or flight)?

Let us be grateful to the people who make us happy. They are the charming gardeners who make our souls blossom.

—Marcel Proust

Gender makes a difference in our response to the amygdala. Women's brains, when stressed, secrete oxycontin at a rate and pace that exceeds that released by men's brains. Oxycontin calms us. The release of oxycontin spurs the desire to connect with others. Under threat, women are more likely to take care of a child, seek out a friend, or sip a cup of tea. UCLA researcher Shelley Taylor identified this uniquely female response to fear as the "tend and befriend" response. Sigmund Freud's term, "fight or flight" has been updated and revised by Taylor's findings. Men are more likely to go it alone and rely on a distraction, like TV or a videogame. Women will call a friend (Taylor et al. 2000).

In either case, the amygdala gland has sparked the response.

OFC to the Rescue

Fortunately, our brains are equipped with an OFC, or orbitofrontal cortex. This part of our brain, located above our eyes and right behind our forehead, can calm or quash the alarm bells of the amygdala. Our OFC, when invoked, returns us to a calmer state. With the OFC, we can step to the side, take a breath, and reflect. This part of our brain allows us to regain perspective, which Amy G. Dala has snatched from us. With perspective, thanks to the orbitofrontal cortex, we can see more clearly and thus reclaim our professionalism.

Keep the power of the OFC in mind. One of the most powerful tools in an early childhood leader's toolkit comes from our knowledge of the OFC. More about this follows later in the chapter. Throughout the chapters that follow, examples are given of situations in which the OFC, if invoked, can empower a leader to act wisely, rather than default into a knee-jerk response.

Crowd Control: Neuroscience of Group Dynamics

So far, we have focused primarily on the two-person relationship. Now let's consider the neuroscience of crowds. Do the same biological systems and reactions click in with groups of people, as well as between individuals? Consider the following example: Have you sat in a movie theater, caught up with the story on the screen, when something surprising or touching befalls the characters? Chances are, a collective sigh or gasp rippled through the audience. Have you watched a football or basketball game with a group and felt the crowd's anxiety just before a big play along with the collective thrill or deflation afterwards? Watch the World Series or Super Bowl on television to witness emotion sweep in waves through the audience.

Crowds can behave as one, for better or worse or both. When Hitler spoke, he galvanized his crowd. When a country's national anthem is performed, many hearts beat as one. When the home team wins the big game, everyone watching feels united. When the team loses, collective surliness can lead to overturned cars and fist fights.

Imagine you are about to walk into your first official meeting with your staff. A collective mood awaits you. That group mood may be anxious, hopeful, skeptical, or all of these. Count on it—you can pick up that collective feeling in the instant you step through the door. The dance of neurons has now become a group gyration.

Goleman refers to this phenomenon as interpersonal "Wi-Fi." We are, he says, wired to connect with each other in groups as we are wired to connect one on one. Moods are as catching as the giggles of young children. Surrounding yourself with can-do, optimistic people will lift your spirits. Hanging around negative people will pierce your optimism. When the morale of an organization heads south, every individual member of the organization will be dispirited.

"In the interpersonal flow of emotion, power matters," Goleman continues (2006, 24). Those perceived to be powerful exert more impact, neurologically, on those who feel they have less power. Knowing that, neurologically, moods and emotions are catching suggests some changes in leadership behavior. Directors who acknowledge the potential power they have on others can use their OFC to ethically exercise that power.

Group dynamics can trump a leader's potential impact. When a leader wants to make changes, she may feel like she is "pushing a rope." That is, her innovation can fall flat as a three-year-old who plops on the floor and won't move. Been there and done that? Let's see how we can use this information on interlocking neurons to change things for the better.

Tavistock Theory of Group Dynamics: "Don't Shoot the Messenger"

After experiencing the devastation of World War II, a number of reflective professionals in London, England, gathered to come up with deeper understanding of how people function in groups. The theories they created became known as Tavistock theory because they met in the Tavistock part of the city of London (www.tavinstitute.org). The following example illustrates the theory in action.

The important thing is this: To be able to sacrifice at any moment what we are for what we could become.

—**Charles DuBois**

Come not between the dragon and his wrath.

—**William Shakespeare**

The feelings that pass through a group can bias how all the group members process information and hence the decisions they make. This suggests that in coming to a decision together, any group would do well to attend not just to what's being said, but to the shared emotions in the room as well.

—**Sigal Bersade,** "The ripple effect: Emotional contagion and its influence in group behavior"

In groups, much goes on beneath the surface that does not get stated in words. (We now know that neurons of each group member tend to synchronize.) At some level, everyone knows what is being avoided. Pressure builds for someone to state the unnameable. The person who volunteers for this task often has a history of being the truth teller or "soothsayer" in any number of group situations. The soothsayer puts into words what everyone feels but no one has consciously admitted.

If the soothsayer's statement is timely and appreciated, that statement brings relief and forward movement to the group. If, however, the timing is wrong, or the message is painful, the soothsayer will be shunned or silenced, usually by the whole group. This dynamic of silencing the truth teller is commonly called "shooting the messenger."

Have you been in situations where the messenger got shot? Were you the messenger? Describe an experience in which you observed this Tavistock principle in action. Did the soothsayer's statement bring relief or pain to the group? How might you as a potential leader use this theory to help your team?

Leaders who find themselves too often in the dangerous soothsaying role do well to let others speak up. Letting go of the soothsayer role may be difficult at first, especially if the pressure to speak up feels almost unbearable. Keeping quiet for a change allows others the opportunity to step up and take leadership by telling the uncomfortable truth that needs to be heard. Someone else's neural pathways will be alerted as you step to the side by relying on your OFC.

✵ Connecting or Disconnecting in Relationships

Laughter is the shortest distance between two people.

—Victor Borge

Humans, according to Abraham Maslow, have a hierarchy of needs. (We will explore Maslow in greater detail in Chapter 9.) Once our survival needs (food, shelter, safety) are met, our "higher" needs (love, self-esteem, spirituality) surface. The desire to be part of a loving, supportive, meaningful community is one of our higher needs. Connecting, feeling part of a community, is crucial to our health and well-being. Not being connected, or being excluded from a community, causes deep and lasting pain. A lone wolf, shunned by the pack, wanders the territory, unable to rely on other wolves for comfort or survival. In isolation, most lone wolves are ill fated.

Early childhood professionals are skilled at making sure that no child is treated like a lone wolf. Timid children are supported in learning how to express their needs. Bullies are helped to find ways to feel good about themselves without having to threaten others. Teachers model acceptance and respect for every child. Throughout the classroom, children and their teacher's neurons get in positive synch, and things run smoothly.

Building nourishing connections, adult-to-adult, adult-to-group, and adult-to-child, is the work of the early childhood leader. How can we use this new information from neuroscientists to further connections and mend disconnections?

Toxic or Healthy Relationships

When a person tells a lie in answering a question, he begins his response about two-tenths of a second later than does a person telling the truth. That gap signifies an effort to compose the lie well and to manage the emotional and physical channels through which truth might inadvertently leak. Successful lying takes concentration.

—Sean Spence, "The Deceptive Brain"

Therapists for years have counseled clients to change or end dishonest, harmful relationships. Harmful relationships damage both our esteem and our bodies. Studies show that our immune systems become compromised while in stressful relationships (Elias 2007). When we get "sick and tired" in a destructive relationship, our bodies become sick and exhausted. Marilyn Elias advises "how to quit your worrying":

- Seek out new friends who prefer to help solve problems rather than indulge in mutual hand-wringing.
- Meditate or pray regularly.
- Schedule limited "over-think" sessions: don't do it at any other time.
- Work on forgiveness and lowering unrealistically high expectations.

Healing relationships, based in hope rather than fear, promote self-esteem and physiological well-being. People in loving relationships live longer. The lower the stress levels in relationships, the higher the levels of contentment. "When we attune ourselves to someone, we can't help but feel along with them, if only subtly—even when we don't want to," Dr. Goleman observes (2006, 26).

This neurological mimicry suggests that we take action to build honest, healthy relationships and step away from toxic, unhealthy ones. Easier said than done? Fortunately, recent neuroscience research confirms the steps we can take toward positive relationships. You will find much more on the practical application of these steps in the chapters that follow. Let's look now at the basic neurological rewiring process for turning toxic relationships into healing ones.

Stepping to the Side of Toxic Situations and People

In the martial art of tai chi, the successful practitioner does little. Instead of resisting or fighting back, she moves aside for the opponent to defeat herself. If a person were to take a swing at you, and you quickly stepped to the side, the attacker would fly off balance and fall. The attacker's angry energy passes you. Your mirror cells do not mimic the other's negativity. By doing little but stepping to the side, you keep your balance and maintain your well-being.

> If you are humble, nothing will touch you, neither praise nor disgrace, because you know what you are.
>
> **—Mother Teresa**

This principle reflects our neurological functioning. As we step to the side instead of taking on another person's toxic energy, we gain perspective to keep a balanced approach. Even if the negative energy creeps up from within ourselves, we can still step aside to reclaim healing perspective. In gaining perspective, we begin to see the situation more clearly. Words of a reggae song describe this process, "I can see clearly now, the rain has gone. I can see all obstacles in my way. Gone are the dark clouds that had me blind. It's going to be a bright, bright sunshiny day" (Jimmy Cliff 1972). Our neurons, with the help of the OFC's functioning, can heal the situation and us.

We lose perspective when our amygdala gland gets hijacked. The amygdala regulates the amount of adrenalin or cortisol in our systems. Both adrenalin and cortisol are enzymes that speed up our metabolism so emphatically that many of us get into a flight or fight state. Each cell in our bodies is affected by the adrenalin or cortisol surge. When our amygdala gets hijacked, it robs us of the ability to see all sides of an issue. We enter the survival mode of hyper-vigilance and self-protection.

The amygdala can be knee-capped instead of hijacked. "Headed off" is a more accurate phrase to describe the intercession we can choose to prevent an amygdala hijack. We can "use our heads" (executive function of the pre-frontal cortex) to stop the adrenalin surge. In emergency situations, however, knee-capping (acting quickly and forcefully to short circuit the amygdala from being hijacked) works.

Using our heads to prevent our sanity from being hijacked is the same as stepping aside from physical attack. In an amygdala hijack, the danger on the outside of us (a threatening person or situation) triggers a dangerous response on the inside. Letting our amygdala run wild is not an option for professionals. We experience few situations as early childhood leaders in which "losing it" is an appropriate response.

When we step to the side and use our heads, we give our systems time to calm down from the initial impact of the threatening or toxic situation. Here's what happens in our neurons:

1. Spindle cells fire shots warning our systems that we are in danger.
2. Mirror cells spur us to imitate the mood/actions of the threatening person.
3. Amygdala gland issues an "all systems alert" release of adrenalin or cortisol.
4. The OFC (orbitofrontal cortex) issues a top-down injunction to amygdala to tamp down the raw emotional surges.

Our neurons in steps 1 to 3 carry us "in the blink of an eye" to a possible misstep. We may well be on the road to doing or saying something regrettable. Step to the side by using Step 4 to take a breath, and hold back from reacting. Doing so invites the rational OFC part of our brain to kick in. Our heartbeat ebbs back to normal, our palms stop sweating, and our professionalism can take charge. This is EQ, social EQ and IQ all operating cooperatively to help us be at our best as leaders.

We can use this stepping-to-the-side remedy when we feel threatened or locked into situations or relationships. We can step to the side to disentangle ourselves from toxic people and environments. "Some potent shaping occurs in our key relationships by repeatedly driving our brain into a given register. In effect, being chronically hurt and angered, or emotionally nourished, by someone we spend time with daily over the course of years, can refashion the circuitry of our brain" (Goleman 2006, 171).

Our new understanding of brain circuitry tells us this locked-in, stuck feeling is not a life sentence. A negative judgment one team teacher makes about another can be lifted. Habits are difficult to transform, but leaders play an important role in helping staff transform unhealthy routines into productive ones. If we are willing to risk the temporary disruption, we can break out of grooves that have become ruts.

Chapter 14 features case studies of difficult situations. A parent may arrive to pick up her child under the influence of alcohol. Such charged situations can trigger our neurons into amygdala overdrive. Fortunately, we have an option. We can step to the side in the "Ask and Listen" process to build partnerships rather than hostile stand-offs.

"Step to the side" is a leadership principle that evokes both EQ and social intelligence. You will be invited to call upon this principle often.

The Danger of Roles

We all play roles, don't we? Roles like friend, sibling, mother, uncle, boss, employee, and devil's advocate carry certain expectations. Playing a role can be comfortable. Expectations are set. When those expectations are met, things go smoothly. If Sahara is expected to take her family to her mother's for Sunday dinner each Sunday, Sahara has a role to play. If Manny plays devil's advocate at the staff meeting, Manny can be expected to bring up all the problems a new idea might engender. If Uncle Fabian's job is to quietly slip $5 bills into children's pockets, Fabian plays the role of benefactor.

Roles bring comfort, but they can also confine us. What if no one else will question a new idea because they are waiting for Manny? If Sahara wants her family to have Sunday dinner at home, Sahara might break a role expectation. Imagine the fit Sahara's mom might pitch: "But we've always done it this way!"

We have choices about whether or not to be cast in a role. A mother may be expected to stay home with her children. She may need to be a breadwinner. Or, she may be expected to be both breadwinner and mother. What will she choose, and will she be happy or unhappy with her choice? Breaking with expectation to be true to our selves, although disruptive, can lead to less slippery pathways.

Our neurons know all about roles. Repeated behaviors create pathways in our brains. Habits are grooves etched in our neurons. Grooves are etched when the same pathways are traversed over and over, just like a pathway through a park. As these grooves are deeply etched in our neurons, our behavior and our brain pathways align. Dinner every Sunday at Mom's no matter what becomes a well-etched groove. Not speaking up at a staff meeting becomes another well-etched groove.

Our neurons are also capable of forging alternate pathways. In fact, adult brains, like children's, have a degree of "neuroplasticity," or flexibility. For sure, children's brains are almost infinitely more flexible than that of a fully mature adult. However, assuming that

Strong people make as many mistakes as weak people. The difference is that strong people admit their mistakes, laugh at them, learn from them. That is how they become strong.

—Richard Needham

There comes a point in many people's lives when they can no longer play the role they have chosen for themselves. When that happens, we are like actors finding that someone has changed the play.

—Brian Moore

our brains are all grown up is a mistake. The PBS show *The Brain Fitness Program,* first aired in 2007, delineates ways our mature brains continue to adapt, grow, and learn. If you have lost the use of your dominant hand, you will experience your brain's adapting and growing process. After a while, you will find you can write adequately, if not gracefully, with your less used hand. Our resourceful neurons forge alternate pathways.

Roles come and roles can go. How does this apply to early childhood leadership? Consider this: everyone you work with has a role to play. But, does that role define who he or she is? We also bring our *selves* to work. Two different directors will act very differently from one another, based on their own identities, personal experiences, and passion for the work.

If we treat another person (or ourself) as a role, rather than a person, we may find a neurological shift occurring. As our neurons etch the groove of seeing another in predictable ways, the neurons no longer create new pathways. Some of their activity shuts down.

If we role-play our lives, we end up with myriads of shut-down neurons. Here's an example: Most of us treat a waiter or waitress as a role, rather than as a person. Our interactions are predictable. The waiter greets us, delivers the menu, and asks what we would like to drink. We play our "customer" and "waiter" role until we walk out of the restaurant.

The next time you order a meal, ask the waiter's name. Ask the waiter what her or his favorite dishes are. Refer to the waiter by name. In other words, engage the waiter as person, not a role player. Continue this until you leave the restaurant. Reflect on your experience. What difference did it make to build a connection, rather than sleep walk through an expected role?

Consider the magic in meeting, greeting, and working with each person in your professional life as a person, rather than a role. Your neurons and theirs will light up and fire away. You won't be bored. Better than that, you may find challenging your neurons in this way daily will fill your life with delightful surprises. Of course, sometimes, resting in a role brings comfort. The good news is that, with this understanding of how our neurons work, we have more choices.

> Being a director is a role; being a leader is each individual's pathway.

> Surgeons who had never been sued spent more than 3 minutes longer with each patient than those who had been sued (18.3 minutes versus 15 minutes). . . . They were more likely to engage in active listening, saying such things as "Go on, tell me more about that," and they were far more likely to laugh and be funny during the visit. The difference was entirely in *how* they talked to their patients.
>
> —**Dr. Malcolm Gladwell,** *Blink*

✖ Leading with Social Intelligence

Being an early childhood administrator opens a new door to each day. Challenges vary like the weather. Opportunities for growth never end. Burnout results from doing work that has no meaning to you. Our work is endlessly rich in meaning. We have little danger of sleep walking through our professional lives. Our spindle cells, mirror cells, amygdala, and orbitofrontal cortex will be busy like bees making honey.

Consider this:

- If you exercise emotional intelligence, you are on a pathway to discover your best and true self.
- If you practice the "stepping-to-the-side" principle of social intelligence, you build partnerships and bridges where stand-offs and roadblocks might have prevailed.

You have choices. Are you ready to explore more?

> The door to happiness opens outward.
>
> —**Søren Kierkegaard**

Reflection Questions

1. Take a day-long inventory of how many times each day you interact with others in a spontaneous, curious, and open way, as compared to the number of times you are locked into role playing with others (and yourself). Once you have gathered this

information, choose to approach at least one of your relationships more authentically and spontaneously, moving from role playing to authentic engagement. Experiment with this new behavior in an "old" relationship or role. Reflect on the difference, the transition process from role to real, in the light of neuroscientific information on building new brain pathways. Write a reflection paper on your experience and what you learned.

2. We all have an amygdala, that gland that stands at the ready at the hint of danger to trigger the alarm response in our systems. Once the amygdala takes over, we can forfeit our ability to keep perspective. Recall at least two work or school situations in which you personally experienced an amygdala hijack, either in yourself or in the people around you. What happened? Describe your experience internally as well as your actions (and/or others' actions). Reread the step-to-the-side information on page 21. Now, reflect on those experiences to imagine using the step-to-the-side approach (with the help of the OFC—orbitofrontal cortex). Record, videotape, or write a reflection on ways you might employ this approach in the future.

3. In future chapters, I will ask you to use your EQ, or take stock of your feelings and the information they are giving you. I will also invite you to use your social EQ to step to the side and find healing perspective in challenging situations. Think of a challenge you are facing today, one that you have not yet resolved. Use both your EQ and social EQ to help you identify and take three steps toward resolving that problem. As if you were recording or writing an act of a play, capture your internal dialogue on your process.

Team Projects

1. As a group, discuss how comfortable each of you is with people who differ from you culturally and ethnically. In what situations do you feel open or anxious? What additional exposure and experience would help you? Now, as individuals, take the Implicit Association Test at www.implicit.harvard.edu. When you have completed the test, meet again to share your ideas and feelings about the test and your results. How does this test relate to the concept that building new brain pathways takes more effort that relying on the grooves already etched in place? Share your observations with your classmates, and offer them the online information on the Implicit Association Test.

2. Early childhood professionals need both EQ and social EQ. Brainstorm as a team the many situations in which EQ and social EQ are either helpful or necessary. Select three of the most important situations (or areas like team or parent relationships) where early childhood professionals need EQ and social EQ. Create three case studies (factual descriptions that describe ambiguous or troublesome situations) that capture these challenges. Make a list of discussion questions to accompany each case study. With the help of your professor, share these case studies with the class for mutual problem solving.

3. IQ tests such as the Wechsler have been around for years. Talk with your teammates about what you think an IQ test measures, and what kind of questions might be on an IQ test. Follow up this discussion by researching the IQ test in a variety of ways (one way per team member). For example, you might interview a person who administers a type of IQ test. You could go online to find any questionnaires for IQ. Or, you can read articles on IQ or, for that matter, EQ tests. Share your research with each other, while discussing: In what ways is the IQ test relevant to the early childhood profession. Report your key findings to the class.

Bibliography

My thanks again to Dr. Daniel Goleman's extensive bibliography in *Social Intelligence*, from which I have selected many of these references.

Anderson, C., D. Keltner, and O.P. John. 2003. Emotional convergence between people over time. *Journal of Personality and Social Psychology* 84 (5): 1054–68.

Blakeslee, S. 2006. Cells that read minds. *The New York Times,* January 10.

Brüne, M., H. Ribbert, and W. Schiefenhövel (Eds.). 2003. *The social brain: Evolution and pathology.* Sussex, UK: John Wiley.

Canetti, E. 1973. *Crowds and power.* New York: Continuum.

Chartrand, T., and J. Bargh. 1999. The chameleon effect: The perception-behavior link in social behavior. *Journal of Personality and Social Psychology* 76: 893–910.

Codependents anonymous: CODA. 2008.

Denby, D. 2004. The quick and the dead. *New Yorker* 80 (March 29): 103–105.

Ekman, P., and W.V. Friesen. 1978. *Facial action coding systems, Parts 1 and 2.* San Francisco, CA: Human Interaction Laboratory, Department of Psychiatry, University of California.

Ekman, P. 1985. *Telling lies: Clues to deceit in the marketplace, politics and marriage.* New York: W.W. Norton.

Elias, M. 2007. Brooding weighs on mind and body: How you handle stress could be shortening your life. *USA Today.* May 8, 7D.

Ellison, R. 1952. *Invisible man.* New York: Random House.

Finley, B., and A. Aron. 2004. The effect of a shared humorous experience on closeness in initial encounters. *Personal Relationships* 11: 61–78.

Gardner, H. 1985. *Frames of mind: The theory of multiple intelligences.* New York: Basic Books.

Gladwell, M. 2005. *Blink: The power of thinking without thinking.* New York: Little, Brown and Company.

Goleman, D. 2006. *Social intelligence: The new science of human relationships.* New York: Bantam Dell.

Hall, J., and F. Bernieri. 2001. *Interpersonal sensitivity: Theory and management.* Mahwah, NJ: Erlbaum.

Hatfield, E., J.T. Cacioppo, and R.L. Rapson. 1994. *Emotional contagion.* Cambridge, UK: Cambridge University Press.

Insel, T., and R. Fernald. 2004. How the brain processes social information: Searching for the social brain. *Annual Review of Neuroscience* 27: 697–722.

Maslow, A. 1943. A theory of human motivation. *Psychological Review* 50: 370–396.

McCraty, Rollin, R. T. Bradley, and D. Tomasino. *The resonant heart.* Online pdf. Boulder, CO: Institute for Heart Math.

Medina, J.J. 2008. The science of thinking smarter: Neuroscience can show managers ways to improve productivity. *Harvard Business Review* (May): 51–54.

Neucombe, M.J., and N.M. Ashkanasy. 2002. The code of affect and affective congruence in perceptions of leaders: An experimental study. *Leadership Quarterly* 13: 601–04.

Neuman, R., and F. Strack. 2000. Mood contagion: The automatic transfer of mood between persons. *Journal of Personality and Social Psychology* 79 (2): 322–514.

Putnam, R. 2000. *Bowling alone.* New York: Simon and Schuster.

Rosenthal, R., J.A. Hall, M.R. DiMatteo, P.L. Rogers, and D. Archer. 1979. *Sensitivity to non-verbal communication: The PONS test.* Baltimore, MD: Johns Hopkins Press.

Seigal, D. 1999. *The developing mind: How relationships and the brain interact to shape who we are.* New York: Guilford Press.

Stern, D. 2004. *The present moment in psychotherapy and everyday life.* New York: W.W. Norton.

Taylor, S.E., L.C. Klein, B.P. Lewis, T.L. Gruenewald, R.A.R. Gurung, and J.A. Updegraff. 2000. Female responses to stress: Tend and befriend, not fight or flight. *Psychological Review* 107 (3): 411–429.

Thorndike, E. 1920. Intelligence and its use. *Harper's Magazine* 140: 227–35.

Whalen, P. J., L.M. Shin, S.C. McInerney, H. Fischer, C.I. Wright, S.L. Rauch. 2001. A functional MRI study of human amygdala responses to facial expressions of fear versus anger. *Emotion* 1 (1): 70–83.

Wheatley, M. 2002. *Turning to one another: Simple conversations to restore hope to the future.* San Francisco, CA: Berrett-Koehler Publishers.

Wraga, M., M. Helt, E. Jacobs, and K. Sullivan. Neural basis of stereotype-induced shifts in women's mental rotation performance. *Social Cognitive and Affective Neuroscience*, Advance Access published on December 7, 2006, DOI 10.1093/scan/nsl041.

Web Resources

What Is Social Neuroscience?
http://www.cognitiveneurosciencearena.com/whatissocialneuroscience.asp

The Brain Fitness Program
http://www.positscience.com/newsroom/news/news/120207.php

Can You Raise Your Social IQ?
http://www.parade.com/articles/editions/2006/edition_09-03-2006/Social_Intelligence

Facial Action Coding System (FACS) Online
http://face-and-emotion.com/dataface/facs/description.jsp

NOVA Science Now: Mirror Neurons Video
http://www.pbs.org/wgbh/nova/sciencenow/3204/01.html

Project Implicit: Take a Demo Test and Speak Your Mind!
http://www.implicit.harvard.edu

Social Intelligence: The Ability to Influence How Others Feel
http://www.timesonline.co.uk/tol/life_and_style/article640746.ece

Time to Toss Your Toxic Relationships
http://www.clubmom.com/display/245147

Leading on Purpose: The Road to Making a Difference

Learning Goals

As you study this chapter, you can look forward to reaching these learning goals:

1. Determine your purpose for your work.
2. Articulate your vision for making a difference.
3. Develop your mission statement.
4. Describe the importance of having core values.
5. Practice how to help your team find its mission and core values.
6. Utilize the S.M.A.R.T. method for turning your dreams into reality.
7. Identify your leadership style, strengths, and challenges.
8. Understand how to communicate with people who are your opposites.

One of our chief jobs in life, it seems to me, is to realize how rare and valuable each one of us really is—that each of us has something which no one else has or ever will have— something inside which is unique to all time.

—*Fred Rogers*

Two roads diverged in a wood, and I—
I took the one less traveled by,
And that has made all the difference.

—**Robert Frost**, *"The Road Not Taken"*

Case Study: Standing Out in Jamilah's Neighborhood

Jamilah's classroom purrs with activity. Senior citizen volunteer Ms. Maisie reads Thomas his favorite stories; Joshua and Trey paint a solar system awash with glittery pearl and gold shooting stars; Eliza and Mimi puzzle over where to dig a pond for frogs' eggs.

Although Jamilah is content with her work, she is ready for something more. She dreams of building her own school. She would name it "Jamilah's Neighborhood."

Looking around her community, Jamilah sees a number of early childhood centers, a Head Start program, faith-based nursery schools, and family providers. "They all want to help children," Jamilah ponders. "How is my dream any different?" Jamilah asks you to level with her: "What is all this vision and mission stuff about? All these programs sound the same to me! I want Jamilah's Neighborhood to stand out and be special."

Purpose is the heartbeat of our existence.

Before emotional and social intelligence theory came about, common practice for identifying one's purpose, vision, mission, and core values was linear and rational. A leader first identified the impact she wanted to make, focused in on drafting her workplace mission, and whittled down from there. Recent management theory suggests that finding our vision and mission is a far more internal, subjective, and individual process. Carter and Curtis (1998, 8) encourage us to search our heart for what is important. This chapter invites you on an adventure to search your heart for the leader you have the potential to be.

✵ Purpose: "Your Heart's Desires Be with You!"

Those who bring sunshine to the lives of others cannot keep it from themselves.

—Sir James Barrie

To lead by inspiration, a leader must first find and tap into her source of inspiration. Purpose is our deepest motivating force. Derived from our life story, purpose is deepened by the difficulties we face. A recent *Harvard Business Review* article (February 2007) encourages leaders to embrace the hard knocks and disappointments in their careers; authenticity is the reward.

Staff trust leaders who are true to themselves and who remain resilient during challenging times. "It's striking to hear teachers describe the contrast between directors who work with a vision and those who settle for how things are. The word 'vision' isn't always used, but they excitedly describe how their director really inspired them to work at the center, how 'she's usually got a twinkle in her eye,' is always 'showing us pictures or little quotes to expand our thinking,' or 'keeps her eyes on the prize even when the budget comes up short'" (Carter 2005, 1). Purpose gives meaning to our lives and intentionality to our work. Purpose gives us clarity in confusion, hope in discouragement, and courage to do the right thing.

Consider how Jamilah's purpose affects her actions in the chapter case study. If you asked her to define her purpose, Jamilah may tell you that she "was born to" instill happiness, respect, and confidence in children. This purpose will inspire her to leave the comfort of her classroom behind and establish her own school. Later, as she develops her vision, mission, and goals for her center, she will return to her purpose again and again like a hiker takes out a compass to find her destination.

Finding Your Purpose: The "Inner Longing"

How do you uncover your purpose? Author Stephen Covey believes each of us intuitively knows our purpose. "Deep within each one of us there is an inner longing to live a life of

TABLE 3.1

Helpful Definitions

1. *Purpose* is your reason for living, your deepest passion.
2. *Vision* is your dream of how you can change your world.
3. *Mission* is the practical way you will turn your dream into reality.
4. *Goals* are specific milestones for accomplishing your mission.
5. *Objectives* are steps you take, and a way to measure your progress toward accomplishing goals.
6. *Core values* remind us what we stand for, while making decisions.

greatness and contribution—to really matter, to really make a difference," Covey advises (2004, 28). Some of us have to dig harder than others to uncover that longing within, and the discovery process often takes a lifetime. No matter how much effort and time your excavating takes, be gentle with yourself. Your efforts will one day hit paydirt: "Choose a job you love and you will never work a day in your life" (Confucius). (See Table 3.1.)

To gain a clearer sense of your purpose, explore each of these activities:

1. Name three traits you had as a child that you still have today. These traits will help you identify your gifts and strengths.
2. Recall a time in your life when you felt you were doing exactly what you were meant to do. This is what living "on purpose" feels like.
3. Identify a person who noticed your potential. What did that person see in you? Others often serve as messengers to help us see what we cannot yet see in ourselves.
4. Describe a time when you experienced "flow" and did not need to think about what you had to do. You may have felt that everything came naturally to you (Csikszentmihalyi 1991).
5. Ask three people you trust and who care about you, "When have you seen me at my happiest? What impact do you believe I can have on the world around me?"
6. What contribution would you most like to make? Some people find it helpful to write the statement/epithet for their gravestone. Others think about what might be said at their retirement party.

Your turn has come. Let go of the need to be perfect, to get it just right, or the mandate to please anyone else. This moment is yours. Complete the following sentence. My purpose on earth is to:

_____.

For some individuals, a purpose will flow like a stream from the tips of their pens. Others will feel stuck. Still others will find themselves squinting to see a purpose that seems just beyond their view. Be kind to yourself. Wherever you are in this process is where you are meant to be. As children need time to grow, an individual's purpose needs time to unfold. Ask yourself, "What am I meant to do?" This will help you discover your purpose. Then ask, "How does knowing my purpose clarify for me the leader I want to be?"

When our inner longing catches fire with our personal vision, we come into our own as leaders.

Vision

Vision is your dream of how your world will be, when you are true to your purpose. Having a vision means taking the long view and looking at the big picture. As you envision the way you want the world to improve, remain true to your purpose as you interact with others and make daily decisions. Leading on purpose is the everyday, lived

As soon as you trust yourself, you will know how to live.

—Johann Wolfgang von Goethe

commitment to make your vision come true. Recall the chapter case study, in which Jamilah's purpose was to instill happiness, respect, and confidence in children. Her next step is to envision a special world where every child feels worthwhile and loved.

Stephen Covey's best-selling book, *Seven Habits of Highly Effective People* (1990), shares ways to successfully problem-solve in both personal and professional situations, a critically important skill for early childhood administrators. Covey's later book discusses an eighth habit, "finding your voice." Covey invites you to cultivate these positive behaviors:

Habit 1: Be proactive.
Habit 2: Begin with the end in mind.
Habit 3: Put first things first.
Habit 4: Think win/win.
Habit 5: Seek first to understand, then to be understood.
Habit 6: Synergize—creatively cooperate.
Habit 7: Sharpen the saw—stay clear and open to possibilities.
Habit 8: Find your voice and inspire others to find theirs.

Each of these habits will help you discover and hone your vision.

Everyone has a pathway that is unique. No one else has exactly the same vision of how to change the world. For early childhood professionals, their vision often focuses on making the world better, safer, and happier for children and families. When you know your purpose and have a vision of how it will manifest on earth, you are ready for the practical step of articulating your mission.

Each person's work is always a portrait of himself.

—**Samuel Butler**

Articulating Your Mission

Your mission is the practical ways in which you will make your dream come true, thereby fulfilling your unique purpose. Jamilah's purpose is to help every child know her preciousness. Jamilah's vision is to create an early childhood program where children are treated as precious. Her program's mission is: "Where children learn their worth as they explore their neighborhood and world." (See Table 3.2.)

T A B L E   3 . 2

Early Childhood Mission Statements

- "Our mission is to provide lots of love to the children whose parents have to work to meet the demands of the society we live in. Our blueprint for this Child Care Center is excellent education, love, guidance, and a home away from home."
  —*Baycrest Academy Child Care Center*
- "'Play with a purpose' guides our unique age-specific programs and curricula, each designed to move your child ahead developmentally, intellectually, and socially in an environment that's warm, nurturing, and fun."
  —*La Petite Academy*
- "A community that shapes and inspires children for the future."
  —*Kiddie Academy*
- "An educated society that contributes to an improved quality of life."
  —*Region 19 Head Start*
- "Provide a safe, stimulating, and nurturing environment in which young children can learn and grow . . . while focusing on healing from past trauma through love, support, and stability."
  —*The Salvation Army Harbor House Childcare Center*

STANDARDS FOR A MISSION. A mission is strong and true when it fulfills these requirements:

- ✓ Inspires everyone who hears it.
- ✓ Empowers staff to find their own purpose within the greater mission.
- ✓ Shines steadily like a lighthouse when storms bluster.
- ✓ Sets a standard for quality performance.
- ✓ Reflects our deepest core values.
- ✓ Informs every decision.
- ✓ Remains timeless.

Above all, a mission is personal, and true to one's purpose and vision.

Margie Carter and Deb Curtis, authors of *The Visionary Director* (1998), can help you discover your mission as an early childhood leader. Think about which bullet represents your highest priority:

- To provide a service for parents while they work.
- To give kids a head start to be ready for school and academic success.
- To enhance children's self-concept and social skills as they learn to get along in the world.
- To ensure children have a childhood that is full of play, adventure, and investigation.
- To create a community where adults and children experience a sense of community and new possibilities for making the world a better place.

- _____

(Add your own words here)

Find and examine your organization, college, or university's mission statement. To what extent does the everyday organization reflect the goals of the mission statement? Now imagine that you are the director of a childcare center and write your own mission statement. How does the mission support your purpose and vision?

The Value of "Core Values"

We all need touchstones. Touchstones keep us grounded. We touch them to remind ourselves of what matters. A touchstone is an object of value we return to again and again for clarity of purpose. Think of a touchstone as a precious sapphire, ruby, or smooth chunk of turquoise. Touching that precious stone can feel reassuring, cool, soothing. Core values are touchstones for your work.

A core value, like a touchstone, reminds you who you are and how you want to lead your life. Leaders who live by their core values act with integrity. Integrity is aligning your decisions with your core values.

One example of a core value is honesty. Leaders with this core value look without blinders at their opportunities, challenges, and blind spots. With honesty as a touchstone, leaders cannot hide in denial or procrastination. Lightheartedness, the ability to keep perspective and not take oneself too seriously, is another core value. Lighthearted leaders have an abiding sense of humor and are optimistic and hopeful.

Other core values include:

- Respect
- Courage
- Inclusiveness

Dreams are the touchstones of our characters.

—**Henry David Thoreau**

A core value is a standard we cannot live without. Core values remind us of our purpose, vision, and mission. We act with integrity when we align our decisions with our core values.

- Compassion
- Humility
- Hope and optimism
- Hard work
- Creativity
- Conflict resolution today
- Community involvement
- Families come first

I work with an early childhood leader whose purpose is to "let people know what is wrong, so we can make it better." As you can imagine, her core values are courage, honesty, and objectivity. What are the core values you could not live without? As you name these, consider your purpose. Your core values and purpose are close companions. List examples of your core values: _____,_____,_____.

Your Team's Purpose and Core Values

Teams, like leaders, need a mission and core values. A helpful exercise is for staff members to write down their individual core values. Then, they can follow that exercise by brainstorming their team's core values together. Core values of highly functioning teams align with individual team members' core values.

Ruby Martin, director of programs and services at the YWCA of York, Pennsylvania, leads childcare organizations through a process of finding their vision, mission, goals, and objectives:

> The process I use is very simple. It starts with the director of the center holding a staff meeting with all her employees and brainstorming what they would love for their center to look like. Someone during the meeting jots down all the key items the employees would like to see. The director then takes all information pulled from the meeting and places it into a paragraph-long vision statement. All employees receive a copy to review and edit and get their feedback to the director.
>
> This Vision is then used as a tool at the next staff meeting to develop goals. The goals are pulled from the vision: areas to improve, disband, initiate. Each goal is then divided into Action Steps where employees are empowered to take on the responsibilities for reaching the goals. A timeline is set and the process begins.
>
> I always encourage centers to hold frequent team meetings throughout the action phase to keep on track. After the vision is fully met, I encourage them to go through the process again about once a year to make sure they are always improving, growing, and remaining focused on areas important to them. This process also works to create a vision for each classroom, only it just involves the teachers and director. (Personal correspondence, September 19, 2007)

Ruby might also invite the team to annually identify their core values. She could post the team's core values and purpose in prominent places around her building as an inspirational reminder for staff. Team decisions are far easier to make when choices are based on agreed upon core values. Many potential conflicts can be resolved by referring to these touchstones.

The S.M.A.R.T. Method

The five-step S.M.A.R.T. method of visioning and planning helps leaders turn their dreams into everyday realities (See Table 3.3). Peter Drucker (1954) is often credited

TABLE 3.3

S.M.A.R.T. Method

- What *Specifically* do I want to achieve?
- How will I *Measure* success?
- What *Actions* do I need to take?
- What *Resources* do I need?
- What is my *Timeline*?

with the concept of "management by objectives," from which the S.M.A.R.T. method has evolved. The first step is to identify goals related to the mission statement. From there, leaders create measurable action items with timelines for success.

> *S:* Develop *Specific* goals that will bring you closer to your mission.
> *M:* Determine how your success will be *Measured*.
> *A:* Make a list of *Action* items that will lead you closer to your goal.
> *R:* Identify the *Resources* you will need.
> *T:* Establish a *Timeline* for meeting your goal.

Examine the S.M.A.R.T. method in relation to the chapter case study. Jamilah's purpose becomes real by using the S.M.A.R.T. method as follows:

- *S:* Jamilah wants to actively engage community members within the daily operations of her school.
- *M:* She will measure success by monitoring weekly sign-in sheets for parents and community volunteers.
- *A:* She needs to write e-mails and letters to parents and community organizations asking for volunteers.
- *R:* She will read relevant books and articles about establishing effective volunteer programs, and she will enlist the help of program staff in identifying areas of need.
- *T:* She and her staff will establish an ongoing volunteer program within six months.

Try using the S.M.A.R.T. method to set and accomplish a goal. You can apply the process to a rainbow of situations, such as a school assignment, workplace project, or issue with a classmate or colleague. Using the five steps, identify a goal and mark your pathway to achievement.

Vision, Purpose, and Leadership

Leaders, confident of the difference they want to make, inspire others to join them on the journey to make a difference. Effective leaders have a vision powerful enough to embrace the vision of others who work with them. Clear on their purpose, leaders inspire the best in others and invite others to live "on purpose" too.

Consider the chapter case study, in which Jamilah takes her enthusiasm with her business plan to her local bank. Jamilah's vision, and her S.M.A.R.T. legwork, inspire the bank-lending officer to grant her requests. That banker will delight in hearing about the progress Jamilah makes and will attend the opening of Jamilah's Neighborhood.

The best and noblest lives are those set to high ideals.

—Rene Almeras

Leaders are everyday, real, "perfectly imperfect" people (Pia Mellody 1989). A teacher is a leader in her classroom. A parent is a leader in his home. A child is a leader in learning all about her world. Leaders connect with fellow travelers to create environments for growth. Dr. Peter Senge calls these "learning organizations," spaces where everyone grows, learns, and supports the growth and learning of others. Does this sound like the early childhood profession? You bet it does.

Servant Leadership: "Paying It Forward"

Consider another valuable management theory in knowing yourself as a leader. This concept is called "servant leadership" (Greenleaf, 1970). Understanding servant leadership will help you move from self-knowledge to knowledge of what motivates others, just as your EQ strengthens your social emotional intelligence.

Servant leaders need not concern themselves with self-promotion. They know helping others grow helps everyone, including themselves. Humility is the servant leader's core value.

One theory of leadership encourages us to be servant leaders. These leaders dedicate themselves to listening to and enhancing the well-being of those around them. Servant leaders ask, "Do those served grow as persons? Do they, while being served, become healthier, wiser, freer, more autonomous, more likely themselves to become servants?"

For women and people of color, "servant" does not usually have positive connotations. Many groups have a history of being coerced into serving others, who have taken the service for granted. Personal dreams are left at some one else's door. This term, "servant leader," reveals the complexity of leadership.

Individuals who feel obligated to be leaders are rarely content or effective. When you choose to be a leader, however, you are doing what you are meant to do naturally. A servant leader, in the kindest meaning of the word, stands ready to work in service to the greater good. Servant leaders serve by choice, not coercion. Servant leaders acknowledge the value of those they serve. Early childhood servant leaders are committed to bettering the lives of children, families, and staff in their care.

Altruism, looking out for others, can be liberating if freed of codependency. Altruism is giving back to the world generously, freely, and without expectation of praise or recognition. Codependency is relying upon others for our self-worth. Codependents manipulate others to gain praise and acknowledgment.

Servant leadership is free of obligation and codependency. Servant leadership is altruism at its best. "Paying it forward" is another way to describe servant leadership. Like paying the toll taker for your toll and the person's behind you, you selflessly brighten another's life. When we are working and living "on purpose," we grace our worlds with our gifts. Servant leaders display heroism by freely offering the best of themselves to children, families, staff, and communities. Altruism leads to an inner sense of serenity and completion.

Take a look back at your purpose, vision, mission, and core values. Articulating each of these clarifies who you are as a leader. Now, you can look at your style of leadership. Knowing your style helps you communicate your vision and purpose to others.

✕ Myers-Briggs Leadership Inventory

The privilege of a lifetime is being who you are.

—Dr. Joseph Campbell

Each of us will have a highly unique leadership style. While directors are not fungible (interchangeable one for the other, like cherry jelly beans), directors can share similar preferences. You may find it helpful to know what you and others have in common, as well as where you are unique. A study of styles to find where you land on the leadership continuum can be enlightening. Insights you gain by learning about leadership styles will enhance your leadership EQ competencies.

Carl Jung, a Swiss psychologist, traveled the world to live among and observe different cultures and people. He concluded that, although we are unique, we also have commonalities. One commonality, for example, is that each of us is either right- or left-handed.

Jung (1961) set about identifying other human commonalities, or preferences. Some people, he discovered, preferred to lead quiet and reflective lives, gathering their energy from within (introverts). Others preferred to be social, outgoing, and gregarious, gathering their energies from the environment (extroverts). Jung placed these preferences on a continuum with two opposite poles. Right- and left-handedness sit at opposite sides of the handedness continuum. Similarly, Introversion and Extroversion anchor opposite ends of the preference continuum:

Right-handed..Left-handed

Extroverts...Introverts

Mother-daughter team Isabella Myers and Katherine Briggs translated Jung's work into a highly validated, easy-to-take leadership inventory. Millions of people around the world have taken the Myers-Briggs inventory since its inception in 1943. Myers-Briggs (also known as the MBTI) research provides us with significant insights into how leaders and their team members function.

Throughout the following sections, you will have a chance to explore your own personal preferences and temperament type. Although this material is not intended to be used as a scientifically validated assessment instrument, it provides an in-depth overview of the MBTI. The following MBTI descriptions are based on my more than twenty years as an MBTI practitioner and certified MBTI administrator. For additional information about the MBTI and online instruments, visit The Myers & Briggs Foundation (*www.myersbriggs.org*).

Using the following information, you will be able to assess your leadership style and temperament type. You also will be able to use this information to grow yourself as a leader, and help others grow.

Your Leadership Style and Temperament

Let's examine the four different preferences people around the world exhibit (Kroeger and Theusen 1992; Myers, McCaulley, Quenk, and Hammer 1998):

- Extroversion (E) .... Introversion (I)
- Sensing (S) ....Intuition (N)
- Thinking (T) ....Feeling (F)
- Judging (J) ....Perceiving (P)

As you read the information, you may find you identify with descriptions of each preference. An outgoing leader may also need quiet time, for example. A spontaneous, free-spirited teacher can also meet deadlines. Jung found, however, that most of us have preferences that place us more toward one end of the continuum than another. Leaders face situations daily that require them to be real and authentic. Jung called this our "true self." As you study the preferences below, ask yourself, "Who am I when I am not playing a role, such as parent, student, director, or

TABLE 3.4

MBTI Overview

Preference	Characteristics	Strengths	Challenges
Introversion (I)	Quiet, reflective, forms one or two deep relationships, thrives on solitude	Skilled listener, soothing, concise communicator	Public speaking, misunderstood by others, viewed as aloof
Extroversion (E)	Friendly, thrives on interaction, gregarious, welcoming	Enjoys team meetings, brain-storming, shares easily	Impatient with silence, difficulty listening, calls too many meetings
Sensing (S)	Uses the five senses to observe, concrete, down-to-earth, realistic	Notices facts and specifics, documents accurately	Misses the "big picture," doesn't like long planning sessions
Intuition (N)	Visionary, open to possibilities, "eyes on the prize"	Welcomes change, dreams "big"	Overlooks details, less interested in practical approaches
Thinking (T)	Objective, critical, task-oriented	Objective and consistent decision maker, direct communicator	Overlooks interpersonal dynamics, can "blame" others
Feeling (F)	Personal, process and people-oriented	Is able to "stand in another's shoes," promotes harmonious workplaces	Takes things personally, avoids conflict
Judging (J)	Prefers clarity and order, punctuality, and organization	Makes a plan and sticks to it, meets deadlines, neat	Can judge too quickly, perfectionism, dislikes surprises and ambiguity
Perceiving (P)	Easygoing, open to possibilities, organizes by piling things up	Adept at inventing alternatives, creates a fun work environment	Has difficulty making decisions, disorganized, last minute

Source: Adapted from material by Otto Kroeger Associates (OKA), Fairfax, VA.

daughter?" Take a look at Table 3.4 to assess which of each of the MBTI types better describes you.

⚔ Extroverts (E) and Introverts (I)

Energetic Gustavo, loved by families, is forever creating new activities for his after-school children. His team teacher, Emma, prefers to stay in the background. Emma is most comfortable helping individual children with their homework. Whenever Gustavo and

Emma attempt to plan curriculum together, Emma sits quietly while Gustavo enthusiastically shares one idea after another.

You are asked to help these teachers "speak each other's language." What recommendations could you make to help Gustavo listen to Emma, and help Emma speak up for what's important to her?

Have you noticed the staff member who rarely speaks up? When, like Emma, she finally shares her thoughts, she amazes everyone with the depth of her insights. This person is an introvert. She derives her energy from within. She prefers to think things through quietly. Introverts make up 51 percent of the U.S. population, making their extroverted counterparts the slight minority (49 percent). Extroverts are noted for their energetic, friendly, and talkative nature. They thrive on social interaction and prefer to talk things through with others.

Are you more energized by interacting with people or by being alone? The E/I preference identifies the source of our energy.

Introverted Leaders

Strengths

Introverted leaders bring well-thought-out solutions to problems. Introverts (I's) create quiet, reflective workspaces where individuals are free to focus on their work or play. Children especially feel soothed by an introvert's serene approach. Introverts are often skilled listeners. Parents and teachers feel heard by an introverted director. Introverts often "craft" their words, taking time to choose the most accurate, concise way to communicate. An introverted director is comfortable with silence.

Challenges for Introverted Leaders

Constant verbal interactions drain an introvert's energy. Public speaking, even addressing a parent group, can exhaust an introverted leader. Introverted leaders can be seen as aloof or uninterested in the ideas of others. Some staff believe introverted administrators withhold information. I's need private time to recharge their batteries. They may avoid brainstorming sessions, when many people talk at once. I's sometimes "pretend" to be extroverts to be able to perform their duties.

TIPS for Introverted Leaders

1. Take quiet time each day for yourself. Recharge your internal batteries. Take a walk, read a book, close your door to meditate.
2. Tell staff: "Thanks for sharing that with me. I need time to consider what you said. I'll get back to you tomorrow morning."
3. Distribute agendas for staff meetings in advance. Introverted individuals need time to reflect on agenda items.
4. When conducting staff meetings, invite staff to work in small groups, especially groups of two. This practice ensures that introverts will have a chance to speak.

Communicating with Extroverts

1. Ask extroverts questions. Listen for the main points. Let go of expecting yourself to take in every word an extrovert utters.
2. Look for an extrovert's strengths, rather than stereotype her as "loud mouthed," "pushy," or a "bulldozer."
3. Find ways to enjoy an extrovert's upbeat energy. Show enthusiasm for her ideas.
4. Communicate as spontaneously as you feel able. Avoid long silences.

Exroverted Leaders

Strengths

Extroverted leaders are friendly, gregarious, and welcoming. Extroverts actively engage with everyone and everything. Comfortable expressing what is on their minds, extroverts

Extroverts derive their energy from a source different from an introvert's energy source. Extroverts gain energy through engaging with people and activity around them. Introverts prefer to find their energy inside.

talk things out to learn what they are thinking. By contrast, introverts think before they talk. Extroverts are at home at brainstorming sessions, team meetings, and social events. Extroverts thrive in lively environments.

Challenges for Extroverts

Extroverts, by virtue of their high energy and need to engage others, can overwhelm introverts. Extroverts, almost one-half of the U.S. population, can assume that everyone should be outgoing, active conversationalists. Extroverts can ask questions and not wait for the introvert's thoughtful response. In fact, extroverts often answer for introverts. Extroverts call meetings frequently, not thinking of how uncomfortable groups can be for introverted employees. Extroverts may be impatient with silence and lose energy when separated from others.

Tips for Extroverts

Extroverts bring upbeat, positive, sometimes ebullient (bubbling) energy to the workplace. Extroverts need to maintain networks of diverse friends and acquaintances outside their programs. If you are an extrovert who works primarily with introverts, use the phone, e-mail, or instant messaging to keep your energy high. Practice your active listening skills to connect with introverts. Remember 65 to 90 percent of emotion is communicated nonverbally. Use your social EQ to appreciate introverted staff. Listening fully to an introvert helps her trust you.

Communicating with Introverts

1. Count to 10 slowly before you answer a question for an introvert. Give introverts time to think.
2. Distribute agendas in advance of meetings to allow introverts preparation time.
3. Schedule individual and one-on-one activities, to balance team meetings.
4. Devote time to inviting the introvert to get to know and trust you.

Assessing Yourself

Where do you get your energy? Do you prefer to actively engage with others, or to quietly reflect by yourself? You may be both an introvert and an extrovert. For purposes of this assessment, select the letter that more accurately describes you.

Question 1: Are you more of an extrovert than an introvert? <u>E</u> _ _ _, or <u>I</u> _ _ _? Fill in the first blank from the left with the letter that indicates your preference. __ __ __ __

You now have determined 25 percent of your MBTI type. If you feel in the middle on this preference, ask yourself, "Which preference could I not live without?" Extroverts, for example, need people around them. Introverts cannot live without frequent, regular time alone, away from all the bustle.

✣ Sensing and Intuition

Serena concentrates on recording every detail accurately for the classroom newsletter, while Roxie keeps coming up with new ideas to include. Serena feels Roxie "upsets the apple cart" and Roxie thinks Serena is a "wet blanket." In fact, Roxie gets bored when she has to focus on details, while Serena feels confused by Roxie's constant innovations.

How can these teachers build upon each other's strengths in creating the monthly classroom newsletter for families?

Jung said we observe the world in one of two different ways. Some of us, skilled at accurate observation, use our five senses to take in facts and details. Others of us prefer using our imagination when observing. These people look for meaning, inspiration, or an unfolding story. Jung's second preference identifies how we take in information and perceive our world.

Seventy-three percent of us prefer to take in information in the "sensing way," noticing facts and specifics. Sensors observe the shape, size, smell, taste, texture, color, and sound of their environment.

Observers who notice specific details are called sensors (S). Observers who see connections, meaning, and possibilities are iNtuitors (N). *Sensors see the trees not the forest. Intuitors see the forest, not the trees.*

Sensors

Strengths

Sensors tend to remember details, including names. Concrete and down-to-earth, sensors are realistic. They report what they observe in accurate detail. In terms of learning styles, sensors learn better when information is presented sequentially, in order, detailing the steps involved. Sensors live in the present and use common sense to create practical solutions. The majority of U.S. presidents have been sensors.

A Head Start slogan is, "If it isn't documented, it didn't happen!" Documentation records the who, what, when, and where of events. Documentation rarely requires the why. Describing exactly what happened in a factual way is essential in reporting children's behavior. Sensors perceive the world in this concrete way.

Challenges

Because sensors notice details, sensing directors can miss the big picture. Planning for the future is uncomfortable for sensors. Sensors focus on what is directly in front of them. When a sensor works with a nonsensing team teacher, the sensing teacher might think her teammate has her head in the clouds or "is a space shot." Sensors can be disoriented when given vague or scant instructions. If asked to plan a holiday party, the sensor will be adrift if she is not given all the details. Her opposite, the intuitor, is more likely to run with a less detailed request. Intuitors will be intrigued by all the possibilities.

Tips for Sensors

Find ways to enjoy the free-spiritedness of your intuitive colleagues. Let them help you see the forest, and not just the trees. Ask them to help you understand how they see things. Sensors tend to be pessimistic; intuitors, who focus on the future, are optimistic. Enjoy the intuitor's upbeat approach. At the same time, value your preference to "tell it like it is" and to accurately observe what is in front of you. Documentation may come easier for you than others. Use your preference to create useful templates and report forms.

Communicating with Intuitors

1. Summarize your main idea first. Hold detailed explanations for later.
2. Identify how your idea will create a brighter future.
3. Let go of expecting intuitors to work methodically: intuitors thrive on novelty and innovation.
4. Allow intuitor's imaginations to soar: do not insist on detailed, sequential explanations.
5. Learn from the intuitor's ability to see connections that you might miss.

Intuitors are like brightly colored helium balloons lifting toward the skies. Sensors are the strings that hold the balloons in place. Sensors and intuitors need one another.

Intuitors

Strengths

Intuitors prefer the big picture, always on the lookout for possibilities. Intuitive leaders keep their eyes on the prize. While sensors prefer familiar practices, intuitors welcome novelty and change. Even though only 27 percent of the U.S. population are intuitors, as visionaries, they have major influence. Martin Luther King, Jr., Gandhi, John and Robert Kennedy, and Abraham Lincoln were intuitors who dreamed of making the world better. Intuitive leaders lift an organization out of the doldrums by inviting employees to step back, gain perspective, and envision positive change.

Challenges

Just as sensors miss the forest for the trees, intuitors miss the trees for the forest. Intuitors, looking for deeper meaning, miss the puddle right in front of them. Intuitors, preferring novelty, can be less suited to taking practical, pragmatic approaches. Intuitors and sensors hear each other's words differently. A common dispute between an intuitor teacher and his sensor team teacher goes like this: "That's not what I meant," sighs the intuitor. "But that's what you said," argues the sensor.

Tips for Intuitors

Acknowledge that the majority of people do not see things the way you do. Pay attention to the details of a situation, and look for the facts. Be ready to "speak the language" of sensors if you want to be understood better. Honor your visionary, optimistic approach, even when those around you are less enthusiastic. Remember, moods are catching. Maintain your hopeful view of the future, and you will uplift and inspire others.

Communicating with Sensors

1. Be practical and pragmatic.
2. Use facts and figures to support your ideas. Give concrete examples.
3. Document your experience in detail.
4. State the steps to be taken to reach the goal in order.

Intuitive students, unlike sensors, do not need teachers to present information sequentially. Intuitors learn when the instructor and/or the subject matter sparks the intuitor's imagination.

Assessing Yourself

What is your preferred way to observe situations? Are you factual and realistic (S), or imaginative (N) and looking for deeper meaning? Early childhood professionals, schooled in documentation practices, learn sensing skills. Being skilled as a sensor does not make you a sensor. Ask yourself: "When I look at something new, do I prefer to see possibilities, or details?"

Question 2: Are you a sensor or an intuitor? _ S _ , or _ N _ _? Place the letter that describes you in the blank that is second from the left. E/I __ __ __

You have determined 50 percent of your MBTI type.

⚔ Thinking and Feeling

Like a duck, every thing rolls off lead teacher Phillipe's back. Phillipe has no time for gossip, and no problem telling people what he thinks. In fact, when Phillipe has a problem with another person, he walks directly up to that person and says, "We need to talk." Other teachers, hurt by or uncomfortable with Phillipe's directness, avoid or placate him. Raylene refuses to speak with him entirely because he is so "insensitive" to people's feelings.

How would you coach these teachers to communicate with one another? Jung's third preference identifies the different ways we make decisions. Some of us (40 percent of the U.S. population and 56.5 percent of U.S. males) prefer to decide things impersonally, by taking an objective, critical approach. Jung named this preference, the thinking (T) preference. Others (60 percent of the U.S. population and 75.5 percent of females) prefer to make decisions more personally, by taking into account each individual's needs, situation, and history. They prefer the feeling (F) decision-making process.

Thinkers

Strengths

Thinkers bring objectivity, clarity, and emotional distance to decision making. A thinker can be counted on to treat everyone fairly. That is, the thinker will not favor one person over another. Thinkers make decisions quickly, unfettered by second guessing themselves. Thinkers often are able to make direct statements, without worrying first about whether the truth will hurt people's feelings. This is not to say that thinkers do not have feelings. Thinkers "rise above" their feelings to make objective decisions. In fact, thinkers are tireless in their pursuit of the objective truth. Thinkers are more task than process oriented.

> Thinkers decide things "evenhandedly," that is, with consistency. Feelers pay attention to individual circumstances. Thinkers use the "letter of the law" process, whereas feelers use the "spirit of the law" approach (Chapter 4).

Challenges

Thinkers, focused on getting the job done, tend to overlook interpersonal data and dynamics. Thinkers, who believe in cause and effect, can "blame" the person perceived to be responsible. Thinkers fail to notice nonverbal cues of coworkers. Thinkers may not be aware of the subtle dynamics that go into building trust between individuals or in teamwork. Thinkers can perceive feelers as "bleeding hearts."

Tips for Thinkers

You may be perceived as "cold" or "overly analytical" in a field that is highly relational. Investigate how to enhance your emotional and social intelligence. Practice noticing and reading nonverbal behavior. Praise staff more readily. According to the Department of Labor statistics, the majority of people who resign do so because they feel underappreciated. Acknowledge employees' strengths and contributions. Practice active listening skills. Slow down your pace. Colleagues need time to "process" how they will work together. Tasks will be accomplished much more easily when you build trusting relationships.

Communicating with Feelers

1. Invest time in building relationships. Find out and ask about what matters to them.
2. Focus on how an idea can improve the quality of people's lives, rather than just focusing on the logic of the decision.
3. Acknowledge that the majority of your colleagues are uncomfortable with conflict. Help feelers focus on common goals in addressing disagreements.

4. Pay attention to how you communicate.
5. Staff members "take things personally." Give them time to talk about their feelings with you. Honor those feelings.

Feelers

Strengths

Feelers are devoted to building a harmonious, comfortable, and supportive workplace environment. A feeler automatically steps up to welcome a new person and help her feel at ease. Feelers pay attention to unspoken clues and signs such as tone of voice, "eye," and body language. Expect a feeler to read people on many levels. Dedicated to making decisions that are compassionate, feelers take everyone's needs and individual circumstances into account.

Challenges

Conflict is often painful for feelers, who can get their feelings hurt more easily than thinkers. Feelers try to avoid confrontation at any cost. Being conflict avoidant leads to misunderstanding, distancing, and indirect behavior such as talking about another person, rather than to her directly. Feelers work well with people they trust. Trust is built by sharing personal information, likes and dislikes. Thinkers who focus on tasks, rather than relationships, can find working with feelers to be overly complicated. Feelers may smile. However, if a feeler doesn't trust you, she won't work with you easily.

Tips for Feelers

Carry a Q-TIP as a reminder to "Quit taking it personally." Not every problem is about you. Feelers focus so much on other peoples' needs that feelers tend to neglect their own needs. Take time to do what you love, even if that means not always saying "yes" to helping out. In the end, with your renewed spirit, you will find you have much more energy to share. Feelers who give themselves away can end up feeling like martyrs with resentments. Practice ways to deal directly with conflicts. Resentments bring feelers down from their usual cordial, friendly ways.

Communicating with Thinkers

1. List the pros and cons for each idea you present. Thinkers base decisions on objective analysis.
2. Make your main point quickly and concisely.
3. Back up your point with objective ideas and supporting facts.
4. Commit to addressing conflicts directly with others. Set a time limit by which you will step up to face each conflict.
5. Use your EQ to identify your feelings, and be open to the data feelings offer. If you find yourself nursing hurt feelings, "step to the side" to look at the situation objectively.
6. Practice looking at a problem through the eyes of a thinker. Analyze the problem critically and impersonally, as if you were a "letter of the law" judge.

Leaders need to use both the thinking and feeling modalities. Neither way is superior to the other. However, since more men than women prefer the thinking modality, women can feel their interpersonal way of making decisions is unappreciated in the business world. Thinking directors are likely to hear they have "ice in their veins." Men in early childhood, appreciated for their compassion and sensitivity, may be stereotyped negatively outside our profession. Work to become comfortable with both decision-making processes, so you can call on whichever you need.

Assessing Yourself

Question 3: Do you prefer to make decisions in a thinking or feeling way? _ _ T _, or _ _ F _? Place the letter that describes you in the blank that is third from the left. E/I S/N __ __

You now have determined 75 percent of your MBTI type.

✠ Judging or Perceiving

Director Jeong decides he has no choice but to delegate tasks to assistant director, Teri, from the growing list in Jeong's Blackberry. Although Jeong believes he can't count on Teri to meet his high standards, Jeong admits Teri gets the job done, if always at the last minute. Teri's "whatever" approach drives Jeong crazy.

Handing Teri a list of phone calls to return, Jeong watches over his shoulder to see how many calls Teri makes. Jeong fears the phone list will get lost in the piles on Teri's desk. Teri claims she knows where everything is. She is chafing under Jeong's "condescending, holier than thou" attitude. How can Jeong and Teri find ways to build on each other's strengths?

According to MBTI data collected on Americans, 54 percent of us prefer to be organized; 46 percent of us prefer to take a "why worry, be happy" approach. In early childhood education, many of us would prefer to go with the flow more than our leadership position allows. We may have taught ourselves to be organized, even though our preference is to spontaneously engage with the children.

The lifestyle preference indicates how we prefer to conduct our lives, either in an organized, planned way (Judging), or in a spontaneous, "go with the flow" manner (Perceiving).

Judgers

Strengths
Accreditation forms are completed, deadlines are met, and airplanes take off from the right runways thanks to judgers. Judgers plan in advance. Judgers favor organization and orderliness, avoiding stress by keeping ahead of deadlines. Judgers "cross their T's and dot their I's." Classrooms are neat, clean, and thoughtfully organized. Clear on where they stand, judgers make decisions quickly. They take pride in accomplishing everything on their lists.

Challenges
Judgers can be impatient with colleagues who need time to check out all their options. Disorganization and disarray annoy judgers. Judgers can judge too quickly, before gathering all pertinent information. Judgers show up early for meetings and roll their eyes when others arrive late. Preferring decisiveness, judgers find living with ambiguity uncomfortable. Perfectionism is the judger's Achilles' heel. Judgers dislike surprises. Flexibility can be difficult.

Tips for Judgers
Much can be learned from living in the moment. Judging directors can stretch themselves by scheduling and taking free time. Judging directors often have difficulty delegating. Few people meet the high standard the judger sets for herself. A judger's worry will

not get the job done by the other person. Delegate, step back, and assume the task will be accomplished, even if not in the way you would have accomplished it. Realize that others prefer to multitask and are comfortable juggling many balls in the air.

Communicating with Perceivers
1. Learn to appreciate the creativity and playfulness of your colleagues.
2. Ask a perceiver to help you identify alternatives and options.
3. Show the perceiver you trust her to get the job done, even if at the last minute.
4. Allow time for exploring all possibilities, and for spontaneous changes to be made to plans.
5. Incorporate lighthearted, fun activities into staff meetings.

Perceivers

Strengths
Perceivers prefer to keep their options open. Adept at creating alternatives, perceivers see possibilities. Perceivers have fun at work. An easygoing work environment suits perceivers. Perceivers bring spontaneity and humor to the workplace. They enjoy the journey, not just the destination. Emergent curriculum is often the perceiver's preferred classroom style. Perceivers describe themselves as human beings, not "human doings."

Challenges
Perceivers, wanting to keep their options open, put off making decisions. Neatness and orderliness are not a priority. Perceivers organize by piling things up. Nonetheless, perceivers know where to find things. Perceivers think meetings start when they get there. This may frustrate on-time colleagues. Perceivers can resent the up-tightness of their judger colleagues. They often complete tasks in the eleventh hour.

Tips for Perceivers
Break assignments into manageable tasks. Set a deadline for each task. Celebrate when you complete a task early. Avoid surprising your colleagues when you change your plans. Give them as much notice as possible to adjust. Since flexibility comes more easily for you, try something different and structure a task. Making the effort will increase your empathy for judgers. Use your sense of humor to help your colleagues lighten up.

Communicating with Judgers
1. Be clear about when you will complete a project.
2. Make small, inconsequential choices more quickly than usual.
3. Demonstrate your ability to complete tasks.
4. Volunteer to clean up, put things away, and organize events.

The majority of senior managers in any profession are judgers. Improvisational theater professionals and inventors are more often perceivers. Perceivers benefit from judgers' predictability and reliability. Judgers benefit from perceivers' easygoing, playful manner. Which describes your preference: are you more organized and structured or laidback, and easygoing?

Assessing Yourself

Question 4: Do you prefer to live your life in a judging or perceiving way? _ _ _ J or _ _ _ P? Fill in the final blank space. E/I S/N T/F __

Congratulations! You have completed all four letters of your MBTI type. Look for your four-letter type in this summary of the sixteen types in Table 3.5 (Otto Kroeger Associates 1997).

For more complete descriptions of each type, go online to *typelogic.com,* or read my MBTI mentors, Otto Kroeger and Janet Theusen's *Type Talk at Work* (1992). In

---

TABLE 3.5

MBTI Type Summary

ISTJ	ISFJ	INFJ	INTJ
"Doing What Should Be Done"	"A High Sense of Duty"	"An Inspiratio to Others"	"Everything Has Room for Improvement"
Organizer • Compulsive Private • Trustworthy Rules 'n Regs • Practical	Amiable • Works behind the Scene • Ready to Sacrifice Accountable • "Doer"	Reflective/Introspective Quietly Caring • Creative Linguistically Gifted • Psychic	Theory Based • Skeptical • "My Way" • High Need for Competency
MOST RESPONSIBLE	MOST LOYAL	MOST CONTEMPLATIVE	MOST INDEPENDENT
ISTP	**ISFP**	**INFP**	**INTP**
"Ready to Try Anything Once"	"Sees Much but Shares Little"	"Performing Noble Service to Aid Society"	"A Love of Problem Solving"
Very Observant • Cool and Aloof • Hands-on Practicality • Ready for What Happens • Unpretentious	Warm and Sensitive • Unassuming • Short-Range Planner • Good Team Member • In Touch with Self and Nature	Strict Personal Values • Reserved Seeks Inner Order/Peace Creative • Nondirective	Challenges Others to Think Absent-Minded Professor Competency Needs • Socially Cautious
MOST PRAGMATIC	MOST ARTISTIC	MOST IDEALISTIC	MOST CONCEPTUAL
ESTP	**ESFP**	**ENFP**	**ENTP**
"The Ultimate Realist"	"You Only Go Around Once in Life"	"Giving Life an Extra Squeeze"	"One Exciting Challenge after Another"
Unconventional Approach • Fun Gregarious • Lives for Here and Now • Good at Problem Solving	Sociable • Spontaneous • Loves Surprises • Cuts Red Tape • Multi-Tasking • Quip Master	People Oriented • Creative Seeks Harmony • Life of Party • More Starts Than Finishes	Argues Both Sides of a Point Brinksmanship • Tests Limits • Enthusiastic • New Ideas
MOST SPONTANEOUS	MOST GENEROUS	MOST OPTIMISTIC	MOST INVENTIVE
ESTJ	**ESFJ**	**ENFJ**	**ENTJ**
"Life's Administrators"	"Hosts and Hostesses"	"Smooth Talking Persuader"	"Life's Natural Leaders"
Order and Structure • Sociable Opinionated • Results Driven Producer • Traditional	Gracious • Good Interpersonal Skills • Thoughtful Appropriate • Eager to Please	Charismatic • Compassionate Possibilities for People • Ignores the Unpleasant • Idealistic	Visionary • Gregarious Argumentative • Take Charge • Low Tolerance for Incompetency
MOST HARD CHARGING	MOST HARMONIZING	MOST PERSUASIVE	MOST COMMANDING

Source: Table Adapted with Permission of Okacotto Kroeger Associates.

Leadership Equations (Barr and Barr 1989) you will find in depth descriptions of each type's leadership style.

To take an abbreviated MBTI, go to *http://www.teamtechnology.co.uk/mmdi-re/mmdi-re.htm*. Upon completion of the questionnaire, you will be given a description of your type. Your instructor also may be able to tell you about MBTI professionals who can administer and evaluate your full MBTI. This service is often available at your college or university's career development office.

⚔ Learning from Our Shadow Preferences

Carl Jung noticed that in addition to our preferences, we all have a "shadow." Our shadow is the least developed part of ourselves, which we keep hidden from most people. Stress nudges us into our shadow. When we have "bad hair days," we fall into using our opposite preferences, at which we do not feel as skilled. A friendly person, under pressure, becomes withdrawn. An easygoing person becomes a taskmaster. The more we learn about our shadow side, the more accepting we become of people who are the opposite of us.

Now that you know your MBTI preferences and type, you can identify your shadow. Write your four-letter type in uppercase letters. Underneath each letter, write the opposite MBTI letter in lowercase.

For example: ESTJ	ISFJ	ENFP	ISFP
infp	entp	istj	entj

The four letters in lowercase are your shadow preferences. The shadow of an ESTJ is an INFP. The shadow of an ISFJ is ENTP. Now, go back to the descriptions of the sixteen MBTI types (p. 45). Read the description for your shadow type. Use your EQ to notice your response. When you are in shadow, do you remind yourself of someone else? Feeling "beside ourselves" is another way to describe being in our shadow (Quenk 1993).

At first we feel cranky and awkward in our shadow. To demonstrate this, sign your name on a piece of paper. Now, place the pen in your opposite hand. Sign your name again. How does that feel and look? When we are in our shadow like this, we are able to complete the task, even though we feel uncomfortable. Consider your shadow as a pathway to learning how to communicate with people who have opposite preferences from you.

Although uncomfortable at first, an extrovert can practice meditation. An introvert can become more at ease with public speaking. A sensor can become more of a dreamer. A perceiver can become more organized. A thinker can demonstrate compassion.

Jung noted that as we embrace our lesser developed or shadow side, we discover our deeper spirituality. The more we find out about our shadow, the more open and accepting we become to different ways of being. To develop our emotional intelligence further, leaders can practice using our shadow preferences. Bad hair days can become opportunities to learn.

⚔ Leadership Temperaments

The MBTI translates readily into four temperaments (Bates and Kiersey 1984) that will help you better understand leadership. Temperaments are our favored ways to behave. When you determined your MBTI type, you identified your temperament as well. The four temperaments are SJ, SP, NT, and NF.

To identify your temperament, write down your MBTI four-letter type again.

E/I **S/N** T/F J/P

TABLE 3.6

MBTI Temperament

SJ	NT
Hardworking	Visionary
Focused	Big picture, systemic approach
Traditionalist	Independent and scientific
Perfectionist	Condescending
George Washington	Eleanor Roosevelt

SP	NF
Problem solver	Utopian thinker
Negotiator	Change agent
Hands on, action-oriented	People first
Avoid paper work	Try to rescue everyone
Theodore Roosevelt	Mahatma Gandhi

Now, write down the second letter of your four-letter type (either S or N). If your letter is S, write the last letter in your type (either J or P) immediately following. If your first letter is N, write the third letter in your type (either T or F) immediately following.

Congratulations! You have identified your MBTI temperament as SJ, SP, NT, or NF.

Find your temperament in Table 3.6. Knowing your MBTI temperament's strengths and challenges increases your emotional intelligence. Pay special attention to the tips on how to grow as a leader. To read more in depth about the four temperaments, see David Kiersey's *Please Understand Me II* (1998).

SJ Leadership Style

SJ leaders are the traditionalists, the bringers of stability, order, and predictability to your organization. SJs lead with authority, instructing others what to do. SJs value hard work and loyalty, a no-nonsense and "can do" attitude. SJs respect authority and exude responsibility. They are highly skilled at detailed follow through. President George Washington was an SJ.

Achilles' Heel

SJs expect excellence, sometimes to the point of perfectionism. SJs can be overly critical of staff, admonishing for their mistakes, rather than praising for jobs well done. SJs have little patience with others who do not embody the hard work ethic. SJs can come across like military generals.

To Grow

SJs benefit from delegating and letting go of expecting perfect results. Focus instead on developing staff strengths. Observe leaders whose "go with the flow" temperaments produce effective results. Praise and acknowledge staff efforts.

SP Leadership Style

The SP leader is the creative problem solver. SP leaders negotiate agreements among people with conflicting viewpoints. SPs are at their best when putting out fires. SPs thrive on activity and prefer hands-on work. SPs are fun to work with, easy to be with, and quick to keep the physical work environment functioning smoothly. Children are drawn to SP's fun-loving, physical, spontaneous ways. "Rough Rider" Teddy Roosevelt was an SP.

Achilles' Heel

If there is no fire to put out, the SP starts a fire. Inactivity is the SP's Achilles' heel, along with paperwork. SPs get bored easily, sitting still, listening to lectures. Detailed follow through is not the SP's strength.

To Grow

Step back out of the action to notice other ways to do things. Teach colleagues how to solve problems, rather than always being the person who puts things right. SPs are often artistic craftspeople. SP leaders need to claim time to work on their own craft projects, and/or to find ways to involve colleagues and families in these creative endeavors.

NT Leadership Style

NT leaders are the visionary logicians. An NT leader's quest is competency and mastery. NTs bring objectivity, intellectualism, and the long view to their organizations. NTs conceptualize systems to streamline work. Like SPs, NTs are pragmatic. An NT leader expects others to learn how to do things by watching the NT. NTs are rarely comfortable giving praise. President Richard Nixon was an NT.

Achilles' Heel

NT leaders' preoccupation with the theoretical makes them appear aloof and condescending. NTs undervalue interpersonal dynamics. NTs judge whether others are competent enough to earn the NT's respect. NTs have little patience with socializing and team building.

To Grow

NTs grow by dedicating themselves to the study and practice of emotional and social EQ. Pay attention to how colleagues feel about their work, not just to the work itself. An NT benefits from researching and learning how to read nonverbal communication cues. Consider the rationale for developing highly functioning teams, and find ways to foster the growth of teams in your program.

NF Leadership Style

The NF leader is a visionary change agent. The heart's desire of the NF leader is to make the world better for children and families. NFs are utopian thinkers, idealistic, and optimistic about changing things for the greater good. NFs lead by encouraging others to fulfill their potential. Unlike authoritarian SJs, NFs are egalitarian, working to bring out the best in everyone through praise and enthusiastic support. NFs are inspiring and charismatic leaders. President John F. Kennedy was an NF.

Achilles' Heel

Guilt and impossibly high ideals can wear an NF down. NFs, like Fs, are conflict avoidant. Confronting inappropriate behavior is difficult for the NF leader.

NFs lose optimism when times are conservative, and social change is unwelcome.

To Grow

Study and practice conflict resolution and effective confrontation skills. Invoke the serenity prayer: "Grant me the serenity to accept the things I cannot change, and the courage to change the things I can." This helps the NF stop carrying the weight of the world on her shoulders. Because NFs take a moralistic approach, they can build unlikely alliances with SJs who also favor moralistic over pragmatic stances.

⚔ The Power of Self-Knowledge

Leaders must learn how to communicate with everyone, especially people who are least like them. An early childhood administrator who understands her own MBTI type, temperament, and shadow is better prepared to respect and honor others' differing gifts. The MBTI helps leaders "read" and understand others, key emotional intelligence competencies.

Leading on purpose, making decisions anchored in core values, and understanding leadership styles empower individuals to be authentic, gifted directors. Self-knowledge is the heart of emotional intelligence. Jamilah knows what she wants. What about you? I hope this chapter has helped you be clearer on the difference you want to make as a leader. To paraphrase the motto of another healing profession: "Director, know thyself."

Whatever you are by nature, keep to it: never desert your line of talent. Be what nature intended for you and you will succeed.

—Sydney Smith

Reflection Questions

1. Core values ground us as we make decisions. We can measure our decisions against our core values to ascertain if we are being true to our values. Think of a decision you need to make. Write (at least three) of your core values. Next, write your purpose. Now, work through your decision. Use any process that works for you: Look back over your core values. Is your decision consistent with what you value? Does your decision align with your purpose? Recall another decision you have made recently. How does that decision measure up to your core values and purpose? Write a reflection paper (or record a statement) on what you are learning about your process of making decisions.

2. Put the S.M.A.R.T. method to work for you. This method turns dreams into realities. Reflect on one specific goal you would like to accomplish. For each of the S.M.A.R.T steps, write the action you will take to reach your goal. Commit to taking the first step by no later than the end of this week. Follow the timetable you set for yourself. Share with your class, or a colleague, how being S.M.A.R.T. can help you as a leader.

3. Investigate how opposites attract. Explore your shadow preferences and type. First, read the information on each of your shadow letters. Next, go online to read your shadow type. How do you feel as you read this information? How do you respond to people who behave like your shadow? Does your shadow behavior show up on your "bad hair days"? Shadow is the lesser known part of yourself. The more you learn about your shadow, the more comfortable you will be with others who have opposite preferences from you. Review how to communicate with your opposites. Write or record a reflection on how understanding your shadow will help you as a leader.

Team Projects

1. Go to page 29 where the steps for finding our purpose are listed. Work through this process in small pairs, one question at a time. At the end of the process, write down your purpose. Discuss with your classmate the degree to which your work or

studies align with your purpose. Brainstorm ways in which you could change your daily activities to fit better with what you are meant to do. Some of us find we need to make career shifts in order to "lead on purpose." If you are one of these people, what are your options?

2. Teams, like individuals, exhibit MBTI preferences. Explain the MBTI to your colleagues. Invite willing team members to take the MBTI online. Ask them if they would be willing to share their MBTI results with you. Collect and tally the results. Does your team have more extroverts than introverts? Do more teammates prefer sensing to intuition? Continue to list the majority letter for each of the four preferences. The four majority letters indicate your team's preferences and type: write down the team's four-letter type. Identify the team's shadow letters. Read up on your team's type. Reflect on how accurately (or not) each of the dominant preferences describes your team. How do your own preferences align with your team's type? Report your findings to your team.

3. In a small group, identify each person's leadership preferences, type, and temperament. Discuss the strengths and challenges of each temperament represented. What percentage of the population does your temperament represent? Discuss how your preferences and temperament help and hinder you as a leader. What steps can you take to communicate better with people who are your opposite in preference and temperament? Name five steps you can take to improve communication with team members, by using your MBTI information.

Bibliography

Barr, L., and N. Barr. 1989. *The leadership equation: Leadership, management and the Myers-Briggs*. Austin, TX: Eakin Press.

Bates, M., and D. Kiersey. 1984. *Please understand me* (4th ed.). Del Mar, CA: Prometheus Nemesis Book Company.

Carter, M., & D. Curtis. 1998. *The visionary director*. St. Paul, MN: Redleaf Press.

Carter, M. What do teachers need most from directors? Staff challenges: Practical ideas for recruiting, training, and supervising early childhood employees, as referenced in *ExchangeEveryDay* e-newsletter, August 15, 2005, *http://www.ccie.com/eed/issue. php?id=1224*.

Covey, S. 1989. *The seven habits of highly effective people.* New York: Simon & Schuster.

Covey, S. 2004. *The 8th habit.* New York: Simon & Schuster.

Csikszentmihalyi, M. 1991. *Flow.* New York: Harper Perennial.

Drucker, P. 1954. *The practice of management: A study of the most important function in American society.* New York: Harper & Row, Publishers.

Greenleaf, R. 1970. *The servant as leader*. Published essay.

Hesse, H. 1932. *Journey to the east.* New York: Picador.

Jung, C.G. 1961. *Memories, dreams and reflections.* Edited by A. Jaffe. New York: Vintage Books.

Kiersey, D. 1998. *Please understand me II*. Del Mar, CA: Prometheus Nemesis Book Company.

Kroeger, O., & J. Theusen. 1992. *Type talk at work.* New York: Delecorte Press.

Martin, Ruby. 2007. Personal correspondence. September 19.

McCaulley, M. H. 1982. *Jung's theory of psychological types and the Myers-Briggs Type Indicator*. Gainesville, FL: Center for Applications of Psychological Type.

Mellody, P., and A.W. Miller. 1989. *Breaking free: A recovery workbook for facing codependence.* San Francisco, CA: HarperOne.

Myers, I.B., M.H. McCaulley, N.L. Quenk, and A.L. Hammer. 1998. *MBTI manual: A guide to the development and use of the Myers-Briggs type indicator.* Mountain View, CA: CPP, Inc.

Quenk, N. 1993. *Beside ourselves: Our hidden personality in everyday life.* Mountain View, CA: Consulting Psychologists Press.

Thoreau, H. D. 1854. *Walden; or, life in the woods.* Boston, MA: Ticknor and Fields.

Web Resources

Exchange Every Day: Free E-Newsletter
http://www.ccie.com/eed/
How to Write Your Mission Statement
www.entrepreneur.com/management/leadership/businessstrategies/article65230.html
Personal Goal Setting
www.mindtools.com/page6.html
Setting S.M.A.R.T. Objectives
www.thepracticeofleadership.net/2006/03/11/setting-smart-objectives
Team Technology
www.teamtechnology.co.uk/mmdi-re/mmdi-re.htm
TypeLogic
www.typelogic.com

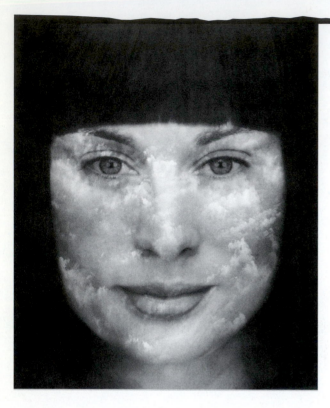

The Art and Science of Decision Making

Learning Goals

As you study this chapter, you can look forward to reaching these learning goals:

1. Summarize at least three effective ways to make decisions.

2. Describe what constitutes "letter of the law" and "spirit of the law" decisions.

3. Improve your capacity to "thin-slice" your decisions.

4. Devise a process for informing staff whether a decision is "mine, ours, or yours."

5. Describe two different ways that groups reach decisions, including the advantages and disadvantages of each way.

6. Examine how a leader's decision-making style affects the structure and functioning of the program.

When you combine your own intuition with a sensitivity to other people's feelings and moods, you may be close to the origins of valuable human attributes such as generosity, altruism, compassion, sympathy and empathy.

—Fred Rogers

We are the creative force of our life, and through our own decisions rather than our conditions, if we carefully learn to do certain things, we can accomplish those goals.

—Stephen Covey

Case Study: Teacher with Attitude about Being Late

Jasmine, a toddler teacher, is scheduled to start her day in the classroom at 6:30 a.m. On Monday, Jasmine arrived at 6:45, and on Tuesday, she showed up at 7:05. Today, Jasmine appeared at 6:50. Jasmine's team teacher is frazzled and parents are tired of waiting to talk with Jasmine. The director needs to finish a grant application but is distracted by having to fill in for Jasmine to cover teacher-student ratios. As Jasmine breezes through the classroom door, she says, "Just change my starting time to 7 a.m. I can get here by 7, no problem!"

The director responds, "Jasmine, arrive in time to be in the classroom with the children at 6:30 a.m. If I bend the rules for you, I have to bend them for everyone." Jasmine is upset and begins complaining about all the burdens of her personal life: battery trouble with her 1991 Chevy, a sick daughter, boyfriend problems, and worrying about her mother with Alzheimer's. Jasmine reminds the director how punctual she was before her husband divorced her and she started feeling depressed.

What would you do as Jasmine's director?

To view decision making in a historical perspective, imagine yourself as a 12th century judge presiding over the Court of Law in the verdant rolling countryside of feudal England. William, a tenant who rents his farmland from a local lord, appears before you, asking that he and his family be permitted to stay on his property.

The law says: Tenants, who rent property from the landlord, must pay their rent on time each season. Failure to pay on time will result in forfeiture of the land. William's rent is due on April 15th. William pays his rent on April 20th. What say you?

As 21st century early childhood professionals, or 12th century judges, we are called upon to make decisions as often as we take a breath. Decision making is both an art and a science. This chapter offers perspective on how to make "good enough" decisions that we can live with, and move on.

❧ A Historical Perspective on Decision Making

As you consider what to do in William's case, you may be reminded of similar situations, such as Jasmine's behavior in the chapter case study. We all want to make decisions that "feel right" and triumph over criticism. But what constitutes a fair or just decision?

The judge's decision in William's case was, "Forfeit the property and quit the land." William had failed to obey the law, and breaking the law had a clearly articulated consequence: forfeiture. The judge did not take into account William's personal circumstances. The judge used a logical, legal, and scientific approach.

Does it matter that William had paid on time for five years and was responsible for his wife and eleven children? What about the fact that William traveled night and day to find a bridge still standing after the spring floods had washed out other bridges over which William usually traveled to deliver his rent? The letter of the law does not concern itself with individual circumstances. With "letter of the law" decision-making process, the law is the law. Fairness is demonstrated by applying the law the same way to every person.

In Jasmine's case, a letter of the law decision could result in disciplinary action such as probation or firing. On the other hand, the director could take into consideration Jasmine's extenuating circumstances. Reflection on the ADA (Americans with Disabilities Act) reminds her that employees with chronic depression may need reasonable accommodations to perform essential job functions.

Jasmine expects the director to pay attention to all her personal concerns. But children, families, and team teachers need Jasmine to meet her professional responsibilities. What decision is fair?

✄ Decision Making by Letter of the Law or Spirit of the Law

With either William or Jasmine, making a decision in the "spirit of the law" may be more appropriate and humane than invoking the letter of the law. When you make a spirit of the law decision, you take into account the totality of the individual's circumstances. You look more deeply to find the root cause of the problem, to make a decision tailored to best deal with each person's personal situation.

Letter of the law decisions meet out evenhanded, often impersonal justice. Each person gets the same treatment under the law. Spirit of the law decisions, which take into account an individual's circumstances, are called "equitable" decisions. Equitable decisions take each person on a case by case basis as a unique individual. Making equitable decisions can be more an art than a science. No one size fits all template exists for spirit of the law decisions.

While letter of the law (legal) decisions are expedient, spirit of the law (equitable) decisions require time and reflection. Similarly, legal decisions call more upon our IQ, and equitable decisions require us to use both EQ and IQ. Discerning which type of decision-making process is more appropriate calls for a leader's intellectual savvy and skillful ability to perceive nonverbal messages. We make both types of decisions by grounding ourselves in the deeper goal: doing what is best for children and families, while leading on purpose.

Think how efficient your work would be if all your decisions could be made like a 12th century judge. Jasmine, like William, would be out the door without recourse. As emotionally intelligent 21st century professionals, we devote hours to accommodating individual needs. Is there a middle path between law and equity? Can equitable decisions take less time?

Come back to the 12th century with me to find some answers. In London stood the Chancery Court (later called the Court of Equity), where controversial cases like William's could be appealed. There, the ecclesiastical member of the king's cabinet, appointed to represent the Church, decided cases using the spirit of the law. The Chancery Court was also called the "star chamber" because the ceiling paint in the great hall was resplendent with stars.

Under those stars, the Equity Chancellor overturned the law court (lower court's) decision and returned the property to William for having made a "good faith effort" (traveling night and day) in the face of an "act of God" (springtime flooding). As the Chancellor of Equity acted on William's claim, he used an artful decision-making process, drawing from an alternative definition of fairness. The spirit of the law became legitimized as an official decision-making process.

✄ Making "Equitable" Decisions

Maxims, created in the Court of Equity, such as "making a good faith effort," are still in common parlance today. Equitable principles evolving from the Chancery Court include:

- Equity will not suffer a wrong to be without a remedy.
- Equity regards substance rather than form.

- One who seeks equity, must do equity.
- Equity acts *in personam* (takes into account the individual's circumstances).
- Equity delights to do justice and not by halves.

William, Jasmine, and countless others over the centuries have benefited from this "softer," more spiritual (looking for deeper meaning) decision-making process.

In the swirl of 21st century complexity, early childhood leaders stand as if we are holding the scales of justice, seeking to balance what is equitable with what is just. Often we feel blindfolded, unclear on the standards to use and troubled by unforeseen consequences of our decisions. We may yearn to be back in the day when decision making was simpler. The law was the law.

In fact, things were never simpler, nor were they ever so difficult. We often must stand, holding two competing realities: fairness means taking individual circumstances into account, while upholding professional standards. In some situations, the objective, analytical decision-making process is appropriate. In other situations, the compassionate, individualized process is more fitting. How can we tell the difference?

Decision Making by Weighing Pros and Cons

Letter of the law decisions are made by weighing the benefits and detriments (pros and cons) of each option. Traditionalists in decision-making theory counsel us to follow a three-step process:

1. List pros and cons of the situation objectively.
2. Analyze the list: which side has the more substantial factors?
3. Make a logical decision in favor of the weightier side.

At times, this process works well. Administrators, pressed by an onslaught of decisions to be made, find the objective approach useful. When a leader makes an impartial decision, she can decide quickly. She does not have to consider the complexity of human emotion. The leader bases her decision on established policies and procedures, and in following precedent or upholding tradition, she furthers predictability and stability. Expectations are met with consistency.

More often than not, however, an impartial decision will be challenged. An administrator may hear complaints that he failed to ask everyone's opinion before deciding or did not notify staff about an impending change. Letter of the law decisions often meet with resistance if social intelligence savvy was not part of the decision-making process. Consider the following example.

> Preschool teacher Joanne decided to tell Aliesha's mom that her daughter needed an evaluation for learning disabilities. Joanne had painstakingly documented all of Aliesha's behaviors warranting an evaluation. Joanne found very few "cons" in her decision: Aliesha needed help. All factors pointed to that.
>
> When Joanne shared her rational decision with Aliesha's mom, Joanne was stunned that her decision was immediately rejected. "Aliesha never behaves like that at home! You must be upsetting her!" the distressed parent cried. Joanne's decision was purely rational and emotion blind. She did not use her EQ to discover and understand the parent's way of looking at her world, and especially at her feelings about Aliesha.
>
> Joanne, in the future, will pay more attention to building a relationship with parents, while continuously sharing information with them. Joanne will practice putting herself in parents' shoes to gain empathy for their situation.

Deciding how to partner with parents like Aliesha's mom is not just a science, but also an art. Parents' feelings of pride, fear, denial, outrage, and shame all need to be factored into a teacher's decision on how best to help the child and her family.

A leader needs to develop skill at both types of decision making and, even more important, at discerning when to use each type. Cut and dried decisions that do not directly affect people are often best served by using the letter of the law process. For decisions that involve other people directly, a leader will likely do better to use the spirit of the law approach. Both approaches require both EQ and IQ. A spirit of the law decision, however, cannot be made without the leader's social EQ. These decisions require us to read people as well as we read books.

Neither decision-making process is superior to the other. Myers-Briggs (MBTI) data helps us understand why staff and others have strong feelings about which process is used. Feelers tend to expect individualized treatment. They are more likely to equate fairness with compassion. Thinkers tend to expect consistency and are not as bothered by making impersonal decisions. Leaders who call upon their knowledge of MBTI preferences will be more able to foresee the consequences of the decision-making style they choose.

Recall your preferred way to make decisions according to the MBTI information. Reflect on how your preference (T or F) has helped and hindered you. How might you utilize both ways of making decisions in the future? Remember, one decision-making style is likely to be less comfortable to you. Practice in that style will help.

Decision Making by Intuitive "Thin-Slicing"

New research on decision making invites us to take a 21st century approach to this age-old dilemma. According to Dr. Malcolm Gladwell, in *Blink: The Power of Thinking without Thinking* (2005), our best decisions are made intuitively, in the "blink of an eye." Rumination, or going back and forth often and second guessing ourselves, according to Gladwell, can be counterproductive. Instinctively, we "know" what needs to be done. Our job is to trust our intuition and take action without dillydallying.

Gladwell calls this decision-making process "thin-slicing." We thin-slice when our brain reaches conclusions without immediately telling us that it's reaching conclusions. The part of our brain that thin-slices is the "adaptive unconscious . . . the giant computer that quickly and quietly processes a lot of the data we need in order to keep functioning as human beings" (2005, 11). Thin-slicing is the act of listening to our inner voice over the cacophony of self-doubt.

How do you discern the sound of your inner voice over the thunder of other voices? Gladwell says we can "teach ourselves to make better snap judgments" (2005, 16).

> Thin-slicing is not an exotic gift. It is a central part of what it means to be human. We thin-slice whenever we meet a new person or have to make sense of something quickly or encounter a novel situation. We thin-slice because we have to, and come to rely on that ability . . .
>
> —Dr. Malcolm Gladwell

The Challenge of Self-Doubt

When making decisions, ruminating too long or second-guessing ourselves about how others will perceive us can detract from our ability to take action. We worry, "What if I'm wrong? What if people misunderstand my intention? What if someone's feelings get hurt?" Ruminating like this wastes time, and worrying devours confidence. While some questioning is productive, overmuch second-guessing harms our decision-making capacity. Employees will wonder if a director like this can make decisions. Dr. Gladwell cautions: "I think that approach is a mistake, and if we are to learn the quality of the decisions we make, we need to accept the mysterious nature of our snap judgments" (2005, 52).

How do we step out of the trap of debilitating self-doubt? An answer lies in "positive self-talk." When repetitive, worrisome voices impede your decision-making ability, quiet down those negative voices with words of self-confidence.

> I am perfectly imperfect.
>
> —Pia Mellody

Each of us can develop our own phrases or affirmations to repeat when we find ourselves slipping into second-guessing. Reflect on situations that erode your confidence, and then say these affirmations aloud:

- Every decision is the right decision, because I learn from each one.
- I make snap decisions with children and my judgments are good. I can do the same with adults.
- Once you make a decision, the universe conspires to make it happen. (Ralph Waldo Emerson)
- What other people think of me is none of my business.
- Write your own positive affirmation: _____

_____

Positive self-talk replaces self-doubt with faith in our ability to make "good enough" decisions. Second-guessing is a rut, a well-established brain pathway. Positive self-talk, with regular practice, helps us climb out of that rut. You can build new brain connections when you remind yourself, "I am a good-enough decision maker." Do your best for today, and move on. Directors recommend these additional approaches for dealing with self-doubt:

1. Set a firm deadline for making the decision. Honor that deadline and move on.
2. Sleep on it. Make a tentative decision by the end of the workday. Sleep on that decision overnight. You are likely to wake up resolved in your decision.
3. Stop second-guessing by choosing to thin-slice your decision in the moment. Write your blink-of-an-eye decision down. Walk away and get involved with something else. Come back later to read what you wrote. You may find your decision has been made.

The right or good enough decision is often already inside of us. This process of defusing self-doubt helps directors cut to the chase to uncover that decision. Leaders have many opportunities to practice replacing worry with positive self-talk. Many directors find they need to let go of the impossible or perfectionist standard they set for themselves to make infallible decisions that will never be questioned. Good enough decisions allow us to move on to the next challenge that awaits us.

Decision Making by "Gifted Improvisation"

In addition to the problem of second-guessing, thin-slicing raises another red flag: bias. For thin-slicing to work well, a decision maker needs a richly developed inner landscape. An inner landscape is the sum of our life experience and decisions to date. Our inner landscapes grow lush when nourished by our interactions with people who differ from us, and by taking risks to grow. Otherwise, we tend to see the world in our own image, expecting others to hold similar values and perspectives. An accurate word for this is "solipsism," the false belief that we are the center of the universe. To let go of solipsistic, biased attitudes, we need thoughtful and heartfelt openness and exposure to diverse people, cultures, and environments.

When I hear I see, when I see I hear.

—Zen koan

Nourishing our inner landscape is a lifelong process. At Harvard University, doctoral students were asked to participate in a study that required them to thin-slice. Each student was shown photographs and asked for an immediate response to each image. These students, both black and white, consistently indicated their preference for images of white people. The students were stunned when told the results.

What if our immediate world is not large enough to embrace, witness, and experience others' cultures? What if the larger world, as evidenced in the Harvard study, conveys bias? Our thin-slicing capacity is limited by the boundaries of our experience, and the barrage of unstated messages.

Gladwell presents a refreshing recommendation for moving beyond bias like this. He invites us to look beyond our own profession to another profession: improvisational theater. Gladwell studied the ground rules for successful improvisation, or "improv."

Improv, he discovered, works only when each actor builds on the previous statement of his or her fellow actor, no matter how absurd that statement appears to be. If the second actor criticizes the first actor's statement, the moment is lost. However, if the improviser finds a creative way to "run with" the statement, magic happens. Energy builds, the audience is engaged, and innovation occurs. Life problems are worked through with humor and originality. The next time you have the opportunity to observe improvisational theater or television, observe this principle in action.

To support the principle of building on another's statements, Gladwell quotes improv expert Keith Johnstone. "In life, most of us are highly skilled at suppressing action. All the improvisation teacher has to do is reverse this skill and he creates 'gifted improvisers.' Bad improvisers block action, often with a high degree of skill. Good improvisers develop action" (114–115). In the blink of an eye, we can find value in what is being offered, or we can turn away and lose the opportunity.

Consider the ramifications of this improv principle for our profession. When a Hmong father describes his practice of healing chest coughs through "coining," what is our response? Do we greet the moment with wonder or judgment? If we judge the parent to be wrong, we lose the opportunity to learn about Hmong culture, the family, and the child. If we build on the moment, trust and knowledge are shared.

To grow away from bias as a decision maker, leaders can explore and build on differences, rather than deny them. Janet Gonzalez-Mena recommends (2001, 42–43), "Be a risk taker. If you are secure enough, you may feel you can afford to make mistakes. It helps to have a good support system behind you when you take risks and make mistakes. Ask questions, investigate assumptions, confess your curiosity—but do it all as respectfully as possible."

Early childhood professionals are skilled at improv. "Multitasking" is our middle name. Each time a teacher practices the "emergent curriculum" approach, she or he improvises by building on the potential of the moment. Children respond with fascination and hunger to learn more. The teachable or learning moment is captured. As a director listens to the messages beneath the words of a parent, the director may surrender one pathway of working with that parent and spontaneously start down another, better suited path.

To improv better decisions like this, we benefit from getting out there more in the world, exposing ourselves to things we do not know, to the people we have avoided, to the life experience we have yet to live. In the process, as we deepen our experience and shine light on our blind spots, we find the conviction of our inner voice. We achieve at last that richly developed inner landscape.

As early childhood professionals, we resolutely encourage children to value themselves and trust their own unique worth. What if we practice what we tell our children? Gavin De Becker, a security specialist, writing before the 9/11 tragedy (1997) counseled: "We have the gift of a brilliant internal guardian that stands ready to warn you of hazards and guide us through risky situations" (13). Develop trust in yourself as a leader. Believe that you are a good enough decision maker. Perhaps, by thin-slicing, the spirit and letter of the law can join hands at last.

❧ Involving Others in the Decision-Making Process: Mine, Ours, Yours

Now that we have studied how leaders make decisions, we are ready to look at involving others in making important choices. Unlike the military, Catholic Church hierarchy, or a monarchy, early childhood programs do not revolve around a general, pope,

TABLE 4.1

Due process is guaranteed by the 14th Amendment of the United States constitution. Due process consists of giving stakeholders:

1. Notice of a possible change that will affect their rights; and,
2. Opportunity to be heard, to speak their minds about the proposed change.

When an administrator fails to give her staff due process, she can expect resistance. "You never told us about that!"

or queen. Generals, popes, and queens are empowered to make decisions, totally by themselves.

By contrast, early childhood leaders work within a community of stakeholders. Stakeholders are people who have an interest, or stake, in the outcome of a decision. Teachers, parents, board members, cooks, and bus drivers can all be stakeholders in early childhood programs. People whose lives are affected by a decision expect to be consulted before that decision is reached. Stakeholders demand "due process," the right to speak up and have their opinion taken into account (see Table 4.1).

For this reason, effective directors need to level upfront with staff about who will be making a decision. Before a director makes a decision, she needs to determine: will this decision be mine, ours together, or yours to make? A leader, who sets clear expectations about who has the authority to make decisions, prevents many misunderstandings.

Decisions that involve groups of people fall into three categories: mine, ours, and yours. To set clear expectations about who has the decision-making authority in each situation, inform everyone whether the decision is to be:

Mine

1. This decision is my responsibility. I'll let you know as soon as I come to a decision.
2. I would appreciate your input before I make my decision.
3. Give me a list of your top three suggestions. I will take those into account as I make my decision.

Ours

1. This decision is ours to make as a team. Let's come to a consensus. We'll start by going around the circle to hear how everyone feels.
2. We all will have an equal vote in this decision. Would you prefer a show of hands or a written ballot?

Yours

1. You can decide how you want to handle this situation. I will back you up.
2. Your team will be the final decision maker on this question. Let me know what you decide.

Think of a decision you are currently facing that involves other people. Which of the three categories best describes who will make the decision? Do you think everyone is clear on who has the decision-making authority or process?

Decision Making by Group

Staff members are more likely to feel responsible for carrying out decisions they have taken part in making. Just as individuals need to understand their personal decision-making process, teams need to be clear on their group decision-making process. Teams reach decisions by one of two methods: (1) consensus or (2) majority vote. Leaders will want to ensure that everyone understands which process will be used.

Groups reach consensus when they come to a meeting of the minds about what action to take. The group gels, is ready to act as one, needing no further debate. With a consensus, no vote is necessary. A consensus is best reached after everyone has spoken on the issue. Before reaching consensus, make sure that concerns and doubts are voiced and resolved. Use your social EQ to sense when the group is ready to reach a consensus. Rushing a consensus can result in a lukewarm commitment or sabotage the decision.

Voting on an issue allows the majority to decide for the whole team. This can lead to a disgruntled minority, who lost the vote. For this reason, decision making by consensus can be more unifying. However, if your team's maturity level is high, voting can work. Those who lose the vote "let go," move on, and support the outcome. Make sure again that everyone who participated in the vote agrees to support the decision. Ask: "Does anyone anticipate a problem carrying out this decision? If so, let's talk that over before we leave the room. We all need to be on the same page."

Decision-Making Structures

Your decision-making style predicts how you will structure your organization. Directors structure their programs internally to let every employee know where she or he belongs in the organization by knowing how decisions will be made that affect them. The clearer the expectations, the fewer the power struggles. Power struggles often come about because decision-making authority is left ambiguous.

The structure you choose indicates your chain of command. In a chain of command, each person is a link in the decision-making chain. Each teacher knows her supervisor. She also knows to whom her supervisor reports. This chain of command simply tells us who is responsible for what decisions.

An organization's chain of command clarifies who reports to whom. A "floating" teacher especially needs to know to whom she reports. Every teacher wants to know who will perform her annual evaluation. The personnel committee of a board is appointed by and responsible to the board chair. A clear chain of command provides security and predictability on who will make important decisions.

With a clear chain of command, a leader has choices about the organizational structure she wants to use. Three types of organizational structures are:

1. Hierarchy (See Figure 4.1);
2. Flat structure (See Figure 4.2); or,
3. Hybrid (See Figure 4.3, combination of hierarchical and flat).

As you study each of these structures, pay attention to your response to each one. Do you find you have a preference for one form over another?

Hierarchy: Directors who make decisions by themselves tend toward "top-down" structures, or hierarchies. In a hierarchy, the chain of command begins with the director at the top, and every other employee reports to the director in some way. In a hierarchy, the person at the top of the organization makes the important decisions. A military general issues a command, which everyone must follow.

Flat: In flat organizations, teams make decisions. Juries, Quaker meetings, total quality management (TQM) quality circles (Chapter 15), and twelve-step groups are examples of flat organizations. Flat structures rely on building consensus among team members. Participation and ownership of decisions are highest in flat structures.

Hybrid: In hybrid organizations, the leader makes some decisions and teams make other decisions. For example, directors make budget decisions (hierarchical), and teams decide how to plan activities that involve parents (flat).

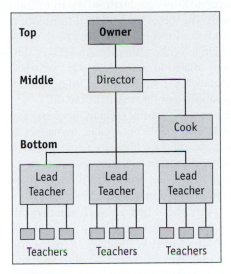

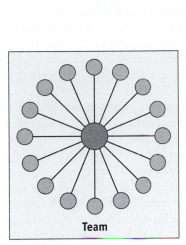

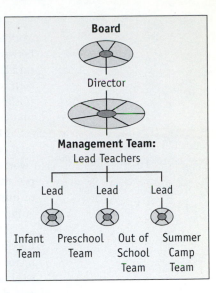

FIGURE 4.1   Decision Making by Hierarchy Mode 1

FIGURE 4.2   Flat Decision-Making Model

FIGURE 4.3   Hybrid Organization Model

How do you perceive decisions are made in your organization? Draw a representation/chart of how your program would look to an outsider.

Use circles to represent a team that makes decisions. Draw a vertical line from the top of each team's circle to the person to whom the team reports. Write the position/name of the decision maker at the top of each vertical line to identify the decision maker.

Here is an example: Draw a circle for the infant toddler teaching team. Next, make a vertical line upward from that circle. At the top of the line, create a box with their supervisor's title or name.

Continue doing this until every individual and team is included. Once you have drawn your representation of how decisions are made in your organization, compare this to your program's organization chart, or "org chart." These charts are often required for grant applications. Each director should have an org chart available for you to view. Is your drawing in line with the official chart? Differences in perception can lead to lively, informative discussions.

Hierarchies: Decision Making by Tops, Middles, and Bottoms

In hierarchies, the top-down decision-making practice has a strong effect on morale. Lower level staff members can have little loyalty to the organization. They see themselves as working for the children and the paycheck. Only a charismatic leader, or an engaging mission, can inspire loyalty to a hierarchy.

Management consultant Barry Oshry (1986, 21) describes the predictable dynamics in hierarchies. Oshry labels employees in hierarchical organizations as Tops, Middles, or Bottoms. The executive decision maker, or Top, wields a great deal of power. Tops (owner, director-owner, director, or board) make decisions with little input. Tops often take a letter-of-the-law approach. Due process, taking time to get employees' input, slows a Top down.

Tops are perceived as "numbers-oriented, distant, arbitrary, out-of-touch, and thinking of people as things, not people," according to Oshry. Tops appear to be dedicated to their own interests, rather than the interests of others in the organization.

Middles (assistant directors, site directors, curriculum coordinators) report to Tops. Middles are limited in the decisions they can make. The job of the Middle is to negotiate between the Top and the Bottoms of the organization. If you have ever felt "stuck in the middle," you know what a middle manager's position feels like. Others see middles as "diligent, well-intended, but also turncoats, weak, and unable to make decisions that stick" (Oshry). Decisions made by Middles are often tentative, pending approval from above. A middle manager says: "I'll have to get back to you on that, or I'll see what I can do."

Bottoms (teachers, teacher's aides, bus drivers, and family support workers) feel least empowered to make meaningful decisions. Bottoms unhappily label themselves as "worker bees, pawns, or peons" at the mercy of those in power. Tops are not required to pay attention to what Bottoms want or need. Bottoms' decision-making power is to strike or quit. Bottoms can drop everything and walk out the door. Frustrated Bottoms resist authority by saying, "That's not in my job description; you don't pay me to do that."

When a director makes decisions autonomously, she or he creates a hierarchy with the director as the Top. Middles and Bottoms can feel insecure and slighted since this director can hire and fire staff at will. Authoritarian structures like this have strengths and weaknesses. Strengths include expedient decision making, clear chain of command, and role clarity. Hierarchies can exhibit these deficiencies: rigidity, stagnation, and restricted top-down communication.

Flat Structures and Decision Making

In flat structures, everyone takes part in decision making. The director knows everyone, and everyone has access to the director. Employees are maximally involved. Everyone is kept informed. Pathways are in place for transmitting information rapidly to everyone in the organization. Due process is at the heart of flat structures. Leaders rarely act unless everyone has been informed and has spoken on each issue. Early childhood organizations almost always include some form of flat, or team, structure.

Flat structures, like hierarchies, have endured through the ages. The Native American process of using a "talking stick" ensures that everyone has the right to speak. Juries sit around a table together for as long as it takes to reach often heartrending decisions. Our legal system assumes that a jury's flat structure ensures that the "voice of the people" will be heard.

Early childhood organizations are imbued with flat structures. Parent advisory committees, team teachers, and other collaborative efforts are often the preferred mode for making decisions. Flat structure strengths include a high level of staff commitment, ownership, empowerment, and involvement.

Flat structures present challenges, however, especially to those who grew up in hierarchical systems. Decisions made by consensus require maturity and accountability by each team member. Without this maturity, individuals in flat structures can slide into power struggles, manipulating others into following their lead. Unlike hierarchies, in flat structures, jobs may not be clear. The chain of command can be foggy. Decision making by teams often takes more time than anyone has. Directors are likely to hear the cry: "Not another meeting!"

Hybrid Approach to Decision Making

As you may have imagined, few organizations are purely hierarchical or purely flat. Most early childhood leaders institute team decision making. Directors who want to develop future leaders encourage employees to make decisions for themselves. Reflective supervision (Chapter 9) is an example of hybrid decision making. Employees are mentored to become more confident and competent in making daily decisions. The supervisor retains the authority to evaluate the staff member.

Team teaching is another example of a hybrid decision-making structure. Both teachers have an equal voice in how the classroom will function. Aides and assistants are encouraged to share their views. Even lead teachers often act as just another voice in the classroom decision-making process. Nonetheless, each teacher is ultimately responsible to the director. Directors decide whether to retain or terminate employees.

Who would want a committee to perform brain surgery? Surely, we want one competent person in charge. Similarly, most directors would not want to change the staff handbook without listening to teachers' ideas and feelings first. Crystal-clear, no-questions-asked emergency evacuation plans are essential. However, without staff input into developing the plan, the staff is less likely to embrace the plan.

Directors have the opportunity to decide how much decision making to share and how much to retain. As a future leader, regardless of the decision-making approach you choose, remember to inform your staff if the decision is mine, ours, or yours. Staff will thank you and the program will run more smoothly.

How we make decisions affects the morale, efficiency, and structure of our programs. Now that you know your options, what works best for you? Are you more likely to make letter of the law or spirit of the law decisions? Would you weigh the pros and cons of each choice before making a decision? Or, are you more at ease thin-slicing, calling upon your intuition? Many administrators are most comfortable using a combination of these approaches, depending on the situation. The choice is yours.

Reflection Questions

1. Complete the organizational chart for your program, as discussed on page 61. Would you say your organization is hierarchical, flat, or a hybrid? Is the chain of command clear? Do you see yourself as a Top, Middle, or Bottom in that structure? If you were to change one thing about your organizational structure, what change would you make? What effect would this have on your program? Include your org chart and reflections in a paper on these questions.

2. Reflect on an important decision you have made. For example, how did you decide to take this course, where to go for your schooling, how to resolve a recent conflict, or who would be your closest friend? Which of these decisions did you make by using the letter of the law (pros and cons) process, and which did you decide by the spirit of the law approach? Do you see a pattern emerging in your decision-making preference? Are letter or spirit of the law more successful with young children? Describe what you have learned about yourself in either an oral or video recording, or in writing.

3. How comfortable are you with thin-slicing your decisions? Give an example of a decision you thin-sliced successfully, and another decision that was not so successfully thin-sliced. Dr. Gladwell suggests that we get better at thin-slicing, the more we expose ourselves to the unfamiliar and unknown. Write a list of steps you might take to deepen your experience and your ability to thin-slice. Be as concrete as you can.

Team Projects

1. Compare your organizational chart with those of your classmates. What decision-making structures do early childhood organizations appear to have in common? Research and share at least one article apiece on what makes early childhood teams effective. What three innovations would you make to ensure that team decisions are made effectively in your organization? Share your insights with your instructor by preparing a summary of your discussion.

2. Morale can be enhanced or harmed by the degree and quality of staff involvement in decision making. Discuss which decisions should be mine (the director and/or administrator), yours, or ours in early childhood programs. Are staff in your programs clear on who has responsibility for each decision? Does your program have Tops, Middles, and Bottoms? If so, how does that structure affect morale? As a group, identify three ways in which morale in your program could be uplifted by making changes in the decision-making process. Lead small group discussions with your classmates on this topic.

3. Find a local improv group or performance, or view one online or on television. One example of an improv television show is *Who's Line Is It Anyway?* Attend or watch the improv performance together. Meet afterwards to share your observations in the light of improv theory discussed in the chapter. Finally, practice doing improv within your team by following quickly on what another person has said. Record or video highlights of your team's efforts in learning about the relevance of improv to our daily decision making in early childhood.

Bibliography

Americans with Disabilities Act of 1990. Public Law 101-336.

Bruno, H.E., and M.L. Copeland. 1999. If the director isn't direct, can the team have direction? *Leadership Quest* (Fall).

Bruno, H.E., and M.L. Copeland. 1999. Decisions! Decisions! Decision making structures which support quality. *Leadership Quest* (Spring).

Buchanan, L., and A. O'Connell. 2006. A brief history of decision-making. *Harvard Business Review* 84 (January): 32–41.

De Becker, G. 1997. *The gift of fear.* New York: Dell Publishing.

Dobbs, D.D. 1993. *Law of remedies hornbook* (2nd ed.). Eagan, MN: West Publishing Company.

Gladwell, M. 2005. *Blink: The power of thinking without thinking* (2nd ed.). New York: Little, Brown & Company.

Golman, D. 1995. *Emotional intelligence: Why it matters more than IQ.* New York: Bantam Books.

Gonzalez-Mena, J. 2001. *Multicultural issues in child care* (3rd ed.). New York: McGraw-Hill.

Greenspon, T. 2001. *Freeing our families from perfectionism.* Minneapolis, MN: Free Spirit Publishing.

Oshry, B. 1986. *The possibility of organization.* Boston, MA: Power & Systems, Inc.

Senge, P. 1990. *The fifth discipline: The art and practice of the learning organization.* New York: Currency Doubleday.

Web Resources

Blink: Thin-Slicing Skills
www.gladwell.com/blink/
Create Organization Charts
www.office.microsoft.com/en-us/powerpoint/HA011327501033.aspx
Group Decision Making Tool Kit
www.extension.iastate.edu/communities/tools/decisions/
Improv Techniques and Leadership
www.salesopedia.com/content/view/1173/10479/
Make Decisions
www.career.berkeley.edu/Plan/MakeDecisions.stm
Thought Awareness, Rational Thinking, and Positive Thinking
www.mindtools.com/pages/article/newTCS_06.htm
Tools for Personal Growth: Overcoming Perfectionism
www.coping.org/growth/perfect.htm

Storming

Identifying, Preventing, and Addressing Resistance to Change

Getting Started:
Wherever You Are
Is the Place to Begin

Learning Goals

As you study this chapter, you can look forward to reaching these learning goals:

1. List multiple pathways for becoming a director.
2. Apply checklists that help new directors get started.
3. Summarize strategies to anticipate and address resistance to new leadership.
4. Identify dynamics of the "founder's syndrome" in organizations.
5. Describe the four stages of organizational development.
6. Discuss the types of "legal entities" early childhood programs represent.
7. Explain differences between not-for-profit and for-profit organizations.

As human beings, our job in life is to help people realize how rare and valuable each one of us really is, and that each of us has something that no one else has—or ever will have—something inside that is unique to all time. It's our job to encourage each other to discover that uniqueness and to provide ways of developing its expression.

—**Fred Rogers**

Courage is the main quality of leadership, in my opinion, no matter where it is exercised. Usually it implies some risk —especially in new undertakings.

—**Walt Disney**

Case Study: Family Ties

Sergio's mother names him to direct one of her centers. Sergio immediately discovers errors in voucher reporting, expenditures, and licensing reports. Some errors are serious enough to approach illegalities. Sergio's mother, the founding director, sees no problem in her record keeping. She says Sergio should just be a good son and follow her lead.

If Sergio asks you for help, what would you advise him to do?

Taking the first step as a leader is both thrilling and daunting for the new administrator. Although she can hardly wait for that lemony pastel infant room to be completed, she worries about infant care costs. Excitement wells up with his first opportunity to lead a center; however, her heart may still be with the children back in the classroom. Combination feelings like this occur frequently as we step up to new challenges. To stay grounded, use your toolkit of emotional and social EQ skills. Allow yourself to stay energized by your purpose and vision of the difference you want to make.

Practical tools will help you. In this chapter, checklists and guidelines will help you chart your course into early childhood administration. Remember as each potential challenge or dilemma of getting started is discussed, the joys of leading on purpose can far outweigh the difficulties. You will make a difference in children's lives.

✷ From Teacher to Director

Nine out of ten directors serve as teachers first. Experienced in the classroom with children, teachers learn how to work with families and colleagues. By taking on additional roles, such as mentor, lead teacher, event planner, union representation, or teachers' representative on the center's board, teachers gain administrative experience. Teachers can gain administrative experience by helping with scheduling, overseeing classroom ratio maintenance, updating immunization records, and covering while the director takes vacation, to "get their feet wet" as assistant director. Many teachers view administration as their opportunity to make systemic changes they cannot make by remaining in one classroom.

Nonetheless, teachers, transitioning directly to administration, feel underprepared for management. Fully three-fourths of directors "report they were not prepared for the issues they encountered when they became directors" (*Research Notes* 1998, 1). Dynamics shift overnight, like tectonic plates under the earth's surface. Becoming a leader changes things.

Suddenly, teachers who were your friends steal wary glances at you. Others expect special favors. Some refuse to accept your new authority. They may want you to remain one of them, a rubber stamp for their desires. Some may feel jealous and even attempt to sabotage you indirectly. Dr. Phyllis Chesler's research substantiates that most women in leadership positions face sabotage from another woman.

To prepare yourself for potential challenges, take steps to deepen your confidence and conviction before starting your new position. As you deal effectively with each challenge to your leadership, you will gain your new team's respect and support. As your confidence grows, their confidence in you deepens. Teachers who become directors of

Approximately 90 percent of directors have been classroom teachers, but only one-fifth report that they always knew they wanted to become a director of a center and actively pursued the position.

—**Research Notes,** Center for Early Childhood Leadership

Be honest with yourself about the consequences and rewards of leaving the classroom . . . because there are both. If you wish you were in the classroom every day, then go back to it! The truth is the job never ends (just like being a teacher), so you need to set limits that are respectful of yourself and your life outside of school. And someday, you will have to give away all those curriculum materials you store in your attic.

—**Wendy,** director and former teacher

TABLE 5.1

Steps for Transitioning from Teacher to Administrator

1. List administration functions you have performed as a teacher; identify the transferable skills you have gained.
2. Assess your administrative strengths and shortcomings; plan how to address the shortcomings. The Myers-Briggs will help you.
3. Ask directors, especially those who took similar paths to yours, to share their experience.
4. Research how to meet your accrediting agency and state's requirements for director credentialing.
5. Enroll in early childhood administration courses through local colleges or online.
6. Seek out and participate in workshops and conferences on leadership and administration.
7. Read at least one article or book each week about leadership (check the bibliography at the end of this chapter).
8. Seek out a mentor or coach. If appropriate, ask your own director to mentor you.
9. Invite trusted colleagues and friends to serve as your transition support team.

existing organizations find the checklist in Table 5.1 useful. These steps will strengthen your credentials, help you assess your administrative talent, give you a broader perspective, and encourage you to build your external support system.

Facing and Embracing Resistance to New Leadership

Tanya, toddler lead teacher, is well respected by the other teachers. Tanya and your predecessor, prior director Maggie, did not see eye to eye. Tanya has come to expect that directors cannot be trusted to pay attention to teachers' suggestions or needs. At your first meeting with Tanya, you sense her reluctance to connect with you. Maggie whispers to you: "Tanya is a troublemaker." Families tell you that Tanya's reputation as a great teacher is one of the reasons they selected your school. What steps will you choose to take with Tanya? What process would you want to set with Maggie to ensure a productive transition of power?

You will need something more, however. That something more is political or "street savvy" EQ to address volatile power struggles that often heat up when leadership changes. "Callousness from a boss not only heightens the risk of losing good people, it torpedoes cognitive efficiency. A socially intelligent leader helps people contain and recover from their emotional stress" (Goleman, 2006, 276).

Much as early childhood programs can be deeply caring environments, they are also especially susceptible to clandestine catfights. Conflicts in women's organizations traditionally are dealt with indirectly, sometimes through "indirect and intimate aggression" (Chesler 2001, 121). Remind yourself not to take resistance personally by saying: "It's not about me." Anyone stepping into leadership is likely to face some resistance to her authority. Change is challenging. Our neural networks struggle with newness. To be successful:

> Yesterday is history. Tomorrow is mystery. And today? Today is a gift. That's why we call it the present.
>
> **—Babatunde Olantunji**

1. Hold reminders of your purpose close to your heart.
2. Knit together and utilize your internal and external support systems.
3. Introduce a process to transform power struggles into productive action.
4. Follow through on that process.

Picture an organization running smooth and clear as a mountain stream. In addition to being a great place to work (Bloom 1997), early childhood organizations can stand at the forefront of positive social change. Face your fear about confronting problems as soon as problems arise. President Franklin Roosevelt reminded us, at times of greatest challenge: "We have nothing to fear but fear itself." Your team will thank you for your courage, although perhaps not immediately. Integrity is your reward. Settle for nothing less. Leading on purpose is liberating.

Winning Over Opinion Leaders

To knit your internal support system together, assess first who the opinion leaders are. Opinion leaders have a following in the organization. An opinion leader's "say" influences how others think. Build strong, positive relationships with opinion leaders by connecting with each one individually, preferably off site. Take her out for coffee at a neutral site, away from peers' observing eyes, to start anew with her.

Once you have made a personal connection with opinion leaders like Tanya, you will be more able to talk over concerns with them. Listen closely as each opinion leader answers these questions for you:

1. What do you feel is important for me to understand to lead this organization effectively?
2. What else would you like me to know about the history/challenges of the organization?
3. What is your dream for the organization? What is your personal hope?
4. In what ways can I count on you to work with me in fulfilling the promise of the organization? What might interfere with your support?

Opinion leaders' answers to these questions, both verbally and nonverbally, gush with information about whom you can trust, what difficulties need to be addressed, and how your vision aligns with others' hopes for the program. This data will give you much to build upon.

If you find resistance to your leadership, welcome this. Often, an employee of the organization harbors resentment that you were chosen and she or he was not. Look for the strengths that person can offer. Consider that person as a candidate to become one of your potentially strongest supporters. Let her know how you plan to utilize and help develop her leadership skills, in return for her active support of your vision.

Be respectfully direct in telling her you expect her to come to you first when she or he disagrees with you. Let her know that you believe differences lead to creative solutions, whereas buried disagreements lead to work disruptions. You and Tanya, after all, are working toward the same worthy goal: quality care for children and families.

Problem Solving with Resistant Staff

Work through each difference she or he brings to you by asking her to:

1. Describe the nature of the problem. "Step to the side" to listen objectively for the underlying issue, while using your other EQ skills to read the emotional data.
2. Tell you what she needs to be able to resolve this problem constructively.
3. Discuss solutions that honor the organization's mission, your vision, and, when in alignment, her needs.
4. Find and implement points of agreement when you can.

If the opinion leader acts in ways that sabotage your leadership, call her in immediately and utilize progressive discipline steps (Chapter 8). If she or he fails to come to you directly to voice her concerns, call her in. Remember, courts hold insubordination as a legitimate cause for terminating an employee. The "directive supervision" process (Chapter 9) gives you a respectful and firm step-by-step approach for holding staff accountable for unprofessional behavior.

I have been through many challenges as a director. What has helped me? Having at least one person you can rely on to tell you the truth; surrounding yourself with people who are willing to follow your dream, and help shape it as you all go; hiring people who are committed to early childhood education and their own professional development; understanding that you can't make everything happen at once; and having an absolute ball, enjoying all the children, families, and relationships. Eating breakfast daily with 3–5 year olds is the best!

—Lori, director

Pay attention to cultural differences. Staff whose cultural heritage promotes saving face may not directly share concerns with you. Others may say they agree with you but secretly harbor misgivings. Many people may be uncomfortable telling you directly that they disagree with you. Take time to observe and listen to each staff member and teaching team. Use your social EQ to notice where their hopes and your vision differ. Suggest possible ways to promote employees' hopes in alignment with your vision and ask for alternative ways to do things. When honoring individual and cultural differences, leaders grow professionally and build a team that better reflects their community.

Waiting Out the Transition Period

Anyone who proposes to do good must not expect people to roll stones out of his way, but must accept his lot calmly if they even roll a few more upon it.

—Dr. Albert Schweitzer

Organizations are organisms. Organisms tend to reject a "foreign object" before adapting to embrace that change. Once you have taken these essential steps to clearing your pathway, you will be able to build individual and team relationships with all your staff. Remember, early childhood organizations are relational. By using EQ to build and maintain relationships, you open a clearing to introduce your organizational vision. Be sure to relate how your overarching vision embraces individual missions of staff members.

Use these guidelines to clear the path relationally in order for all the other organizational systems to work properly. Fiscal, physical plant, marketing, curriculum systems—all depend upon your personnel system's effectiveness. Your entry as a new leader can take time, patience, and the long view. Your transition period can feel lonely, especially in comparison with the comfort of the classroom you left behind. Keep your eyes on the prize.

⚔ Three Different Paths

Walking the "Inside Path" to Leadership

People who become directors in the organizations where they work take the "insider's path." This path has pros and cons. Insiders benefit from knowing and being known by the organization, the families, and community. Remember Amy and Jane (Chapter 1), who team taught for years and struggled when Amy was named director? Peers sometimes resent the promotion of an insider into a management position. To move up successfully within an organization, consider these Guidelines for Insiders:

1. Before you accept the offer to become director, pay close attention to the hiring process. How participatory was the process? Who were other internal applicants? What was the "scuttlebutt" among the teachers during the process?
2. Work with the current director to plan and hold staff meetings to outline and discuss the transition to new leadership. At that meeting, form small heterogeneous groups to surface staff fears, hopes, and practical questions. Address what emerges directly.
3. Meet individually with former peers. Ask them to describe what they will need from you as their boss. If that question is too direct, ask instead: "What will you miss about the way things are when I become director? What can we do to continue to work together as a new team?"
4. Be clear about and explain the difference professionally between being boss and being a colleague. You will make decisions differently, focusing on the needs of the organization first. Friendships at work will become more professional. This does not mean that you will stop caring about each person.

Insiders who have been successful at stepping in to leadership positions tell me that accompanying former peers through their discomfort professionally helps confirm your leadership.

Taking the "Outside Path" to Leadership

Being an outsider brings another set of opportunities and challenges. You may have heard the adage: "The devil you know is better than the devil you don't know." Like clans, organizations tend to favor insiders and suspect outsiders. Again, the "foreign" body may have to endure an uncomfortable initiation process before the clan adapts to a new leader. Initiation rites usually involve testing and some discomfort. Patience, difficult as that virtue can be to come by, sustains outsiders most. Keep the long view, while waiting out the adaptation process.

Being an outsider feels painful like any rejection or abandonment. Call upon your external support network. Share your feelings and frustrations as they emerge with trusted colleagues. At the same time, be proactive. Your staff may grieve the loss of their former director, and this can take the face of anger as well as sadness. Connect with one person at a time. Word about your integrity will begin to spread.

Susan describes her transition in this way: "Meeting continuously with board members was invaluable. Having the support of the board helped me through what might have been a lonely transition period. Keeping my sense of humor and letting others know I could laugh at my own mistakes also eased the tension. It took three years before my leadership was fully accepted."

Founder's Syndrome

Early childhood programs usually spring like lilac buds from the stem of one person's dream. Creating a promising new program requires a deeply felt life passion. The creator of the program becomes the founding director. This founder, acting like Mom or Dad of the organization, perceives the program as "my baby." Original staff members feel more like family members than employees. Fierce loyalties form. Memories of the good old days when everyone worked tirelessly creating the organization evoke wistful expressions and damp eyes. An "inside" group, with strong attachments, forms. Anyone not in on the founding of the organization can feel like an "outsider."

This leads to the "founder's syndrome" where the departing director's style firmly establishes expectations, written and unwritten, about the way the next administrator should function. Founder's syndrome can be a setup for failure. No subsequent leader can be a founding director. Saying goodbye to the founder can be disruptive for staff. Employees may feel they are losing a family member and, in particular, a caring parent. Grieving their loss is essential. The departing director can do much to ease the pathway for her replacement by creating rituals and forums with her staff for closure and moving on.

Should you accept a position in which you follow a founder, you will find these pointers useful:

1. Observe organizational dynamics while the founder is still director.
2. Assess whether your personal style and vision are aligned with the founder's style and vision. Your new vision must closely align with the founder's vision to be acceptable to staff.
3. Dialogue with the founder about activities she plans to ease her departure.
4. Ascertain what ongoing relationship the founder wants to have with you and the center. Be clear on how much contact you feel is appropriate.
5. Create activities with the founder, including staff, family, community, and team meetings that will signal the change in leadership.
6. Acknowledge that your leadership of the organization will initiate a different, but essential, phase of organizational life.

Founders, like parents, stamp organizations with personal patterns and expectations. The founder's vision, identity, and style form the organization's vision, identity, and style. Replacing a founder can be one of the prickliest pathways to leadership.

✄ Stages of Organizational Development

Forming, Storming, Norming, and Performing

As you step into leadership, whatever your pathway, an understanding of organizational dynamics will be a helpful EQ tool. Organizations, from classroom teams to families to early childhood programs, progress through predictable stages (Tuckman 1965). Each team or program you participate in, in some way or another, works through similar dynamics. Leaders can gain perspective on the growing pains of their organization by identifying its current phase and guiding the organization on to the next phase. Understanding these stages is a useful social EQ tool for directors.

Forming

In this "honeymoon" period, everyone is at her best, looking good, feeling hopeful, and expecting the best. Team teachers greet one another, anxious to share their dreams and ideas for the children. (See "Forming," Chapters 1–4.)

Storming

When the honeymoon is over, all those little things that seemed so charming before begin to bother us. Staff, who may have smiled in welcoming a new director, return to business as usual, resisting any changes. In organizational terms, certain predictable questions need to be cleared up to free team members to move on (see "Storming," Chapters 5–8):

- Leadership (who is in charge);
- Task (what our work is);
- Ground rules (clear, written expectations for working together, especially how decisions will be made and by whom);
- Membership (who is on the team, and who is not); and
- Time frame for accomplishing the task (goals and measurable objectives).

Norming

The resolutions agreed upon in the Storming phase now are put into place as the norms of the organization. Expectations become clear on who does what. (See "Norming," chapters 9–13.)

Performing

With systems in place, and problems addressed, everyone is ready to get down to doing the work of the organization. (See "Performing," chapters 14–15.)

Re-forming

In reality, a fifth stage occurs: Re-forming. When new issues pop up, new people are hired, or changes to policies or practices are proposed, the organization can return to the beginning stage. The team is re-formed with fresh players, new challenges can bring on thunderclouds and ice storms, and the same list of issues needs to be resolved before the new group can function effectively. (See "Re-Forming," Chapter 16.)

Several years later, another likely phase was added to these styles of organizational development (Tuckman & Jensen 1977): Adjourning. Not every team, partnership, or program is meant to last. When a committee finishes its work, the committee disbands. As new teachers are hired, teaching teams change. Directors move on. In some cases, schools and programs close down. Adjourning is similar to Re-forming in that a new phase takes place. However, adjourning is the final phase in the life of some organizations. As with any change, leaders need to pay attention to the feelings of individuals and the mood of the whole organization to better guide them through the transitions.

Reflect on a long-term friendship, relationship, or team you have been part of in the context of the stages above. Did you experience the honeymoon? How did you address the storming times? What stage are you in now?

Here is a more descriptive take on how organizations evolve through the forming, storming, and norming phases. This description provides insight on a leader's job during these stages (Greiner 1998). Beginning organizations will grow through (1) Initiation and (2) Administration. Initiation is another way to describe the Forming or honeymoon stage. The Administration stage covers what must happen for the organization to flourish in the long run, after the honeymoon is over. As you can imagine, not all organizations survive to the Administration phases. Some organizations collapse when the founder departs.

Initiation Phase of Organizational Growth

The founding stage is the birth of the organization. This initial phase is characterized by high energy, strong feelings of commitment, and job fluidity. All are caught up in the excitement of creating something new. The founder's words and spontaneous actions become the living core of the organization. Staff pitch in to perform necessary functions, and roles and responsibilities are unchartered. Procedures and policies, forms, and job descriptions are created as needed. Decision-making and problem-solving processes are worked out on the spot. The Initiation phase suits a visionary, flexible, and dynamic leader. Staff members often report that they feel like part of the founder's family.

Administrative Phase of Organizational Growth

Stabilizing the organization for ongoing survival after the founder's departure is essential. This phase is the "clean up" phase for the organization. Every important task that was done spontaneously now must be reduced to writing. Policies and procedures need to be codified. Job descriptions are written. Staff and parent handbooks are created or significantly rewritten. Meeting schedules with agendas are set well in advance. A chain of command replaces ad hoc, on the spot, decision making. The Administrative phase best suits a leader who enjoys stability, predictability, and structure.

Your knowledge of these organizational development dynamics will serve you well as a leader. By understanding the predictable stages of any group or organization's growing pains, you can offer them the light of perspective, as well as practical tools on how to move more gracefully on to their next phase.

With these principles in mind, let's look at additional pathways into leadership.

⚓ We Are Family:
Becoming the Director of a Family Organization

Directors who take over a family-run organization face another set of "getting started" dynamics. Have you noticed the number of sisters and brothers, aunts and uncles, cousins and in-laws who work for the same early childhood organization? Families often employ people they know best and trust most. Stepping up from family member to director of a family-run business presents its own set of opportunities and challenges.

The job of the new director in a family enterprise is to build upon the functional and address and/or diminish less functional family dynamics.

Family secession planning, intent upon keeping the business "in the family," can work. What makes family secession plans work, while others fail? Most families, as human systems, exhibit functional as well as dysfunctional characteristics. These dysfunctions can carry over into the program and undermine its quality and day-to-day operations. By emphasizing professionalism, a new director can focus the family organization on enhancing quality.

Tips for Taking Leadership in a Family Organization

1. Begin by inviting everyone to a family business meeting.
2. Bring in an outside facilitator to keep discussions productive.
3. Ask everyone to reflect on these questions: "What are this organization's strong points to build upon? What are the ways we need to reinvent ourselves?" Go around the circle, inviting each family member to share his or her experience.
4. Use your EQ to listen for what is unsaid as well as what is verbalized. Watch for whose contribution commands the greatest attention. Chances are good that the family has one or two members whose opinion matters most. Your job is to work with that person(s) to ensure a transition of leadership to you. If you have used the services of a facilitator, be sure to ask for that person's observations and recommendations.
5. Discuss professionalism with family members. How can objectivity and fairness be maintained when making decisions? If family meetings are not part of the program's culture, meet individually and follow similar processes.
6. Finally, pay attention to "insider versus outsider" dynamics. Nonfamily employees may feel like outsiders. Meet individually with employees to discuss their hopes and goals for themselves and the organization. Honor legitimate hopes by incorporating them into the organization's evolving mission. Mentor promising staff. Introduce an employee evaluation system and apply it consistently to everyone.

Above all, keep a sense of humor. Humor brings perspective and relief to sticky family situations.

✇ Founding Directors: Creating a Childcare Organization

Each year, a small but dedicated number of my students in this course envision opening their own centers. This trend is reflected nationwide. If you become one of those dedicated founders, the checklist in Table 5.2 can guide your steps. Remember, you will not have to reinvent the wheel. Benefit from the experience of others who have taken the same path. They would want you to stand on their shoulders.

Every new director can benefit from knowing the bases that must be covered to create programs. Not all founders have had classroom teaching experience. Founding directors often leave behind another career for the dream of starting their own business. Retailers, accountants, parents, attorneys, financial planners, and musicians have all founded early childhood organizations. Many skills are transferable to early childhood.

T A B L E   5 . 2

Starting Up an Early Childhood Organization Checklist

1. Ask yourself, "What is my dream?" Envision your center after five, ten, and twenty-five years of operation.
2. Contact your state licensing department and legislators for information, regulations, and help.
3. Assess the need. How would your center complement current childcare programs? Ask your Resource and Referral (R&R) agency and other directors, "What needs are unmet?"
4. Meet with your local small business association: use their service for setting up new organizations.
5. Study accreditation standards.
6. Work with a trusted realtor. Assess possible sites to construct, upgrade, or utilize.
7. Decide, with an attorney's help, what "legal entity" is best for your purposes (see below).
8. Create your business plan.
9. Seek financing. Which alternative is best for you?
10. Join your local chamber of commerce. Ask for assistance, especially in marketing and network building.

❈ Types Of Early Childhood Organizations

Creators of early childhood programs can choose from a variety of types of organizations, from nonprofit to franchised center. Each of these types has been formalized into a legal entity. What does "legal entity" mean? Entity indicates an institution that can enter into contractual agreements (like renting a site or accepting vouchers) and can be sued for their actions. Forming a legal entity sets a useful boundary between the personal and professional realms. Over the years, different types of childcare organizations have been (and will continue to be) created. Each type of entity differs from the other types. Each legal entity must meet a set of standards developed especially for it.

Our government regulates businesses to ensure that essential public safety standards are met. Your local small business association can help you study your options, while you decide what best fits your goals. Work with an attorney to draw up and file legal forms necessary for each type of program.

In considering your options, ask yourself if you want to:

1. Undertake the venture by yourself, or partner with others?
2. Found your own program, or be part of an established program, for example, a franchised corporation?
3. Report to a board of directors?
4. Make annual reports and hold meetings with shareholders?
5. Qualify for government grants?

Your answers to these questions indicate the type of business entity that will fit you best. Options include:

Sole Proprietorship

If you create your own center and maintain responsibility for making all decisions, you are its sole proprietor. This is the equivalent of going solo as a businessperson. "Proprietor" signals that you own your organization. You do not need to form a board of directors, nor must you accommodate requirements of a larger sponsoring agency.

Sole proprietors appreciate the freedom to design the program in alignment with their personal vision. People who like to work without a boss will be happiest as sole proprietors.

Because a sole proprietor forms a business, that business must comply with state and federal laws and requirements. Legal forms must be completed and filed with local, state, and federal governmental agencies. A sole proprietor has the right to name her organization. A sole proprietor will want to check first, however, to make sure that the name she chooses has not already been chosen. Otherwise, she may be accused of "trademark infringement," by using a name that has been registered. You can contact your small business association and/or attorney for guidance on these matters.

Consider how trademark issues can affect Jamilah in the Chapter 3 case study on page 28. If Jamilah fears that another center may be named "Jamilah's Neighborhood," what steps does she need to take?

Sole proprietors can face the challenge of isolation. Independent owners often long for more contact with peers. Meeting other director/owners at conferences and workshops can provide a community of peers. Forming owner/director support groups with other directors helps end isolation.

While a sole proprietor owns her program, this individual does not necessarily serve as the director. Owners often hire directors who report to the sole proprietor. This owner-administrator relationship works best when job descriptions and boundaries are clear. Otherwise, staff may be confused about who is in charge.

Partnerships

If you do not wish to venture alone into founding your own center, consider joining forces with another compatible person(s). Two or more people can form a legal entity called a "partnership." Partnerships form when people develop a program together, or when one person solely cannot afford the costs.

Partners have choices about who is most responsible, both financially and administratively. Some partners split everything equally. Imagine three teachers who want to collaborate, pool resources, and start a new center. They could each be responsible for 33 percent of the partnership they create.

Partners can also designate differing financial interests in the business. One partner may own 60 percent of the center, while two others are each responsible for 20 percent. Another option is having a "silent" partner. Silent partners invest financially, without requiring a voice in the everyday running of the program. Family members often serve as silent partners who offer seed money to get a new program under way.

Franchised Centers

If you file your income taxes with the help of a local branch of a national tax preparation service, you are familiar with franchises. Fast-food restaurants also are usually franchises. At a franchise, customers can expect consistent service at each location.

Early childhood organizations can also "franchise" themselves. The originating program can franchise its physical plant and curriculum design, mission, mottos, staff, and parent handbook. Others can purchase the franchise and all that comes with it. The purchaser must legally meet and adhere to the practices and standards of the original organization. Additionally, the purchaser of the franchise pays a percentage of her gross profits to the original organization.

Franchising works best for a well-established organization ready to branch out over a greater geographical area. Maintaining quality at each new franchise can be a challenge.

Corporations

Forming corporations can be especially complex due to the work involved in meeting numerous standards. Founding a corporation requires administrators to complete and file "articles of incorporation." Bylaws, the rules an organization adheres to, must also be filed with the secretary of state's office. Corporations are required to form a board of directors, with clearly written responsibilities for oversight (making sure everything is done properly) of the program.

Instead of individual owners or partners, corporations have "shareholders." A shareholder holds a share in the profits of the corporation, and shareholders elect directors to run the corporation. These directors are not the same as the center directors. Corporate directors select members of the Board of Trustees, the group of people who are vested with oversight of the organization. Directors may be personally liable for corporate actions and can be sued. If you are thinking of establishing a corporate legal entity, discuss your plans with directors of existing corporate centers and learn from their experiences.

Annually, Roger Neugebauer of *Child Care Exchange* lists the largest corporate early childhood programs. Bright Horizons Family Solutions and La Petite consistently are in the top five corporate programs.

Nonprofits

Nonprofit centers can make a profit! However, nonprofits are required to use that profit to meet organizational goals. For example, imagine that St. Bartelemeo Family Service System brings in more money than it spends. That extra income must be used directly to fund St. Bartelemeo's programs. Teacher bonuses, classroom books or equipment, and/or expansion to new sites are examples of where nonprofit early childhood programs have placed their profits. A board of directors governs and oversees the organization's work.

Examples of nonprofits include:

1. Agency-sponsored programs. Community agencies like faith-based groups (St. Bartelemeo) and community service agencies such as CAPs (community action programs);
2. Individually sponsored programs. Early childhood organizations that rely upon grant funding and that serve the "greater good." An example of this is Project Hope in Dorchester, Massachusetts. Project Hope serves children and families without homes.

Nonprofits are also known as 501c3's. The title comes from federal legislation that sets compliance standards nonprofits follow. Completing, filing, and being approved as a 501c3 allows you to apply for grants available only to nonprofits.

For Profits

Profit-making organizations aim to do just that: make a profit. For-profits meet different organizational standards than nonprofits. For-profits have stockholders, who own shares in the organization. A "share" is a percentage of the business. Some shareholders may own more shares than others. If a for-profit organization clears $10,000 at the end of the fiscal year, that profit may be distributed to shareholders. Shareholders vote on what to do with the profits: reinvest the profits in the organization? Upgrade the playground? Add on an infant room? Take their share of the $10,000?

Stereotyping of nonprofits and for-profits is nonproductive. For-profits are not "out for themselves, dedicated only to the bottom line." For-profits often give back to their communities. Bright Horizons Family Solutions, for example, funds programs to improve quality in targeted areas. Nonprofits are not "poorly run, bleeding heart" organizations. Nonprofits use sound business practices and can have effective leaders. Both nonprofit and for-profit early childhood programs may have a mission for the greater good.

✂ Are You Ready?

Getting started as a new leader means making practical choices, while being uplifted by your dream. Winston Churchill, who led Great Britain through the perils of a world war, advised: "The pessimist sees difficulty in every opportunity. The optimist sees the opportunity in every difficulty." Brain research (Kliff 2007) reaffirms the power of optimism. Where will your optimism take you on your journey toward leadership?

Reflection Questions

1. Considering all the pathways to leadership of early childhood and school age programs, what was or is likely to be your pathway? Describe in a written or recorded reflection what is most (a) challenging, (b) encouraging, and (c) special about your process.

2. Reflect on your leadership style that you learned about by studying the Myers-Briggs in Chapter 3. Identify how your leadership style will help you get started as a leader. What steps are likely to be the most challenging for you? How might you use the tips for communicating with people of opposite preferences as you picture yourself building relationships with new team members? Write a reflection on how your knowledge of your Myers-Briggs leadership style can help you get started as a leader.

3. Laws and regulations can be difficult to put into plain language. Review website literature and small business association booklets. Write a 3 to 5 page commonsense guide on (a) the different types of organizations or (b) tips on how to choose the legal entity best for you.

Team Projects

1. Your instructor will organize small affinity groups from your class depending upon which pathway to leadership you have taken or expect to take. Review the section of this chapter that applies directly to your path. Meet with your small group members to research and discuss common problems and resources available to you. Prepare and present a summary of your findings to your classmates. As you listen to other small groups' presentations, look for similarities and differences.

2. To find out more about your entry into leadership, interview current directors by first creating as a team an interview questionnaire. What would you like to find out about their entry into leadership? Conduct at least one interview apiece. Summarize and report your findings to the class.

3. Discuss either the founder's syndrome or family-run program dynamics. Which of these presents more difficulties in your estimation? Create a case study that captures these special situations. Share the case study with your class, and facilitate a discussion of possible solutions. Compare your case with Sergio's situation (p. 67). Utilize NAEYC's *Code of Ethical Responsibility* or the NACCP Code of Ethics (p. 251) in your presentation.

4. Shakespeare said, "Uneasy is the head that wears the crown." Resistance to change, especially a change in leadership, can be fierce. Research, discuss, write, and prepare a coaching session or video for potential new directors on how to effectively deal with resistance to new leadership. Take into account resistance from within yourself as well as from outside individuals and constituencies. Share your presentation with the class.

Bibliography

Bloom, P.J. 1997. *A great place to work* (revised ed.). Washington, DC: NAEYC.

Brinkman, R., and R. Kirschner. 2002. *Dealing with people you can't stand.* New York: McGraw-Hill.

Carter, R.T. 2000. *Addressing cultural differences in organizations.* New York: Sage Publications.

Chesler, P. 2001. *Woman's inhumanity to woman.* New York: Plume Books.

Click, P. 2004. *Administration of programs for young children* (6th ed.). Clifton Park, NY: Delmar.

Dalai Lama. 2003. *Destructive emotions: How can we overcome them?* New York: Bantam Dell.

Goleman, D. 2006. *Social intelligence.* New York: Bantam Press.

Gonzalez-Mena, J. 2001. *Multicultural issues in child care* (3rd ed.). Mountain View, CA: Mayfield Publishing Company.

Greiner, L. 1998. Evolution and revolution in organizational growth. *Harvard Business Review* (May 11).

Jordan, J.V., ed. 1997. *Women's growth in diversity.* New York: Guilford Press.

Kliff, S. 2007. This is your brain on optimism. *Newsweek,* October 24. http://www.newsweek.com/id/61572.

Neugebauer, R. 2007. Annual review of for-profit child care organizations. *Child Care Information Exchange* (January).

Research Notes Center for early childhood leadership. National Louis University. *Centerforearlychildhoodleadership.com* (Summer 1998).

Sciarra, D., and A. Dorsey. 2003. *Developing and administering a child care center* (5th ed.). Clifton Park, NY: Delmar.

Shapiro, A. 2003. *Creating contagious commitment to change.* Hillsborough, NC: Strategy Perspective.

Shoemaker, C.C. 2000. *Leadership and management of programs for young children.* Upper Saddle River, NJ: Prentice Hall.

Tuckman, B.W. 1965. Developmental sequence in small groups. *Psychological Bulletin* 63: 384–399.

Tuckman, B.W., and M.A. Jensen. 1977. Stages of small group development revisited. *Group and Organizational studies* 2: 419–427.

Web Resources

Legal Entities

The 'Lectric Law Library *(www.Lectlaw.com)*

InvestorWords Investing Glossary *(www.Investorwords.com)*

501c3's

LegalZoom *(www.Legalzoom.com)*

Foundation Group *(www.501c3.org)*

Internal Revenue Service: Charities & Non-Profits *(www.irs.gov/charities/)*

Thompson & Thompson Transactional Law Firm *(www.t-tlaw.com)*

Management Resources

Free Management Library *(www.Managementhelp.org)*

Help 4 NonProfits: Community Driven Institute *(www.help4nonprofits.com)*

Surviving Founder's Syndrome *(www.Ccfbest.org/management/survivingfounder.htm)*

Wikipedia *(www.Wikipedia.org)*

Partnering with Change

Learning Goals

As you study this chapter, you can look forward to reaching these learning goals:

1. Discuss the nature of change.
2. Explain the difference between "managing" and "partnering with" change.
3. Address changes from the inside out rather than the outside in.
4. Examine the degree to which people welcome or resist change.
5. Explain the relationship between grieving a loss and experiencing a change.
6. Summarize models for partnering with change.
7. Describe ways to foster resilience in the midst of change.
8. Recognize the role of optimism in facing the unknown.

Human growth is full of slides backward as well as leaps forward and is sure to include times of withdrawal, opposition, and anger, just as it encompasses tears as well as laughter.

—*Fred Rogers*

If you don't like something change it. If you can't change it, change your attitude. Don't complain.

—*Maya Angelou*

Case Study: New Director, New Changes

New director Amalie bustles with hundreds of new ideas to enliven Best Friends Pre-school. Amalie's heart beats hopefully as she walks into her first staff meeting. "We'll bring in an exciting new curriculum. Research shows children love it," Amalie bubbles.

Looking expectantly around the room for approval, Amalie is shocked to find teachers stiff and still as gravestones. Amalie huffs to herself: "What is their problem?"

Change is many things. For the person who initiates change, like Amalie, change is energizing. To the person who feels at the mercy of change, change can be threatening and unwelcome. Our attitude toward change derives from the amount of choice we feel we have to create, accept, reject, or modify the change.

We are exposed to change every moment, despite our yearning for stability and security. Heraclites, a Greek philosopher, observed, "You can never place your foot in the same river twice." Rushing river water that flows over our toes can never be called back. Each day as we arrive at work, something changes. A spat over the treasured tyrannosaurus rex toy erupts between preschool pals. Rain splatters cupcakes on the playground picnic table. The cook asks to go on maternity leave.

The river keeps on flowing beyond our view. This chapter provides helpful models for partnering with inevitable changes.

> Change is the status quo.
>
> —Gwen Morgan

⚔ The Challenges of Change

The Brain and Change

Humans resist change because our brain pathways are wired to click into hyperalert when something new occurs. An innovation may be a threat. Adrenalin revs up our systems in response. We jump from "at ease" to tensed and itchy discomfort. Adrenalin junkies like race car drivers and skydivers experience the heart pounding adrenalin surge as pleasurable. For the rest of us, the physiological effects of change are far from appealing. Self-preservation is an ancient motivation, "If it ain't broke, don't fix it."

To experience this resistance dynamic for yourself, clasp your hands together like you usually do. This feels "normal." Now, re-clasp your hands in a different way, lacing your fingers in a new pattern. How does that feel? If even a small change in how we join our hands together feels uncomfortable, imagine our body's reaction to an important change.

Our brain pathways settle into routine patterns. Changes to those patterns can feel abnormal. New brain pathways need to be established for each new pattern. Time and practice are needed for the new pattern to feel as comfortable as the old. Have you moved to a new residence or rearranged your room? Do you recall how conscious and alert you needed to be to adapt? Your brain was establishing new connections.

> Anticipate the good so that you may enjoy it.
>
> —Ethiopian proverb

Definitions of Change

Change, as a noun, according to *Merriam-Webster's Dictionary*, is:

a. Alteration
b. Transformation
c. Substitution
d. Passage
e. Menopause

As a verb, Webster's defines "to change" as "to switch, transfer . . . break." Which of these definitions of change gets your attention?

For me, "break" and "menopause" call up physical reactions. Ouch! I broke both of my wrists as a child. I broke my left wrist falling from a schoolyard swing. My right wrist fractured in a wrestling match with my best friend's brother. Both wrists now warn me when rain clouds are on the horizon.

Menopause? Oh my! Women talk about "the change" with knowing glances. Have you heard of the Broadway show *Menopause, the Musical*? Writer/producer Jeanie Linders transformed an inevitable (and often disorienting) female life transition into a bevy of humorous songs and dances. Linders is rumored to have written the show "after a bottle of wine and a hot flash." Linders' approach to unbidden change reminds me of the power of humor to bring healing perspective.

Clearly, change, while inevitable, can also be uncomfortable. This dynamic leaves us again holding two opposites in our hands at once. On the one hand, change happens. On the other hand, we resist change. How can leaders, conscious of this paradox, flow with and/or initiate change in a helpful, functional, useful manner? Are you ready? Let's take a look.

Who Is the Boss of Change?

When I was in elementary school, my Mom cautioned me, "The only things you can be sure of on earth are death and taxes." As I looked around, I saw a neighborhood full of predictability. Hadn't our elm tree stood straight as a candle for 100 years? Didn't snow blanket our hillsides every December so I could sled down at breakneck speeds? Mom couldn't prove that purple lilacs adorning Margery Sage's farm wouldn't bloom every May, or that hot fudge sundaes weren't the yummiest dessert ever. Brownie scouts "flew up" to become real girl scouts. Each September, I regretfully said good-bye to blackberry-picking summer days to trudge my mile to school. As far as my young eyes could see, death and taxes didn't live on my street.

My Mom, of course, had a point. My magically thinking child's mind was not ready to accommodate the concept that just about everything changes. As my colleague Gwen Morgan notes, "Change is the status quo!" Even as a young adult, I was ready to make a long list when a well-intended teacher asked, "What do you have control over?" As I ponder that question today, I can place only one thing on my list. How would you answer that teacher's question?

Much as I may like to think I can control outcomes, events, and, I admit, other folks' behavior, I have come to understand that the only thing I can control about change is my own attitude. I admire author, Viktor Frankl. Despite overwhelming agonies as a concentration camp prisoner during World War II, Frankl remained clear about his freedom. He found hope within even though he lacked control over anyone or anything outside of him.

Theologian Rheinhold Niebur, who visited war-ravaged Europe, allegedly penned these words, "God, grant me the serenity to accept the things I cannot change, the courage to change the things I can, and the wisdom to know the difference." Twelve-step addiction recovery programs, such as AA (Alcoholics Anonymous) and CODA (Codependents Anonymous), embrace this "Serenity Prayer," as a daily reminder to keep perspective when problems knock on our door.

Think about situations you have tried to change or wish you could change. Write these challenges down. Next, consider your list in the context of the serenity prayer: what do you have the power to change and what lies beyond your power to make change?

> The last of the human freedoms is the ability to choose one's attitude in any given set of circumstances.
>
> —**Viktor Frankl,** *Man's Search for Meaning*

Break down Niebur's words to find useful leadership insights regarding your "change" list:

1. *Serenity* is mine when I let go of thinking I can control others (people, places, or things). These are all "things I cannot change";
2. *Courage* is the virtue I need to change my thoughts, attitudes, and actions. The "things I can change" lie within myself. My power derives more from letting go of attempting to control than from holding on to the belief that I can control others;
3. *Wisdom* evolves from learning to discern what I have the power to change, and what I need to let go of trying to "fix" beyond myself.

For managers, directors, and leaders of any sort, control seems essential to authority. Administrators must control budget spending, accomplish tasks on time, comply with licensing regulations, and maintain positive relationships with boards of directors. If you take a closer look at these functions, however, you will discover that what you can control is *your* action, not others' reactions.

For example, a director may work hard to build productive relationships with board members; however, she cannot control a board member's response to her efforts. Similarly, a director may think he maintains tight control over fiscal spending until the March winds blow a tree down over the school van.

"Crash" goes the transportation budget. The director had placed just enough funds in the account to anticipate rising gasoline costs. A manager's control rests, curiously, in acknowledging what is beyond our control.

> Walk on the rainbow trail . . .
> Walk on a trail of song . . .
> And all around you will be beauty . . .
>
> **—Navaho song**

⚔ Leadership and Control

Who is the boss of change? Back we come to the challenge of leadership: holding opposite realities in each hand. On the one hand, directors are responsible for the budget. On the other hand, they cannot fully predict budget spending. On the one hand, directors think they have all the bases covered should the state licensor drop by. Over many years, licensors and directors can develop a strong and collegial working relationship. But things change instantly when a new licensor arrives unexpectedly with a different emphasis from her predecessor. "Crash" goes the expectation!

Many directors tell me when they began as administrators, they believed, "If I only work hard enough and long enough, I will finally get everything in order and under control." New directors work diligently, checking one task after another off the "to do" list.

> Keep what is worth saving, and with a breath of kindness, blow the rest away.
>
> **—Dinah Mulock Craik**

Like mushrooms after a storm, one unanticipated challenge after another pops up. The lead toddler teacher resigns the first week of school; energy costs go through the roof; reaccreditation standards change; cicadas devour luscious leaves on trees shading the playground. Andi Genser said of her early days as director, "The hardest and most important lesson for me to learn as a director is that the challenges never end. I went into the position thinking I would work on everything until it got resolved. Eventually, my program would be problem free. I learned to become comfortable with the fact that a new challenge presents itself all the time" (see Table 6.1).

Here is a helpful principle to keep in mind, "Someone else's action does not have to predict my response" (Dalai Lama as quoted in *Life's Journeys according to Mr. Rogers* 2005, 6). If a frantic parent loses his temper and yells at a teacher, does the teacher have to yell back? Despite how upsetting the parent's behavior may be, the teacher can choose a professional response. Remember the amygdala hijack? Adrenalin may spurt through our veins causing us to feel out of control in the moment. Nonetheless, we can choose to wait out that intense, heart-stopping moment before taking action we might regret. In this way, we can be the "boss of change."

> A leader's work is never done. Putting out a fire, reaching a summit, slaying a monster only clears the way for the next and greater challenge, be it organizational or personal.
>
> **—Don Moyer,** *Harvard Business Review*

TABLE 6.1

Challenges That Come with Change

1. Change is constant;
2. Change happens whether I am ready or not;
3. The only control I have in the face of change is to choose my own attitude and actions.

Knowing When and How to "Focus on Yourself"

"Keep the focus on yourself" may sound selfish. The phrase, "It's all about me" signals immaturity. In the survival stage of staff development, for example, teachers cannot see beyond their own needs. Imagine a novice teacher who frets so much about preparing for each day that he cannot pay attention to parents with questions about their child's day. At that stage for the teacher, "it's all about me" rings true.

Even directors can get stuck in it's-all-about-me thinking. Consider a director who gets tangled up in fear about confronting staff members who gossip. She cannot see beyond her own fear. Meanwhile the gossipers, unchecked, spread destructive, untrue rumors. Self-centered it's-all-about-me thinking can cause an individual to be unaware of what's going on around her and rob her of perspective. She cannot see her responsibility to address negative behavior if she cannot see beyond her own worries.

A director in New Jersey told me, "Guilt is a selfish emotion." I was stunned! I always thought feeling guilty was the first step to accepting responsibility for what I need to change. For her, prolonged guilty feelings block action to make changes for the better. "Guilt is all about me" and is paralyzing in that case. I came to see her point. As H. B. Sanders observes: "Worry is a mental attempt to control the future" (2005, 55). Guilt is an attempt to control the past. We cannot control the past. Worry does little to improve the future.

When it comes to change, "It's all about me" can signal a more positive, mature perspective. Keeping the focus on ourselves, on our power to change the things we can, is an asset. The director who waits for other people to change can wait a lifetime. The director who keeps the focus on herself and the action she can take is the director who makes a difference. Using energy to worry about what others will or won't do wastes precious time. As one of my employees observed, "That's like trying to push a rope." Keep the focus on what you can change. Let go of trying to change others.

When I speak about change to large groups of people, I like to ask, "Who has either been married or in a partnership for a long time?" At first, many people raise their hands. "OK, who has been in a relationship for over twenty years?" Hands drop. "Thirty-years? Thirty-five years?" I continue asking until the number of hands raised has diminished to one or two. The rest of the audience at this point, almost always applauds anyone with her hand still raised. I then ask our long-term relationship experts, "Have you been able to change your partner?" "No," they always respond. Some add, "I wouldn't want to," or "Together we have changed." Learning to change together as director and team is one of the rewards of leading on purpose.

How Welcome Is Change?

Changing what we can and letting go of trying to fix or change others is a powerful director's tool. In your experience, how welcome is a new idea? What percentage of people affected by the new idea "buy in" eagerly? Does "But we've always done it this way!" sound familiar? Let's look at information on how people respond to a change. Does your experience match Neila A. Connors' (2000, 47)?

> When you're stuck in a spiral, to change all aspects of the spin you need only to change one thing.
>
> **—Christina Baldwin**

> What other people think about me is none of my business.

TABLE 6.2

The 4 *P*'s to Remember When Communicating to Staff about Transitions

1. *Purpose:* Why we have to do this.
2. *Picture:* What it will look and feel like when we reach our goal.
3. *Plan:* Step by step, how we will get there.
4. *Part:* What you can (and need to) do to move us forward.

Source: William and Susan Mitchell Bridges, 2000.

The truth is that through any change:
5% of the people will accept it immediately,
25% will slowly adapt and accept,
60% will take a "let's wait and see" approach and will eventually accept the new idea if it
works to their advantage, and
10% will never accept change.
The most astute leaders recognize this and DON'T WASTE TIME FERTILIZING ROCKS
OR WATERING WEEDS. The Japanese term for never-ending pursuit is kaizen. *It is a*
never-ending pursuit to improve and advance. Effective leaders promote this philosophy.

Reflect for a moment on your response when another person wanted to change something that affected you. Were you instantly enthusiastic, slowly accepting, sitting back with a wait-and-see attitude, or refusing to budge? The answer to this question often depends on who initiated the change and how it was initiated. When individuals feel someone else is imposing change on them, they are more likely to resist.

Leaders who inspire staff to buy into new ideas have often resisted change themselves. As a result, these leaders have learned the power of "due process." By involving others from the beginning in developing a change, a leader avoids resistance. Remember Amalie's experience in the chapter case study? When her staff felt left out of the process, they dug in their heels and resisted. If Amalie had solicited and listened to their ideas about a new curriculum, the teachers most likely would have been more open. In fact, their input may help focus, redesign, or otherwise improve the proposal. Buy-in to change depends on an open, engaging, affirming, and appreciative process (see Table 6.2).

Trauma and Transitions

Children and adults who have survived trauma may find change especially wrenching. The child subjected to unpredictable, neglectful, or violent parenting aches for safe places, dependable routines, and soothing relationships. Sadly, statistics show that the younger a child is, the more likely that child is to be maltreated (Center for the Study of Social Policy 2004). In fact, "of the 825,000 substantiated cases of child abuse or neglect in 1999, 14 percent represented children under one year of age; 24 percent represented ages from two through five" (2004, 23–24). For guidelines on steps childhood professionals can take to help traumatized children, see "Teachers may never know: Building professional relationships with children and families that heal" (Bruno, *Southern Early Childhood Association Journal,* Fall 2007).

If you notice that an innovation causes significant anxiety and resistance for a staff member, take time to invite that person to talk with you about her fears and reservations. When an everyday problem overwhelms adults, we may be reminded of a past problem that remains unresolved. Therapists, not directors, are best suited to help traumatized people. However, listening in a caring way may go a long way to help the staff member relax out of rigidity into flexibility. That staff member may become a strong ally for the change.

Change and "Cognitive Dissonance"

Driving home from work one day, I listened to an NPR (National Public Radio) interview with Elliot Aronson, coauthor of *Mistakes Were Made (but Not by Me): Why We Justify Foolish Beliefs, Bad Decisions, and Hurtful Acts* (2007). Aronson first coined the term "cognitive dissonance," the internal, squirrelly tension we feel when we act in a way that does not honor our value system.

Imagine a director whose core value is integrity. When he finds himself favoring one infant teacher over another, he may feel the tension of cognitive dissonance. He may be able to convince himself that he is not showing favoritism. Employees, reading the director's non-verbal cues, sense that he feels guilty and out-of-sorts, despite the smile on his face. In early childhood environments, cognitive dissonance is not a secret that can be kept by silence. The high level of EQ leads to being "read," even when we might prefer our feelings to be invisible.

According to Aronson (Tavris and Aronson 2007), when our anxiety with an internal conflict looms into something impossible to bear, some of us pretend or forget we have a problem. Denial is another way to describe cognitive dissonance. For the director who feels she must be flawless, making a mistake ignites cognitive dissonance. That director might feel a mistake was made, but certainly not by her! Denial kicks in when we cannot face the fact that we made a mistake.

Change can be disturbing as an earthquake. The earth moves under our feet. I will never forget my office chair "walking" across the floor during an earthquake in Augusta, Maine, in 1980! I can picture that chair now. Our brains have a remarkable capacity to recall emotionally powerful changes in living detail.

In the calm that follows an earthquake, some of us get right back to work as if nothing happened. Denial can feel productive at the moment. Denial, however, cannot negate the reality that is taking place. Living in cognitive dissonance or denial takes a toll on our stamina. Consider the case in which a staff person, Kathy, senses her director is displeased with Kathy's telephone etiquette. If the director says nothing to Kathy directly, Kathy can try to brush off the feeling of disapproval. Kathy may try to avoid making phone calls when the director is near, but her denial of the problem does not make it go away. Because neither Kathy nor her director initiates discussion about the problem, the problem grows between them like ragweed or skunk cabbage. Trust goes down the drain.

The following "Partnering with change" model offers ways to acknowledge inner conflict, step out of denial, and take action to embrace change. Resistance to change, while inevitable, can be transformed into acceptance and eventual constructive action. Awareness of the problem must come first before acceptance and action can follow.

❈ Partnering with Change

Have you ever placed a new frame on a familiar wall hanging? If so, you probably discovered that reframing showcases colors and shapes previously unnoticed. In the past, organizational development consultants commonly presented "managing change" strategies to receptive programs. The popular thinking was and still can be, "You can take charge of change, rather than having change take charge of you." Being the boss of change seems ideal. Who wants to be buffeted like a kayaker in unexpected whitewater?

Over the years, I have come to appreciate that storms rain down, whether I anticipate them or not. These days, my preferred approach is to go with the flow of change, rather than believe I can anticipate and manage the torrents. The adage "If life gives you lemons, make lemonade" works for me.

My son, Nick, has taught me many lessons. When Nick was little and didn't do things the way he thought he should, he would shrug his shoulders, throw up his hands, and say, "Silly me." When his experiment didn't go the way he anticipated, Nick again would say, "Silly me." I have always loved Nick's self-accepting phrase. This chapter evolved from years and years of "Silly me" experiences, times when I thought I knew how to manage change. Please! Now I am content to partner with change.

Choosing to partner with, rather than manage, change allows us to see unanticipated opportunities as they emerge. I can be sure of this: Only I can choose my attitude.

Keeping Perspective on Change

Patterns emerge even in the most unpredictable of times. Dr. Meg Wheatley (1999) reminds leaders to look beneath the surface. Wheatley's deeper view offers refreshing perspective and her work reveals one "fractal" after another. A fractal is a pattern that shows up repetitively in nature. Consider the leaf of a tree as a fractal. Every oak tree's leaves exhibit the same shape. Every palm frond spreads out according to the same pattern. Every crystal begins with the same elemental structure. Brain cells begin with the shape of a neuron. Fractals are everywhere. Take a look around you. See if you can identify a fractal, or repetitive pattern like a honeycomb or a flower petal.

Soothing perspective comes from finding patterns in the midst of change. Resistance, the human response to change, is predictable. Reluctant acceptance follows. Buy-in eventually occurs and the change becomes the new norm. A pattern seems to emerge. Understanding this pattern helps us name where we are and what our options are. Keeping perspective is the first step to partnering with change.

An example of an emotional "fractal" is this: Every change brings about a loss. For sure, a change may lead to new gains. Something must be left behind for the new idea to replace it. When we close the door on something familiar to us, we often feel a loss. Elisabeth Kubler-Ross described the grieving process when we experience a loss, specifically, the death of a loved one.

Sometimes we love institutions and familiar ideas as much as we love an individual. When that institution changes, or an idea becomes out-of-date, we feel loss. The "partnering with change" model in the next section incorporates a number of Kubler-Ross' stages of grieving, such as denial, anger, and acceptance.

William Bridges (1991) writes about transitions and offers another fractal in the pattern of change. Much as Kubler-Ross writes about the grieving process, Bridges writes about the courage we need to change. Bridges observes that humans prefer to hold onto something known, even at the expense of finding something better. The "known," even if troubling or inadequate, is often preferred over the unknown. The unknown, healthier, more pleasant, and more fulfilling option cannot be discovered without courage.

Bridges likens resistance to change to the challenge of a trapeze artist. To be able to swing over to the other side of the circus tent, the trapeze artist must let go of the trapeze he is holding. Only with courage, can he "fly through the air with the greatest of ease" to the waiting new trapeze. Paralyzed by fear of risk taking, the trapeze artist holds on to his trapeze, swinging endlessly back and forth with white knuckles and arms aching.

Like the trapeze artist, many of us hold tight to what we know, sometimes at great expense. Bridges calls the space between the old and the new, the "neutral zone." To shorten the amount of time in the neutral zone, Bridges (1991) provides practical coaching on how to take a "leap of faith":

> You see things and say "Why?" But I dream things and say "Why not?"
>
> **—George Bernard Shaw**

1. *Learn to describe the change* and why it must happen *in one minute or less.*
2. *Understand who has to let go of what,* what is ending for staff members and what is beginning.
3. Take steps to *help staff respectfully let go of the past.*
4. Name the skills and attitudes staff need to make the change, and *provide training and resources to help staff develop new skills and attitudes.*

My "partnering with change" model that follows can free us from staying stuck with white knuckles, aching arms, and weary souls.

Partnering with Change Model

Take a moment to identify a change that you need to make, but may have avoided. What are you thinking, how are you feeling, and what, if anything, do you want to do? Look at the model below to find where you are in the change process.

To partner with changes, the first step is to acknowledge where you are. Once you have named your stage in the change process, you can more readily make choices about where you want to go. The perspective that comes from using this model can free us to take constructive action more quickly, with confidence and a relieving sense of humor.

Figure 6.1 illustrates the change pattern, informed by Kubler-Ross, Bridges, and my own observations.

My "back burner" gets very crowded; does yours? Fires can start that way. Here's an approach that gives me energy to move back burner items to the front burner so I can "get cooking."

Let's say my back burner item is discomfort with my boss's management style. Specifically, every time my boss loses his temper and yells, I get agitated inside. Here is the pattern, often predictable, that many of us follow when a challenge like a boss's yelling knocks on our door.

1. *Denial*: avoiding the issue, imagining everything is fine when it is not, hoping the problem will disappear if I do not dwell on it. Denial is similar to taking a snooze. For the moment, I escape what I know I need to face. I pretend to myself that my boss is just having one bad hair day.

2. *Isolation*: cutting myself off from others, not telling anyone about the problem. In the isolation stage, I may appear at ease to others. However, I know I am keeping a secret: I am afraid of my boss' temper. This secret separates me and leads to loneliness.

3. *Guilt*: berating myself over action I have not taken, or have taken inappropriately. Guilt pops up when I violate my core values. Honesty is a core value. I am being honest neither with myself nor with my boss about my concerns. *Guilt* can also involve blaming another person so I can avoid changing.

4. *Despair*: hitting the bottom and feeling helpless and hopeless. By not facing the problem, the problem only grows. As the problem grows, my self-esteem goes down the drain. Most of us cannot tolerate *Despair* for long. We become sick and tired of being sick and tired.

5. *Anger*: outrage about not having faced the problem. Anger leads to clarity about who is responsible for what. I am responsible for talking with my boss about my boundaries. My boss is responsible for dealing with emotions productively.

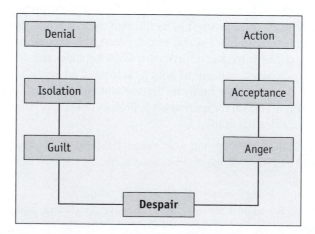

FIGURE 6.1   Partnering with Change

6. *Acceptance*: acknowledgement of the problem (the opposite of denial), willingness to face the issue. *Acceptance* brings a sense of calm and resolution. I accept responsibility for allowing behavior that I do not appreciate. I decide what I need to do.

7. *Action*: addressing and resolving the issue, moving out of inaction into productive behavior. I ask my boss if we can discuss our different styles in order to work together as productively as possible. At our meeting, I tell him I am uncomfortable and my productivity decreases when he raises his voice. Identifying and addressing problems before they become crises works better for me.

Notice how long I took before I acted. Can you picture the time I wasted by avoiding, fearing, and isolating? None of us has to take this tortuous, long road. Consider this: each stage (denial, isolation, guilt, despair, anger) offers a direct pathway to acceptance and action. Leaders can leap across that chasm, rather than fall into the valley of despair.

These are the tools directors can use:

1. *Acknowledgement* overcomes *Denial*: facing facts, admitting that I have a problem, owning that I am denying something that bothers me. As I *Acknowledge* my upset feelings about working with my boss, I *Accept* the feelings. This prepares me to take *Action*.

2. *Connecting* replaces *Isolation*: reaching out, asking for help. Resourceful colleagues are in the wings, just waiting for me to ask them for assistance. As I reach out to another person, I gain energy to take *Action*.

3. *Accepting Responsibility* overcomes *Guilt*. Wallowing in *Guilt* does not change anything for the better. As I accept my responsibility to take action, I move on from stalemate to *Action*.

4. *Trust* relieves *Despair*. Have you ever felt sick and tired of being sick and tired? Few of us can tolerate being face down for long. Any action feels better than being debilitated or overwhelmed. *Trust* or faith that things have to improve lifts us out of the pit. Each of us has access to our own source for trust, faith, or both.

5. *Clarity* is the gift of *Anger*. Have you ever felt grateful that you could finally get angry? The adrenalin flow of anger sweeps us toward clarity about the *Action* we need to take. Our OFC (orbitofrontal cortex) empowers us to step to the side of the adrenalin rush to gain that clarity.

6. *Acceptance* leads to a peaceful heart. I worked with a woman in Ohio who described herself as "an absolute nervous wreck" about surgery she was facing. Nothing seemed to comfort her. She was scared to death. The day she went to the hospital, peace surrounded her like a warm fleece blanket. She had accepted the necessity of the surgery. Studies show that patients who lessen their preoperative tension hasten their own recovery.

7. *Action* frees us. When we carry the weight of an unresolved problem on our shoulders, we become bent over. When we release that weight, as a Head Start director in New Hampshire sighed, "I stand tall."

Describe a change you are facing or an issue that you know you need to address in order to "stand tall." Review the stages of the change process. In which stage are you now? Are you in denial about the issue? Are you feeling guilty about it? At any stage, you can leap across the chasm into action by using one of the seven tools. Select the tool that would be most helpful for you now.

What steps do you need to take to partner with change? Like a trapeze artist, your leap of faith will carry you to the other side and save you from crashing to the bottom.

Notice the loss. To leap, leaders must let go of the known, the predictable. To leap, leaders need courage. Fear of loss can hold individuals back. I can tell myself loss is part

In spite of illness, in spite of the archenemy sorrow, one can remain alive long past the usual date of disintegration if one is unafraid of change, insatiable in intellectual curiosity, interested in big things, and happy in small ways.

—**Edith Wharton,** first woman to win Pulitzer Prize, 1921

of life, but the pain of loss still tears at me. If I have moved on too quickly and not grieved my losses in the past, I can build up a fear of facing another loss. In this way, partnering with change involves accepting the feelings of sadness, anger, fear, loneliness, and despair. Who wants to feel those emotions?

Emotional intelligence, knowing our strengths and our limitations, helps. By acknowledging how we feel about change and loss, we know better where we need to grow. This is the first step toward finding the help we need.

For example, if I am skilled at isolating myself, I know I need to take one step toward reaching out to another person for help. If denial is my middle name, I need to face facts. By having a support system, directors can ease their process of partnering with change.

When a Relationship with a Boss Needs to Change

"Managing up," or attempting to change a relationship with a supervisor, requires substantial social EQ. We walk a tight rope between overstepping our boundaries and forging a more effective relationship with our boss. To our boss, we may be perceived as either insubordinate, appropriately honest, or anything in between. Early childhood professionals frequently tell me they face this dilemma. They ask: "What can I do if my boss gossips and I am disciplining staff for gossiping?" and "What do I do if my supervisor reverses decisions I have made, if employees complain to him about my decisions?"

When you feel your relationship with your supervisor is a problem, use these EQ tips for managing up:

1. Devote energy to forging as honest a relationship with your boss as possible;
2. Ask your boss how she or he prefers you to bring up difficulties;
3. Check in with your boss about the best time and way to share your concern;
4. State the change you hope to make;
5. Identify the pros and cons the change will bring;
6. Remain as objective as possible to be able to hear your boss' perspective;
7. If your boss sees no reason to make changes, decide if you can be effective in your job without the support you want from above; and
8. Be ready to let go and move on if you feel you are not making headway.

Not every supervisor is open to a change in the supervisor-supervisee relationship, when the supervisee initiates the change. In that situation, present the change in such a way that the boss can feel the change is in her or his best interest. Your boss may need to feel that the change is her idea, not yours.

Leading Organizational Change

John J. Gabarro says bluntly, "The all-purpose general manager who can parachute into any situation and succeed is a myth" (2007, 116). In many ways, Gabarro's research is relevant to early childhood, even though his research sample was seventeen male business executives. Gabarro notes these predictable stages new managers experience as they attempt to make changes:

1. Taking hold
2. Immersion
3. Reshaping
4. Consolidation
5. Refinement.

See Table 6.3 for more on each of these stages. "Remain open to new developments" and "Deal with underlying causes of residual problems" are tall orders. Openness and courage are required.

TABLE 6.3

Five Developmental Stages of Being a Manager

Taking Hold	**Tasks**
Orientation and evaluation	• Develop an understanding of the new situation
Corrective actions	• Take corrective actions
	• Develop initial set of priorities and "map" of the situation
	• Develop initial set of expectations with key subordinates
	• Establish the basis for effective working relationships
	Dilemma
	• How quickly to act on apparent problems?
	Act too quickly—risks:
	• Make a poor decision because of lack of adequate information or knowledge
	• Take actions that constrain subsequent decisions that cannot be anticipated yet
	Act too slowly—risks:
	• Lose advantages of the "honeymoon period"
	• Lose credibility because of apparent indecisiveness
	• Lose valuable time
Immersion	**Tasks**
Fine-grained, exploratory learning and managing the business	• Develop a deeper, finer-grained understanding of the new situation and the people
	• Assess consequences of taking-hold period actions
	• Reassess priorities
	• Settle questions and problems concerning key personnel
	• Reconfigure "map" of the situation; fill out or revise the concept
	• Prepare for reshaping actions
Reshaping	**Tasks**
Acting on the revised concept	• Reconfigure organization based on finer-grained understanding
	• Deal with underlying causes of residual problems
	• Be open to unanticipated problems that emerge as a result of second-wave changes
Consolidation	**Tasks**
Evaluative learning, follow-through, and corrective action	• Follow through on reshaping actions
	• Deal with unanticipated problems that emerge as a result of reshaping stage
	• Remain open to new developments
Refinement	**Tasks**
Refining operations, looking for new opportunities	• Focus on fine-tuning operations
	• Look for new opportunities, such as staff development, curriculum innovation, technology integration

Source: Adapted from John J. Gabarro, *Taking Charge: Tasks and Dilemmas* (2007, 114).

In picking your battles, ask yourself, "How important is it?" Your answer to that question will help you in almost every leadership challenge. Professor Kathleen Reardon (2007, 61) asks, "Does the situation call for immediate, high-profile action or something more nuanced and less risky? Courage is not about squandering political capital on low priority issues." An example of using your "political capital" is calling on someone you know for a favor. That person may in turn expect you to do her a favor.

⚔ Resilience

What a magical attribute resilience is! It is the ability to bounce back, maintain hope, see the bright side, never lose trust, and maintain spirit. Resilience is an essential EQ ability for a director. How do directors become resilient? How can they remain resilient in the midst of challenges?

Research on resilience is uplifting. A Harvard University study revealed that the unconditional loving support of one other adult can restore resilience to a person who has experienced an abusive or neglectful upbringing. Similarly, unconditional loving kindness from one adult to a child exposed to the destructive effects of cortisol in utero (before birth) can help heal the child's nerve endings. That child can grow and develop in a healthy way. Her EQ and IQ will develop, in large part due to the care of a loving adult.

Optimism's Role in Resilience

I was happy to discover that our children's optimism about themselves is a greater predictor of their first semester grades than their SAT scores. My sweet daughter, Lily JinHee, is an excellent student. Gifted as she is (isn't every child gifted in his or her own way?), Lils does not score well on standardized tests. Fortunately, her grades were strong enough to win her admission into the university of her choice. In her first semester in college, my Lily aced her advanced placement chemistry and calculus courses, as part of an overall excellent first semester average. I was not surprised when I found this research finding come true: Lily's (or any student's) optimism about herself is a greater predictor of her first semester college grades than any of her SAT scores.

Optimism is a powerful force in every stage of our life. Studies show optimistic people are able to see more options, recall more, and think more flexibly than pessimists. Optimists also share the gift of humor. Humor, after all, provides perspective and allows us to step to the side to see things anew.

Optimism can lead to greater longevity, freedom from illness, and, if the optimist gets sick, she or he will heal more rapidly than the pessimist. If you see that glass as half full, rather than half empty, you will become a more resilient leader.

Researchers in a study of Dutch men note that optimistic people ask for help, cope better with difficulties, and stick with their medical treatment plans. Optimistic men appear to spend more time happily reminiscing about the past. The study suggests that by devoting 20 minutes each day to recalling happy memories, we become more cheerful and upbeat than on days when we are not happily nostalgic.

Moods are catching. All who are in your presence will feel your optimism. A person up to five feet away can sense our heartbeat. That heartbeat conveys optimism or pessimism, welcome or rebuff. The optimistic leader, who looks for the bright side in every challenge, models resiliency for her team.

Can optimism be learned? Have you ever been able to turn a pessimistic viewpoint into an optimistic one? Chances are if you were able to do this, you allowed yourself to grow through that uncomfortable "neutral space" of change. Transitioning from negativity to being upbeat is in large part through choice. As the saying goes, "When we change

---

If you can keep your head when all about you are losing theirs and blaming you, you're a better man than I am.

—Rudyard Kipling

A good laugh is sunshine in a house.

—William Makepeace Thackeray

Success is not the key to happiness. Happiness is the key to success. If you love what you are doing, you will be successful.

—Albert Schweitzer

A 15-year study of 545 Dutch men revealed optimistic men had a 50 percent lower risk of dying from cardiovascular disease than the least optimistic men.

—Archives of Internal Medicine

the way we look at things, the things we look at will change." This is not to shortchange the difficulty of letting go of beliefs and attitudes. Letting go is rarely an easy path.

Superdirector? Not.

Directors who believe they should be all things to all people, neglect to take care of themselves (Bruno 1999, 8). Have you noticed how flight attendants advise fliers to use oxygen masks? "Place the mask over your own face first," they remind us. Many of us would help the person next to us before we took care of ourselves. This is a downside of emotional intelligence—those who are exquisitely attuned to reading other people's needs too easily forget to take stock of their own. Sound familiar?

A support system makes self-care easier and more fun. Support system members show up in different places—in our communities, professional organizations, our families and friends, as well as at our jobs. The support system model below identifies needs that have to be met for a director to maintain resilience.

I invite you to fill in the boxes in Table 6.4 with names of people you count on for support. Who is your "cheerleader"? Who "keeps you honest" and encourages you to face what you prefer to deny? Who celebrates you with a card, an e-mail, or a party?

Across the top are the places you can find these people, in your personal life, professional relationships, and your neighborhood or community. Vertically, on the left, are needs we must have met to stay resilient. Directors need unconditional acceptance, "tough love," or a push to get out of denial, and celebration of ourselves as human beings and human "doings" (our accomplishments).

Are you ready? Name your current support system members:

TABLE 6.4

Support System for Change

	Personal	Professional	Community
Unconditional Support			
Pushes You to Get Out of Denial			
Celebrates You			

The people whose names you filled in on Table 6.4 form your support system today. Do you see areas where you might need to reach out? Are you, like I once was, relying on one person to meet all your needs? I nearly wore out my best friend! Today, my support system is more expansive, thanks in part to connective technologies like e-mail and listservs.

I invite you not to judge yourself. Consider your answers as data, information for you to ponder, as you prepare yourself to partner with change.

Promoting Resilience for Others

Early childhood author Jim Greenman (2004) reminds us that every person touched by change brings a different perspective. Each perspective needs to be solicited and heard. As long as the director hears each perspective, "A participatory process in planning, design, and implementation does not have to mean an endless, egalitarian process, culminating in a compromised end product that serves no one well" (Greenman 2004, 334–335). Informal conversations with constituents prior to staff meetings can reduce meeting time.

As employees feel acknowledged, heard, and appreciated, their resilience grows. If employees feel left out, unacknowledged, and underappreciated, they withdraw.

Practical tips to promote staff buy-in to change:

1. *State your vision:* Be clear, strong, and articulate about your vision for change.
2. *Identify the benefits:* Name the benefits for staff and the program the change will bring.
3. *Use "due process":* Involve staff at every stage of the change process. Ask their opinion, problems they anticipate, adaptations they recommend.
4. *Mobilize "opinion influencers":* Employ staff who are enthusiastic about the change to engage in dialogue with others who resist change.
5. *Demonstrate willingness to adapt:* Show that you have heard your staff by altering the innovation to align with their helpful input.
6. *Take "baby steps":* Gwen Morgan, with whom I teach, reminds me that staff accept change more readily if the innovation is broken down into bite-sized pieces, or "baby steps."

Effective leaders use EQ in each of these steps. They pay close attention not only to what is verbalized, but to the energy, the demeanor, and other nonverbal cues staff exhibit.

Taking Care of You

Take rest; a field that has rested gives a bountiful crop.

—Ovid

Stress goes with the territory of early childhood administration and leadership. Ten- to twelve-hour workdays leave little time for rest and relaxation. Even with all this hard work, none of us can control the future, hard as we may try. We can, however, put support systems in place, lay groundwork for improvements, and take steps toward making things better. As we promote constructive change, we need to take time to take care of ourselves to keep our energy high. Each of us finds our own ways to refresh and rejuvenate.

Replacing Stress with Reassurance

Directors need to get physical to take care of themselves. We all hear about the value of good nutrition, getting enough rest, and exercising regularly. Did you know that we have the potential to lower our blood pressure in 30 seconds? *Harvard Women's Health Newsletter* offers this process, which we can do anywhere. Before doing this exercise outlined in the steps below, check how you feel. Check in with yourself again once you have completed the exercise. Chances are good that you will feel calmer and more grounded. Feeling reassured of our well-being defuses the stress frenzy.

Begin by picturing a place, an actual physical setting, if possible, where you feel safe, at home, comfortable, and at ease. Strolling down a beach at sunset, soaking in a bubble bath surrounded by candles, sitting by the fireside with a good book, or singing a lullaby to a child all qualify. I picture myself hugging my yellow lab puppy, Toby, whose whole body wags when he sees me.

Next, recognize that distractions almost always flit across our minds. Controlling distractions is almost impossible. At best, we can acknowledge the barrage by saying, "Thanks, but no thanks. This is my time to relax." Third, we need to find a location where we will be free from interruption.

With these three guidelines in mind, follow these steps to lower your blood pressure in 30 seconds:

1. Go to a place where you are free or protected from interruption.
2. Acknowledge that distracting thoughts, although likely, do not have to rob you of your quiet time.
3. Picture yourself in that place where you can relax, feel at home, comfortable, and welcomed. If you feel safe, close your eyes.
4. Recall the scents, the texture of the surroundings, the quality of the light, anything specific that will help you travel to that welcoming place.
5. Breathe in and breathe out, while placing your right hand over your heart. Feel your heart beating as you breathe.
6. If/when distracting thoughts interrupt your quiet, just say, "Thanks, but no thanks. This is my time to relax."
7. As you feel your spirit and heart calm, rest in that place of quiet as long as you can before saying good-bye and returning to your present surroundings and responsibilities.
8. Open your eyes, and give yourself credit for taking care of yourself in the moment.

Nominated for the Nobel Peace Prize, Thich Nhat Hanh, suggests we accompany our breathing with these words, "Breathing in, I calm my body. Breathing out, I smile. Dwelling in the present moment, I know this is a wonderful moment!" (1991, 10).

Remember, you cannot take care of anyone else unless you take care of yourself. This can be hard for directors to remember in the moment. Transitioning from taking care of others to taking care of you takes one step at a time. Just like any change, we may feel uncomfortable at the beginning. Know that as you practice self-care, you model pathways to resilience for your staff.

> There is a vitality, a life-force, and energy, a quickening that is translated through you into action, and because there is only one of you in all of time, this expression is unique. And if you block it, it will never exist through any other medium and be lost.
>
> **—Martha Graham,** dancer, teacher, choreographer

Fired Up or Burning Out?

Burn out, or losing one's energy, passion, and optimism, is a danger in service professions. One psychologist has established a website to offer tips on "caregiver's syndrome." His major tip, of course, is to take care of you first. Authenticity, or acting in ways consistent with our true selves, helps us stay fired up. Being authentic is the beginning of self-care.

Using authenticity to convey our hopes for change is vital. A program's staff can read how important the change is to a director. According to the authors of *Crucial Conversations: Tools for Talking When Stakes Are High* (Patterson and colleagues 2002), managers need to:

> Your heart's desires be with you!
>
> **—William Shakespeare**

- Start from the heart with a caring, hopeful motive.
- Stay on track, and turn away from temptations to enter into power struggles.
- Ask yourself: What do I really want for myself, for others, and for our program?
- Reflect on: How would I behave if I truly believe in my dream?

So much depends on our attitude toward change, and our courage to lead on purpose.

Recognizing staff that make successful changes is essential for fostering a learning community where change for the better is valued. Ellen Clippinger, interviewed in *School-Age Notes* (September 2006), describes her approach for burnout prevention. Recognizing that very few staff members can advance by becoming the program's director, Clippinger created a five-step ladder for staff professional growth. A program review panel listens as employees report on accomplishments, workshops and courses attended, and as they share projects completed by children in their classrooms. When a staff member moves up the ladder, that employee is acknowledged and rewarded. You can read more about Clippinger's approach by going to *www.SchoolAgeNotes.com*.

> In dealing with those who are undergoing great suffering, if you feel "burn out" setting in, it is best for the sake of everyone, to withdraw and restore yourself. The point is to have a long-range perspective.
>
> **—H. H. The 14th Dalai Lama**

Paula Jorde Bloom, early childhood author, who has now survived two bouts with cancer, advises leaders, "Peeling away the layers of our motivations is not always a comfortable process, but it is a necessary step if our goal is to become an authentic leader known for integrity. Central to this process is gaining clarity about what we perceive our purpose in life to be and how we define success" (2007, 2).

We burn out when our work loses its meaning. In early childhood we are surrounded by real-life opportunities to change things for the better. If we get to the point where we cannot see those abundant opportunities, we have come to a time when we need to nurture our own spirit.

Who is the boss of change? I hope that as a result of reading this chapter, you feel even more equipped and, perhaps, inspired to make changes to uplift the lives of children, families, and your own. You are the one to do it.

Reflection Questions

1. Is there an issue you need to address, but have been avoiding or putting off? Now, review the Partnering with Change Model, on page 88. What stage are you in now? Denial? Guilt? Anger? Look next at what you need to do to break out of that "stuck" place into acceptance and action (p. 89). Write an analysis of how you might utilize the Partnering with Change Model to help with (a) the issue you identified and (b) future issues you might face.

2. Would you describe yourself as an optimistic, "the glass is half full," person? Do you, in a "the glass is half empty" manner, more quickly visualize problems that a change will bring? How has this attitude affected your desire to take risks to change things for the better? What are the strengths and challenges of each stance, optimism and pessimism? Research at least two studies on optimism. Write a reflection paper on what role optimism plays in your decision making.

3. What can you change? Can you give an example of a time you were successful in changing another adult's behavior? In terms of child development, do you think adults change children? Write a reflection paper on the serenity prayer as it applies to a particular situation you have faced with both an adult and a child whose behavior has troubled you.

Team Projects

1. Self-care is invaluable to everyday leadership. Make a list of those things you currently do, as an individual, to maintain and restore your energy. On a scale of 1 to 10, rate yourself (1 = neglect yourself; 10 = take excellent care of yourself). Discuss your feelings and thoughts about self-care and self-mentoring. Average your scores, as a team. With your team members, develop and present (a) a list of reasons we resist taking care of ourselves, (b) daily self-care steps we can take, and (c) strategies for incorporated self-care and self-mentoring into our lives on a long-term basis, especially during hectic and stressful times.

2. Identify and share situations in which someone you know, including yourself, has attempted to make a change for the better. What was the change? How was it presented? Describe how people responded to the proposed change. As a team, review Neila Connors' statement (pp. 47–48) on people's responses to change. Do her figures surprise you or confirm what you have observed? Reread the pointers

on how to successfully promote change for the better (p. 94). Looking back at the situations you each identified and forward to situations you face or may face, how might you promote a more positive response to change?

3. Elisabeth Kubler-Ross named stages of the grieving process. William Bridges likened taking risks to the moment a trapeze artist lets go to catch hold of a swinging trapeze. Both of these authors wrote in the 20th century. Research more fully what each author had to say. Which of their insights hold true today? How might advancing technology affect our risk taking or grieving processes? Do you believe any philosophies or values are timeless? Engage your whole class in a discussion of these issues as you present the work of Kubler-Ross and Bridges.

Bibliography

Bloom, Paula Jorde. 2007. *From the inside out: Self-mentoring.* National Louis University Press.

Bridges, William. 1991. *Managing transitions: Making the most of change.* Reading, MA: Addison-Wesley.

Bridges, William, and Susan Mitchell Bridges. 2000. Leading transition: A new model for change. *Leader to Leader* 16 (Spring): 30–36.

Bruno, Holly Elissa. 2007. Teachers may never know: Building professional relationships with children and families that heal. *SECA Journal* (Fall).

Bruno, Holly Elissa, and Margaret Leitch Copeland. 1999. Professionalism in challenging times: A new child care change management model. *Leadership Quest* (Fall).

Bruno, Holly Elissa. 1999. SUPERDIRECTOR: All things to all people but one. *Leadership Quest:* 8.

Clippinger, Ellen. 2006. Staff "lifers" in after-school and summer programs. *School-Age Notes* (September). *www.SchoolAgeNotes.com*

Connors, Neila. 2000. *If you don't feed the teachers, they eat the students.* Incentive Publications.

Frankl, Vicktor. 1959. *Man's search for meaning.* Boston, MA: Beacon Press.

Gabarro, John J. 1985. When a new manager takes charge. *Harvard Business Review* 63(3): 110–123.

Greenman, Jim. 2004. *Caring spaces, learning places: Children's environments that work.* Oregon: Child Care Exchange Press.

Kubler-Ross, Elisabeth. 1969. *On death and dying.* New York: Macmillan.

Moyer, Don. 2007. The final test. *Harvard Business Review,* January, p. 128.

Patterson, Grenny, McMillan, and Switzer. 2002. *Crucial conversations: Tools for talking when the stakes are high,* New York: McGraw-Hill.

Protecting children by strengthening families: A guidebook for early childhood programs. Center for the Study of Social Policy, 2004.

Reardon, Kathleen. 2007. Courage as a skill. *Harvard Business Review.* January, p. 61.

Rogers, F. 2005. *Life's journeys according to Mr. Rogers: Things to remember along the way.* New York: Hyperion.

Sanders, H. B. 2005. *The subconscious diet: It's not what you put in your mouth; it is what you put in your mind!* Azusa, CA: Liberation Press.

Tavris, Carol, and Elliot Aronson. 2007. *Mistakes were made but not by me: Why we justify foolish beliefs, bad decisions, and hurtful acts.* New York: Harcourt Brace.

Thich Nhat Hanh. 1991. *Peace is every step: The path of mindfulness in everyday life.* London: Bantam Press.

Wheatley, Meg. 1999. *The new science: Discovering order in a chaotic world revised.* San Francisco, CA: Berrett-Koehler Publishers.

Work and Family Life (December 2006). *Workfam@aol.com* (summary of "Archives of Internal Medicine").

Resources

Bridges, William. 1980. *Transitions: Making sense of life changes.* New York: Addison-Wesley.
Co-dependents Anonymous, Co-dependents Anonymous, Phoenix, AZ (1995).
Harvard Business Review, January 2007.

Web Resources

Articles and Tools for Leading Organizational Change
http://www.beyondresistance.com/change_migraines/leading/articles.html
Getting Employees to Not Only Embrace Change, but Ask for It!
http://www.zeromillion.com/business/managing-change.html
Emotional Resilience: Optimism
http://www.mentalhelp.net/poc/view_doc.php?type=doc&id=5789&cn=298
Radical Self-Care for Stress Reduction and Inner Peace
http://www.mentalhelp.net/poc/view_doc.php?type=doc&id=5789&cn=298
The Kubler-Ross Grief Cycle
http://changingminds.org/disciplines/change_management/kubler_ross/kubler_ross.htm

Preventing Legal Issues: Policies and Procedures

Learning Goals

As you study this chapter, you can look forward to reaching these learning goals:

1. Maintain perspective while in the midst of potential legal challenges.
2. Confirm commonsense legal principles for program leaders.
3. Know your rights and responsibilities when asked to provide a reference for a former employee.
4. Ask appropriate interview questions for all applicants, including applicants with "known" handicaps.
5. Understand key elements in the Americans with Disabilities Act (ADA).
6. Prevent disputes at the end of the day about who has the right to take the child home, especially if the parent appears impaired by alcohol or a custody issue flares up.
7. Prepare and practice how to handle potential crises when families pick up children.

My personal introduction to the Dalai Lama was by way of television—in a hotel room. I was in Washington, D.C., preparing for a conference on children and the media and was looking for a certain news program when I happened on His Holiness saying, "Someone else's action should not determine your response." I was so intrigued. I wrote down those words, turned off the television and thought about nothing else the whole evening. . . . It sounds so simple, doesn't it? And yet what if someone else's action should be shouting angry words at us or hitting us with a rotten tomato? That doesn't affect what we do in response? Not if our compassion is genuine. Not if our love is the kind the Dalai Lama advocates.

—**Life's Journeys according to Mr. Rogers** *(Fred Rogers)*

What do we live for, if not to make life less difficult for each other?

—*George Eliot (aka Mary Ann Evans)*

Case Study: Parental Pick-Up Policies

Lupe Hernandez-Jones listed only her brother and sister on the authorized list for pickup when she enrolled her daughters, Rosa and Yvette. The girls are anxious to please, obedient, and seem fearful of changes. Lupe faithfully picks the girls up each day; her brother and sister have never appeared.

At the end of their first year at your program, Lupe comes to your office anxiously requesting a confidential meeting. She tearfully tells you she and the girls escaped from the girls' abusive dad, Buster, in Tampa. At enrollment, Lupe did not mention the children's father. The director, at the time, did not ask Lupe for information about him. Lupe begs you to prevent Buster from seeing the girls. Before you can respond, a respectful Buster, baseball cap in hand, appears at your door, requesting to take his daughters out for ice cream.

How might you prevent this situation from arising?

Directors can take steps to prevent problems from exploding into mushroom cloud disasters. The more preventative measures they take, the more confident and effective they become as leaders. Directors can protect their programs, and the children and families in their care, by planning in advance. Some problems, of course, cannot be prevented. Even for those crises, directors can prepare by having in place and practicing model crisis procedures. (See Table 7.2.)

This chapter provides guideposts, sample forms, and background information on the law to assist you in creating model policies and courses of action for the future. Please note that nothing in this chapter (or textbook as a whole) serves as legal advice. Consult with an attorney directly for legal advice.

⚔ Lawsuits Wield Power

Just one lawsuit has potential to put a childcare center out of business. One accusation of wrongdoing, even a false one, can cause parents to withdraw their children. An accusation of sexual abuse will inevitably and understandably trigger a fierce community reaction. Successful early childhood programs, carefully co-created with families and staff over the years, can be destroyed by one lawsuit, even before the suit is adjudicated in a court of law.

Our legal system guarantees the presumption of innocence until guilt is proven. Public opinion is often quick to assign guilt, even before the evidence is in. Directors in the field report that their fear of the consequences of lawsuits detracts from their confidence as leaders.

A New England director mourned, "My worst fear has come true," when one of her teachers was accused of child molestation. Everyone, especially the director and accused teacher, wanted proof that abuse had not taken place. Everyone, from children to teachers, parents and administrators, felt anxious about the potential lawsuit.

Her center survived and still thrives by continuously offering open forums for parents and staff to discuss their concerns. In the end, the charges were dropped. Nonetheless, the center initially lost families as soon as the accusation was uttered.

Commonsense principles help prevent legal crises. A review of the case law (decisions made by courts) relevant to early childhood employment law reveals underlying commonsense principles. Leaders who practice these principles, both in

TABLE 7.1

Honor Civil Rights

Check your state's and municipality's definitions of whose rights are protected. New Jersey, for example, has broader employment and public accommodation antidiscrimination laws than federal law mandates. New Jersey's protected categories against discrimination include race, creed, color, national origin, nationality, ancestry, age, sex (including pregnancy and sexual harassment), marital status, domestic partnership status, affectional or sexual orientation, atypical hereditary cellular or blood trait, genetic information liability for military service, or mental or physical disability, including AIDS and HIV-related illnesses.

establishing policies and in making decisions, can feel more confident that they are on the right track. These principles reflect emotional and social emotional intelligence in practice:

- *Be consistent.* Hold employees to the same standards. Favoritism is suspect. Courts want to make sure every employee has equal opportunities.
- *Stay objective* and act reasonably. Use the step-to-the-side process to prevent the amygdala from hijacking professional perspective. Make decisions keeping "your eyes on the prize" with the long view in mind. Wait until the adrenalin surge has subsided before acting, when possible.
- *Document* and report facts. Remember the Head Start saying: "If it isn't documented, it didn't happen." Document concrete and essential facts. Writing a novel or short story is not required. Just the facts will suffice.
- *Follow written policies* and procedures. The employee and parent handbook documents program standards and practices. These are "living" documents that should be added to and changed as needed.
- *Honor civil rights.* Ensure that everyone is welcomed, respected, and treated without bias, especially with regard to ethnicity, religion, cultural, and age differences. (See Table 7.1.)
- *Exercise "due process."* Give notice or information in advance of making a change to all those affected. Provide staff the opportunity to share their responses to the change by providing a "right to a hearing."

The emotionally intelligent leader maintains perspective in the midst of threatening situations. Rather than being devastated by crises, the leader with EQ can make choices. Fortified by these principles, a leader can act more confidently. Effective leaders not only respond calmly during threatening situations, but also have preventative policies and practices in place to minimize such situations from occurring.

✖ Preventative Policies and Practices

The question to ask, before getting paralyzed by fear of a lawsuit, is, "What choices do I have, above and beyond my immediate reaction?" Stepping back from a potentially overwhelming threat frees leaders to use their emotional intelligence. You have options that free you from doing or saying something in the moment that you may later regret. Let's look at some policies you can institute as a leader that will afford you choices and a longer-range perspective.

TABLE 7.2

Three Common Issues Directors Face

1. Giving references for former employees.
2. Using appropriate job interview questions in the hiring process.
3. End-of-the-day disruptions: Parents arrive under the influence or in custody disputes.

By instituting preventative measures, administrators can nip potential problems in the bud. Each problem, if not handled preventatively, could mushroom into a lawsuit. When planned for in advance, the problem loses its power to alarm and, perhaps, overwhelm the director and the program.

Giving References for Former Employees

Consider what you would do in the situation below. Next, think of policies you could put into place that might prevent problems like this from arising.

Evangeline, a director from across town, calls you with this request: "Jenna, who says she worked for you, is applying to be my new lead toddler teacher. Jenna says you will give her a wonderful reference. What did you think of Jenna's performance?" What would you say to Evangeline in the following four scenarios?

1. You were grateful Jenna quit because you were about to fire her for continually arriving late.
2. Jenna's classroom skills were adequate; however, her gossiping and negativity troubled other teachers.
3. Jenna was one of your best toddler teachers. You believe Jenna is ready to become a lead teacher. However, you do not have a position available.
4. Something bothered you about Jenna that you couldn't quite identify. Frankly, you were relieved when she left.

Directors often wish they could tell the whole truth about their experience with a past employee. Employees who perform well deserve glowing references. Directors want to warn prospective employers against hiring poor performers. A leader's sense of fairness tells her she should be able to share accurate, documented information. After all, if Jenna presents a danger to children, aren't we obligated to warn future employers? Sometimes the law and common sense do not align.

Legally, the answer to Evangeline's question would be the same, regardless of which scenario were true. Most centers are instructed by their attorneys to abide by the written policy in Table 7.3.

TABLE 7.3

Policy on Requests for References

Our organization's policy on responding to requests for references on current or former employees is to provide only the following information:

1. *Confirm or deny the applicant's employment.* For example: "Yes, Ms. Jenna Wrightson worked for our organization" or "No, our organization has not employed Ms. Wrightson."
2. *State the dates of that person's employment.* For example: "Ms. Wrightson was employed by our organization from March 15, 2007, to January 10, 2008."

This policy precludes sharing any information on Jenna's performance. Jenna's potential employer, Evangeline, has learned little to help her make an important hiring decision. On the other hand, Jenna has been protected. No negative information about her has been released. How does this policy serve the interests of children and families? What additional policy would allow directors to share accurate information when called for a reference? Consider the sample "Reference Consent Form" in Table 7.4, to be signed by new and current employees.

TABLE 7.4

Reference Consent Form

I, _____, an employee of _____, agree to hold harmless _____ for the reference that organization may give me, on my employment with the organization.

(Employee, your initials on the topics below authorize us to discuss your performance in these areas. We will not comment on areas you do not check.) In particular, I authorize _____ to comment on my

___Punctuality

___Classroom management ability

___Usage of DAP (developmentally appropriate practices)

___Ability to partner with families

___Professionalism

___Skill as a team member

___Teaching abilities

If Jenna had signed this statement, Jenna would have consented to your sharing accurate information about her performance. This consent form could free you to answer Evangeline's questions such as: "Would you rehire Jenna? Do you have any reservations about Jenna's performance? What skills did you observe in Jenna that would indicate her ability to be lead toddler teacher?"

Administrators are bound to convey information in an accurate, unbiased manner, which honors the employee's confidentiality. By using the Reference Consent Form you isuse that ethical and legal standards will align. As long as a director shares her professional opinion based on accurate information, she will not be committing slander. *Slander is saying something false that would cause the person's reputation in the community to be damaged.* If a director shares false information about a former employee, she could be sued for damages. Telling the truth is the best defense to a charge of slander.

Instituting the Reference Consent Form (see Table 7.4) with staff will ward off the problem of not being able to share your professional opinion about a former employee. By taking this preventative step, directors can better ensure that competent people are hired and that poor performers are not recommended.

Asking Appropriate Interview Questions

Equal Employment Law requires directors to treat each applicant for a position fairly, regardless of race, religion, age, gender, or (in most cases) national origin. When interviewing possible employees, directors are required to give each person equal opportunity to respond to the same questions. If an applicant is asked, "Can you describe a time when you faced a discipline challenge in the classroom, and how you handled that challenge?" all other applicants for that position must be given the opportunity to answer the same question. If an interviewer were to use different questions for different applicants, she could be accused of favoring one applicant over another. This is why many directors choose to have a written set of interview questions and scenarios that is consistent for each applicant. Consider what you would do in this situation:

Jason's written application for preschool teacher indicates he can perform the job functions. His associate's degree in early childhood education is from a nearby community college. In his cover letter, Jason notes his military service in the Middle East strengthened his desire to work with young children. When Jason arrives for the interview with a smile, he shrugs off his coat. Jason's right arm appears to have been amputated. The interviewing team becomes anxious about what they can ask Jason about this visible handicap. What could you do in advance to help all parties to the interview feel welcome and prepared?

Essential Functions of the Job

When directors interview applicants to fill a position, they seek to hire the person who is best qualified from those who can "perform the essential functions of the job." The Childcare Law Center's booklet, "Employing People with Disabilities," defines essential functions as: "*The tasks and duties that describe the job, but only those that are essential to the performance of the job.*" For example, an infant teacher must be able to diaper a child. In the event of a fire or similar crisis, teachers must be able to assist in evacuating children from the building while immediately responding to an emergency situation. Infants must be taken to a designated safe place. Both being able to diaper a child and assist in an emergency situation are essential functions of the job.

Essential functions of the job should be stated in terms of the tasks the employee will complete, rather than as a physical attribute. This allows applicants like Jason to demonstrate their own way of accomplishing the task. Jason's way may not be like anyone else's. *Physical and mental attributes, and skills based on them (like lifting, driving, and reading), should be avoided to the greatest extent possible in the list of essential functions of the job. If a physical attribute seems unavoidable to perform the job, accompany that attribute with a description of the task or goal intended to be accomplished,*" advises the Childcare Law Center.

For example, diapering a baby properly is an essential function of the job. This skill is different from focusing on the teacher's physical attribute of being able to lift 20 pounds. In making this subtle shift from physical attribute to skill, leaders can open the door wider to potentially qualified candidates. As part of the interview process, all candidates, including Jason, can be asked to demonstrate how they would diaper a baby. If Jason shows he can safely and properly diaper a baby, as well as meet other functional requirements of the job, Jason will be considered along with other applicants who can demonstrate the same abilities.

✂ The Americans with Disabilities Act (ADA)

The ADA supports employers' efforts to find the person best qualified for the job. The ADA also ensures that applicants, who are "handicapped," or otherwise able, have equal access to employment and to maintaining their employment. The ADA does not require employers to favor a handicapped applicant over other equally qualified applicants. The ADA does require employers to make "*reasonable accommodations*" to allow qualified applicants to perform the job. Jason, for example, may request reasonable accommodations to be able to fully perform his duties if hired.

Handicap and Reasonable Accommodations

According to the ADA, a *handicap "restricts an essential life activity."* Essential life activities include breathing, sitting, standing, walking, seeing, hearing. Employers are required to make accommodations that allow a person with a handicap, *who is otherwise qualified,* to perform the duties of the job.

Consider applicant Selena, who is diabetic, and otherwise qualified to be a teacher's aide. To perform her job, Selena says she needs to test her blood sugar level at predictable intervals during the day. She also needs to ingest or inject insulin as needed. If you were to hire Selena, what "reasonable accommodations" would you make?

Selena's employer must make reasonable accommodations to allow Selena to test and maintain her blood sugar levels. Making sure Selena has a safe storage location for her testing equipment and insulin, as well as adequate time to test and maintain her blood sugar, are both reasonable accommodations her employer can make. If Selena and her physician state Selena needs a container of orange juice refrigerated nearby, her director will also reasonably accommodate this request.

Administrators often worry about whether their budgets will cover the cost of making accommodations. Interestingly, federal statistics show that the average cost per reasonable accommodation is approximately $240, and more than half are $500 or less.

These reasonable accommodations need only be taken if Selena is otherwise qualified for the job. If Selena lacks the required coursework or experience for working with children, Selena is not otherwise qualified for the job. She cannot be considered for the position until she meets the essential requirements listed in the job description. This is why job descriptions must be written with care.

ADA Exceptions to Making Reasonable Accommodations

Undue Hardship: The ADA envisions a workplace where every qualified person, regardless of handicap, is given equal opportunity to find employment and to continue that employment productively. In some cases, the accommodations required for a potential employee with a handicap are too costly for the program to bear. The ADA does not require an organization to endure an undue hardship for the sake of one employee.

In other cases, an applicant, even with the necessary accommodations, might still pose a *direct threat* to herself or others. An employee with chronic progressive multiple sclerosis who cannot hold a child without the strong possibility of dropping him poses a direct threat to her own and others' safety.

If either of these exceptions is present, undue hardship or direct threat, the ADA does not require employers to hire or retain the employee. In those cases, the well-being of the program outweighs the individual's needs.

To prevent difficulties like these from arising, directors can focus on two preventative measures. First, write the job description as a list of essential functions and/or tasks to be performed. Avoid listing physical attributes. "Must be able to diaper a child" can replace "must be able to lift 20 pounds." An alternate approach is to link the physical attribute directly to the task to be accomplished, "Must be able to lift at least 20 pounds to be able to diaper a child."

Second, invite the applicant to demonstrate how she or he would accomplish those tasks. Consistency is important. Recall the example about Jason. If everyone interviewed is asked to demonstrate diapering a child, Jason will not be singled out. Jason may well demonstrate his own way to safely and effectively diaper a child. If so, everyone has benefited by the interviewing process. If Jason names the accommodations he requires to be able to perform this task, the interviewers can explore in greater detail what those accommodations might involve. However, if Jason does not voluntarily request accommodations, the interviewers may not be the first to ask.

Appendix A contains a sample job description that focuses on tasks rather than attributes. By revising your job descriptions to focus on tasks, administrators can prevent difficult moments at job interviews. Interviews can be restructured from question-and-answer format to include scenarios and demonstrations. In this way, applicants can share their own ways of meeting the essential functions of the job.

⚔ Preventing Custody Disputes When Parents Pick Up Children

Sometimes divorce decrees are clear as "March mud puddles." Courts may grant joint custody, without clarifying the details. What happens if both parents arrive to pick up their baby on the same day and an argument ensues? When parents are not married, who has the right to create the authorized list for pickup? Can one parent leave the other parent off the list? What if a mother changes her mind frequently about whether the father can pick up their child? The last thing anyone wants at departure time is a disruption that leaves a child feeling unsafe and unsettled.

A director's job is not to decide who has the right to the child. The task, instead, is to obtain complete information at enrollment to prevent power struggles from occurring. Table 7.5 contains a policy for parent handbooks that clarifies enrollment practice and can prevent custody ruptures later on.

Consider how having this clear custody policy could have changed the outcomes in the chapter case study. If at enrollment, Lupe supplied an up-to-date restraining order against Buster, you would have been better able to do your job. If Buster appeared, you could advise him that the girls cannot be released to him, because of the restraining order against him. If at enrollment, Lupe did not supply you with an appropriate document demonstrating her custody of the girls, Buster could claim Lupe kidnapped the girls from him.

To prevent a program and its children from getting caught in the middle, directors can take preventative measures. The policy on "both parents' right to pick up the child" can be added to the parent handbook. The policy can be enforced at enrollment so that parents provide necessary court documents (restraining order, sole custody decree, or divorce decree) from the beginning. With documentation on file, leaders and staff will be prepared for end-of-day custody issues. The right to place people on the authorized list for picking up the child will also be established. The parent with custody has this right.

Perhaps Lupe and Buster share custody of their children. However, their anger at each other makes it difficult to foresee who will pick up the girls. Worse than that, the girls might be exposed to a blistering disagreement between Lupe and Buster at the entrance of the center.

TABLE 7.5
Both Parents' Right to Pick Up the Child
Under the laws of the state of _____, both parents may have the right to pick up their child, unless a court document restricts that right. The enrolling parent, who chooses not to include the other parent's name on the authorized list for pick-up, must file an official court document (e.g., current restraining order, sole custody decree, divorce decree stating sole custody, judgment of adoption). Absent that document, the center may release the child to either parent, provided that parent documents biological or adoptive parenthood of that child.

TABLE 7.6

Shared Custody Parental Agreement

We, _____ & _____, parents of _____, agree that _____, (parent 1) will pick up _____on Mondays-Wednesdays; _____ (parent 2) will pick up _____on Thursdays and Fridays. If a parent attempts to pick up _____ on the other parent's day, that parent must document the consent of the other parent to the change in schedule. Should continuous changes occur, both parents will file a revised agreement with the program promptly.

To keep all children safe from harm, the Shared Custody Parental Agreement policy in Table 7.6 can be included in a parent handbook as an option for parents who share custody.

By requiring parents at enrollment to complete these forms, the director has prevented headache and heartache for everyone, especially the children. Lupe and Buster will become responsible for following their own written agreement. If one parent wants to change the agreement, she or he will have to communicate directly with the other parent before any changes can be made. This approach allows directors and staff to focus on their responsibilities, rather than get stuck in the middle of an upsetting custody battle.

✂ Planning for the Unplanned: Crisis Prevention

Directors can't always prevent crises. They can, however, use their emotional intelligence to deal as effectively as possible with each crisis. Just knowing, as Fred Rogers did, that another person's action, no matter how frightening or threatening, does not have to determine our response is deeply empowering.

Ways to Prepare Staff for Managing Crises

Margaret Leitch Copeland's (1996) "Code Blue! Establishing a Child Care Emergency Plan" walks us through a step-by-step process of preparing for the unseen. She advises:

1. Brainstorm with staff all the possible crises that can occur.
2. Utilize the assistance of local crisis management experts when developing plans.
3. Post crisis plans and regularly practice carrying them out.
4. Establish a system of how to inform and communicate with parents.
5. Name a spokesperson for the organization, preferably not the director.
6. Anticipate and prepare information the media may need, and make sure the spokesperson has that information in writing.
7. Inform all others to refer questions to the spokesperson.

Rehearsing these seven steps with staff on a regular basis helps prevent fear and anxiety from overwhelming when crises erupt. State licensing standards mandate procedures for dealing with natural disasters. Sometimes, the "unnatural' disasters can be just as unsettling. What if a snake slithers onto the playground, a hazardous waste truck tips over on the front lawn, or Uncle Jack pulls a knife on a teacher? Preparing in advance for all possibilities is the best preventative medicine.

Sometimes, parents who appear to be under the influence of drugs or alcohol arrive to pick up their children. How can a director help her program prepare in advance for this possible scenario? What would you do in the following situation?

Mr. and Mrs. McClure share custody of three-year-old Cole. Cole used to be a bubbly, curious, playful boy. Lately, Colde's withdrawn, timid manner has concerned you. Both parents try to win you over to their side by telling stories about the other parent's wrongdoings and shortcomings. You feel like you are witnessing *Days of Our Lives*. You try to stay neutral and understanding. It's Friday afternoon, just before the December holidays, when Mr. McClure careens into your program to pick up Cole. You think you smell alcohol on his breath. He yells "Ho! Ho! Ho!" at everyone he encounters. Cole hides behind his teacher.

Preventing an Intoxicated Parent from Driving a Child Home

Consent to call others on the authorized list if a staff member is concerned about the child's well-being: Parents agree to the program's calling another person on the authorized list, when a staff member believes that the safety of a child is better served if the parent does not drive.

Remember that agreements made with parents at enrollment serve as preventative medicine. Directors can consider adding the *"Consent to call others on the authorized list if a staff member is concerned about the child's safety"* policy in Table 7.6 to their parent handbooks. If the McClures sign this agreement, they agree to a process that helps keep all parties safe. Talking with parents about this policy at enrollment and enlisting their sign-off on the policy puts into place a calming practice. Families can be reminded of the policy and their agreement to it, as well as the discussion at enrollment. By affording families due process, a leader prevents wrenching disruptions.

TABLE 7.7

Model Release Time Crisis Procedure

This crisis management system carefully guides staff through a possible end-of-the-day crisis. This procedure can be added to a staff handbook and practiced at staff meetings in advance. Employees can be invited to brainstorm any possible disruption that might occur when family members arrive to pick up their children. Use these as examples in applying the crisis procedure that follows.

Should an unanticipated crisis erupt at the end of the day, directors can take these steps for everyone's well-being:

✓ Do not immediately release the child. Discuss your concerns with the person. Engage the child in an activity with another staff member.

✓ Contact the other parent or another responsible adult on the authorized list. Enlist them in solving the problem.

✓ Offer alternatives. Offer to call another person on the authorized list to pick up the child.

✓ Release the child with reservation. As a mandated reporter,*call the appropriate state and/or municipal agency to report your concern. For example, ask police to shadow the car of a parent who may be under the influence.

✓ Call the authorities. When someone's well-being or safety is in jeopardy, notify the police, the Department of Social Services, your licensor, along with any other appropriate authority.

It's not that I'm so smart. It's just that I stay with problems longer.

—Albert Einstein

The adage "an ounce of prevention is worth a pound of action" holds true in child-care administration. Directors aim to maintain perspective and to remain professional.

---

*Mandated reporters are professionals who are responsible for children's well-being and safety. State law requires mandated reporters to contact authorities if a child appears to be exposed to or in danger of abuse or neglect. Driving while intoxicated could be considered neglectful or abusive action toward a child.

They can take many steps to prevent crises from emerging. Written policies and procedures in staff and parent handbooks ward off later disruptions. Safeguards can be instituted, such as the "Model Release Time Crisis Procedure," to guide programs through crises that cannot be prevented. Whether the worry is a potential lawsuit or an emotional disruption at the end of the child's day, directors who plan ahead will have tools to use that respect everyone's rights and ensure children's well-being.

Reflection Questions

1. Recall a work-related problem you have faced. Describe that problem and how you handled it at the time. Can you think of policies, procedures, or steps you might have had in place that would either have prevented the problem or made the problem less disruptive? Describe that policy or procedure.

2. Make a list of ten questions you would like to ask a person who is applying for a position in your organization. Review and rewrite those questions to make them welcoming and unbiased toward persons with handicaps. How can you make sure the questions focus more on the tasks of the job than on personal attributes? Having created these questions, would you recommend ways to rewrite the job description to be in compliance with ADA requirements?

3. Imagine that a single dad, Thomas, wants to enroll his twin sons, Ryan and Rocco, in your program. As Thomas completes the authorized list for who can pick up Ryan and Rocco, Thomas does not include the twins' mom. Describe the steps you would take to balance the rights of both parents, while keeping the best interests of the twins in mind.

Team Projects

1. Discuss professional experiences you have had where you feel you reacted too quickly to someone else. Consider what Mr. Rogers learned from the Dalai Lama: "Someone else's action should not determine your response." Brainstorm with each other the options you have instead of reacting immediately; use websites or other sources on stress management. Develop a list of five tools you can use to remind yourself in the moment to step back, rather than to overreact. Prepare a video or other demonstration for your classmates on how to keep cool while under pressure.

2. Read aloud the case study about the McClures. Role-play how to apply the "Model Release Time Crisis Procedure" with Mr. McClure. Now think of how you could prevent that scene from taking place. How many indications of potential problems can you find in the case? Name the steps you could take with family members in advance to prevent the incident that occurred. Brainstorm together other potential crises that could occur when families pick up children. Select one of the most powerful crises and discuss how the "Model Release Time Crisis Procedure" might help.

3. Research your organization's policy on giving references on current or former employees. What, if anything, would you change about that policy? Imagine that your cell phones ring: Evangeline is calling to ask you to give a reference on Jenna (p. 102). What would you say, according to your current policy on references? If Jenna had signed a "hold harmless consent form" allowing you to speak freely, how would you respond to each of the hypothetical situations listed about Jenna?

Bibliography

Bruno, H.E. 2005. At the end of the day: Legal and ethical issues at release time. *Child Care Information Exchange* (September–October): 66–69.

Child Care Law Center. 1996. Employing people with disabilities: The Americans with Disabilities Act and child care. San Francisco, CA: Child Care Law Center.

Copeland, M.L. 1996. Code blue! Establishing a child care emergency plan. *Child Care Information Exchange* (January–February): 23–26.

Copeland, T., and M. Millard. 2004. *Legal and insurance guide: How to reduce the risks of running your business*. St. Paul, MN: Redleaf Press.

Copeland, T. 1997. *Contracts and policies: How to be businesslike in a caring profession*. St. Paul, MN: Redleaf Press.

Podell, R. 1993. *Contagious emotions*. New York: Pocket Books.

Web Resources

American with Disabilities Act Home page
http://www.usdoj.gov/crt/ada
U.S. Equal Employment Opportunity Commission
http://www.eeoc.gov/
Practical Information on Crisis Planning
http://www.ed.gov/admins/lead/safety/crisisplanning.html
Ethical Learning and Development Resources
http://www.businessballs.com

Creating a Community of Problem Solvers: Winners Not Whiners

Learning Goals

As you study this chapter, you can look forward to reaching these learning goals:

1. Identify what gossip is and why people gossip.
2. Examine steps to create a zero tolerance for gossip workplace.
3. Describe how to establish boundaries to end whining and negativity.
4. Replace gossip and negativity with problem-solving practices.
5. Discuss how to help employees take responsibility for solving their own problems.
6. Promote a welcoming multicultural community for all children, employees, and families.

When I was young and would see scary things on the news, my mother would say to me: "Look for the helpers. There are always people who are helping."

—**Fred Rogers,** You Are Special

The person who says it cannot be done should not interrupt the person doing it.

—**Chinese proverb**

Case Study: Team Teacher Tension between Gabriella and Maude

Gabriella is a free spirit. Children jump up and down in anticipation when she enters the class-room. Gabriella lives and breathes the "emergent curriculum" approach. When Javier finds a "hop" toad on the playground, for example, Gabriella spontaneously invites the children to imag-ine Mr. Hop Toad's world. Emma and Esther scrunch down to hop like Mr. Toad. Xavier wants to find "Hoppy" a snack. Because Gabriella must leave at 3 p.m. for her second job, she quickly passes out finger paints and paper. "Let's imagine Mr. Hop Toad's world!" Gabriella croons. Gabriella asks the children to spread their wet creations around the edge of the classroom floor to dry. "Tomorrow," she smiles, "we will tell each other all about Mr. Hop Toad's day." She breezes out of the classroom waving at teacher's aide Tiara while ignoring Maude.

Maude, who thrives on order and organization, believes children learn best in a structured environment with sequential lesson plans. Children pay attention to Maude because she brings engaging, "hands on," planned activities to class. Maude works hard to gather and organize materi-als for each lesson. When Maude notices scattered wet papers on the floor, she gasps: "Some one will slip and fall!" Quickly, before parents arrive to pick up their children, Maude throws the slip-pery "mess" into a large garbage bag. "Another law suit avoided!" Maude proudly sniffs.

Maude and Gabriella complain and gossip about each other to their peers. Gabriella calls Maude "Ms. Prissy Control-Freak." Maude righteously persuades everyone how disgusting it is to be stuck working with "Slobby Gabrielly." Children can't miss the unspoken tension between their teachers.

The next morning, Gabriella, stunned, glares at Maude and demands: "What did you do with the children's finger paintings?" You walk into the classroom as the explosion is about to detonate. What would you do?

Directors often say: "I just want everyone to be happy." In the best of worlds, everyone would appreciate everyone else. Differences would fascinate us. We would want to learn more about what we do not know. When we stumble and bump into each other, we would stop to talk directly about how to honor each other's space. We would value everyone's right to see the world in her own way. We would model for children how to respectfully solve problems. Author Kurt Vonnegut reminisced about such an ideal world: "Everything was beautiful and nothing hurt."

In this chapter, we will explore ways to create a community of problem solvers and transform whiners into winners.

✸ Open Communication, Welcoming Community

Envisioning early childhood programs as open, caring, lively multicultural learning communities is ideal. To get there, many of us will address challenges that may be un-comfortable. Confrontation is a scary concept for the majority of early childhood pro-fessionals. Can we become a welcoming community if we cannot openly identify, discuss, and resolve our inevitable differences? Perhaps these practices can help:

1. We can agree to disagree.
2. I don't have to love everyone, as long as I respect everyone.
3. Facing my blind spots can be rough.
4. "My way or the highway" is the fast track to isolation.
5. I have the right not to be right.

Shall we get to work on how to create a community of problem solvers? Imagine that—a place where everyone is respected for who she or he is!

Supervising employees of very different temperaments, heritages, values, and backgrounds can be like herding cats. Everyone thinks she's right, and no one wants to bend. Confronting each other directly can be perceived as rude, aggressive, and distasteful. Teachers may form cliques, gossip about each other, whine to the director, and complain to parents.

Children imitate everything we do. Their "mirror neurons" are already hard at work, imitating adult role models. Imagine preschooler Emma whispering to her playmate Esther, "I'm not going to play with Xavier for a hundred years, are you?" Esther has already learned her only response is "no." Children quickly learn the unwritten rule: "If you gossip to me, you will gossip about me."

Check in with yourself: Do you believe our programs can be free of gossip, negativity, backbiting, and whining? Or, do you believe we have to work around them?

I invite you to consider the strategies that follow. By using these tools, directors have successfully overcome gossip to create communities of problem solvers: winners not whiners. Help is on the way. Early childhood accrediting agencies set codes for ethical conduct. NAEYC's *Code of Ethical Responsibility* and the National Association of Child Care Professionals' (NACCP) *Code* contain language against gossip. If it were possible to summarize both codes in one word, that word would be *respect*.

When we have a concern about the professional behavior of a co-worker, we shall first let that person know of our concern, in a way that shows respect for personal dignity and for the diversity to be found among staff members, and then attempt to resolve the matter.

NAEYC Code of Professional Responsibility

✖ Gossip

What Is Gossip?

Gossip is an outmoded way to gain and maintain power at the expense of community. "Some women cannot bear to experience themselves as lesser lights; in order to shine more brightly, they must rid the stage of greater lights" (Chesler 2001, 465). Complaining about coworkers separates peer from peer. Cliques replace teams. Isolated fiefdoms crop up. Power struggles replace problem solving. Children learn how not to problem solve, even as we advise them to "use words." (See Table 8.1.)

Why Gossip?

Like bullies, gossipers wield power. Recall the chapter case study in which Maude uses "lateral violence" (peer-to-peer threats) and "pleasantly" bullies teachers into siding with her against Gabriella. Colleagues fear the consequences of standing up to a gossiper. Anyone who courageously resists Maude's bullying is likely to be isolated, shunned, or mocked by Maude's followers. Gabriella, of course, will have her own clique of supporters against Maude. Who is thinking of the children?

TABLE 8.1

What Is Gossip?

Gossip Is:

-Communicating about another person,

-who is not present,

-with the intention of harming that person's reputation;

-listening to gossip.

Gossip Is Not:

-sharing accurate, necessary, appropriate information; or,

-holding an opinion about another person.

Gossipers establish power bases by promoting their own spin on reality:

> Lying, in order to manipulate others, is an art. A liar-artist often believes her own lies—What she's saying must be true, no one has ever stopped her, she's been able to get away with false, unethical reports, she's even been rewarded for them. Emboldened by reward, she thinks what she's saying has to be the truth. . . . In one's own very small circle, the *psychological executions are real.* (Chesler, *Woman's Inhumanity to Woman*, 432)

Gossip is avoidant, manipulative behavior. We use it to express resentment or dissatisfaction towards individuals indirectly without having to take responsibility for confronting them face-to-face. Women's lateral and indirect violence to one another inflicts painful and long-lasting wounds.

According to our research with over 500 early childhood leaders (Bruno and Copeland, 1999), 80 percent of early childhood leaders are conflict-avoidant. They fear direct confrontation and hope problems eventually will go away. Administrators hope staff will magically get the message to improve by observing appropriate role modeling. Indirect communication like this feeds unhealthy relationships and dysfunctional workplace environments.

Myers-Briggs data show that 70 percent of women take things personally, seek harmony, fear conflict, aim to rescue others, and can hold grudges. Women can forgive but do not forget a slight. The minority (30 percent) of women conduct themselves in an objective, analytical, impersonal manner. For this minority of thicker-skinned women, interpersonal issues are not unsettling. The majority of men (56 percent), like this minority of women, do not let interpersonal slights get to them. They focus more on getting the job accomplished than on who likes whom in the process.

Gossip in Early Childhood Programs

Do you think our colleagues identify gossip as a concern? To find out, I queried a diverse variety of over 700 early childhood professionals across the country. More than one-half of the respondents named gossip, backbiting, catfights, and power struggles as female work dynamics. Three times as many respondents named destructive dynamics as compared to those who named constructive dynamics (friendship, caring, humor, empathy). Twelve percent listed both destructive and constructive dynamics. Of those I asked, 68 percent had experienced gossip at work and expected it to continue.

Do men as well as women engage in gossip? Research shows that men may be neurologically wired to deal with conflict differently (Cahill & Kilpatrick, 2004). Male confrontations are typically direct, aggressive, and aimed at determining who has the greater status. Anthropologist Margorie Harness Goodwin notes that once males have engaged in "battle," they quickly move on (as cited in Chesler, 2001). As a "recovering" attorney, I recall mornings in the courtroom, advocating for my clients against formidable opposing attorneys (mostly men). Immediately afterwards, my "opponents" would jovially say: "Let's do lunch." I, meanwhile, needed time to recover from the intensity of the battle. Unlike men, women tend to avoid direct confrontation, while choosing to seek support from other women (Tannen, 1990).

What about different ethnic groups and gossip? Three groups were studied (Chesler 2001, 273), Anglos, Latinas, and African-American women. What is your hunch about who gossips most? White women, who are taught that "if you can't say something nice, don't say it at all," gossip the most. Latinas, according to research by Theresa Bernandez, also gossip. Bernandez notes religion may factor into this. Of the three groups, black women gossip the least. Dr. Beverly Green, in commenting on her research, observes that because they have been exposed to both racism and sexism, black women have learned to be direct.

Feeney and Freeman (2000), in speaking about the use of NAEYC's Code of Ethical Conduct, note (73): "Ethical behavior requires thought and reflection, pride and humility, a willingness to change, and the courage to stay steadfast." Instead of a community of problem solvers, warring cliques fight clandestinely with smiles on their faces.

Creating Gossip-Free Zones

"Houston, we have a problem," astronauts confessed to the Houston NASA command, while attempting to guide their sputtering space craft home. "Early childhood professionals, we have a problem." Historically, staff and directors have avoided conflict and "resolved" their problems indirectly through gossip, negativity, sabotage, and backbiting. We need a makeover to our organizational culture.

> To create a climate of trust and candor that will enable staff to speak and act in the best interests of children, families, and the field of early childhood care and education.
>
> **—NAEYC Code of Ethical Conduct**

Are you ready to consider changing the way we do business? Here are practical, everyday approaches to transform pettiness into professionalism.

Strategies to End Gossip and Negativity

- *Update employee job descriptions.* Add and enforce this statement as a functional requirement of the job: "Maintaining a gossip-free work environment."
- *Be vocal and clear about your stand against gossip.* Picture a director who posts this sign in her office: "Is this good for children and families?" That director can place every instance of gossip in its proper perspective. "Gabriella, when you spoke to Javier's mom about your team teacher, how was that helpful to Javier and his mom?"
- *Apply the five steps and principles of directive supervision* (Chapter 6) *to gossipers.* "Maude, referring to your team teacher as 'Slobby Gabrielly' is out of line. This program has zero tolerance for gossip. What will you do to change your behavior?"
- *Prominently display your organization's mission statement.* Motown legend Aretha Franklin got it right: *Respect* is crucial. Early childhood mission and philosophy statements hold respect for others and ourselves as essential. Respect is demonstrated through effective communication, placing organizational goals over personal gain.
- *Problem-solve using NAEYC's Code of Ethical Responsibility or NACCP's Code of Ethics at staff meetings.* Devote staff development sessions to skill building in how to create gossip-free zones. Ask staff to practice applying the ethical code to case studies (examples are included in this chapter).
- *Provide peers with empowering statements and practices to stop gossip.* "I need to focus on the children right now" or "I am not comfortable talking about someone who is not present" stop gossip in its tracks. A list of *gossip stoppers* follows (pp.117–118).
- *Educate and guide employees in effective problem-solving techniques.* Three techniques are highlighted later in this chapter.
- *Select and train a team of peer coaches.* Reward employees who demonstrate problem-solving expertise by designating, training, and honoring them as peer coaches.
- *Contract for a gossip-free program.* Following sessions in effective problem solving, invite employees to read, discuss, and sign the Problem Solving Agreement in Table 8.2. Add this policy to your staff handbook and place signed commitment statements in employee files.
- *Update your staff handbook.* Add this statement to your policies: "Our program has zero tolerance for gossip" or "This program is a gossip-free work environment. We are committed to respectful, problem-solving communication. As professionals, we do not have time for gossip."

Using Directive Supervision to Weed Out Gossip and Negativity

When ethical standards are not enforced, gossip spreads like the flu. Trish, a Bright Horizons director in Massachusetts, was "sick and tired of being sick and tired" of the debilitating effects of gossip on her program. Trish and her assistant director called a staff meeting dedicated to creating a gossip-free work environment. After much discussion, staff were asked to sign the "Problem Solving Agreement" in Table 8.2. The next day, when gossip resumed, Trish called each gossiper into her office to walk her through the five steps of directive supervision (Chapter 12). Trish reminded each gossiper that her behavior was being documented; the next steps were probation and termination. Within a month, one staff member resigned and the other one was fired. Staff morale rose, uplifting children and families.

Peer Power to Stop Gossip

For sure, employees feel supported in doing their part when they observe supervisors enforcing the gossip-free zone. What power does each staff member have to stop gossip? Consider the chapter case study, in which Maude may decide she will not gossip from this day forward. She vows not to talk about Gabriella to others. Maude also resolves not to say anything when a gossiper complains to her. Maude, with her director's prodding, has decided to change her behavior in important ways.

Will these strategies be enough to stop gossip? Remember this definition of gossip? "Listening to gossip is gossiping." By listening to gossip, we enable the gossiper to continue spreading negativity without interruption. The gossiper may even boast that others agree with her!

Instead of tolerating gossip by listening to it, teachers need effective statements to stop gossip from spreading. At the same time, some peers may not yet feel confident enough to directly confront the gossiper. Teachers may fear becoming targets for gossip if they challenge the gossiper.

 The next time someone gossips to you, try one of these *Gossip Stoppers*. By using one of these statements, you take responsibility for your own behavior, without becoming the next bull's eye for a gossiper.

As director, you can offer staff these *Gossip Stoppers* to say to gossipers:

- I am not comfortable talking about a person who is not present.
- I need to focus on the children now.

TABLE 8.2

Problem Solving Agreement

I, ____, an employee ____, agree to promptly and directly raise any issue I have with another staff member. I agree to work with my colleague to find a mutually agreeable solution, building on both of our strengths. If, after a good-faith effort, the conflict remains unresolved, I will request a meeting with my director (or designee) and my colleague. I agree to take to that meeting at least two possible solutions that will honor the organization's and both persons' needs. I agree neither to gossip about, nor hold back from, resolving an issue that affects the quality of care and education. I will participate fully in staff development sessions on problem-solving techniques.

_____ (Signature)   _____ (Date)

- Would you be willing to talk with X about your concern with her?
- I'll go with you so you can share your concern with X.
- I promised not to gossip.
- Let's not go there.
- Since I can't help you with that problem, please don't raise it with me again.
- Diana Ross says: "Stop, in the name of love, before you break my heart! Think it over."
- Remember, we signed an agreement not to gossip?
- Our mission statement on the wall says we respect differences.

Each of these statements is respectful and effective at stopping the spread of gossip and negativity. As a leader, you can help staff say no to gossipers by including these statements in a handbook or discussing them during a meeting.

Can teachers really take a stand against gossip? Preschool lead teacher Danielle Donati Gulden recalls, "I found the hardest part of working with women was gossip. I used to crave it like a drug, but have since recovered. I let my co-teachers know that I had my fill of gossip and to leave me out of the mix. Whenever I would hear gossip, I would say to myself 'Walk away, walk away.' Eventually they just stopped including me in the gossip. It never felt so good to be left out."

Case Study: LaVonda

LaVonda was hired to replace Betty, who stole from the petty cash. Teachers resent that Betty was fired. No one wants to work with LaVonda. They avoid LaVonda, make up stories about her, and leave her out of conversations. This afternoon, Wanda and Trixie invite you to go shopping after work. LaVonda is standing beside you. They look right through her.

Imagine you are LaVonda's team teacher in the case above. What could you do as a peer to stop the damaging behavior? Alternatively, as director, what could you do to help resolve the conflicts involving this new hire?

How do you feel about this response? "That was rude. LaVonda is a teacher here too. Show her respect." Taking this direct approach stops gossip in its tracks, but not every teacher feels ready to be so direct. Administrators need to work with staff to help them develop courage and skills in such situations. Directors can invite staff to create case studies to role-play at team meetings. With practice, each employee will hone her own style at stopping gossip.

✄ Problem-Solving Practices

We have looked at important steps directors and peers can take to confront gossip. Other common behaviors can be equally damaging to a healthy workplace community.

What can leaders do to resolve issues with staff members who are negative because they don't know how to solve problems with others? What about individuals who can't find the courage to stand up to a whining peer? Consider also the employee whose cultural background does not favor directness.

Many early childhood professionals are more at ease helping children resolve conflicts than they are comfortable facing their own adult conflicts. All of these instances bring us to the heart of creating a community of problem solvers: problem-solving techniques that work. Let's take a look at our options for resolving, rather than denying or avoiding, conflicts.

We shall provide staff members with safe and supportive working conditions that permit them to carry out their responsibilities, timely and non-threatening evaluation procedures, written grievance procedures, constructive feedback, and opportunities for continuing professional development and advancement.

—NAEYC Code of Ethical Conduct

Modeling Problem Solving for Children

Remembering that children learn how to resolve their conflicts by observing adults work through their disagreements is valuable. This encourages us to keep our problems in perspective. Detaching from a heated "my way or the highway" stance, although difficult at times, rewards us with cooling perspective. The key question is: *How can we resolve this issue in a way that models problem solving for the children? If children were observing us at resolving our problems, what would we want them to notice?* By remaining focused on helping children as we help ourselves, we might feel a stronger motivation for respectful conflict resolution.

Adults ask children to work through problems by saying "Use words." When children learn to use words instead of shoving, hitting, or snatching a toy away, children learn an approach to resolving their difficulties. How often do we as adults use words to state the issues we have with each other? Unless we use our words effectively, we cannot demonstrate mature, cooperative behavior for children. Finding the words to use is especially difficult when a child or an adult feels angry, hurt, resentful, fearful, or helpless. For this reason, step by (empowering) step practices work best.

Does Venting Help or Hurt?

Some employees need to vent or express their upset feelings before they can calm down to problem solve with the other person. Some directors and supervisors encourage staff to "blow off steam" and get upset feelings out in the open prior to problem solving. Can we expect employees to problem solve effectively when they are still feeling wounded or "hot under the collar" about the other person?

In the chapter case study, if Gabriella labels Maude her "enemy," Gabriella is not in a mental or emotional state to work through problems with "evil" Maude. Gabriella takes the moral high ground and assumes she is right; Maude is totally in the wrong. Throwing out children's precious art work is hateful in Gabriella's eyes.

Of course, Maude may label "Slobby Gabrielly" the enemy too. "How anyone in her right mind could put children and families in danger of slipping and breaking their necks is beyond me!" Maude insists. Time for both teachers to vent in order to come back to their senses may be needed. Venting is like taking the top off a boiling pot. Releasing the steam eases the intensity of the boiling.

Recall from Chapter 2 the concept of the amygdala hijack. Dr. Daniel Goleman (1997) warns us of the temporary power of our amygdala gland to "hijack" our emotional intelligence and our IQ. When we feel threatened, the amygdala (a small almond shaped gland in the center of our head) triggers adrenalin or cortisol to speed through our system. If you have ever felt internal pressure to run away from, yell at, or punch another person, you may know what an amygdala hijack feels like. We enter the "fight or flight" mode. Professionalism temporarily flies out the window until we can "step to the side" to calm down.

The danger in venting is that venting does not solve the problem, even though it relieves the person venting. For venting to be a productive first step in problem solving, venting needs to be:

1. Limited in time (e.g., no more than 10 minutes);
2. In private, in the presence of a supervisor; and,
3. Followed up within a day by a meeting to resolve the problem.

Venting per se not only does not solve the problem but also can be gossiping. However, when venting adheres to the three steps above, venting can be useful to some who may be more susceptible to an amygdala hijack.

✖ Strategies for Resolving Conflict

The Z-Method

One effective problem-solving method, which has been adapted from a Myers-Briggs model, follows the contour of the letter *Z* (Kroeger and Thuesen 1992, 163). At each starting point, ending point, and joint in the letter *Z*, we ask a different question or set ourselves a different task.

T A B L E 8 . 3

The Z Method

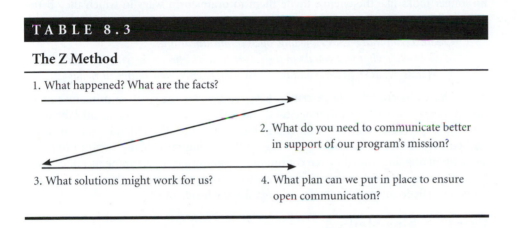

1. What happened? What are the facts?

2. What do you need to communicate better in support of our program's mission?

3. What solutions might work for us?

4. What plan can we put in place to ensure open communication?

As "opponents" share answers, each person is invited to listen to how the other person perceives the situation. In the process, each may discover the value in letting go of the belief that she can control another person.

Let's walk with Gabriella and Maude through the *Z* method's four turning points:

1. *What happened? What are the facts?* Focus on your own observations: no blaming, shaming, or inflaming the other person. Keep the focus on yourself and what you experienced. A leader can keep the discussion on track by asking questions like:

    Gabriella, could you describe what activity you did with the children on the playground yesterday afternoon?

    Maude, please describe, as factually as possible, what you observed and what action you took shortly after Gabriella left for work yesterday.

Once each person describes her actions and observations, we may see a shift in one or both people. Often, we are reminded that we are both looking at the same glass, even though one sees it half-full and the other sees it half-empty. Facts are concrete and non-judgmental. Once we have elicited the facts, we ask:

2. *What do you need to communicate better in support of our program's mission?*

    Maude, what do you need to feel the classroom is safe and structured, but also can allow for emergent curriculum?

    Gabriella, what do you need to feel the classroom is open to spontaneous learning, while affording children the predictability they also need?

In this step, one or both teachers may still feel the need to attack the other person. Gabriella may call Maude uptight and inflexible. Remind her to keep the focus on finding solutions. Maude may continuously glance at her watch and imply that the discussion is pointless. Ask them both: "How can you work together to resolve this problem in a way that models problem solving for children?"

3. *Brainstorm solutions that work for the program and build on each person's strengths.*
   Maude, can you name at least one solution that honors both Gabriella's and your teaching styles?
   Gabriella, what do you respect about Maude's teaching?

Help each person name something she honestly values about the other person. As each person hears something positive about herself from her "opponent," that opponent no longer looks like the enemy. Invite them to brainstorm ways in which they better serve children by sharing strengths and meeting each other's needs.

4. *Create a plan that ensures ongoing, open communication.*
   Gabriella, what will you do in the future to work effectively with Maude?
   Maude, what steps will you take to work more effectively with Gabriella?

I have observed that 98 percent of peer conflicts are the result of miscommunication. When a teacher feels misunderstood and unappreciated, she "turns off" the other teacher. Employees need systems for continuous communication. Maude and Gabriella's problem is solved temporarily by putting up the drying rack. Invite them to find and agree upon ongoing ways they can continuously communicate. Planning meetings every Friday afternoon? Using a shared notebook to write notes to each other? Gabriella can create an artistic cover, and Maude can organize the inside of it!

Peer Coaching Method

A peer coach is an on-call, trusted resident "expert" who helps colleagues work through conflict. Directors can call upon these skillful problem solvers to serve as peer coaches.

Transitioning from indirect to direct behavior can be awkward for all of us. Some team members will be quicker than others to master problem-solving skills. Beginner problem solvers may require a director's special time and assistance to help them hone their skills. Peer coaches support the director's efforts by reinforcing problem-solving practices.

In addition to using the *Z* method, peer coaches can draw from this five-step coaching process, made popular by professional coaches:

1. What is your *vision* of how you could work together effectively?
2. What are the *barriers* to working together?
3. Name *three steps* you can take to improve the situation.
4. *Take one step at a time.*
5. *Meet again* to discuss, "What is our vision/hope now?"

The peer coach asks colleagues about their hopes, barriers that get in the way, and steps they can take to make their program and classrooms a highly functional learning environment. This collaborative process invites coworkers to share responsibility for resolving their problems. Coaches remind each person to focus on what is best for children and families.

Apply the five steps of the peer coaching process to Gabriella and Maude. What would you ask? How might they respond? How can you keep them on track?

"Getting to Yes" and "Difficult Conversations" Methods

These strategies emerged from work by the Harvard Negotiation Project on peaceful resolution of conflict, and they share three powerful concepts:

1. Rather than waste time arguing over who should win, devote energy to understanding and accepting that each of us sees the world through different eyes.

2. Compromise often results in "unfinished business" and resentment. Aim instead for a deeper solution that honors each person's values.
3. If we look deep enough, we will find a point of agreement between the opposing parties.

President Jimmy Carter used this strategy as he negotiated a peace agreement between warring rivals, Menachem Begin of Israel and Anwar Sadat of Egypt. In the summary that follows, notice how President Carter helped both leaders find the "Yes!" upon which they could agree. Consider how you might use this strategy as you apply the Z and/or Peer Coaching methods of conflict resolution. What, for example, is the deeper value Gabriella and Maude share, which might offset the sting of their biases?

President Jimmy Carter invited Egyptian President Anwar Sadat and Israeli Premier Menachem Begin to meet at Camp David. The President's goal was to negotiate a peace accord between the leaders, whose differences were deep, long lasting, and painful. Neither man was willing to budge. President Sadat was about to walk out of the sessions.

At that point, President Carter asked Premier Begin, "Do you have grandchildren?" Begin softened and responded that he did. Carter then asked: "Can you show us their pictures?" The proud grandfather spread photos of his energetic grandchildren on the table. "Tell us about each of these delightful children," Carter encouraged. As Begin lovingly told a story about each child, Sadat began to edge closer to see and hear who these children were.

Carter next turned to Sadat and asked the same questions: "Do you have grandchildren? Could you show us their pictures? What is each one of these glorious children like?" As Sadat beamed with pride, Begin inched closer to see and to hear.

At the end of the day, the two men agreed they wanted a better future for their grandchildren. They signed the peace agreement that brought freedom from fear to both of their countries. They agreed wholeheartedly that all grandchildren deserve a promising future, free of fear and warfare.

The "difficult-conversation" method answers the question "Can I change another person?" with a resounding "No." When I try to persuade another person that I am right and she or he is wrong, I cannot win. If I focus instead on listening to "where the other person is coming from," and she or he, in turn, listens to my view of reality, we are more able to find a solution. Have you ever been able to change another person?

To apply these practices to the case study scenario, when Gabriella hears that Maude feared for the children's safety, Gabriella has the opportunity to see the situation through Maude's eyes. As Maude hears how important the children's creative artwork is to Gabriella, Maude is invited to pay attention to what matters to Gabriella. With practice, team members will begin to expect differences, rather than attempting to deny or destroy differences.

This difficult-conversation strategy focuses problem solvers on three questions (Stone, Patton, & Heen 1999):

1. What happened?
2. What feelings were triggered, both expressed and unexpressed?
3. What matters to you most?

As President Carter knew and leaders Begin and Sadat came to see, creating a better world for our grandchildren matters most. In early childhood education, what matters most? When we agree on that, we agree to resolve our interpersonal conflicts for the sake of the children. To do this, we need to detach from the desire to prevail over another person. As we look more deeply at what we all want, we can find our way back to why we are in this profession after all.

Strategies for Dealing with Negative People

Moods are catching. Common sense tells us that. Have you ever walked into a room where everyone is complaining, and before you know it, you find yourself being negative too? Neuroscience research substantiates that our neurons line up harmoniously with the neurons of the people nearby. Otherwise, we feel at odds in our environment. Often, negative people prevail. One whiner can rip shreds in a team's morale.

How can we end whining and negativity? Brinkman and Kirshner (2002) offer insight about two kinds of whiners: situational and chronic. "Situational" whiners are stuck on a situation they can't resolve. "Chronic" whiners complain for the sake of complaining. Like gossiping, whining is an indirect way of getting attention and power.

Situational whiners stop whining when they get help resolving their specific problem. Once they see that help is on the way, they stop whining. The bad hair day is over.

Chronic whiners, on the other hand, need a more assertive approach. Brinkman and Kirshner advise us neither to agree nor to disagree with the whiner. In either case, the whiner will keep whining, either because she has a captive listener, or to prove herself right. The authors also advise us not to "fix" the whiner's problem. According to the well-known adage: "Give a person a fish and they eat for a day. Teach a person to fish and they eat for a lifetime."

Take these steps with chronic whiners when they begin to complain:

1. Interrupt and ask for a concrete, specific example of the problem.
2. Work with the whiner on coming up with strategies to solve the problem by focusing on the concrete example.
3. When the whiner complains: "That will never work! Things will never change" use this empowering statement: "Since I can't help you with that problem, please don't bring it to me again."

If whiners find they have no audience, the point of whining is removed. Everyone else is modeling or encouraging resilience through effective problem solving. The whiner's effectiveness has ended.

In some cases, a whiner may be suffering from depression. Anyone with the illness of depression deserves help. Peers can recommend that the depressed person talk with the director, or accompany the person to the director. The director or human relations personnel can offer assistance, counseling, and medical intervention. Respect the employee's confidentiality. The Americans with Disabilities Act includes chronic depression in the list of disabilities "that effect a major life function" and administrators must provide reasonable accommodations. With help, the employee may return to being an effective colleague.

Once boundaries are set and help is offered, whining behavior can eventually become winning behavior.

Multicultural Problem-Solving Approaches

Kioko relocated with her parents from Japan when she was in high school. As a bright, creative, sensitive teacher, Kioko is viewed with great respect and caring by her peers. Kioko's cultural heritage encourages her to help everyone "save face." She takes care to make sure conflicts do not come out in the open. Kioko is more comfortable listening to people complain and gossip than she is to saying anything to stop or divert them. The program has just agreed to become a gossip-free zone. This statement, in particular, troubles Kioko: "If you listen to gossip, you are gossiping." How can you honor Kioko's culture while upholding program policy?

Given the richness of cultures represented in our programs, diverse approaches to conflict are to be welcomed and expected. Some cultures encourage directness. People in direct cultures need little physical distance from each other as they communicate. Israeli culture might be described this way. Other cultures encourage reserve and reticence. To stand too close to a person of this culture could be offensive. Japanese culture might be described in this way. How can we honor cultural differences, while upholding program problem-solving policies?

The first question to ask is, Does the policy respectfully embrace cultural differences? When introducing a policy, like the Problem Solving Agreement, invite employees to discuss the change at a staff meeting and to individually comment on the change. If you know a policy may conflict with a staff member's culture, invite that person to share her thoughts and observations with you first.

From there a leader has at least two options: revise the policy to make it more culturally sensitive, or find ways to institute the policy while encouraging each staff member to bring her own heritage to the practice of the policy. Look also to the spirit of the policy. The Problem Solving Agreement, in spirit, is aimed at requiring adults to take responsibility and resolve their problems together. Regarding the previous scenario involving Kioko, you could ask her what processes work in her culture when people have unresolved conflicts. Then, you could incorporate as many of those practices as possible. Alternatively, you could work with Kioko on what she is comfortable doing and saying to promote the spirit of the policy. In the end, you may discover some approaches you never envisioned.

Dr. Debra Ren-Etta Sullivan, who wrote an account of the successfully multicultural Pacific Oaks Northwest learning community she cocreated with colleagues in Seattle, Washington, knows the work is never done. Nonetheless, in an online interview with Redleaf Press, Dr. Sullivan optimistically reminds us: "When I see those who educate and care for young children advocating for the rights of all children to have a strong, healthy start in life, that makes me smile because we are growing leaders and their leadership may make all the difference in the world to the one young child who needs it most." A multicultural community of problem solvers leads to a strong, healthy start in life.

> Never let your sense of morals get in the way of doing what's right.
>
> —Isaac Asimov

⚔ Community

Without the capacity to resolve our inevitable differences, we cannot live in community. Community is living and working together in support of each other's and the community's well-being. The African adage, "It takes a community to raise a child," fits early childhood programs like a beloved pair of blue jeans.

I asked colleagues around the country to share the guidelines they would use to establish multicultural communities. Here are three responses from three corners of our country to my question: To fully participate in a multicultural community, what three ground rules would you most need that community to follow?

Donna Rafanello, California

1. All contributions are welcomed and valued.
2. Participants need to commit to the process and be willing to actively engage in change and be willing to be changed by it.
3. Enter into the conversation with awareness that others' way of doing things and thinking may be as good as, or better than your own.

Dr. Cathy Jones, South Carolina

We will:

1. Hold at the core of our community: *respect* for the right to be different.
2. Have the freedom to express our differing opinions without fear of retribution.
3. Work through issues with love and respect and never walk away until consensus or resolution is reached.

Attorney Arthur LaFrance, Oregon

Our community must:

1. Have a purpose/function beyond itself.
2. Agree upon a process for inclusion, action, and dissolution before commencement.
3. Have leadership that is time-limited.
4. Recognize me as leader for life and anyone who doesn't like that should get out now!

Thank you, Art, for being direct (and tongue in cheek)!

 What are at least three ground rules you would establish to promote a multicultural community of problem solvers? Reflecting on all the ideas and approaches in this chapter, what strikes you as most important? What does it take to build a community of problem solvers?

I have come to see that my sense of humor is one of my most valuable emotional intelligence capacities. I know too, that when I am able to detach, step up to the balcony, and get perspective on a heated issue, I am more able to see what matters to everyone, not just to me. Humor and perspective: I don't leave home without them! At least that is what I remind myself when my old friend, "my way or the highway," comes calling. What are your most valued EQ capacities for creating a community of problem solvers?

Reflection Questions

1. What phrases and principles can you find in NACCP's Code of ethics to support a director's efforts in ending gossip, negativity, and other unproductive behavior? Apply these principles to one of the cases in the chapter.

    National Association of Child Care Professionals (NACCP)
    Code of Ethics

    The National Association of Child Care Professionals is an association of people who are leaders in the field of early care and education. As an association, we believe that child care is a profession and that it is our responsibility as professional women and men to lead our centers in an ethical manner. Recognizing that the association is a vital link in this process, we determine to govern our individual centers as follows:

    1. To maintain the ethical standards of the National Association of Child Care Professionals to more effectively serve our children, their parents, and the field.
    2. To continually remember that ours is a service industry. We are committed to providing quality child care to our children and their families, and we place this service above personal gain.
    3. To conduct our business in a way that will both maintain good will within the field and build the confidence of parents, the community, and fellow professionals. . . .

        • • • •

    8. To avoid sowing discontent among the employees of competitors with the purpose of embarrassing or hindering their business.
    9. To avoid possible damage to a competitor's image by purposefully misleading parents, members of the community, or fellow professionals. . . .

        • • • •

    11. To conduct ourselves at all times in a way that will bring credit to our association and the child care field.

2. Reflect on your own experience of working, studying, and/or living with women. What strengths and difficulties predictably emerge? Is your experience different when you work with men, or when you work with both men and women together? Do you attribute these differences to nature, nurture, both? Find at least one research study to support your theory, and one that differs from your theory. "Nature and nurture" is a phrase used to acknowledge that some traits are genetic or inborn (nature), while others are learned and/or result from our environment (nurture).

3. Take a look at your cultural background. Begin by reflecting on each of your names (first name, surname, middle names, or confirmation names). Why was each of these names chosen? Were you named after someone? What heritage does your name carry? What is your family's history in this country? Was the family name changed or lost at any point? Write a reflection paper on how your cultural background contributes to your view of building community, and conflict resolution.

Team Projects

1. Read the case about Betty below. Present a plan to your class on how to (a) prevent Betty from disrupting the program and (b) hold Betty accountable for changing her behavior.
   What tactics or "weapons" does Betty use to gain power? In what ways might Betty's behavior affect team members and program morale? Have you known and/or dealt with a person who behaved like Betty? Look at the approaches described in this chapter: What action do you think you might take, both as a peer and as Betty's supervisor?

   > If **A**lice has offended **B**etty, **B**etty will tell **C**arolyn & **D**iane about it—but in such a way as to enlist **C**arolyn & **D**iane against **A**lice by persuading them that **A**lice has not only unfairly offended **B**etty, but offended **C**arolyn & **D**iane as well. Of course, **A**lice may have done no such thing. **B**etty will carefully manage how she presents "past events." She will do so in order to gain the support of a clique imbued with righteous indignation, which will then assist **B**etty in any future confrontation with **A**lice, or in a decision to shun **A**lice. **B**etty must accomplish this without appearing to intend to (Chesler 2001, 111).

2. Research additional (to the ones described in this chapter) problem-solving approaches. Select two approaches that appeal most to you. Prepare a presentation for your class on each of these approaches. Apply the approaches to Gabriella and Maude.

3. Investigate and discuss how conflict is viewed and dealt with by at least two cultures other than your own. How do you feel about these diverse approaches? What can you learn from other cultures on conflict resolution? As a leader of a program, what actual steps could you take to ensure that cultural differences are respected as conflicts arise?

Bibliography

Brinkman, R., and R. Kirshner. 2002. *Dealing with people you can't stand: How to bring out the best in people at their worst*. New York: McGraw-Hill.

Bruno, H. E. 2007. Gossip free zones: Problem solving to prevent power struggles. *Young Children* (September).

Bruno, H.E., and M.L. Copeland. 1999. If the director isn't direct, can the team have direction? *Leadership Quest* (Winter).

Cahill, L., and L. Kilpatrick. 2004. Sex-related hemispheric lateralization of amygdala function in emotionally influenced memory: An MRI investigation. *Learning & Memory* .

Chesler, P. 2001. *Woman's inhumanity to woman.* New York: Plume.

Code of ethical conduct and statement of commitment: Guidelines for responsible behavior in early childhood education. 2005. Washington, DC: NAEYC.

Copeland, M.L., and H.E. Bruno. 2001. Countering center gossip and negativity. *Child Care Exchange* (March).

Feeney, S., N. Freeman, and Eva Moravcik. 2000. *Teaching the NAEYC Code of Ethical Conduct.* Washington, DC: NAEYC.

Fisher, R., and W. Ury. 1983. *Getting to YES: Negotiating without giving in.* New York: Penguin Books.

Goleman, D. 2003. *Destructive emotions: How can we overcome them? A scientific dialogue with the Dalai Lama.* New York: Bantam Dell.

Goleman, D. 1997. *Emotional intelligence.* New York: Bantam Books.

Gonzalez-Mena, J. 2005. *Diversity in early care and education.* New York: McGraw-Hill.

Gonzalez-Mena, J. 2008. *Foundations of early childhood education.* New York: McGraw-Hill.

Jordan, J., ed. 1997. *Women's growth in diversity.* New York: Guildford Press.

Kroeger, O., and J.Thuesen. 1992. *Type talk.* New York: Delacourte Press.

Kyle, A. 2007. *The God of animals.* New York: Scribner.

National Association of Child Care Professionals (NACCP). *Code of ethics . http://www.naccp. org/displaycommon.cfm?an=1&subarticlenbr=287.*

Stone, D., B. Patton, and S. Heen. 1999. *Difficult conversations: How to discuss what matters most.* New York: Penguin Group.

Sullivan, D.R. 2003. *Learning to lead: Effective skills for teachers of young children.* St. Paul, MN: Redleaf Press.

Sullivan, D.R. *Interview with Redleaf Press. http://www.redleafpress.org/client/archives/features/rl_ Aug2005_feature.cfm.*

Tannen, D. 1990. *You just don't understand.* New York: Ballantine Books.

Tanenbaum, L. 2002. *Catfight: Women and competition.* New York: Seven Stories Press.

Vonnegut, K. 1969. *Slaughterhouse-five.* New York: Dell.

Woolsey, L.K., and L. McBain. 1987. Issues of power and powerlessness in all-woman groups. *Women's Studies International Forum,* 10.

Web Resources

Are Your Workers Whiners or Winners?
http://www.humannatureatwork.com/Workers_Whiners_Winners.html
Conflict Resolution and Negotiation Articles
http://www.abetterworkplace.com/conflicts.html
NAEYC Code of Ethical Conduct and Statement of Commitment
http://www.naeyc.org/about/positions/PSETH05.asp
Managing in a Multicultural Workplace
http://www.enewsbuilder.net/theayersgroup/e_article000935108.cfm?x=b11,0,w - a935108
Problem-Solving Techniques
http://www.mindtools.com/pages/main/newMN_TMC.htm
Stop the Gossip, Save Your Career
http://hotjobs.yahoo.com/career-articles-stop_the_gossip_save_your_career-208

Norming

Establishing Management Systems

Supervision and Staff Development: Social EQ in Action

Learning Goals

As you study this chapter, you can look forward to reaching these learning goals:

1. Define supervision.

2. Explain "discernment" as a supervisory competency.

3. Describe and compare the types of supervision: directive and reflective.

4. Identify and explain staff development stages.

5. Determine which type of supervision is more appropriate to use.

6. Practice directive supervision's five principles and five steps.

7. Connect the "progressive discipline" process with directive supervision steps.

8. Identify reflective supervision practices that inspire employees and teams to perform at their best.

We'd all like to feel self-reliant and capable of coping with whatever adversity comes our way, but that's not how most human beings are made. It's my belief that the capacity to accept help is inseparable from the capacity to give help when our turn comes to be strong. It can sometimes be difficult to ask for support when we need it, but having someone we can count on to stick with us through the tough times can make those times much more bearable.

—*Fred Rogers*

If your actions inspire others to dream more, learn more, do more and become more, you are a leader.

—*John Quincy Adams*

Case Study: Tailoring Supervision to Fit Each Employee

Francia, outstanding toddler teacher, is a dedicated mom to her four young children. Francia's husband expects a homemade meal on the table every evening, a clean house, and time with the wife he loves. Francia is highly motivated to earn her early childhood degrees. With English as her second language, no money to spare, and fears about feeling inadequate in a college classroom, Francia asks you, her director, for guidance.

Jasmine, Francia's team teacher, is due to arrive by 6:30 a.m. daily. On Monday, Jasmine arrived at 6:45. On Tuesday, she walked through the door at 7:05. Today, Jasmine showed up at 6:50 without apology. Jasmine's behavior stresses Francia. Clarence's parents, who told Francia they couldn't wait any longer to speak with Jasmine, stormed out yesterday. To cover ratios in the toddler room (make sure enough teachers are in the room, given how many children are there), you increasingly reschedule early morning meetings and phone calls to cover for Jasmine. Once Jasmine settles into the classroom, she is a creative and loving teacher.

If you were Francia and Jasmine's director and supervisor, how would you assess the situation? What steps would you take?

Supervision is helping employees perform at their best, in service to their organization's mission. Supervision fosters professionalism in every employee and team. By working to build forthright, caring, and respectful relationships with each teacher and team, supervisors create communities of problem solvers. Supervision both invites and requires conscientious, creative, and dedicated performance.

A leader's vision sets the standard for how she supervises. In this way, supervision is a "super" way to implement a leader's "vision." Supervision, like emotional intelligence, is common sense but not necessarily common practice. When a director leads on purpose, her supervision practice hums.

This chapter will help you successfully tailor your supervision to fit the needs of each staff member. You will learn how to discern when a teacher needs to be told what to do (directive supervision) and when she can be invited to innovate (reflective supervision). Much depends on the maturity level of each staff member and each team. You will also study how to establish a system of supervision with useful policies, procedures, and forms. Because supervision practice aligns with legal requirements, you will track the close and necessary relationship between the law and a director's actions.

While supervision is hard work, it is also a joy and an honor. Skilled supervisors, in exercising social EQ, mentor our next generation of leaders. Helping a teacher develop and soar can be just as fulfilling as helping a child discover her world.

⚙ Supervision Components

Social EQ Capacities

Managing people who care for and educate children requires more than an annual evaluation meeting. Supervision is the day-to-day, often moment-to-moment, responsibility to support each employee's professional growth and to ensure the program runs smoothly.

Supervisory EQ entails the mindful, heartfelt work of continuously assessing and building upon:

1. What inspires and motivates employees; as well as,
2. Staff strengths, blind spots, and developmental needs.

I've been doing supervision for 40 years and I'm just beginning to get the hang of it.

—**Jeree Pawl**

With supervision, staff members are invited to take responsibility for their own actions, attitudes, and relationships. Supervisors help employees learn to fish. As the saying goes: "Give a person a fish; the person eats for a day. Teach a person to fish; the person eats for a lifetime."

As courageous nurturers, supervisors take stands for quality. Acting quickly to discipline a nonperforming staff member requires courage. Because children learn by observing adults, children benefit from their teachers' professionalism. Confronting employees promptly for inappropriate behavior, difficult as that is for many administrators, is an essential supervisory practice.

Insight and empathy are just as useful to a supervisor as courage. Reading our staff accurately lets us see talent and gifts they might not yet see. Supporting each employee to claim and build on her strengths, while working through her weaknesses, will call on all three virtues: courage, insight, and empathy.

> If you are new to supervision, take heart. Consider all you have learned about "developmentally appropriate practice" for children. Draw upon that knowledge when working with adults. Adults, like children, grow through stages of development. Each stage predicts the type of supervision we use.

Adult Developmental Stages

The type of supervision a director chooses depends in large part on the maturity level of the employee. Just as teachers use developmentally appropriate (DAP) practices with children, directors gear supervision to the developmental stage of each staff member.

In the stages of staff development section below, the adult developmental levels identified help leaders determine what supervision practice will fit. Less mature staff members are likely to need to be *told* what is expected. More seasoned employees, who already take responsibility for themselves, can be *asked* to take charge of new ventures and come up with creative possibilities. Age is not the determinant of an adult's developmental stage. Maturity and accountability are better predictors. A fifty-three-year-old teacher can be fourteen on the inside. A twenty-year-old can have the maturity of an elder.

Consider how we apply principles of developmentally appropriate practice when working with both children and adults. For example, we might respectfully guide toddlers through the process of redirection. We might guide teenagers by balancing firmness with their need for autonomy. We might mentor a gifted classroom teacher into confidently presenting a workshop at an early childhood conference. As Jasmine's supervisor in the chapter case study, we are likely to enforce the boundary for punctuality and consideration for others.

Respect the Person, Address the Behavior

> We seek in supervision to find where our professionalism lies.
>
> —Jeree Pawl

Regardless of her developmental level, each employee, like each child, deserves unconditional positive regard. Although a person's behavior may be inappropriate, she is still worthy of respect. The person's behavior, not the person's worthiness, is the issue. Teacher Jasmine's lateness for work does not make her a "bad person." Jasmine's behavior, however, is unacceptable. Toddler Israel's biting is not acceptable. Regardless of having hurt another child, Israel, is still worthy of love and respect, as is the child Israel hurt. No one wants or deserves to be put in a box and labeled a bad or unworthy human being. If an employee, or a child, senses she has been labeled inadequate as a person, she will resist her supervisor's efforts, however well-intended.

No question about it, as a supervisor, you will call upon all your social EQ skills and develop new ones along the way. Knowing what you stand for will put you in good stead as a supervisor.

The Vision in Super-"Vision"

Ask yourself: "What do I stand for?" Complete this sentence: I stand for _____.
Do you stand for quality, equality, fairness, kindness, doing the right thing, holding people accountable?

Be assured, whatever you stand for, your purpose predicts how you will supervise others. Should you lose sight of your purpose in the midst of a particularly heated situation, "step aside" (Chapter 2) to recall your core values and why you do the work you do. Regaining perspective will reenergize you to face what you need to face.

At a minimum, supervisors ensure that staff comply with licensing and accreditation standards, and personnel policies. On their busiest days, administrators may feel they merely "watchdog" or oversee staff to ensure essential functions of their jobs are performed. Just as border collies patrol tirelessly to keep the flock within boundaries, supervisors can practice hypervigilance as their core function. But trust is not instilled by watchdog supervision and watch dogs grow weary after long days of being "on alert."

Keep the *vision* in your super*vision* alive in your heart and mind. Imagine your vision as a home that remains cozy and welcoming regardless of the weather outside.

Supervision entails far more. Supervision with vision and social EQ can be an elegant, dynamic and creative, individualized and systematized, rewarding endeavor. The Latin prefix *super* means having sight that goes "above, over, beyond." Emotionally intelligent supervision keeps leaders' eyes on quality care as they encourage each staff member to perform at her best. A leader's unique vision for quality informs and inspires every interaction with her staff. Each of us leads best by being true to our "super" vision (Chapter 2).

Discernment, the Core Competency for Supervisors

Directors make choices. Discerning what action to take is what leadership is all about. Whether we use thin-slicing, letter of the law, or spirit of the law (Chapter 4) to make decisions, our decisions will be measured by their effectiveness. In supervising, directors employ case by case methods to tailor their approach to each individual. In creating and implementing a supervision system, directors use letter of the law discernment. Any way you "slice" it, supervision is a continuous judgment call.

How can a director find time to effectively discern what's right for each employee, given all the director's other management and administrative responsibilities? Leaders are responsible for creating a community of problem solvers, an environment where adults and children alike can bloom. Childcare staff report that to bloom, they need more feedback, interaction with and attention from their directors (Kilbourne 2007). Because a director's time is limited, supervision needs to be quality time.

Consider staff members Francia and Jasmine in the chapter case study. Francia and Jasmine represent two of the most common challenges for supervisors:

1. The willing employee who needs significant support to develop professionally; and,
2. The unwilling employee, who does not take responsibility for her own actions.

Which staff member would you prefer to supervise and why? What are your concerns about dealing with the staff member you did not select?

Professional development may be the last thing on Jasmine's mind. Jasmine's director must supervise Jasmine to help her become more consciously professional, or to find another career better suited to her style. Discerning when to "counsel staff out the door" is a useful supervisory competency.

The early childhood education field is trending toward increasingly higher standards for professional credentialing. As you discern the course you would take with Francia and Jasmine, keep in mind that supervision occurs in the context of evolving professional standards and expectations (Chapter 15). The 2006 *NAEYC Accreditation Criteria for Leadership and Management Standard*, for example, requires accredited programs to have a plan in place for staff professional development. Francia's personal goal to earn a degree fits into her director's goal of ensuring 75 percent of her staff members have a CDA, associate, baccalaureate, or advanced degree by 2011.

Supervision is many things: a vision, commitment, style, system, and a relationship. You can count on supervision to provide you every opportunity for growth as you discern each course you will take (see Table 9.1).

Discerning Who Needs What and When

In directive supervision, we *tell;* in reflective supervision, we *ask.*

Directive supervision holds employees accountable when their performance does not meet expectations.

Reflective supervision invites employee and supervisor to grow together in the context of a supportive, introspective relationship.

⚒ Types of Supervision: Directive and Reflective

Directive Supervision is a process for holding employees accountable for their professional performance when they do not demonstrate ability, capacity, and/or intentionality to take responsibility for their own actions.

Reflective supervision is a process that invites and empowers staff to examine their performance and grow professionally within a nurturing, honest relationship.

Which type of supervision would you use for Francia? Jasmine? What type would work best for you if you were being supervised?

Later in this chapter, as we explore directive and reflective supervision in detail, we will look back at the choices you make initially about these teachers.

Supervision systems incorporate both directive and reflective procedures. Placing these two practices in the context of a broader supervision system helps directors formulate and create a plan for supervision. A supervision system will include:

✓ Regular, ongoing assessment and evaluation practices, along with
✓ Spontaneous interventions.

Reflective supervision is instrumental to a director's ongoing evaluation, mentoring, and assessment system. Directive supervision requires spontaneous corrective intervention, backed up by a system of progressive discipline procedures. See the Appendix for sample forms and procedures for developing a professional supervision system. With a standard system of supervision in place, employees will know what they can expect from their director and what is expected of them.

Assessing What the Employee Needs

The first question to ask is, "What does each staff member need to do her best work?"

To supervise successfully, managers need a method to assess what each staff member needs to help her develop. In effective supervision, "one size fits all" does not apply. Each employee's stage of development indicates the type of supervision employed. What steps will ensure that teachers arrive on time? What supervision style will help them build partnerships with families?

Paula Jorde Bloom (1972) has given us a clear method for measurement. Her stages of staff development identify employee needs at different times in their career (Figure 9.1). Let's examine what each of these stages entails, and how that stage of adult development predicts the style of supervision to be used. Let's study these stages from the bottom up. More staff members are likely to be at the bottom or beginning stages of staff development than at the mature professional stage at the top.

Survivors make it through the day. Everything feels new to the survivor, who has little experience or expertise to rely on. Remember how you felt in your first job or on the first day of school? You may have gone home exhausted, wondering how you would survive until the weekend. Classroom teachers at the survival stage feel overwhelmed by

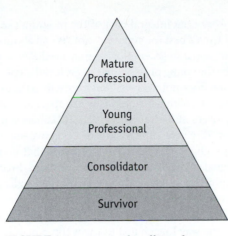

FIGURE 9.1 *Stages of Staff Development*

the demands of the job: parents' needs, classroom management issues, required documentation, lack of planning time, children who require one-on-one care. Survivors, caught up in getting through the day, do not yet see beyond their own needs. A survivor rarely has or takes time to "step aside" to see the program from a larger perspective.

Even seasoned professionals can return to the survivor stage. Each time a person takes on a new challenge or position, she may feel she has to start at the bottom. A teacher who suddenly finds herself in the director's position can feel overwhelmed and in the survivor stage. An "A" student can feel like a survivor the first day of each new course she takes. Fortunately, we do not have to remain at the survival stage. As we develop and grow professionally, we move up to the next stage of staff development.

Consolidator

Once a professional has survived the beginning stage, she is ready to "consolidate" her successful experiences and growing knowledge base. For the consolidator, not everything is new. Past successes can be built upon.

If her lesson plans on butterflies fascinated preschoolers this year, the consolidator can supplement that curriculum with additional teaching strategies. A consolidator may have gleaned useful tips from an *Exchange* article on classroom activities or have participated in a workshop that equipped her with tools on classroom management. Her lead teacher may have modeled how to partner with families whose children have ADHD. Her supervisor may have offered alternative teaching strategies.

Consolidators begin to braid these diverse strands of knowledge and competency together. Confidence develops as their skills grow. Unlike survivors, consolidators enjoy more of a comfort level with their work. Like survivors, consolidators, still early in their development, focus more on themselves than the program as a whole. Consolidators continue to require supervision that provides clear expectations and boundaries.

Young Professional at the Renewal Stage

Having survived and consolidated their knowledge, employees through appropriate supervision step up to the young professional stage. At the young professional or renewal stage of development, an employee becomes more enthusiastic and able to "direct" herself. She might feel confident with parents, curriculum, and children.

The "young professional" can be fifty years old. Age is not the determinant. Skills and competencies are. The young professional has grown to be a self-starter, initiator, and creator. She or he is more likely now to see the bigger picture. She or he acknowledges that as a team member, her work is an integral part of the program's success. A young professional thinks first about what's best for *everyone*, not "it's all about *me*."

At the young professional stage, employees may need *Renewal*. This is why Renewal is another way to describe the young professional stage. Ideally, a person at this stage knows enough to know what she does not know. She is ready to reflect on how she needs and wants to grow and contribute, with her supervisor's support and mentoring.

To supervise employees at the renewal stage, the supervisor shifts from authority to guiding partner, from directive supervision to reflective supervision. We supervise young professionals through a collaborative relationship that invites them to reflect on their performance and goals. We also continue to offer them direction when needed.

Not every young professional is ready to transition to reflective supervision, however. Have you worked with a person who does the same thing over and over, year after year? She may feel, "If it ain't broke don't fix it." She is likely to resist new ideas: "Why should I have to change the way I teach just to meet some new accreditation standard?" An employee with this attitude, still focusing more on herself than on the big picture, may still need directive supervision.

Elders

Mature professional "Elders" in Native American tribes are respected for their wisdom. Their opinion carries weight in their community. Many early childhood programs are fortunate to have "elders" on their teams. Early childhood elders take responsibility for themselves, while encouraging and inspiring professionalism in others. Seasoned staff members "walk the talk" of quality.

My colleague, Susan, with over thirty years in the field, continuously delights me with new insights and enthusiasm about being a director. Last year, Susan traveled to Italy to study Reggio Emilia methods. This year, Susan joined a directors' discussion group on how to enhance infant programs. Susan, like most of us, has her uninspired times too. On balance, however, she uses her lifelong learning skills to take risks for personal and professional growth.

Elders benefit from collegiality, appreciation, acknowledgment, and opportunities for continuous improvement. Like Susan, they need to stay inspired and avoid burnout by discovering fresh ways to find meaning in their work. Perhaps Gladys is ready to write an article for the *Young Children*. Gladys may have the desire to mentor others. She may ask you to help her apply for a directorship at another center. Because you have come to know Gladys well, you will be able to hold heart-to-heart conversations with her about her hopes and goals. You will also have learned more about yourself as you have accompanied Gladys on her journey.

Age is not a trustworthy predictor of an employee's stage of development. Some of the most mature and responsible teachers are in their twenties. Some of the least mature employees may be forty-five on the outside but eighteen on the inside. Supervisors can use their emotional intelligence radar to assess the true stage of a staff member's development.

Stages of Adult Development

As you have probably noticed, early childhood leaders can draw from many fields to better understand "what it's all about." We can learn, for example, from psychologists, like Abraham Maslow, who studied adult development. Maslow's "hierarchy of needs" offers perspective on stages of staff development (1943). Notice the parallels between Maslow's model in Figure 9.2 and the Jorde Bloom model in Figure 9.1.

Again, we start at the bottom and work our way up. Maslow calls the survivor stage the "physiological" stage. This beginning stage of adult development is the time where we put a roof over our head, food on the table, and clothing on our backs. We need to

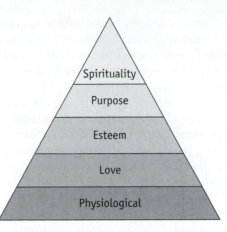

FIGURE 9.2   *Maslow's Hierarchy of Needs*

Source: Maslow 1943, 370–396.

feel safe and secure first, before we feel confident to take risks to grow. Maslow's physiological stage closely aligns with the survivor stage of staff development.

With our physiological needs met, we are freer to interact more meaningfully with others. At this point, we grow upward through levels of love and esteem. At these levels, we view the world from a less self-centered perspective and begin to see ourselves as connected to others in meaningful ways. These are the consolidation and young professional stage in the Jorde Bloom model.

As we more fully mature, we are able to claim and to live out our purpose. At the pinnacle of adult development, we seek deepest fulfillment. This is the stage Maslow calls "spirituality." Spirituality is the quest for a life of deeper meaning. Being religious is one of many pathways to spirituality. A mature employee may decide to work with young children without homes as part of her spiritual practice of "paying it forward," or giving back to others.

Using either the Maslow or Jorde Bloom model, a supervisor can determine an employee's stage of development. To "manage through relationships," we need to ask and assess what each person needs both in the moment and in the long run. Each accurate assessment we make empowers us to discern better what type of supervision to use.

Matching Supervision Type to Staff Developmental Stage

Remember Francia and Jasmine? What indicators do their behaviors and words tell you about their developmental stage? Are Jasmine and Francia at different stages, or the same one?

Once you determine an individual's stage of development, you know better how to match the type of supervision to each person's needs. Let's look at how that assessment process works. Fortunately, for each stage of staff development, one particular mode of supervision works better. A manager's challenge is:

1. Assess the staff member's stage of development.
2. Apply the supervision style best suited to that person at that stage.

To Tell or to *Ask:* When Should Each Mode of Supervision Be Used?

Use directive supervision at the early stages of staff development (survivor, consolidator, and, at times, young professional). At these stages, staff are better served when supervisors set boundaries, establish professional expectations, and make clear what the consequences of their behavior are.

Blessed is the influence of one true, loving human soul on another.

—George Eliot (Mary Ann Evans)

For sure, Jasmine requires directive supervision to help her take responsibility for getting to work on time. Jasmine's focus, like any survivor, seems to be self-centered. She does appear to be thinking about how her lateness harms children, parents, other staff, and program quality. In directive supervision, the leader directly and clearly *tells* the employee what's expected.

Use reflective supervision with employees at a stage of maturity, either elder or young professional, whose performance indicates their ability to observe, assess, and change to meet the needs of the program. Unlike Jasmine, Francia's desire to improve herself professionally may indicate she has the bigger picture of program quality in mind. Francia's willingness to look at herself and her openness to establish a career pathway indicates her supervisor can use reflective supervision. With reflective supervision, a leader *asks* her employee to reflect on what she values and needs.

Identify a coworker, staff member, or peer whose behavior troubles or offends you. Perhaps this person is perpetually late, like Jasmine, or dispirits others with her negativity. Maybe she always presents herself as a victim and fails to take responsibility for herself. In her mind, someone else is always to blame. List three facts that capture this person's problematic behavior. Be specific and concrete. "Jasmine arrived at 7:05 today, although her 'start time' is 6:30" is a concrete fact. Avoid generalities like "Jasmine is always late."

Once you have written three facts, find a crayon or felt marker and a blank piece of paper. Picture yourself as supervisor of the person whose behavior is offensive. Imagine you have decided to call this person in for a directive supervision session. Your task is to help her take responsibility for changing her inappropriate behavior.

Picture how you would feel in the moment before you confront this person about her behavior. You do not need artistic talent to do this next task. Take your marker or crayon and draw what you would feel like and/or what your mental state would be just before you sit down with this person.

Congratulations. Now, set your list of facts and drawing to the side for a moment. We'll come back to them after we look at some helpful research.

For 80 percent of early childhood leaders, supervision that requires confronting staff for inappropriate behavior is so daunting that they avoid doing it (Bruno and Copeland 1999). Directors around the country report unpleasant physical symptoms like shortness of breath, sweaty palms, stomach butterflies, and stress headaches when asked to picture direct confrontation. Seventy percent of women and 44 percent of men tend to take things personally, seek to keep the peace, and avoid conflict. For the majority of early childhood leaders, reflective supervision's nurturing process flows naturally. Affirming comes more easily than confronting.

Where would you place yourself in these statistics? Would you be part of the 80 percent who fear conflict, the 20 percent who face conflict, or in between?

> Adversity is the first path to truth.
>
> **—Lord Byron**

Five Principles and Steps of Directive Supervision

Being able to tell employees directly that their behavior needs to change is part of leadership. For the majority of early childcare professionals who are conflict avoidant, learning the skills of direct supervision is liberating. At the early stages of development, employees learn best when told directly what is expected of them. This means stating the "1, 2, 3" steps of the task and spelling out in detail what needs to be done. Many supervisors prefer to imagine staff will "catch on" by imitating model behavior. Avoidance makes the problem grow larger.

Take a look at your drawing. Do you find signs of comfort or discomfort, confidence or fear? The majority of people who have completed this exercise draw people who look like they have put their finger in a light socket. Frowning faces, fearful faces, or butterflies in their stomachs are common. Some draw thunderbolts or turbulent weather like rain clouds. Only a few have drawn smiling faces. When asked to describe how they feel about confronting another person, they say, "Anxious, afraid, upset, angry." Is it any wonder so many early childhood professionals are not comfortable with directive supervision? Let's take directive supervision one principle and one step at a time.

Directive supervision is based on five principles. It can be challenging for directors to use directive supervision when an employee doesn't want to take responsibility for her own actions. Table 9.2 provides tips for how to apply each principle and remain objective and focused on finding a positive solution.

Let's revisit the chapter case study and put these principles to the test. Jasmine behaves like a survivor, and she needs to take responsibility for the impact of her behavior on others. Her performance will improve only if she learns to take responsibility for her actions through directive supervision.

Imagine calling Jasmine in for a supervision session about her behavior:

Director: Jasmine, when you arrived this Monday at 6:45 a.m., Tuesday at 7:05, and today, Wednesday, at 6:50, that was inappropriate. You need to be in your classroom, ready to begin by 6:30 a.m.

Jasmine: Why are you picking on me? Melanie is late half the time.

TABLE 9.2

Principles of Directive Supervision

Principle 1

Focus on the person's behavior, not the person	The employee's behavior is at issue, not her worthiness as a person.

Principle 2

Be factual, concrete, and accurate when identifying the behavior.	Tell the facts about what she or he did, accurately and in sufficient detail, without shaming or blaming the employee or "sugar-coating." *Res ipse loquitur,* a Latin saying, translates: "The facts speak for themselves."

Principle 3

Don't get hooked by taking what is said personally; use a "Q-tip."	Because employees can become defensive, focus the conversation on "What changes will you make to be sure you do what's expected?" Do not get ensnared in a power struggle. Step to the side, use your OFC (Chapter 2) if you feel your amygdala may be hijacked. Put a Q-tip in your pocket. Squeeze it to remind yourself: *Quit Taking It Personally.*

Principle 4

Expect employees to take responsibility for their behavior.	Focus the employee on problem solving by asking: "What will you do to change your behavior?" Do not rob the employee of her chance to take responsibility by stepping in to "fix" it for her. Find a solution that is right for everyone, especially children and families.

Principle 5

Come to a "meeting of the minds" and enforce it with a follow-up plan.	Tie a bow on this supervision meeting by making sure the employee understands what she will do differently, when you will meet to follow up, and what the consequence of her failure to change would be.

Director: Jasmine, we're talking about your behavior, not anyone else's. The actions I take with staff members are confidential.

Jasmine: I work really hard and give my heart and soul to these children. Why isn't that enough for you!

Director: The children need you in the classroom on time. What will you do to make sure you arrive on time each day?

Jasmine: Change my start time to 7:30. You let Taylor come at 7:30!

Director: We need you for the early morning slot. Tell me what you can change to make sure you are in the classroom, prepared and ready to start by 6:30.

Jasmine: (crying or yelling) You don't appreciate anything I do! I'm a better teacher than half the staff you have here!

Director: Yes, Jasmine, when you are with the children, you are an excellent and caring teacher. That's not the issue. You need to get here on time. Here's a Kleenex. Take a five-minute break. Come back ready to share what you will do to be here on time each day.

Jasmine: All right, I suppose I could take the earlier bus, the #79 that leaves a half-hour earlier. Would that make you happy!

Director: Sounds like a plan, Jasmine. Are you agreeing to take the earlier bus?

Jasmine: If I have to I guess.

Director: We'll meet one week from today at this time. Taylor will cover your class. I'll also stop by each morning to check in with you. The children, their parents, and Francia will all feel better when they can count on you to be on time. If you do not arrive on time, however, the next step is probation. Please sign this Corrective Action form to indicate you agree to this plan.

Jasmine: This is hard for me. I have never been an on-time person.

Director: I understand and I support your making the effort.

Directive supervision is respectful and not mean-spirited. "Holding the line" with Jasmine will help her learn how to become a professional.

Having examined the five principles for holding staff accountable, let's develop a script for putting the principles into practice. Table 9.3 shows what Jasmine's director could say when applying the steps of directive supervision:

How do you feel about the directness of direct supervision? Take stock of your emotions. Let them give you information about your response to this process, which is counterintuitive (feels unnatural), or as if we are in shadow (Chapter 3).

For that 80 percent of us, directive supervision's straightforward, no-nonsense, "thinking" approach can be problematic (Chapter 3). Being direct and being respectful are not mutually exclusive. In fact, this process respectfully informs the employee what is expected of her and encourages her to take a mature approach. In twelve-step (AA or Alanon) parlance, directive supervision is "tough love."

The steps of directive supervision comply with legal requirements. The progressive discipline steps that follow are synchronized with the five steps.

Directive Supervision's Compliance with Legal Requirements

Courts require supervisors to make a "conscientious rescue effort" to help employees, like Jasmine, learn skills and attitudes to effectively perform their jobs. Conscientious rescue efforts include "enhanced supervision," such as meeting with Jasmine, being clear with her on what is expected, developing a plan for how she can improve her performance, and documenting the process.

"Weeble wobble"—help from an old-fashioned children's toy:

Picture a weeble wobble, the inflatable plastic children's toy, with a weight at the bottom. No matter how many punches the weeble wobble takes, it bounces back to standing tall. Directive supervision steps help you come back to your center, like a weeble wobble. When you lead on purpose, nothing can take you off center for long.

T A B L E   9 . 3

Putting Directive Supervision into Words

1. State the inappropriate behavior.	"Jasmine, when you arrived Monday at 6:45, Tuesday at 7:05, and this morning at 6:50 a.m., that was inappropriate."
2. Name the expected behavior.	"You need to be here ready to start by 6:30 a.m. each day."
3. Ask what changes the employee will make to meet expectations.	"Jasmine, what will you do to get here, ready to start in the classroom by 6:30 a.m. daily?"
4. Hold the employee responsible for identifying a solution that is best for children and families.	"Changing your start time is not an option, Jasmine. Your idea of taking the earlier bus will work well."
5. Make a plan for follow-through.	"Please tell me what you agree to do differently. We'll meet one week from today at 1 p.m. naptime in my office. Millicent will cover for you. I'll check in with you daily to see how things are going. This is your written notice, Jasmine. If you do not get to work on time, you will be put on probation. Thank you for coming up with a solution that will help children, families, and your team members."

The good news is that the five steps and principles of directive supervision align with the conscientious rescue effort courts require of employers. Most of us work in "at will" states where an employee can resign "at will," and an employer can terminate an employee's work "without cause." An employer can say: "It's just not working out." Why aren't more employees simply told: "It's just not working out"?

Most organizations afford employees opportunities to improve their performance. This policy is called "progressive discipline." Progressive discipline is just what it sounds like: "You get three strikes before you are out."

The three steps of progressive discipline are:

1. *Written notice.* The employee is called in, inappropriate behavior is identified, and a plan is developed for corrective action with a timetable for improvement.
2. *Probation.* If the employee's behavior does not change for the better, she is informed in a meeting and in writing that her employment will be terminated if she fails to meet expectations one more time. A second written plan is put into place for enhanced supervision.
3. *Termination.* The employee is fired for not meeting program standards and expectations. Document the behavior that led to the termination and the meeting at which the employee was terminated.

The *Informal Alert* precedes the three steps. An employee is informally alerted when a supervisor notices a behavior that needs to change and reminds the employee what is expected. A challenge many directors have is that they stay at the informal alert stage, fearful of moving on to progressive discipline steps.

If employee policies name the steps of progressive discipline, supervisors need to follow those steps. There are two exceptions. First, during the probation period, usually

"Management by walking around" (MBWA) is the management process of greeting, interacting with, and connecting informally with each employee early and often. Staff welcome this attention. Supervisors see indications earlier of problems and successes in their walkabouts. MBWA was first described by Tom Peters.

TABLE 9.4

Employee Improvement Plan of Action: Corrective Meeting with Supervisor

Employee's name: Date & Time:

Present at meeting: (Names and job titles)

Director's concern (Briefly and factually, identify incident and/or observation):

Expected behavior (Attach/refer to center policy, job description, program mission, licensing/accreditation standard, Code of ethical behavior, etc.):

Plan for correcting problem:

Follow up meeting set for _____ (date and time).

Employee will:

Director/supervisor will:

Consequence if problem behavior is not corrected:

Signatures of those present:

_____

Employer

_____

Employee

_____

_____

Witness (name and title)

Employee's comments (optional):

---

the first ninety days that the employee works in your program, managers have the right to let the person go "without cause" as long as the employer is not discriminating against the person in any way. The second exception is if an employee commits what courts term a "major offense." Major offenses include stealing, abuse, violence, drinking, or abusing other substance at work.

Table 9.4 contains the form for documenting the steps you have taken, pursuant to both directive supervision principles and the progressive discipline process:

Return now to the offensive situation you identified with your own coworker, staff member, or peer. Apply the five principles and steps to your situation. Although directive supervision is designed for employee-employer problems, do you think the principles may work in other situations?

When Reflective Supervision Is Appropriate

Reflective supervision is what it appears to be: holding a mirror up for staff to see their own behavior in a supportive, ongoing, relational way. Reflective supervision invites staff to acknowledge and affirm strengths, grow, take risks, overcome obstacles, all in the context of a supportive relationship. In reflective supervision, strengths are built upon

If we did the things we are capable of, we would astound ourselves.

—Thomas Edison

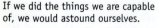

while problems are worked through in partnership. "You never have to make a decision alone" is a reflective supervision principle.

Principles of Reflective Supervision

Self-assessment, collaboration, and frequency are hallmarks of reflective supervision. As Trudi Norman-Murch and Ginger Ward note: "If staff in leadership positions do not themselves practice collaborative problem-solving, fail to provide a safe, respectful work context, allow meetings to be dominated by administrative concerns, or are inconsistent in their expectations for regularly scheduled supervision, the impact will be felt across the agency" (1999, 10). Reflective supervisors and supervisees together build relationships that:

- Foster safety and trust.
- Support and honor differences.
- Invite growth, risk taking, and humor.
- Acknowledge and build upon strength.
- Become aware of blind spots.
- Partner on vulnerabilities.
- "Slow down the process".

Reflective supervision is social EQ in action.

For reflective supervision to work, the employee must have the capacity to look objectively at herself, to identify her strengths and her weaknesses. Survivors and consolidators are rarely ready for this type of supervision. Young professionals, possessing the ability to be self-critical, aware of strengths and limitations, are candidates for reflective supervision. They are eager to make changes to become even more effective.

Reflective Supervision in Practice

Practical steps to take with an employee in reflective supervision practice have been articulated by the Michigan Association of Infant Mental Health (2002):

- Agree on a regular time and place to meet.
- Arrive on time and remain open, curious, and emotionally available.
- Protect against interruptions, e.g., turn off the phone, close the door.
- Respect each supervisee's pace/readiness to learn.
- Invite the sharing of details about a particular situation, infant, toddler, parent, their competencies, behaviors, interactions, strengths, and concerns.
- Observe and listen carefully.
- Strengthen supervisee's observation and listening skills.
- Ally with supervisee's strengths, offering reassurance and praise, as appropriate.
- Listen for the emotional experience that the supervisee is describing when discussing the case or response to the work, e.g., anger, impatience, sorrow, confusion.
- Respond with appropriate empathy.
- Invite supervisee to have and talk about feelings awakened in the presence of an infant or very young child and parent(s).
- Wonder about, name, and respond to those feelings with appropriate empathy.
- Encourage exploration of thoughts and feelings that the supervisee has about the work . . . as well as about one's responses to the work, as the supervisee appears ready or able.
- Remain available throughout the week if there is a crisis or concern that needs immediate attention.
- Suspend harsh or critical judgment.

If you are irritated by every rub, how will your mirror be polished?

—Djalal ad-Din Rumi

TABLE 9.5

Self-Assessment Tool #1 Goals Blueprint

Teacher's name _____   Date _____

Strengths as a teacher:

1.

2.

3.

Areas in need of improvement:

1.

2.

3.

Goal: _____

Objectives:

1.

2.

3.

Source: Jorde Bloom, 1998.

As the Teacher Grows, the Supervisor Grows

The mirror that supervisors hold up to employees reflects the supervisor's image as well. Reflective supervision invites the supervisor to examine and stretch along with the supervisee. Often supervisors see areas of their own that need improvement. A supervisor might find she needs to assess herself:

- Am I patient?
- Can I delegate?
- Am I jealous of this employee in any way?
- Was that my own "blind spot" I just bumped into!
- Can I accept honest feedback from my employees without getting defensive?
- Am I willing to change, as I expect my employees to change?

As seasoned supervisor Emily Fenichel observes (2002, 14): "Supervisors and mentors need to resolve their own conflicts about exercising priority before they can establish clear expectations of their students or employees." Reflective supervision opens a manager's eyes to her own strengths and challenges as well as to those of the person being supervised. Reflective supervision is a gift to everyone.

Jorde Bloom's *Blueprint for Action* (1998) in Table 9.5 provides helpful written tools to support our reflection with employees like Mary Catherine. Remember, the purpose of reflective supervision is to help each employee reach her full professional potential while furthering program vision and mission.

Case Study: What Do You See in the Mirror?

Mary Catherine is gifted one-on-one with children. She has shown patience, understanding, and encouragement with Solomon, a three-year-old with developmental delays. Mary Catherine painstakingly built trusting relationships with Solomon's divorced parents. Her gentle persistence and clear documentation were instrumental in the parents' agreement for Solomon to be evaluated by early intervention specialists.

Prior to being in Mary Catherine's room, Solomon's parents blamed the center for Solomon's difficulties. Mary Catherine turned all of that around. However, her classroom management skills are lacking. Her classroom grows out of control while she focuses on one child at a time.

As her supervisor, what are your options?

Complete the form above to assess yourself. Replace "teacher" with the term that describes your work, if necessary.

Reflective supervision practices, as evidenced by Bloom's form above, include:

1. Self-assessment accompanied with supervisor's assessment.
2. Sharing these assessments.
3. Identifying strengths and challenges.
4. Affirming strengths and partnering on challenges.
5. Selecting three goals.
6. Developing a plan for change including objectives, steps, and a timetable.

What Additional Skills Would You Like to Gain?

Through reflective conversations with Mary Catherine, we support her in gaining the skills that she needs to improve (see Table 9.6). Should Mary Catherine not master that skill, we may, through reflective supervision, help her find a position or a workplace that can use her one-on-one skill. Or, we may rely upon directive supervision to hold her accountable for not developing classroom management skills.

Reflective supervision promotes quality by calling upon the director's insightful, nurturing skills. Directive supervision requires the director to take a stand for quality, no matter how intimidating the situation may be. Both directive and reflective supervisory skills are essential for program quality.

The practice of reflective supervision carries over to the whole organization. Just as individuals are encouraged to grow, so is the community. To promote "slowing down the process," leaders can include these items in staff meeting agendas:

- *Affirmations:* Each staff member, one at a time, shares with the person to her left one thing she appreciates about that person. This continues until everyone has spoken.
- *Good news:* Go around the circle, inviting each staff member to state something she has done at work that she feels good about.
- *Team problem solving.* Encourage staff to discuss something about the program that needs improvement or that an individual requests help on. Devote time to problem solving together.
- *Rumor mill grinds to a halt here.* Use humor to let staff know they can bring rumors they have heard to the meeting for clarification and answers. Facts will win out over the rumors.
- *Treasure hunts* (Chapter 15). Send small teams on a treasure hunt by handing them checklists to inspect for quality. Reward the teams when they report.

> What we see depends mainly on what we look for.
>
> **—John Lubbock**

TABLE 9.6

Self-Assessment Questionnaire

What are:

1. Three successes you have had in your classroom?
2. Your strengths that are most helpful to children and families?
3. Additional skills that you would like to gain?

Employees feel respected by a supervisor who reserves time for mutual problem solving at staff meetings, and who dedicates one-on-one time to reflecting over a cup of tea with employees about their dreams and challenges.

Creating Your System for Supervision

Skilled supervisors use both directive and reflective supervision as part of their overall plan for supervising staff. Let's look now at how the two approaches can be embedded into a system that continuously encourages staff to do their best work for the program.

A Supervision System Must Meet These Four Functions

1. Creation and enforcement of policies, procedures such as evaluation tools, as well as ongoing posting of new information.
2. Continuous assessment and recognition of each staff member's developmental needs, accomplishments, and "stretch" goals.
3. Intervention early, especially when change is required.
4. Maintenance of individual supervision within a system that upholds the organization's vision.

To regularize these processes, directors rely upon standard forms, such as the corrective action (see Table 9.4) or teacher self-assessment (see Table 9.5) form. Policies, procedures, and evaluation tools, all placed in the employee handbook, create and communicate the system for supervision. Directors can create, share, and/or purchase standardized forms for ongoing employee evaluations. Sources of online supervision forms and checklists include:

Supervision Series
ncchildcare.dhhs.state.nc.us/providers/pv_supervision.asp

Teacher Self-Evaluation Form
www.eced-resources.com/index.php/2005/11/11/teacher-self-evaluation-form/

Child Care Online: Forms
childcare.net/catalog/catalog/default.php?cPath=22_29

Completed forms must be signed or initialed before copies are placed in the employee's personnel file. Annual staff evaluation forms also require a standardized form. Employees come to count on being treated fairly in the usage of these forms. Standardized forms for the employee's annual review are essential.

At the annual review, employee and supervisor share their assessments of the employee's work record and progress toward goals in the past year. Stretch goals are mutually agreed upon for the year ahead. Table 9.7 contains an example of an annual staff evaluation instrument, to be completed by both supervisor and staff member:

Evaluation Time

360-Degree Evaluations

Some supervisors choose to include a "360-degree" evaluation tool. A 360-degree evaluation invites everyone who is part of the team circle (360 degrees) to evaluate one another. The employee evaluates the supervisor. Employees evaluate each another. The supervisor evaluates herself and each employee. An excellent example of a 360-degree instrument is Bloom's *A Great Place to Work* (1988). In that resource, you will find both evaluation instruments and scoring templates.

TABLE 9.7

Annual Employee Evaluation Instrument

Employee name _____ *Date* _____

Employment period reviewed _____

Employee accomplishments:

Progress toward annual goals:

Goal 1:

Goal 2:

Goal 3:

Areas for improvement:

Goals for next year:

Goal 1:

Goal 2:

Goal 3:

Overall rating: average _____ good _____ outstanding _____ other _____

Employee comments:

Signatures: _____

Date:

Garbage Can Dynamic

The first time a supervisor asks staff to evaluate her or the program, she is likely to experience the phenomenon known as the garbage can dynamic (Cohen et al. 1972). Staff often "dump their garbage" all over a 360-degree program evaluation form the first time they are asked to complete it. Any stored up issues, unspoken hurts, snippets of anger, or resentment get dumped.

Supervisors need to step to the side, remind themselves not to take the results personally, and examine information objectively. By the second or third 360-degree evaluation, employees will have dumped their stored up issues and are likely to express more timely and constructive views. (See Table 9.8.)

Avoiding Annual Evaluation Pitfalls

First, schedule annual employee evaluations to take place at each employee's anniversary date (of hire). Programs that, instead, conduct everyone's annual review at the same time each year can find productivity takes a tumble. Fear is contagious and can affect even the most seasoned and professional staff member. Anxiety spreads like the measles. To prevent collective annual review jitters, space out the evaluations by individualizing them to fall on each employee's start date.

Second, make sure that annual evaluations are not the only time you and your employees sit down together to assess their performance. Understandably, employees fear annual evaluation meetings if they have not received steady feedback throughout the year.

By using the five steps of directive supervision, and continuously encouraging staff via reflective supervision, managers prevent unwelcome surprises. Employees know where they stand. More important, employees have benefited throughout the year from a supervisor's ongoing interest in them and their improved performance.

Third, give employees notice of personnel policy changes that affect them, and the opportunity to discuss their feelings and thoughts about these changes. This goes a long

> Treat people as if they were what they ought to be and you help them to become what they are capable of being.
>
> —Johann Wolfgang von Goethe

TABLE 9.8

Slowing Down the Process

"*Slowing down the process*" is a reflective supervision practice that entails taking time with employees individually and at staff meetings to ask:

- How was your week?
- What is going well?
- Do you have anything that is bothering you?
- What do we need to think about?
- Has anyone heard a rumor you want to check out?

This practice surfaces issues early and lets employees know you are open.

way in meeting the requirement of providing staff with notice about what affects them. Tack up any new policy that comes across your desk, and post any changes made to policies and procedures. By dating each posting, you can periodically check to make sure all postings are timely and up-to-date.

Bring these policies to everyone's attention at staff meetings. When appropriate, make one copy for each employee, ask her or him to initial it as evidence that they have read and understood the policy, and place that initialed statement in each employee's file. This meets the supervision function of "ongoing posting of new information."

✶ Supervision as an Evolving Process

Consider a system of supervision as both a noun and a verb. Nouns, like an apple or a post office, are solid and stable. Verbs, like to throw or to stir fry, are more active. As a noun, supervision is a protective, well-maintained system shored up with written standards and procedures; ongoing, shared information; evaluation processes; staff meetings that inform as well as slow down the process; individual reflective sessions; and daily management by walking around. In this way, a supervisor establishes and maintains an overarching system to meet each employee's needs in the context of the organization's mission.

As a verb, systemic supervision works like "emergent curriculum" in the classroom. Managers employ the most effective supervisory style required in the moment. "Teachable" moments, mutual learning opportunities, pop up at any time. Supervision is a richly challenging daily opportunity to model for employees the way we want them to interact with children Today, Jasmine may learn best from directive supervision; tomorrow she may be more prepared to reflect on how she can help Clarence's family.

✶ Supervision and Staff Development Plans

In 2005, NAEYC introduced its *Leadership & Management: A Guide to the NAEYC early childhood program standard and related accreditation criteria.* NAEYC's standards require accredited programs to comply with:

- *Criteria 10.E.10 (summarized)* An individual professional development plan is generated through the staff-evaluation process and is updated at least annually and ongoing as needed.
- *Program Standard # 6 Teachers:* The program employs and supports a teaching staff that has the educational qualifications, knowledge, and professional commitment necessary to promote children's learning and development and to support families' diverse needs and interests.

Directors are expected to create and implement a plan that places each employee's professional development goals into a comprehensive program plan. This plan must ensure that teachers meet academic course requirements within a certain number of years. Annual stretch goals for employees must include pathways for staff members to further their education and complete degrees. By meeting these goals, programs can meet NAEYC professional standards for a well-educated staff. A supervisor who does her job well will be on her way to meeting and exceeding these standards.

Supervision, like any other EQ practice, is both an art and a science. The more open we are to learning and practicing, the more proficient we become.

Reflection Questions

1. Think back over the supervisors and/or teachers you have experienced so far. Who was your favorite? What competencies did this person demonstrate with you? How would you describe the person's supervision and/or teaching style? What in particular about that style endeared the person to you? In rerospect, was this person using directive, reflective, or both practices with you? Now reflect on a supervisor or teacher whose style did not work for you. Can you identify what in that person's style was mismatched with your learning style? What does this tell you about supervision practice? Write a summary about the kind of supervisor or teacher you need to perform at your best.

2. Dr. Cathy Jones, with over thirty years' experience in early childhood education, makes the following observation on challenging employees: "*Difficult employees often just want to be heard. To get attention, like difficult children, they engage in annoying and nonproductive behaviors. Providing a mechanism for them to have a voice is often helpful. They also need to be guided to find solutions. I think many of them have a lifetime of 'center stage' because of their negative behavior. When given a way to shine for doing the right/good/productive thing, the focus can change. Sometime folks in childcare are negative because the field is not an appropriate choice for them. Sometimes the best we can do is counsel them into another line of work. Allowing negative employees to continue disrupting and stirring up things is so disrespectful to the children and those employees who are trying their best. Turning a deaf ear has to be strategic and seldom used. When good employees consistently complain about a negative employee, that should be an immediate red flag!*" Do you agree? What have you learned about dealing with difficult people? How do their needs differ from your own? How are their needs the same? Write a reflection on your experience with difficult colleagues.

3. Complete the Supervision Exercises on pages 142 and 143. Based on your responses, assess your potential strengths and challenges as a supervisor. What steps might you take to expand your competencies as a supervisor.

Team Projects

1. Reread together Mary Catherine's case on page 142. Identify and discuss the supervision challenges, as well as the approaches, you might take if you were her supervisor. Do the same with Francia's case (page 129). Present a report to your classmates on the important points in your discussion.

2. Investigate what makes an effective supervisor by interviewing people who supervise employees. Meet first as a group to develop interview questions for the supervisors you plan to interview. Create questions that will help you track down answers that will be useful to you. Possible questions include: "What has been your greatest challenge as a supervisor?" "What part of supervising do you most enjoy?" "Do you have forms you can share on how you document supervision?" Once you agree on the questions, each of you will interview three supervisors. Regroup to develop a PowerPoint report on your findings for the class.

3. As a group, create at least two factual cases of employees like Jasmine with problematic behavior. Make a video that captures the difficult behaviors in your case studies. Practice together how to apply the five principles and steps of directive supervision to each situation. Show your video to your class and facilitate small group discussions on applying directive supervision to the cases.

Bibliography

Bloom, Paula Jorde, Marilyn Scheerer, and Joan Britz. 1998. *Blueprint for action: Achieving center-based change through staff development.* Beltville, MD: Gryphon House.

Bloom, Paula Jorde. 1988. *A great place to work: Improving conditions for staff in young children's programs.* Washington, DC: NAEYC.

Bruno, Holly Elissa, & Margaret Leitch Copeland.1999. If the director isn't direct, can the team have direction? *Leadership Quest.*

Cohen, Michael D., James G. Murch, and John P. Olsen. 1972. A garbage can model of organizational choice. *Administrative Science Quarterly*, vol. 17, No. 1, pp. 1–25.

Fenichel, Emily. 2002. Learning through supervision and mentorship. *Zero to Three.*

Guidelines for reflective supervision and consultation. Michigan Association for Infant Mental Health. Online MI-AIMH.

Katz, Lillian. 1972. Developmental stages of preschool teachers. *Elementary School Journal*, 73: 50–55.

Kilbourne, S. 2007. Performance appraisals: One step in a comprehensive staff supervision model. *Exchange* (174): 34–37.

Kloosterman, Valentina. November 2003. A partnership approach for supervisors and teachers. *Young Children*, 72–76.

Maslow, Abraham. 1943. A theory of the human motivation. *Psychological Review*, 50, 370–396.

Michigan Association of Infant Mental Health. 2002. *Guidelines for reflective supervision and consultation. http.//www.mi-aimh.msu.edu/aboutus/29-RecommendedReferencesforPreparingforEndorsement/09-GuidelinesforReflectiveSupervisionandConsultation.pdf.*

NAEYC. 2005. *Leadership & management: A guide to the NAEYC early childhood program standard and related accreditation criteria.* Washington, DC: NAEYC.

Neugebauer, Bonnie and Roger. 2004. *Staff challenges.* Redmond, Washington: Exchange Press.

Norman-Murch, Trudi, and Ginger Ward. 1999. First steps in establishing reflective practice and supervision: Organizational issues and strategies. *Zero to Three*: August–September.

Parlakian, Rebecca. 2001. *Look, listen, and learn: Reflective supervision and relationship-based work.* Zero to three. Washington, DC: National Center for Infants, Toddlers and Families.

Pawl, J., & M. St. John. 1998. How you are is as important as what you do. In *Making a difference for children, toddlers and their families.* Zero to three: Washington, DC.

Peters, Thomas J., and Robert H. Waterman Jr. 1982. *In search of excellence: Lessons from America's best run companies.* New York: Harper and Row.

Progressive discipline. University of Indiana Human Relations services. *www.indiana.edu/~uhrs/training/ca/**progressive**.html.*

Web Resources

Directive Supervision
http://www.paperboat.com/index.php?option=com_content&task=view&id=34&Itemid=49
Implementing Progressive Discipline
http://www.nfib.com/object/IO_35002.html
Reflective Practice and Supervision in Action
http://cdd.unm.edu/ecspd/news/updates/2007-06/practice.html
Self-Assessment for Directors and Administrators of Child Care Programs
http://www.ncchildcare.org/admin.html
Supporting Teachers, Strengthening Families
http://www.naeyc.org/ece/supporting/default.asp

Financial Management: Holding the Purse Strings

Learning Goals

As you study this chapter, you can look forward to reaching these learning goals:

1. Expand perspectives on the symbolism of money.
2. Summarize money management skills needed by early childhood directors.
3. Develop an understanding of a budget as both a program vision and a road map toward that vision.
4. Identify practices and tools to maintain a balanced budget.
5. Discuss common pitfalls to avoid when managing a budget.
6. Create a checklist for setting up a budget.
7. Define money management terminology.

Often, problems are knots with many strands, and looking at those strands can make a problem seem different.

—*Fred Rogers*

I am always doing that which I cannot do, in order that I may learn how to do it.

—*Pablo Picasso*

Case Study:

Adrienne, a seasoned and talented lead toddler teacher, was recently named director of her pro-gram, "Heaven on Earth." Founding director Rosalia followed her dream by returning to Hon-duras with funding to establish a Montessori preschool. Adrienne told the board in her interviews how inadequate and inexperienced she was with budgets. "Don't worry, we'll help," board members assured her.

Working overtime to reinvent relationships with her staff and deal with power struggles in the board, Adrienne delays learning about financial management. When a freak tornado devas-tates the playground, Adrienne forces herself to look at the budget. Numbers swim like sharks before her eyes. "I don't have a clue!" she cries frantically.

You are the first person Adrienne calls to ask for help. What kind of assistance can you offer her?

If social EQ is crucial for managing interpersonal challenges, which intelligence is essen-tial for money management? Depending on people skills for cash flow reports, comput-ing depreciation, and FICA allocations sounds like "putting lipstick on a pig" (as my friend Marylou says). "Reading people as well as we read books" may not be helpful when what we need to read is the budget. Have we come to the end of the usefulness of EQ?

In this chapter, we will discuss best practices and tools for setting up and manag-ing balanced budgets for early childhood centers. Through the case study experiences of Adrienne, we will see the ways in which she uses her IQ and EQ to achieve financial management success.

⚓ Money: Loaded in More Ways Than One

Olivia Mellan and Karina Piskaldo (1999, 47) explain why money is a loaded topic.

> For most people, money is never just money, a tool to accomplish some of life's goals. It is love, power, happiness, security, control, dependency, independence, freedom and more. Money is so loaded a symbol that to unload it—and I believe it must be unloaded to live in a fully rational and balanced relationship to money—reaches deep into the human psyche. Usually, when the button of money is pressed, deeper issues emerge that have long been neglected. As a result, money matters are a perfect vehicle for awareness and growth.

We often relate to money as if money were a person. Sometimes we are indirect and fearful. Other times we are forthright and confident. Our relationship with money is often complex and deeply emotional. In the chapter case study, Adrienne's early learn-ing about managing money is likely to hold clues to her approach today.

Recalling messages about money that we "caught" when we were children is infor-mative. Low confidence as a money manager usually has historical roots. Mellan and Piskaldo continue, "We grew up in families where nobody talked about money. Most people will immediately protest, 'Not true. My family talked about money all the time.' When I ask, 'How did you talk?' they reply, 'My father worried about not having enough, and he yelled at my mother for spending too much'" (150).

Studies show men and women view money differently. Jennifer Harper (2006), in a *Washington Times* article, notes, "They may have money in their purses and a decent salary, but many women fear they'll lose their income and end up a bag lady, forgotten and destitute."

"Bag lady syndrome is a fear many women share that their financial security could disappear in a heartbeat, leaving them homeless, penniless and destitute," *MSN Money*

Folks with plenty of plenty, got a lock on the door. 'Fraid somebody's gonna rob 'em, while they're out making more. What for? I got no lock on the door. That's ok with me. They can steal the rug from the floor, that's ok with me, cause the things that I prize like the stars in the skies are all free.

—"I Got Plenty of Nothing," George and Ira Gershwin's *Porgy and Bess*

When a man keeps hollering, "It's the principle of the thing," he's talking about the money.

—Kin Hubbard

columnist Jay MacDonald (Harper 2006) wrote. "Lily Tomlin, Gloria Steinem, Shirley MacLaine and Katie Couric all admit to having a bag lady in their anxiety closet."

This "great depression" about money derives, in part, from the Great Depression of the late 1920s and early 1930s. Children who grew up with out-of-work parents and empty plates felt lucky to have a roof over their heads. My mother dropped out of high school in tenth grade to support her family of seven siblings and a single mom.

Slogans like "a penny saved is a penny earned" or "waste not want not" conveyed Great Depression coping strategies. My mother taught me how to darn socks, grow my own vegetables, and hunt like a lioness for bargain prices. My family dressed in hand-me-downs even when we could afford new clothing.

Children learn about money through their parents' attitudes and actions, the media, and other people in their environment. For early childhood programs, decisions about how money is spent communicate messages to children, families, and staff as well. Program directors play a key role in allocating money in a balanced way. The following sections show how Adrienne, the director in the chapter case study, works hard to keep a balanced budget and adapt to unexpected expenses.

✦ Coming Clean Is Not the Same as Money Laundering

Managers, like me, often feel less confident about managing finances than they do about managing other day-to-day program operations. When it comes to budgets, new directors may feel as though they are bumping around like a toddler in a high-tech grown-up world. They feel behind on the learning curve and fear they will mess things up.

> When I dare to be powerful—to use my strength in the service of my vision, then it becomes less and less important whether I am afraid.
>
> —Audre Lorde

Liz, who directed programs in New Jersey for years, offers this advice:

> Hire someone who does nothing but budgets, contracts, money issues, etc. Running an early childhood program is a business, but the humanization of the business is what is critical. The person hired needs to be able to communicate with parents in a warm and welcoming way. You don't want a budget person or financial secretary to be nasty to those parents who might be late with tuition, or to be rude to a vendor. Her or his actions reflect on how the children are treated in the center.

When I was a new manager, I struggled to handle numbers by myself. Asking for help felt like admitting I was the great imposter. I was in awe of leaders with Donald Trump-like confidence. Tell me you love "number crunching" and you have my attention. Trust me; I know this is one of my blind spots.

I sympathize with Adrienne, the new director in the chapter case study. Yet, somehow, my business runs smoothly at a profit. I keep fastidious records. Bills are paid on time, vendors (salespeople) are content, and the checkbook balances. My profit and loss statements (P&Ls) are more comforting than worrisome.

How have I learned to work through my fears and deal with budgets, financial planning, bookkeeping, and balance sheets? First, I hire competent, trustworthy professionals. My wise accountant, Tony, breaks chunky problems down into pieces I can grasp. My bookkeeper, Denise, continuously updates me on the status of budget items, flagging anything that needs my attention. One click on Denise's software program puts everything in instantaneous perspective. My financial planner, Gerry, devotes hours to explaining financial planning concepts to me, with ample real-world examples and generous time for my plodding questions.

Second, I gave up feeling like an imposter. Assuring myself, as I do others, that we all have different strengths, I ask for help. "Break it down for me like I'm in second grade" is my straightforward and useful request. My uncle, Arthur Bruno, says in Sicilian dialect,

"Sometimes we have to walk into the mouth of the wolf." Hello wolf! Slowly, I am coming to understand the basics of managing the purse strings. Every step of the way, I call upon emotional intelligence to grow and ask for help.

That's my story and I'm sticking to it! What is your story? What childhood messages did you receive about the meaning of money and how to manage money? How do you think these messages impact your confidence and money management skills today?

✖ Budget as Both Policy and Map

Keeping "our eyes on the prize" in financial management is especially helpful (Table 10.1). A budget follows our dream and turns it into reality. Details make better sense in a larger context. If a director sets "staff development" as her priority, scheduling and financing a staff retreat will bring that priority to life.

In this way, *the budget is the policy statement for a program.* What a director targets for the greatest expenditures is what she values and needs most. In early childhood programs, staff salaries are the greatest expenditure. The well-being of our employees is a high priority. The purpose and goals of a program become enfleshed through dollars dedicated to make them real.

Like a map, a budget predicts and guides. The budget is a center's financial framework. It predicts what a director will spend and shows whether spending aligns with the prediction. In practical terms, according to colleague Dr. Cathy Jones (who coauthored this chapter), a budget:

1. Predicts the cost of running the center;
2. Keeps track of actual costs; and,
3. Flags changes to make, when the prediction and the reality are at odds.

Expenses, like an unexpected tornado, can hit a program out of the blue. Energy costs for heating can skyrocket. Gasoline prices can prevent staff from making a long commute. The original budget must be brought up to date to account for what really happens (actual expense budget). The good news is that with each passing year, a director will be able to use the current year's actual cost budget for making the next year's prediction budget.

TABLE 10.1

Top Ten Financial Management Pointers

1. Remember the big picture. Your program needs to be able to pay its bills on time.
2. The amount of money you take in needs to at least equal the amount you pay out, plus allow for enough "wiggle room" (liquidity or cash flow) to pay your bills on time.
3. Employee compensation is the largest expense in early childhood program budgets.
4. Tuition is the primary source of revenue.
5. Last year's budget is usually the best resource you can use in preparing next year's budget.
6. Each month, make sure your income is at least equal to your expenditures.
7. Regularly provide up-to-date budget reports to people who need to know.
8. Ask for help any time you need it. Outside auditors bring perspective.
9. Hire competent people to work with you on the budget.
10. Do a "cash flow analysis" and maintain a reserve fund to have money when you need it.

Ask, "Are we bringing in enough money to operate a quality program while covering our expenses?" That simple question keeps everything else in perspective.

TABLE 10.2

Adrienne's Revenues

Revenues	January	February	March
Tuition:			
Parent Fees	$14,429	$14,438	$13,224
Subsidy	15,773	14,498	16,112
Food Program	4,900	5,087	5,243
Other:			
Accreditation Grant	2,000		
Total Revenues	$37,102	$34,023	$34,570

Recall the chapter case study and walk through Adrienne's budget in Tables 10.2 and 10.3 to get a sense of her program's *"viability"* (financial well being). For an indication, let's start by looking at the first three months of last year's budget. Use your EQ to assess how you feel about delving into budgets and numbers. If fear arises, not to worry; we will walk through this process one step at a time. Above, you can see Heaven on Earth's money inflows ("revenues").

TABLE 10.3

Adrienne's Expenses

Expenses	January	February	March
Payroll:	$21,249	$20,877	$20,854
Workers Comp	614	599	599
Payroll Deductions (incl. FICA/Social Security)	2,100	2,064	2,067
Insurance	579	623	612
Retirement @.02	425	418	418
Supplies	200	76	183
Telephone	98	98	98
Utilities:	843	765	824
Electricity			
Water			
Garbage Fee			
Rent	1,270	1,270	1,270
Food	2,986	2,077	2,664
Liability Insurance (due quarterly)			533
Advertising	212		
Accreditation fee Step 1	350		
Custodial Services	1,000	1,000	1,000
Loan Repayment	1,000	1,000	1,000
Total Expenses	$32,926	$30,867	$32,122

TABLE 10.4

Reconciliation Budget

Reconciliation Budget	January	February	March
Revenue	$37,102	$34,023	$34,570
Expenses	32,926	30,867	32,122
Net Income	$ 4,176	$ 3,156	$ 2,448

Look at the left-hand column in Table 10.2 to locate funding sources. Tuition brings in the largest amount of money. *"Subsidy"* (tuition paid by the state for some children) is a second form of income. Tuition and subsidy add up to the money flowing into Adrienne's program. Other income in the left-hand column also contributes to the inflow.

Like most programs, Adrienne's center receives funding for food. States provide monies to make sure children receive nutritious meals and snacks. The last item in the revenue column is a $2000 grant from a local agency to help Heaven on Earth prepare for reaccreditation. The sum of the items in each column shows Adrienne's revenue for that month.

Now examine how much money was spent each month in Table 10.3. Compare the income to the expenses to assess if Heaven on Earth made money, lost money, or broke even.

This *"reconciliation"* budget in Table 10.4 shows remaining money after bills were paid. Good news for Adrienne! For each of those three months, her program earned money, or *"net income."*

Given the program was *in the black* (made more money than it spent) during this time period last year, Adrienne feels more confident to look back over the remaining 9 months of last year's budget. She is keeping her fingers crossed that she has enough of a budget surplus to accomplish her goals for the upcoming year:

- Hire an infant teacher to replace Lonni who retired at a salary of $23,000.
- Purchase new playground equipment and surfacing. Bids have come in between $12,000 and $18,000.
- Resurface the playground @$2000 for wood mulch, $8000 rubber mulch.
- Fund a staff team-building retreat, off-site @$500.
- Bring in a consultant @$700 to help teachers build classroom portfolios, or investigate to see if childcare resource and referral has a trainer at no cost.

For Adrienne's program to afford these changes, what will the additional expenses be?

The Budget Seesaw

Picture this scene on Adrienne's new playground: 20 pound Brady sits on one side of the seesaw, while his friend Marshall, 40 pounds, climbs on the other. Clunk! Brady yells, "No fair!" Teacher Tamjin captures the teachable moment and helps the boys analyze what happened. Tamjin pushes down on Brady's side. Balance is achieved.

Budgets are all about money coming in and money going out. Money coming in is *revenue* or *income;* money going out is *expenditure* or expense.

This commonsense principle applies to budgets. Buying playground equipment must be balanced by spending less on something else, or by raising additional funds. Figuring the options can be, in Dr. Cathy Jones' experience, a treasure hunt. Fortunately, early childhood management has evolved to a place where many budgeting tools are available to help. Finding the software package that fits your program's needs can be the beginning of that treasure hunt.

Software for Early Childhood Financial Management

More good news: directors can choose and use budgeting software, such as *EZ-Care2*, *Childcare Manager*, and *ProCare Software*. Childcare financial management software provides a framework that can be continuously updated (see Table 10.5). In the click of a key, directors can use software to enter and sort data to show:

- Percentage of children enrolled compared to a program's licensed capacity.
- Actual cost per child.
- Attendance records.
- Payroll from a particular week.
- How to develop a new annual budget, step by step.
- The reconciliation budget: predicted expenses vs. actual expenses.
- Eligibility for and reimbursement amounts for the food program.
- How to plan menus.
- Children and family records, like inoculations and medications.
- How to post reminders to families on the system.
- Employment records.
- Professional development hours and staff scheduling.

Each year, updates to early childhood management software include new "bells and whistles." For the latest information, go to *http://childcareexchange.com*.

Line Items and Consistency

Adrienne thinks she can find additional money for playground expenses by saving money on Lonni's replacement, Regina, since she has fewer years of experience. Regina will start at a salary of $17,500, and Adrienne wants to know if she can use that savings toward equipment.

    Her predecessor's annual budget predicted "business as usual." The budget did not include plans for playground equipment replacement costs, nor did it include funds for an off-site staff retreat. Adrienne needs to fund both of these while operating within the projected budget for this *fiscal year*. A fiscal year begins and ends the same time annually, typically July 1 through June 30. Some programs start their fiscal year on January 1. Adrienne's text message says that she hopes to replace Lonni (who earns $ 23,000 annually) with Regina (whose salary will be $17,500). Project the difference in Regina's salary from Lonni's salary, beginning October 1, for the rest of the fiscal year.

TABLE 10.5

Help in Finding Financial Management Software That Meets Your Needs

- Ask other directors what software works for them.
- Meet with a director to learn more about the software she or he uses and how student, family, and program data is used.
- Tell vendors you would like to try out the system before you purchase.
- Attend conferences with exhibit halls. Most of the software vendors there will be glad to help.
- You may have a trusted family member who is a capable accountant. Let her or him design a financial management plan to meet your specific needs. This will ensure that your software investment pays off and aligns with your needs and expectations.

Source: Dr. Cathy Jones, Assistant Professor, Early Childhood Education, Spadoni College of Education, Coastal Carolina University.

TABLE 10.6

Money Management Advice for New Directors

1. Don't sell yourself or your staff short. If you wear yourself out, you wear out your human *"capital."* Capital is an asset of your program. In the end, you will just be worn out and will not save anything.
2. Do your homework before you start. Being a quality program is much more than "just loving the kids."
3. Don't underestimate your real costs. Otherwise, you may end up paying for quality out of your personal budget.

Source: Dr. Cathy Jones, Assistant Professor, Early Childhood Education, Spadoni College of Education, Coastal Carolina University.

Use your EQ to help Adrienne brainstorm low- or no-cost ways to replace playground equipment and surfacing (donations from local businesses, workdays by parents). Ask Adrienne to investigate off-site retreat locations that might be free or low cost (local foundations, nature centers, someone's home).

Adrienne worries that the money she saves on Lonni's replacement is in a different *"line item"* (Salary) than the playground equipment line item (Equipment). Each *line item* lists one type of expense, such as salaries or rent. Adrienne does not know if she can mix these apples and oranges. She wants to know, "Will I be 'robbing Peter to pay Paul'?" (See Table 10.6.)

In the short term, income from one line item can be moved to cover an expense in a different line item. Replacing playground equipment is a *"one-time expense"* (paid in full in one payment). Adrienne may be able to transfer salary savings to cover the one-time expense of replacing playground equipment. Money from the "salary" line item can be moved to the "equipment" line item.

In the long term, however, Adrienne needs enough money to attract and keep excellent staff. If Adrienne wants to promote quality, will paying new staff a lower salary achieve that goal? Saving money in this way may bolster the *"bottom line"* (keeping your program in the black), but a short-term increase to the bottom line may lead to a long-term decrease to quality.

Playground expenses may be covered, but at what expense? By funding playground expenses from salary savings, Adrienne can make a *"short-term fix"* (immediate solution). Eventually, Adrienne hopes to increase salaries and provide incentives to keep quality staff. She will need a plan to meet this goal.

Ongoing expenses, like salaries, are a predictable budget line item. Ongoing expenses demand ongoing revenue. Rent or mortgage payments are ongoing expenses. To pay monthly rent, Adrienne needs a steady influx of money ($1700 each month). Short-term gains cannot be relied upon for ongoing expenses.

Depreciation

Depreciation shows how much value equipment loses each year after purchase. Heaven on Earth's eight-year-old playground equipment is not likely to last more than two years. The original purchase price for the equipment was $15,000. To report her loss to the insurance company, how does Adrienne compute the actual value of the equipment?

Here is a simple, easy method for computing depreciation:

1. List the purchase cost of the product.
2. Find the number of years the product was guaranteed to last.
3. Divide the purchase price by the number of years of the warranty.

TABLE 10.7

Depreciation of Adrienne's Playground Equipment

Purchase price—first year	$15,000
Second year	13,500
Third year	12,000
Fourth year	10,500
Fifth year	9,000
Sixth year	7,500
Seventh year	6,000
Eighth year	4,500
Ninth year	3,000
Tenth year	1,500
Eleventh year +	0

Adrienne's first task is to find how long the equipment was guaranteed to last. The playground equipment vendor's guarantee was for ten years. If each year the equipment drops in value by 10 percent, by the end of eight years, the equipment has lost 80 percent of its value, or $12, 000. Subtract this amount from the purchase price, and you can see how products quickly "depreciate."

$$8 \text{ years} \times 10\% \text{ or } \$1500/\text{year} = \$12,000$$

As Adrienne subtracts the depreciated amount ($12,000) from the purchase price ($15,000), she discovers the equipment's value has decreased to $3,000. This is very helpful for Adrienne as she budgets for replacement of large items. Adrienne computes the depreciation of the playground equipment in Table 10.7.

Try computing the depreciation value of classroom furniture, your computer, or some other item. You can even go online to look up the "blue book" value of your car. To what degree have your items depreciated? Now you will be able to confidently compute the depreciation of items in your early childhood center!

An accountant will have to help you figure the depreciation of large equipment and real estate items. The chart in Table 10.7 is for budgeting purposes only and not to be used for audits or financial reports.

✵ Budget Reports

Adrienne wants to work with her board to be sure everyone is apprised of important budget information (Table 10.8). Adrienne invites the board's Finance Committee to work with her on funding the playground and staff retreat. She already has worked with the Personnel Committee for her new hire, Regina.

In the chapter case study, Adrienne "inherits" a power struggle among board members. Lawyer Roderick, chair of the Finance Committee, competes with financial planner Placido, chair of the Planning Committee. In an effort to "bring Placido down to earth," Roderick demands a *cash flow analysis.*

Roderick argues the program may look good on paper but could put itself out of business due to cash flow problems. As Gwen Morgan (2008) notes in *The Bottom Line,* far too many well-intended programs have failed for lack of cash flow. Tuition was owed, but not enough was paid on time to meet the payroll. Roderick also requests information on *fixed* and *variable costs.*

TABLE 10.8

Help from Your Board

Board members can bring professional expertise, such as accounting, financial planning, legal skills, and marketing savvy.

Boards of early childhood programs often do the bulk of their work in subcommittees:
- Finance and Fund-Raising
- Personnel and Policy
- Planning
- Executive

The Executive Committee is composed of board officers: president, vice president, secretary, and treasurer (or secretary-treasurer) plus chairs of each of the three other subcommittees above. Work closely with your board's Executive Committee.

In cooperation with her Finance Committee, Adrienne uses her software to prepare and present the following reports:

Cash Flow Analysis

A *cash flow analysis* is a record of how money flows into and out of a center. This analysis shows how much money was received and spent during a given period of time. A budget may predict an income of $37,000 in January. If the food program or tuition subsidies are late that month, the actual amount a center takes in will be less. Paying staff salaries may be difficult. Just getting by every month does not allow the center to generate enough revenue for unexpected costs or periods of low enrollment.

For this reason, maintaining a *cash reserve* is wise. A cash reserve, like an old fashioned savings account, holds funds a director may need to use for unexpected reasons. Adrienne may have been able to use funds from the cash reserve to cover the cost of the playground equipment. She adds *cash reserve reports* to the list to give her board on a regular basis.

Knowing monthly revenues and expenditures is rarely enough. A safer approach is to generate a cash flow analysis. This analysis shows whether there is money "in hand" to pay bills on time. Take a look at the information Adrienne can generate for her board by doing the cash flow analysis in Table 10.9.

Remember Adrienne's budget. For the first three months there was a positive cash flow, meaning every month the center took in more revenue than was expended. A storm

TABLE 10.9

Cash Flow Analysis

Cash Flow	January	February	March	April	May
Revenue	$37,102	$34,023	$34,570	$35,221	$37,000
Expenses	32,926	30,867	32,122	38,765	32,763
Net Income	4,176	3,156	2,448	(3544)	3,737
Cumulative Cash Flow	$ 4,176	$ 4,176 + 3,156 = $7,332	$ 7,332 + 2,448 = $9,780	$ 9,780 − 3544 = $6,236	$ 6,236 + 3,737 = $9,973

in April causes unforeseen roofing damage that was not covered by her insurance. How did that affect her cash flow?

Notice that the budget loss of $3544 in April is indicated by parentheses ($3544). In a cash flow analysis report, amounts that appear in parentheses are *"in the red"* (not enough money to cover expenses).

✄ Collecting Money Owed

Adrienne uses her EQ to stay on top of situations where tuition is *"in arrears,"* or has a history of being unpaid. To keep cash flowing, directors can use these strategies recommended by experienced peers (Neugebauer 2007, 86–89):

- Spell out policies at enrollment.
- Keep in close touch with families.
- Be alert for freeloaders.
- Make it easy to pay.
- Collect fees in advance.
- Collect a deposit.
- Enforce late payment policies.
- Offer to deal with problems in advance.
- Act quickly on delinquencies.
- Offer repayment options.
- Have parents sign a promissory note.
- Sue in small claims court.
- Stop providing care.

Telling a family they can no longer enroll their child can be painful, for the child and everyone who cares for the child. Effective directors are proactive and tell parents immediately that money is due. Directors also can collect a deposit in advance of at least two weeks' tuition. By using "letter of the law" skills, you will be able to hold everyone to the same standard. Otherwise, within just a few weeks, a single family can owe a substantial portion of a center's projected monthly revenue.

A *promissory note*, signed by one or both parents, commits the family to pay the full amount owed plus interest. Promissory notes help when significant tuition payment sums are in arrears. Should legal action be taken, a promissory note supports the center's case and documents the parents' acknowledgment of responsibility. Promissory note forms are available online or at office supply stores.

To keep a child enrolled in a program, the family needs to pay both current tuition and past due payments on time. *Garnishing* the parents' wages or suing for past due tuition requires a lawyer's action. When wages are garnished, an amount is taken off the top of the earnings and sent directly to the center. Going to court costs time and resources—having effective financial management practices in place helps prevent costly situations from arising.

✄ Budgeting for Part-Time Children and Teachers

Imagine that an automobile manufacturer in Adrienne's community lays off employees, several of whom have children in her center. Due to their new financial hardships, many of these parents request part-time childcare slots. Can toddler Tarak come Mondays, Wednesdays, and Fridays? Marta's Mom finds a job from noon to 5 p.m. and wants to bring Marta for afternoons only.

Offering parents part-time slots is a family-friendly, but not always business-friendly, practice.

To assess Adrienne's ability to provide part-time care, use this checklist:

——Program has a waiting list of children who need care at different times.
——Parents' needs match up with another family's needs.
——Teacher and family needs match.
——Families are charged for part-time slots, whether the child attends or not (just as with full-time enrollees).

Similarly, teachers may want to *"job share"* (together do the work of one full-time teacher). Bertie wants to work Monday through Wednesdays; Jamie prefers Thursdays and Fridays. Together they make up one *"full-time equivalent"* (FTE) teacher. Regina wants to work only afternoons. She has not found another teacher to job share. To schedule part-time teaching, Adrienne must ask:

• Can children's need for quality care be met with this arrangement?
• Will this new staffing pattern align with enrollment? For example, if afternoon enrollment is higher than morning enrollment, Regina is needed more in the afternoon.
• Is another staff member willing to job share, effectively creating an FTE with Regina?
• How will this change affect other staff?

Adrienne wants to help her families and staff. Can she schedule for part-time teachers and children and still come out with a balanced budget? As long as Adrienne can ensure that all the children will receive the best possible care, she is willing to be flexible.

Part-time options require careful tracking and bookkeeping. Often, directors offer part-time slots only when children from different families attend as if they were one full-time child. This allows two children the opportunity to attend without financial risk for the center. Similarly, job sharing allows two part-time teachers to share the work of one full-time teacher. Each part-time employee is paid according to the percentage of full time work she or he does.

Utilities, personnel, and rent costs continue to accrue even when no children are attending. Adrienne must plan enrollment, schedule teachers, and charge tuition in a way that keeps her program operating smoothly. Adrienne offers this schedule to accommodate two families needing part-time childcare:

	Monday	Tuesday	Wednesday	Thursday	Friday
A.M.	Tarak	Marta	Tarak	Marta	Tarak
P.M.	Tarak	Marta	Tarak	Marta	Tarak

Similarly, Adrienne develops this schedule for two teachers requesting a job share arrangement:

	Monday	Tuesday	Wednesday	Thursday	Friday
A.M.	Bertie	Bertie	Bertie	Jamie	Jamie
P.M.	Bertie	Bertie	Bertie	Jamie	Jamie

In both cases, each slot is filled each day. Programs can charge a daily fee that is a little higher than the weekly fee for part-time slots. Directors can refuse a request for a part-time teaching position if that change will affect children and the program negatively.

For Adrienne to budget for part-time children and teachers, she needs to think in terms of full-time equivalents (FTE). Adrienne computes percentages of a full-time enrollee or a full-time teacher. She asks what percentage of an FTE is Tarak? Marta? How about Bertie and Jamie? What percentage of an FTE is each teacher?

Since Tarak attends 60 percent of the week instead of filling a full-time slot, Tarak's slot is .6 FTE. Marta balances Tarak with her .4 FTE, or 40 percent enrollment.

Help Adrienne by computing Bertie and Jamie's FTE percentages.

Allowing staff to work part-time can be both a family-friendly and program-friendly policy. Job sharing can be beneficial to the budget's bottom line if less is paid to each teacher in terms of benefits. *Benefits* include health and dental insurance, 401(k) contributions, life insurance, disability insurance, and discount on childcare.

Both Bertie and Jamie assure Adrienne that their spouse or partner's benefits cover them. Each teacher's schedule is 50 percent of full-time, or .5 FTE. Because neither is full-time, neither qualifies for benefits. Job sharing for Regina is not an option until another teacher joins her to make one FTE.

Benefits for one full-time teacher can add approximately 28 percent to the cost of employing that teacher.

❧ Fixed and Variable Costs

Roderick, Finance Committee chair, e-mails a reminder to Adrienne to report on fixed versus variable costs as soon as possible. Adrienne uses her common sense to understand the difference between a fixed and a variable cost. Although few things are permanent, Adrienne expects monthly rent to be a *fixed* cost. The landlord has promised not to raise the rent for two years. Repaying a loan at the same amount each month is another fixed cost.

Other expenses, *variable* costs, are less predictable. If Tarak's family moves to Arizona, for example, their tuition payment ends. If Heaven on Earth implements a *"sliding scale"* (allows families of different economic means to pay what they can afford), tuition is variable, not fixed. Variable revenues can change suddenly. Adrienne's budget must account for the variable in income.

Adrienne assumes correctly that fixed costs are best met by predictable sources of income. With this in mind, Adrienne can better estimate how many variable expenses, like new equipment and a staff retreat, she can take on. She e-mails her report to Roderick.

❧ Wage and Hour Considerations

All this work on FTEs and benefit packages raises another issue for Adrienne: how does Heaven on Earth comply with federal wage and hour laws? Adrienne heard a nearby center was penalized for not paying staff properly under these laws.

The bottom line of wage and hour laws is that "staff must be paid for the hours they work" (Morgan 2008, 35). That three-credit hour required course, the weekend "spruce-up" of school grounds, and attendance at the annual statewide early childhood conference are all work time for which a teacher must be compensated. Gwen Morgan (2008) provides this summary of wage and hour law considerations:

- Staff must be paid for the hours they work. No employee can work 40 hours or more per week unless she is compensated. Hours in excess of 40 must be compensated at a time-and-a-half rate. If the Department of Labor determines that you have violated these rights of employees, you will have to make substantial back payments.
- The concept of "compensatory time" does not apply to any employee covered by wage and hour laws, unless it is used within the same workweek and is less than 40 hours.
- If the employer requires the employee to do anything, the employee must be paid for the time spent doing it. This includes training, conferences, and parent

meetings. For example, if the center requires an assistant teacher to take a course in order to do her job better, the center director must pay for the course, and for the hours spent taking it. However, if the employee is taking the course because the employee aspires to become a lead teacher (or achieve any role advancement), then the center director is not required to pay for the time or the course. In that case, the employee is not required by the employer to take it, and the benefit is to the employee rather than to the center.

- Audits may be routinely conducted by the government or can be initiated in response to complaints by disgruntled employees. Wage and hour officials do not reveal to you whether or not there was a complaint.

✕ Starting from Scratch: Your First Budget

Now that Adrienne feels more confident managing a budget, she is freer to dream of founding her own center. Like Adrienne, most new directors step into leadership of an already established program, with a budget in place. With her dream of "going out on her own" tucked tightly under her heart, Adrienne looks for help to develop her business plan and start-up budget.

Fortunately, Adrienne can turn to many helpful resources, including:

- Small business association (SBA);
- Resource and referral agency (R&R) for early childhood programs locally;
- State regulatory agencies, especially Licensing;
- Legislators such as members of Congress;
- Utility companies for cost estimates and package plans;
- Online websites for cost comparisons of equipment and supplies;
- Information on salaries in the field and, if available, in a particular locale;
- State and local professional organizations;
- Workshops on finances at early childhood conferences;
- A local directors' support group; and
- Software programs for early childhood financial management.

A business plan, including the proposed start-up budget, needs to be thorough, detailed, and clear before potential lenders or partners can be approached.

New directors can easily underestimate start-up costs. The local small business administration (SBA) will help aspiring business owners think through unforeseen expenses. Some SBAs can provide links to small business "incubators," which specialize in setting first-time entrepreneurs up for success.

List all the costs a new program will have. Next, list all the sources of income. When you finish each list, go back to see if you can add even more possibilities.

Start-up directors can be tempted to choose lesser quality items for the sake of saving "upfront." Think long term when it comes to quality. Less expensive, lower quality equipment and furnishings help today but harm tomorrow. Cheaper items can wear out before the budget can afford to replace them. Every purchase, from toys to tables, needs to stand up to daily wear and tear. Vendors of toys and classroom and playground equipment often set up display booths at state and national conferences. Online schedules for conferences list participating vendors.

Tips for designing a start-up budget:

- After space is secured and furnished, personnel will be your greatest ongoing costs. Remember Adrienne's operating budget? Personnel costs ran between 57 and 62 percent.

What's the secret to financial management?

There are no secrets. The key is in being detailed, comprehensive, and staying up-to-date. Thinking "I'll get to the budget tomorrow" just doesn't work.

—Dr. Cathy Jones

- The costs of furnishing a room can range from $5000 to $35,000 depending on the room size and children's ages.
- Are you comfortable with your staffing plan? Have you considered how many staff you will need when you open?
- Build in a *"cushion"* (financial safety net) to carry your center while enrollment builds. Initially you will not need as many staff as you need at full operation.
- Plan for advertising costs. Sometimes a local newspaper will feature your new center as newsworthy. Continued advertising costs money. Have you developed a website? Have you posted jobs or advertisements on Craig's List *(www.craigslist.org)* or *Monster.com*? Have you listed in the yellow pages or joined the Chamber of Commerce to put the word out?
- Basic office equipment will be required such as two computers, office supplies, a copier, and desk with chair. Used and donated office equipment can lower expenses.

Adrienne plans to use all the assistance she can find to help her get started. She wants to be confident and prepared when she tucks her business plan under her arm and takes her dream to the bank for funding.

Start-Up Budget

Adrienne's start-up budget will include items in Table 10.10, along with their estimated cost. The column on the right will be filled in as soon as Adrienne makes the purchases. Being able to compare actual costs with estimated costs will be useful information.

TABLE 10.10

Start-Up Budget

Before Opening	Estimated Costs	Actual Cost
First month's rent/mortgage plus any deposits		
Utilities:		
Water		
Electricity		
Garbage		
Other		
Remodeling costs		
Furniture for classrooms		
Kitchen equipment		
Office equipment		
Toys and manipulatives for children		
Consumable supplies such as toilet papers, napkins, drawing papers, art materials		
Licensing fees		
Taxes		
Liability insurance		
Director salary for one to two months		
One week's personnel salary for training		
Advertising for the center		
Advertising for staff		

EQ Plus IQ in Managing Money

"I have a legal problem," directors often tell me. To listen, I shift into my "lawyer brain." Approximately 80 percent of the problems turn out to be personnel problems not requiring legal skills. Interpersonal problems can feel beyond our understanding, so much so that we imagine them to be legal problems. How refreshing to know that a manager's EQ can help her resolve these dilemmas. Imagine the relief on a director's face when she remembers that human problems, and budget problems, can both become manageable when we use our EQ.

As Roger Neugebauer (2007, 7) reminds us, "Directors of child care centers must be as effective at managing money as they are at caring for children." (See Table 10.11.) We have helped Adrienne use her EQ to guide her IQ in managing her program's finances. Could it be we know more than we think we do about finances?

How do you think Adrienne can handle the power struggle between her two board members? Attorney Roderick is competing with financial planner Placido to be seen as the board's expert on budgeting. What would you recommend? Use your social EQ.

TABLE 10.11

A Voice from the Field on Overcoming Budget Problems

1. A center, in operation for over fifteen years, lost a hefty source of funding. The director thought the center would have to close. She called her staff together, met with them and, after that, with the families.

   Throughout both meetings, she invited each group to brainstorm solutions to this problem. In the end, they were able to come up with enough good ideas to save the center. Additionally, they felt they had a stake in the solutions. That "buy-in" was the best part.

   The director's attitude was positive in public, even though in private moments she cried many tears. I don't think the families and staff ever knew her agony. They saw instead her hope and her love for the children.

2. I served on an advisory board that worked with a program having financial problems. No one had ever worked with this center to uncover the "real costs" involved in its operation. The director's budget showed no reconciling between the "predictor budget" and the "actual costs."

   Our board helped the director identify and tabulate the actual costs. Once the figures were out in the open and decided upon, we were able to support the director in making necessary changes. She began to make better use of staff time. She changed policies on part-time slots for children. A new after-school program brought in more funding. Parent fees were raised a little.

   Often, just getting help to see your program through new eyes makes all the difference.

Source: Dr. Cathy Jones, Assistant Professor, Early Childhood Education, Spadoni College of Education, Coastal Carolina University.

Reflection Questions

1. Our values about money, as well as our confidence about managing money, can have a lot to do with the way we were raised. Make a list of five to ten "messages" you got in your early years about money and its management. What memories stand out more than others when it comes to learning about money?

Write a paper about whether or not the "bag lady/bag man" fear applies to you. Note what you can do or have done to gain confidence and expertise in managing money.

2. Balancing your personal checkbook and figuring your own budget both serve as starting points in learning about program budgets. List your own fixed costs and your revenues. From those figures, create your personal start-up budget for the rest of the year, beginning tomorrow. Look through your checkbook to identify variable expenses and unexpected income. With these figures, create a budget of income and revenue for the remainder of the year. Can you create a balanced budget for yourself in advance? Your professor will keep this assignment confidential.

3. Shopping has become an American pastime. My mother taught me to be a huntress for the best bargains. If you are a shopping machine, how can you be sure your "shop 'til you drop" approach does not torpedo your budget? List ten realistic strategies to help you keep within budget, regardless of the allure of buying "just one more thing." Teachers often spend their own money to create hands-on classroom activities and to decorate anew each season or month. Can you think of alternative resources and ways for teachers to access ample creative supplies without using their own funds? Again, list at least ten alternative resources and/or approaches.

4. Research early childhood financial management software options. Write a comparison with recommendations for beginning directors.

Team Projects

1. Imagine being a director who must raise some "hot button" budget issues with teachers. The most pressing issue is whether to continue to offer reduced childcare tuition for employees as a benefit. Your generous policy has attracted excellent teachers, but loss of income has become a serious drawback. The second "hot button" issue is how to design and fund a family-friendly space and atmosphere where families drop off and pick up their children. Finding room, easy chairs, a "muffin and coffee" service is your goal. Later on, you hope to provide teachers with a lounge of their own. Create a budget for each project with estimated costs. Make a chart listing the pros and cons of both major items to be discussed. Strategize how to present and discuss these issues effectively with the teachers. Present this to your class as if they were your staff members. If possible, create a PowerPoint presentation to help visual learners.

2. Go on a well-planned "treasure hunt" to investigate resources available to help a new director get started. Decide first what specific area or topic each person will investigate. Pointers on page 162 will help. When done investigating, prepare together a "Financial Resources Notebook" for new directors. Include organizations and individuals' names, contact information, Web addresses, fact sheets, regulatory standards, and other useful information. Present this to your classmates.

3. Interview up to three early childhood administrators apiece about their "learning curve" in mastering all the facets of financial management. Create a list of interview questions including (a) what stages did you pass through in gaining expertise? (b) what helped and hindered you along the way? (c) what advice would you give new directors? Create a list of tips for your class based on the interviews. As a team, create a "director's map to financial management expertise" to show the stages a director passes through on the way to becoming a confident fiscal manager.

Bibliography

Copeland, T. 2002. *Getting started in the business of family child care*. St. Paul, MN: Redleaf Press.

Copeland, T. 2004. *Family child care record-keeping guide* (7th ed.). St. Paul, MN: Redleaf Press.

Copeland, T. 2007. *Family child care tax workbook and organizer*. St. Paul, MN: Redleaf Press.

Gross, M., R.F. Larkin, and W. Warshauer. 1994. *Financial and accounting guide for non-profit organizations* (4th ed). New York: John Wiley & Sons.

Harper, J. 2006. Nearly half of women fear life as a bag lady. *The Washington Times,* August 23.

Jack, G. 2005. *The business of child care: Management and financial strategies*. Clifton Park, NY: Delmar Learning.

Mellan, O., and K. Piskaldo. 1999. Men, women and money. *Psychology Today* (January–February), pp. 46–50, 74, 76.

Morgan, G. 2008. *The bottom line for children's programs: What you need to know to manage the money*. Waltham, MA: Steam Press.

Neugebauer, R., ed. 2007. *Managing money: A center director's guidebook*. Redmond, WA: Exchange Press.

Web Resources

http://childcareexchange.com **Includes articles on financial management.**

http://childcare.net **Forms for recording monthly income and expenditures, attendance tracking, family files, medical information, menus.**

http://nationalchildcare.com/formspackage.htm **Sample forms for managing money.**

http://www.naccrra.org **National Association of Child Care Resource and Referrals.**

http://www.sba.gov/-41k **Small Business Administration information.**

Managing Facilities and Equipment: Do No Harm

Learning Goals

As you study this chapter, you can look forward to reaching these learning goals:

1. List guiding principles for designing environments that "do no harm."

2. Determine sources of support and expertise for facilities management.

3. Discuss legal requirements that will ensure safety and health.

4. Identify practical policies, procedures, and practices that will prevent harm.

5. Devise disaster or crisis plans that will keep everyone as safe as possible if a crisis occurs.

6. Examine ways to honor cultural differences while promoting safe and healthy environments.

The roots of a child's ability to cope and thrive, regardless of circumstances, lie in that child's having had at least a small safe place (an apartment, a room, a lap?) in which, in the companionship of a loving person, that child could discover that he or she was lovable and capable of loving in return.

—Fred Rogers

The path of learning and development is more like a butterfly than a bullet. Our job is to provide a setting where a group of energetic, idiosyncratic seekers go about this task and where all—adults and children—thrive amidst the daily rigors of group living.

—Jim Greenman

Case Study: Different and/or Harmonious?

Beatrice and her cousin Aurora have taught preschool and kindergarten for years. The cousins promised themselves that one day they would start their own program. Aurora yearns for the pine trees and clear streams of her childhood. Beatrice, raised in the city, prefers cozy window seats to getting her feet muddy. Their grandmother names Beatrice and Aurora as beneficiaries in her will. "Aurora! We can do it! Nonna has made it possible for us to build our own center!" Beatrice cries. The cousins hug and cry in joy, but neither one's vision of the perfect center looks anything like the other's.

What building and grounds design do you think could integrate the visions of both Beatrice and Aurora?

Author Ernest Hemmingway's short story entitled "A Clean Well Lighted Place" was set in a European café protected from the troubles and dangers of the world around him. As Hemingway wrote about the warm golden light in the café, the darkness of the Spanish Civil War chilled the hearts of villagers around him with fear.

In ways both literal and metaphorical, our children and families live on the edge of danger. Safety is not guaranteed. Good health is more a gift than a given. Many children are left behind when it comes to being assured of clean, well-lighted, happy environments.

Early childhood leaders have the honor and challenge of creating environments for children where no harm can befall them. To learn, a child needs to feel safe first. Danger or fear of danger impedes a child's learning ability. Studies show children who do not feel safe in their environments will focus on self-protection, rather than being relaxed enough to explore and learn in their environment (Goleman 1997; Hannaford 2002). Our job is to remove danger, prevent harm, and provide welcoming, inspiring, healthy environments, all of which evaporate fear from a child's psyche.

In this chapter, we will focus on standards for safety and health. These standards are the cornerstone for early childcare building designs, policies, and practices. The principle of "do no harm" underlies every system leaders build and manage, from playground safety to food service, and from classroom equipment to emergency procedures. When adults take responsibility for healthy and safe environments, children are free to discover their world without barriers to impede them.

> Trifles make up the happiness or misery of human life.
>
> —Alexander Smith

✖ Guiding Principles

Guiding principles are touchstones to return to in our commitment to create safe spaces, policies, and practices for children to learn. Just as a person or program has "core values" (Chapter 3), administrators need guiding principles to make sure each step they take furthers those values. If a leader's core value is "Do no harm," she will ask herself the following questions to be true to her core value. Guiding principles for health and safety are embodied in the questions.

Is every structure, piece of equipment, policy, and practice designed to:

1. Comply with established standards for health and safety?
2. Anticipate possible harm, and prevent that harm as much as possible?

3. Utilize "universal precautions"?
4. Attend to special need's: do we meet and exceed ADA requirements?
5. Welcome children's and families' ethnic and cultural differences?

Whether an administrator is designing a building, playground, classroom environment, or drafting a policy for administering medicine or selecting equipment, she will benefit from asking these questions each time.

⚓ Help Is on the Way: Resources, Experts, Advisors, Support

As a leader, your vision, core values, and principles will become the guiding light that brightens every meeting, debate, and groundbreaking. You will not have to be an expert on how to renovate or build from the ground up. Nor will you have to be an expert on equipment, playground design, or medical procedures. You will, however, need willingness to:

1. Learn the essentials (concepts, terminology, alternative approaches).
2. Explore resources (from people to websites to places to visit).
3. Ask for help (experts, practitioners, and governmental agencies).
4. Involve your communities (families, staff, business communities).
5. Engage your board and/or other advisors.
6. Manage your budget wisely (Chapter 10).
7. Keep your eyes on the prize: does every step further our goal?
8. Ask: Is this safe? Is this healthy? Are we preventing hazards?

Architects and builders are ready to help early childhood administrators create safe, healthy, and happy environments. Leaders can ask around to find architects who are available, reasonable, and compatible. They also can call other local programs to ask about their experiences with architects. Resource and referral agencies may be able to provide names of architects other programs have used. Clients' ratings of architects also can be investigated online.

Administrators may find—once they share their vision, lists, pictures, or sketches with an architect—that not everything they had in mind is possible. Although a leader won't always get exactly what she wants, she will be given realistic alternatives. The architect's job is to know what is feasible, reasonable, and meets standards. As an administrator, you will be able to ask the architect for designs of the building or renovation or for a computerized "virtual tour" of the designs. As with a doctor's visit, you, as a client, have a right to ask for a "second opinion" from another architect.

Partnering with a Board of Advisors

If a board of directors or advisors is in place, administrators will benefit from partnering with that board. Invite them to help. Chances are good that someone on the board is, has worked with, or knows of an architect. Work with board subcommittees. The Finance Committee chair can help project a budget for building or equipment costs. A Planning Committee, involved from the start, can help administrators envision how proposed changes will improve the program. Work closely with the Executive Committee, the board leadership team, to look at the proposal from all directions.

If a board of advisors is not in place, administrators can form a design team to help during construction or renovation. Family, friends, neighbors, and businesspeople can provide support and also play devil's advocate. Select people who are not all yea-sayers (rubber stamps) or nay-sayers (pessimistic or negative about change). Ground rules should be set with this team, especially on decision making. Will the design team be a group of advisors to you? If so, make that clear. If design team members will have more authority, spell that out. Otherwise, team members may build contradictory expectations. Any building erected on shifting sands instead of solid ground is likely to collapse.

Community input sounds like a mechanical process. Inviting people to share their dreams and hopes for a children's learning space, however, can be anything but mechanical. I have seen whole communities mobilized by wanting something better for their children.

Consider the "focus group" process. Focus groups often sit in a circle and individually share ideas as equals, without fear of judgment. An administrator (or other individual) prepares the questions, facilitates the focus group meeting, and records responses. Everyone shares ideas. Children express what they want: a farm with animals. "Can we milk cows? Make ice cream? Fly on an airplane in the sky?" Families discuss what they need and would love to see: overnight care, bilingual classrooms, a "one stop shop" to drop off dry cleaning and pick up wholesome meals when they pick up their children. Community leaders may even want to publicize the early childcare program free of charge in order to attract new businesses to the area.

As with a board of advisors or a design team, administrators must be clear on the role of focus groups from the start. *An administrator who is gathering ideas is not taking orders.* Brainstorming sessions for community input can lead to unrealistic expectations. Not everyone's "wish list" will come true. As a leader, set ground rules and expectations in writing and announce them verbally. Tell community members up front that although you do not guarantee you will meet everyone's needs, you value their input. This due process approach creates community interest, generates great ideas, and may elicit volunteers and contributions.

Help is all around if you ask and ask wisely.

NAEYC Program Standard #9: The program has a safe and healthful environment that provides appropriate and well-maintained indoor and outdoor physical environments. The environment includes facilities, equipment, and materials to facilitate child and staff learning and development.

National Association for the Education of Young Children

❧ Fundamental Building Blocks for Safety and Health

Not everything that is beautiful is safe; not everything that is safe is beautiful. Recall Beatrice from the opening chapter case study. She sketches a tree house she remembers happily from her own childhood, high in the branches, with a retractable rope ladder. When her friends uttered the magic words "Rapunzel, Rapunzel, let down your hair," she unfurled the rope ladder so they could climb up. Enchanting, but is the tree house safe?

Or consider Maximilian's case:

Maximilian's synagogue elders decide a childcare program would serve many young Orthodox families. Max, an elementary school teacher, is enthusiastically selected to "pull it all together" as the first director. "No problems, Max," congregation leaders croon. "We have Sunday school classrooms and the city park is one block away. We're faith-based so we can set our own curriculum and standards. How soon can you get us up and running?"

Maximilian, devoted congregation member for as long as he can recall, feels he cannot refuse the elders to whom he owes so much. Silently, Max fears the historic *shul* (synagogue building) will not meet standards for safety, classroom space, or food preparation. The start-up budget is limited. Praying he can honor the elders' vision, Max gasps as he reads licensing requirements and building standards online. In Max's program, families come from the Ukraine, Poland, Israel, and Russia, bringing different traditions and expectations for what a space should look like. Uniformity may ensure safety, but does sameness support diversity? Can a child's imagination be sparked in the midst of such uniformity?

Do No Harm: Is the Structure Safe?

"Do no harm," a guiding principle for early childhood leaders, can be summarized in this way: In everything we do, are our families and staff free from danger?

The following health and safety standards guide the design of a physical plant to prevent injury while maximizing learning:

1. State licensing requirements.
2. Local building and sanitary codes.
3. Fire and emergency codes.
4. Federal laws: OSHA, ADA.
5. Accreditation standards.
6. Environmental rating scales.
7. Quality checklists.

Lawful Standards for Health and Safety

Whether an administrator is building a center from the ground up or renovating an existing facility, she needs to be mindful of requirements for creating safe and healthful places. Chances are, an administrator will be working with architects, builders, and/or other facilities professionals. These professionals can expand the knowledge you will need about federal, state, and local standards. Anyone involved in building must keep in mind the "do no harm" goal by making sure governmental health and safety standards are met and, hopefully, exceeded.

State licensing standards are the first place to investigate what "do no harm" means in a particular state. Licensing standards set the bottom line, or baseline standard for safe and well-run programs. Although standards can look like "legalese," they are usually broken down into commonsense steps. Not to worry if standards appear overwhelming. Administrators can ask for assistance every step of the way.

You can start by going online to read your state's licensing requirements. While reading the requirements, keep a running list of questions about how your current or envisioned building can meet each standard. Call your state's early childhood licensing office, and ask who might be able to work with you if you design, build, or renovate your facility and develop safe practices.

Each program and director is assigned her or his own licensor, usually by region. Licensors are there to answer questions and to help programs meet the standards. Administrators will benefit greatly if they cultivate a good working relationship with licensors. To become better educated about your region's licensing requirements and procedures, consider the following guidelines:

- Contact directors of nearby programs for names of their licensing representatives.
- Call your local resource and referral agency for information about licensors in your area.
- Use your social EQ to develop a working relationship with your assigned licensor.
- Licensors can be extremely helpful in answering a variety of questions.
- Ask as many as you can imagine. No question is a "stupid" question.

Having had the honor of keynoting at the National Licensing Seminar, an annual conference, I can assure you that licensors want to help. Unfortunately, licensors are often viewed like the dentist. Everyone knows going to the dentist is necessary, but who would visit a dentist more than required? As you build a relationship with your licensor, you will likely discover a fellow traveler who cares deeply about quality. The sooner you develop a working relationship with your licensor, the faster and more confidently you will be able to proceed in your projects.

Licensing standards, crafted by state legislators, can be unique to each state. Nonetheless, some standards are "universal" nationwide. Each state sets a minimum amount of space for each child in each classroom. Generally speaking, *in the classroom, each child needs 35 square feet of space.* On the *playground, square footage per child rises to 75 feet* to allow children to be able to "cut loose" and whoop with energy. Go online to find your state's standards for space per child.

Licensing requirements for safe and healthy practices for groups and individuals usually include:

- Written parental permission for program staff to administer medication to children.
- Certification that all program staff are tuberculosis free.
- Mandatory reporting of child abuse and neglect.
- Permission to seek emergency care for children.
- Records of medical examinations and immunizations.
- CPR training for staff.

Remember, licensing requirements are the bottom line. You are free to substantially exceed the bottom line to strengthen your program.

Local Zoning, Building, and Sanitary Codes

Local zoning, building, and sanitary codes vary by community. Just as the state has standards for early childcare programs, so does the local government of any town, city, or county.

Zoning laws specify where childcare programs can be built. Since you, as a future administrator, will be in charge of a business, think of zoning laws that allow for businesses, rather than residential dwellings. When possible, programs should be built in an area zoned for the business of childcare. This is especially important if an individual wants to convert a residential home into a childcare facility. Zoning *variations* (exceptions to zoning code requirements) can be formally requested. However, zoning boards can be strict about granting variations.

Building codes set standards for quality of construction and usage of space. Just as licensing standards vary by state, building codes can vary from city to city, or town to town. Nonetheless, some standards are universal. *Most building codes establish the first floor as the location of infant and toddler classrooms.* This "do no harm" requirement makes sure the youngest and less mobile children readily can be evacuated in an emergency. Requirements for building and grounds safety usually include provisions for:

- Minimum square footage of usable floor space for each child in activity rooms,
- Exterior doors and windows,
- Stairways, ventilation, and lighting,
- Bathroom facilities,
- Food preparation area,
- Drinking water,
- Minimum square footage for outdoor play area, and
- Outdoor play area equipment and cushioning materials, such as mats, wood chips, or sand.

Building code inspectors can make visits before, during, and after construction. Inspectors make sure materials and processes meet standards. If, for example, an administrator is renovating an existing building, an inspector will most likely check for lead paint, asbestos, and radon gas. Administrators and builders will do well to develop a cordial, professional relationship with building inspectors to promote efficient, timely inspections. Social EQ is a leadership asset in virtually every undertaking.

Sanitary codes focus on keeping buildings clean. Being well lighted, with proper bathroom facilities and fresh air quality, all quash the spread of disease. Sanitary codes determine air circulation patterns so that each center space is guaranteed freshly replenished air. Sanitary codes set the hot water temperature, usually in line with state licensing requirements, to prevent scalding, while ensuring cleanliness.

Convenient location of bathroom facilities also falls under sanitary code requirements. Are sinks and toilets close and accessible for children and staff, whether children and staff are inside the building or outside on the playground? Effective lighting contributes to keeping areas mildew and mold free. Being able to see clearly is essential to safety at all times of the day and night. Lighting must meet sanitary code standards.

Town or city offices and the local Chamber of Commerce can provide zoning, building, and sanitary codes. Before administrators build or renovate, they will need to submit plans to each of these authorities for approval. Directors tell sad tales about being sent back to the drawing board for making (often costly) changes without authorization.

Administrators can ensure that health and safety standards are upheld daily by using Cleanliness Policies like the sample in Table 11.1. When "do no harm" becomes second nature to every staff member, cleanliness is a guaranteed practice.

Fire and Emergency Evacuation Plans

Do you recall the last time you waited outside during a fire drill for the "all clear" signal? For years, when we evacuated buildings, we assumed fire or another fire drill was the reason. For centuries, wood was the dominant building material, and because wood ignites easily, fires were common.

TABLE 11.1

"Do No Harm" Policies

Cleanliness Policy

All staff personnel at _____ are responsible for the cleanliness of your area of responsibility. While ongoing cleaning throughout the day is essential, programs should ensure a clean-up is conducted upon completion of projects, snacks, lunch, and during rest so that the area is clean for the next activity and contributes to the professional atmosphere of the center. Each teaching team is responsible for the care and cleaning of their class space daily, and the entire staff shares in the cleaning of the center common areas.

Minimum Clean-Up Times

- Transition between morning activity and morning snack.
- Transition between mid-morning activity and lunch.
- At completion of lunch.
- Transition between afternoon activities and afternoon snack.
- At the end of the day.
- Please remember tables must be sanitized before and after all snacks and meals.

Source: Lee, Live & Learn Early Learning Center, New Hampshire, staff handbook.

TABLE 11.2

Emergency Backpack Supplies

Flashlight
Nonperishable snacks
Smart or cell phone
Water
Games, books, toys
Lightweight blankets
First aid supplies are in the administrator's backpack

After 9/11, early childcare programs began developing evacuation plans for unforeseen disasters. Homeland security is setting new standards for safety, and communities are updating fire codes and broadening evacuation plans for whatever danger may arise.

The variety of disaster situations that can arise in early childhood settings is remarkable. Listed below are emergencies that programs have already experienced. Some of these emergencies may be unsettling to read about. Call upon your emotional intelligence for help if this list troubles you.

- Parent arrives with a loaded weapon.
- Wolf ambles on to playground; children rush to pet the "doggie."
- Truck with hazardous waste overturns near center.
- Homeless man uses center grounds for shelter.
- Prison escapee makes a beeline for the center.
- Enraged boyfriend violently attacks teacher on playground.
- Drive-by shooting occurs when children are outside playing.
- Zoo animal gets loose while children are on a field trip.
- Sleeping child is left behind on school bus.
- Van driver falls asleep when driving and crashes van.
- Teacher has mental breakdown in the classroom.
- Child dies during classroom activity.
- Intoxicated and belligerent family member threatens children and staff.

Of all the emergencies administrators need to plan for, fire is only the beginning. For this reason, administrators must ensure that their programs comply with fire codes, emergency evacuation, and homeland security standards (Table 11.3).

Make a list of possible emergency situations, and then consider the previous list as you design emergency procedures for a variety of possible dangers.

OSHA, the federal Occupational Safety & Health Act, requires programs to take *"universal precautions"* for the safety and health of children, families, and staff. Universal precautions are actions to prevent the spread of dangerous illnesses by "blood borne pathogens" or germs. Hand washing is a universal precaution against the spread of pathogens. Disinfecting toys, classroom surfaces, and "mouth-ables" (anything acceptable for young children to put in their mouths) is another universal precaution.

These precautions are "universal" because they assume anyone might be infected, not just one or two children. In this way, children are not singled out. Instead, with universal precautions, early childhood professionals assume that every child may be infected with

---

TABLE 11.3

Code Blue

In an *Exchange* article entitled "Code Blue! Establishing a Child Care Emergency Plan," Margaret Leitch Copeland (1996) recommends we prepare for emergencies well in advance by:

1. Brainstorming, discussing, and practicing with staff how to deal with all possible emergencies.
2. Preparing backpacks equipped with emergency supplies for each classroom (see Table 11.2 for backpack contents).
3. Designating one person (preferably board chair, not director) as program spokesperson for television and press reporters.
4. Preparing a fact statement on your program in advance for the spokesperson to share with reporters.
5. Designating a building nearby where children can be relocated.
6. Creating a communication tree for families to inform one another quickly.
7. Dedicating a phone line/number, not tied to the building, for families to call.

When staff and children have more planning and practice time, they will feel safer and more competent when disaster strikes.

---

an illness like AIDS, or be HIV positive. Universal precautions apply to all programs that bring children and/or adults together, including early childcare programs, hospitals, and restaurants.

The Americans with Disabilities Act (ADA), discussed in Chapter 7, was enacted into law because people with disabilities found themselves unable to enter, use, or enjoy facilities and employment with the same ease as a nondisabled person. Perhaps because European countries dealt with war on their own soil, those countries were ahead of the United States in making provisions for injured veterans. Seats on European buses and trains were reserved for handicapped individuals. Ramps for people in wheelchairs were commonplace.

In 1990, the United States caught up with European countries in making spaces safe and welcoming for handicapped people. Passage of the ADA ensured that anyone who enters a childcare center has equal access to the facilities. A child in a wheelchair can gain access to the center by means of a ramp, an ADA mandate. Similarly, the ADA requires bathroom facilities designed for the use and safety of disabled children and adults.

As directors build or renovate, they need to consider how every child, family, and staff member, regardless of disability, can participate in and enjoy program activities. The ADA does not require administrators to expose their programs to "undue hardship" by spending the majority of a construction budget on ADA accommodations. Usually, a reasonable, considerate approach suffices.

Architects, builders, and licensors can work with directors on meeting ADA standards. Administrators can also go online (http://www.usdoj.gov/crt/ada/) or simply call 800-514-0301 for assistance from federal government agencies. For assistance in creating and coordinating plans for children of special needs, directors can contact the American Public Health Association (APHA) and American Academy of Pediatrics (AAP) for national health and safety guidelines.

OSHA 1910.1030(b):
Blood borne pathogens means pathogenic microorganisms that are present in human blood and can cause disease in humans. These pathogens include, but are not limited to, hepatitis B virus (HBV) and human immunodeficiency virus (HIV).

Accreditation Standards

Each accrediting agency, such as NAEYC and NACCP, sets detailed standards for safety and healthfulness of physical facilities, including classroom and playground space and equipment. Accreditation agencies usually set more rigorous standards than states. Although directors may not immediately apply for accreditation, they can use the standards to guide the overall creation and subsequent operation of their programs. Later, when directors do apply for accreditation, they will be "ahead of the game." Staff will be accustomed to working with the higher standard.

Environmental Rating Scales

Are additional tools to assess your program's strengths and weaknesses in providing safe and healthy spaces for children and adults. Thelma Harms, Richard Clifford, and Debby Cryer (2005), from the University of North Carolina at Chapel Hill, are leaders in the design and implementation of these scales. Detailed rating scales include:

- Family day care rating scale (FDCRS).
- Infant toddler environment rating scale-revised (ITERS-R).
- Early childhood environment rating scale-revised (ECERS-R).
- School age care environment rating scale (SACERS).

Marcy Robinson (2005, 23) notes: "For many directors, the environmental rating scales provide a quality tool through which to view their programs, to support and involve their staff, and to measure their progress. In the United States, the scales have also been attached to state licensing initiatives and other methods of insuring quality, such as quality ratings for child care centers."

After directors design or renovate a building with these standards in mind, they must consider additional practical policies and procedures to promote health and safety once the building is completed.

✤ Policies and Practices to Ensure Health and Safety

Meeting requirements from the start puts a program's physical plant and policies in good stead for everything that follows. Now let's look at practices and policies that continue our guarantee to "do no harm." I have chosen key policies and practices. You may think of others of particular importance to you. Policies and practices often come about because a director sees a need to create protections that were not in place.

At the end of this chapter, I will give you some examples of current, evolving policies to think about that have not yet been fully tested.

Checklists for Weekly "Walks around the Center"

Checklists can be formulated on a number of health and safety topics. One checklist might focus on cleanliness procedures and practices. Another checklist might address readiness for evacuation. Still another checklist can assess whether toys and equipment are well maintained and safe. Checklists can help administrators focus on all the different ways a program is safe, secure, and healthful for children, families, and staff.

Cathy Abraham (2007) turns what might be a "been there, done that" job into an adventure. Abraham notes that the important task of covering child care licensing regulations every year can be dry and repetitive. Her scavenger hunt activity adds fun to the topic and gets staff interacting. The first task on the hunt sends employees off with the checklist in Table 11.4 and instructions: "Physically locate the following items within the building—no guessing!"

An example of an NAEYC accreditation standard for physical environments is as follows:
The outdoor play area is arranged so that staff can supervise children by sight and sound.

TABLE 11.4

Licensing Scavenger Hunt

Item	Location
• Thermometer	
• Fire extinguisher	
• Parent handbook	
• Licensing regulations	
• Tissues	
• Fax number to program's supervising office	
• Extra children's clothing	
• Children's emergency cards	
• Child abuse hotline	
• Choking/CPR chart	
• Employment posters	
• The lost and found	

Other lists can focus on cleanliness measures and specifics such as square footage requirements for infants and the number of puzzles in the four-year-old classroom. To make these valuable exercises even more engaging, administrators can roll lists up and tie them with a ribbon like treasure maps, divide staff into heterogeneous (different classroom) teams for the hunt, and reward winning teams.

You can create your own checklists from any number of sources. Checklists based on state licensing standards like Abraham's are always useful. Not only may your licensor arrive unannounced at any time but, more important, you and the licensor will have the same goals in mind: keeping everyone safe from harm. If your program is accredited, use accreditation standards as the basis of your checklists. Inviting and engaging your staff in creating classroom checklists can increase "buy in" to complying with checklist requirements. Ready-made checklists are also available.

Procedures for Handling and Reporting Accidents

Preventing accidents by keeping buildings and grounds safe is the goal. With children's high energy and quest for exploration, along with their proximity to other children, some falls and scrapes cannot be prevented. Administrators can prepare staff and families in advance to deal with and report accidents.

Keep "due process" in mind: give people the information they need and the opportunity to talk about what happened. As my retired friend Frank, a priest in the mountains of New Mexico, advises: "Facts have dimensions. Fear has no dimensions." Keeping accurate accident reports and sharing the information about the accident immediately with families is the best policy.

Steps directors can take (Click 2004, 297):

1. Ask parents at enrollment to sign a form authorizing emergency medical treatment for the child.
2. Keep this signed form in the child's file.
3. Create/use a standard form to document details of the accident. (See Table 11.5 for the sample accident form that is used by Johanna Booth-Miner, seasoned director of Live & Learn Early Learning Center, New Hampshire.)

TABLE 11.5

Child Care Injury Report

TO BE COMPLETED FOR ANY INJURIES THAT REQUIRE TREATMENT, OTHER THAN MINOR SCRAPES OR BRUISES, AND RETAINED ON FILE AT THE PROGRAM FOR 3 YEARS FROM THE DATE OF INJURY.

NOTE: FIRST AID TREATMENT MUST BE PROVIDED BY A STAFF PERSON WHO IS CERTIFIED IN FIRST AID.

_____

NAME OF CHILD CARE PROGRAM

_____   _____

NAME OF INJURED CHILD   DATE OF BIRTH

DATE OF INJURY: _____   TIME OF INJURY: _____

WHERE WAS CHILD WHEN HE/SHE WAS INJURED?_____

_____

WHAT WAS CHILD DOING AT TIME HE/SHE WAS INJURED? _____

_____

_____

HOW DID IT HAPPEN? _____

_____

TYPE OF INJURY & BODY PART INJURED:

_____

WHAT FIRST AID TREATMENT WAS GIVEN, & WHAT TIME AND DATE WAS THE FIRST AID PROVIDED?

_____

_____

_____

NAME OF STAFF PERSON WHO ADMINISTERED FIRST AID

IF INJURY REQUIRED ADDITIONAL MEDICAL TREATMENT, IDENTIFY THE INDIVIDUAL OR MEDICAL FACILITY THAT PROVIDED THAT TREATMENT:

_____

_____

DATE, TIME & METHOD OF PARENT NOTIFICATION:

_____

_____

I HAVE REVIEWED THE ABOVE INJURY REPORT AND CERTIFY IT IS TRUE AND ACCURATE TO THE BEST OF MY KNOWLEDGE
WITNESS _____   DATE _____
_____   DATE _____
STAFF PERSON RESPONSIBLE FOR SUPERVISION OF INJURED CHILD AT TIME OF INJURY
_____   DATE: _____
CENTER DIRECTOR/FAMILY CHILD CARE PROVIDER

I HAVE READ THE ABOVE INJURY REPORT AND HAVE EXAMINED MY CHILD'S INJURY.
COMMENTS: _____
_____
_____   _____
PARENT'S SIGNATURE   DATE SIGNED

4. Accident forms include time of accident, what occurred, what was done for the child, and follow-up.
5. Depending on the severity of the accident, call 911.
6. Tell parents their child has been in an accident, the status of the child's health, and what steps have been/will be taken.
7. If the child has been taken to a health care facility, give the family members contact information and clear directions to the facility.
8. If another child has bitten a child, write this up as an accident report. However, the identity of the biter should be kept confidential. (See the "Biting Policy" section for more information.)
9. Inform all staff members working with or nearby the child to use extra care in observing the child in case further complications develop.
10. Comfort all children involved to reassure them they are safe and are being watched after. This includes children who observed the incident, not just the injured child.

Biting Policy

Two-year-olds bite. Before children can adequately express themselves with words, they need to make their point. Biting another child says, "Hey, I'm angry!" or "No, you can't take my toy!" When my son Nick was two, I encouraged him to "use words" instead of biting or hitting. Nick's teachers followed the same plan. Nick, like other children, outgrew his need to bite as his verbal ability grew. Of course, until Nick outgrew the biting phase, I kept my fingers crossed each day!

Biting upsets parents. Consider the following scenario in which a child bites toddler Djabril. When you inform Djabril's mother that her child was bitten, the parent reacts strongly. Seeing the bruise on Djabril's cheek is alarming. The director shares with the parent a completed accident/incident report detailing the facts: what happened, when, and what steps were taken. *One fact will not be included in the report: the name of the child who did the biting. This is confidential information.* Imagine how the "biter" might be shunned if the information were freely released.

One parent in West Virginia, an attorney, threatened to sue a director who would not reveal who had bitten the attorney's son. Fortunately, the director had the Biting Policy in Table 11.6 in the parent handbook:

TABLE 11.6

Sample Biting Policy

In the event that another child bites your child, we will make every effort to keep your child safe and prevent the biting from recurring. We will report the biting incident to you, using our Accident Report Form. We keep the identity of the child who did the biting confidential. We work with that child to help her/him learn other ways to express feelings.

When the attorney parent continued to threaten a lawsuit, the director took another approach. She investigated why the biter's identity is confidential. She discovered that the child who is bitten is not likely to be at risk. The biter, if she or he breaks the skin of another child, is the one exposed to blood borne pathogens. In the end, the father dropped his threat. More important, the child, like Nick, outgrew the biting stage. Staff took special precautions to work with the biter as they saw his frustration rise.

Mildly Ill Child Policy

Parents know children need to be home to heal from illnesses and hurts. Families, however, do not always have the luxury of staying home with a sick child. Hourly wage earners experience a particularly difficult bind if they stay home with the child. Not every employer is "family friendly" enough to support parents taking days off. Family members may fear they will lose their jobs if they stay home with their child.

Teachers frequently report children arrive without a fever, but within two hours, the child's temperature rises. Teachers suspect the child was given Tylenol or aspirin before school and that the fever returned once the medicine wore off. Phoning a parent at work to pick up her ailing child can be difficult for everyone involved. Some parents react with frustration, desperation, or anger. An administrator's hope of balancing individual family needs with program needs becomes mutually exclusive:

- Relocate the child to a safe, loving, and healing home environment.
- Keep staff and children safe from the spread of illness.
- Support the family in staying gainfully employed.

For a time, some programs attempted to remedy this dilemma. "Mildly ill" children were cared for in a separate room with specially assigned nurses. Hospital childcare programs seemed best suited to take on this responsibility. But the number of children needing this service is unpredictable, and nursing care is expensive. Costs quickly became prohibitive for most centers. Only a handful of programs for sick children are currently in operation.

How can administrators ensure health and safety while honoring family needs? Some conditions are nonnegotiable. Children cannot come to or stay in childcare if they exhibit:

1. Ongoing diarrhea.
2. Temperature above 100 degrees (armpit temperature).
3. Vomiting twice in one day.
4. "Pink eye" or conjunctivitis.
5. Other contagious illnesses, including measles, rubella, mumps, strep infection, head lice or scabies, impetigo, pertussis (serious coughing), hepatitis A virus, influenza, chicken pox, and tuberculosis.
6. Other changed behavior that may be indicative of serious illness (crying, crankiness, listlessness, disorientation, difficulty breathing).

A director's written policies should state the action a program will take if a child becomes ill. In addition to forewarning parents, administrators can help them find resources in the community for backup care. Some family home providers will care for mildly ill children. Resource and referral agencies may also provide a list of programs or individual providers who can help.

Note that HIV/AIDS is not listed in the illnesses that would keep a child out of a program. In fact, HIV/AIDS is an ADA-protected disability for which directors must make reasonable accommodations. Universal precautions shield everyone from blood borne pathogens and ensure HIV positive children, staff, and directors the confidentiality they deserve.

Sex Offenders

People convicted of sex offenses, such as child molestation and rape, are free once they have served their sentences. The severity of the sexual offence dictates the "level" of each offender. Usually a higher number (level 3 or 4) indicates a more serious offense. States and communities keep lists of registered sex offenders by residential address. Sex offenders are required to report to authorities if they relocate. Lists of sex offenders are available as a matter of public record. Contact police for a list of sex offenders in your vicinity. What can early childhood programs do with this information?

Remember I said we would take a look at safety and health challenges that have not yet been consistently resolved by policies and practices? Here is an example. I invite you to consider what you would do if you were the director in each of these not-unlikely scenarios.

CORI searches (criminal offender record information) are mandated as part of the early childcare hiring process. Sometimes, however, CORI checks take more time than a director has. Imagine that Rhonda's infant teacher enlists in the army without telling her. Rhonda's program is in crisis until she replaces the teacher. One applicant, Ryan, appears to meet all the requirements for infant teacher. Rhonda hires Ryan one month before Ryan's CORI reaches Rhonda. If Ryan's CORI reveals Ryan is a "level 3" sex offender, what can or should Rhonda do?

Most directors tell me they would terminate Ryan's employment. If Ryan is in the probationary period of his employment, especially in an "at will" state, Ryan can be terminated. This action aims to protect children. A director who faced this issue wanted to terminate the employee. She met with significant resistance from the employee's job counselors. Her desire to protect children and families was not the "slam dunk" she had hoped for. In such instances, I think of the director from Dorchester, Massachusetts, who said, "When the law doesn't make sense, I make my decision based on the fact that I have to live with myself when I go home for the day."

What would you decide in this case? Consider parents' concerns for their children. In the "spirit of the law," also assess Ryan's rights. In this country, convicted felons who have served time and "paid their debt to society" can be entitled to equal employment opportunities. Ryan's job counselors and advocates assure Rhonda that Ryan has made a turnaround in his life. If you were Rhonda, what would you do?

An equally complex dilemma arises if a parent is a registered sex offender. Assume Ryan's son and daughter are enrolled at your program. Because Ryan has custody, he has the right to drop off and pick up his children. Other parents feel they have the right to protect their children from exposure to sex offenders. How do you ensure safety while respecting parents' rights? Ryan's son and daughter, Mark and Maura, are worthy, as all children are, of respect. Mark and Maura want their Dad to come to family night with them. What would you do?

One program worked through the challenge in this way. The director, after listening to everyone's point of view, spoke with local police and her licensor. The father agreed to be accompanied by a third party when he engaged in center activities. The third party could be the family social worker, staff member assigned by the director, or another respected party known to the program and to the families, but most important, to the children.

Keeping Medical Records

A medical history for each child is collected at enrollment, and these records need to be updated and maintained while the child is within the care of the center. The medical data must be documented in concise, accurate, and up-to-date ways. Software packages (Chapter 10) make the task of tracking this information easier. Each child's file should contain:

Health and Medical Data

- Record of immunizations.
- Doctor's examination records and findings.

EPI training for staff:
EPI (epinephrine) shots restore normal breathing after a bee sting or other allergic reaction. As with other medications, parents need to complete and sign your medication administration form and provide doctors' dosage instructions. Promote health and safety by providing and requiring EPI administration training for staff. Only staff who have completed this training can administer an EPI.

- Medical history of conditions and/or allergies that may affect the child while in your program.
- List of ADA accommodations agreed upon and signed by doctor and family.
- Details of treatment plan for early intervention.

Family Data

- Signed release to get emergency care for child.
- Authorized list of persons who can pick the child up.
- List of people to be contacted in an emergency if parent is not available.
- Field trip permission form(s) completed and signed.
- Authorization to administer medication, including specific instructions as to dosage, timing, and other instructions from the doctor.
- Permission to use photographs of the child for educational purposes (with special consent forms for online photos, however).
- Completed application form with all relevant information.
- Family history information relevant to the child's care.
- Cultural preferences and preferred practices.

Child's Growth and Development

- Child's *in utero* (mother's pregnancy) relevant information.
- Record of physical and developmental growth.
- Comments submitted by professionals working with child, including teachers, speech pathologists, therapists.
- Progress on treatment plans.

✂ Food Program Management and Safety

Headlines scream out warnings about contaminated foods. Manufacturers recall once-trusted food products. Studies on childhood obesity warn us against foods that families may serve regularly. With food preparation and service, "do no harm" is again the non-negotiable bottom line.

As with any other aspect of our programs, the government sets standards in health and safety in handling food. Food must be fresh, healthy, prepared and served in a hygienic way. Meals and snacks must be age appropriate. The federally approved food pyramid, revised in 2005, tells us what percentage of each food group is appropriate daily.

Infants and preschoolers' diets will differ accordingly. At six months, children will likely have developed enough to be able to swallow and digest solid food of the proper consistency and amount. Preschoolers can be served a fuller range of healthy food options.

Some programs employ cooks who prepare meals and snacks daily. Other programs rely on catering services to deliver prepared food. In either case, the director's job is to make sure children are given fresh, nutritious food under hygienic circumstances. An outbreak of salmonella would be disastrous.

Just as with building design and renovation, state and federal standards are in place to guide directors through the essential bottom lines of serving food safely and healthily. How often children are provided with nutritious food is determined by the amount of time a child is in a program's care. Use your leadership EQ in hiring food service staff whose competencies include attention to health and safety.

Hours of Operation and Required Meals

State licensing standards connect hours of operation with number of meals provided. Traditional half-day schools, often called "nursery schools," are required to provide a nutritious snack at mid-morning or mid-afternoon. The child is expected to have eaten a main meal before she arrives and will eat one soon after she returns home.

On the other end of the care continuum, programs providing 9 hours of care (or more) must provide two-thirds of a child's daily food requirements. The assumption is the child will eat at least one meal at home each day.

When it comes to infants, some general guidelines apply to ensure that each child receives proper nutrition. However, *infant classrooms utilize individualized feeding plans.* Each baby is on her own schedule. Children who are breastfed may not take solid food. A mother may breastfeed at the center and/or leave adequately labeled bottles of breast milk for her child. Directors need to pay attention to families' cultural values in determining together what each child needs and when.

The longer children are in a program's care, the greater percentage of their daily nutritional requirement directors must meet.

Food Pyramid

The latest revision of the food pyramid (2005) changes some of the recommended food portions and physical activity priorities (see Figure 11.1). Educators can download the revised Food Guide Pyramid and other resources online (*http://www.mypyramid.gov/tips_resources/*). Whole grains, fruits, and vegetables have risen to a higher step on the pyramid of required foods. Protein, while important, can be found in nonmeat sources, such as fish, nuts, and legumes. For the federal government's guidelines on the new food pyramid, go to *http://www.mypyramid.gov/*.

FIGURE 11.1   *Food Guide Pyramid*

Food Allergies

Children and adults are increasingly diagnosed with a variety of food allergies. Some of these allergies, especially peanut allergies, can result in critical and sometimes fatal reactions. Other foods causing allergic reactions are tomatoes, milk and dairy products, and chocolate.

At enrollment, directors should ask each parent whether her child has any food allergies or dietary restrictions. A child's medical examination record should also state diagnosed allergies and procedures for prevention and treatment for allergic reactions. Anyone serving food to children needs to read labels closely for "hidden" ingredients. Eliminate foods or food products that cause allergic reactions for children or staff.

Cultural and Religious Preferences

In some religions and cultural practices, certain foods are not allowed. For example, serving ham or pork products to Muslim families is disrespectful. When Jewish families follow kosher diets, a number of dietary practices must be honored. For example, dairy products cannot be served along with certain other products. Some Catholic Latino families follow the precept of not eating meat on certain days. Invite parents to share their cultural and/or religious food requirements. When possible, honor the family's requests.

Potluck Meals, Out of Luck?

For years, early childhood programs have invited families to "bring a dish to share" as part of a potluck meal. Families were especially encouraged to bring dishes that reflected their ethnic or cultural heritage. Potluck gatherings provided a natural way for families to enjoy and learn about one another's different traditions.

Today, holding potluck meals is under question. Might centers be liable if some one becomes ill after eating a potluck dish? Directors have attempted to prevent this problem by asking families to display a list of ingredients used in the dish. This would enable people with food allergies to make informed decisions about which dish to sample.

Another challenge with potluck dishes derives from families' different hygienic standards and traditions in food preparation. One family may be rigorous in washing all surfaces and implements. Another family might have more relaxed standards.

If a program sponsors a potluck meal and a participant becomes sick as a result, the program might be liable. This concern has led some directors to eliminate food brought from home, including children's birthday cakes.

 After hearing these warnings about potluck meals, how do you feel? What has been lost and what has been gained? If families, excited about sampling foods of many cuisines, were to say, "Let's have another potluck family night. What fun we had the last time!" what would you say?

⚔ Safe and Sound

The "do no harm" standard for early childhood programs makes sense. We want everyone to be safe. We want to offer nutritious, healthy meals. We want buildings and grounds to be free of danger. With the help of established standards, we will know how to prevent harm.

If a crisis occurs, we want procedures in place to respond quickly and fully. This "do no harm" precept is the cornerstone for all early childcare buildings and environments, from classrooms to food preparation to emergency medical procedures. Now that we have established the cornerstone for health and safety, we can step up to creating environments for children to learn, grow, and thrive. Are you ready?

Reflection Questions

1. Imagine you have chosen to build a childcare center "from the ground up." What is your vision for the new structure? What environment do you want to create for children and families? In what ways would your new building be beautiful? What would you do to make sure each space is safe and inviting? Investigate and list all the resources available to you to help you accomplish your goal. Write a comment next to each resource on your list explaining the assistance that resource provides.

2. Maximilian (case study, p. 170), over coffee, asks your advice in converting the temple Sunday school into a viable and appealing early childhood center. Help Max identify the various groups of people who have expectations for the program. Advise Max how he can use both his EQ and "social EQ" to work with each group and with his whole community. What questions do you feel Max needs to ask himself about his goals and how realistic they are? Where might you and Max look to find information on renovating the existing building? Write or record a summary or a dialogue between you and Max on important points in your discussion.

3. Kindergartner Philippa (Pippa) has asthmatic reactions where breathing becomes labored. Her doctor has prescribed an "EPI" device. This device enables epinephrine to be injected into Pippa's thigh. The injection works quickly. Pippa feels like her energetic self again. Pippa's mother, a nurse, says Pippa knows how to use her EPI. Mom explains she has shown Pippa how to use the EPI at home. Mom feels Pippa needs to be able to help herself more quickly than a staff member could. How would you respond to Pippa's mom? What policy might you put into place or call upon to support your decision? Present your policy and summary to the class.

Team Projects

1. Reread Beatrice and Aurora's case (p. 168). What might Beatrice, who loves nature and the great outdoors, want to incorporate into an early childhood building? Now imagine "city girl" Aurora's vision of a new building. As far as Aurora is concerned, the farther away she is from "vermin" (mosquitoes, spiders, snakes, crows, and "smelly" animals), bad weather, and sunlight, the happier she is. As a team, envision a center, indoors and out, that incorporates the best of both cousins' visions, without "creating a monster." Now, research just how much of the great outdoors can safely be included in an early childhood building. For example, what about animals? How "wild" can the outdoor playground environment be? Visit local early childhood programs to see how they answer these questions. Present a conceptual design that incorporates the "forever wild" elements Beatrice craves, in a safe enough way for Aurora.

2. Brainstorm what you imagine to be in the job description of an early childhood licensor in your locale. What might be the licensing agency's mission? What do you expect the core values and code of ethical behavior for state licensors to be? What procedures do you think the agency has in place if a program is out of compliance with standards? What else would you like to know about your state's licensing agency? Divide these questions among team members for research. Be sure to interview at least one licensor. Present a PowerPoint of your findings to the class.

3. Keeping in mind that licensing standards are the basic, rather than the ultimate, standards for health and safety, compare other professional standards. Look into NAEYC and NACCP's accreditation standards. Examine a copy of a quality rating scale, such as the ECERS-R (2005). Check out Head Start's directives on health and

safety. Research actual "checklists" used by directors to make sure their programs are safe and healthful. Which of these standards, or what combination of standards and practices, do you recommend to your classmates and why?

4. Childhood obesity has grown to epidemic proportions in this country. The Food Guide Pyramid, recently revised, sets new standards for healthy eating. If you were directors of early childhood programs, what are at least five things you could do to promote healthy nutrition and eating habits at your programs? Consider the foods, cooking, and eating practices of at least three cultural groups. How can your initiatives honor the practices of diverse cultures while working to eliminate childhood obesity? Prepare a presentation of your five ideas as if your audience included parents from various ethnic groups.

Bibliography

Abraham, C. 2007. Licensing scavenger hunt. *Exchange* (January–February): 80–82.

American Academy of Pediatrics. 2002. *Caring for our children: National health and safety performance standards* (2nd ed.). Chicago, IL: American Academy of Pediatrics.

American Academy of Pediatrics and National Association of School Nurses. 2005. *Health, mental health and safety guidelines for schools.* Chicago, IL: American Academy of Pediatrics.

Carter, M. 2006. Rethinking our use of resources—Part 2. *Exchange* (January–February): 18–20.

Click, P. 2004. *Administration of programs for young children* (6th ed.). Clifton Park, NY: Thomson Delmar Learning.

Copeland, M.L. 1996. Code blue! Establishing a child care emergency plan. *Exchange* (January–February): 17–22.

Decker, C.A., and J.R. Decker. 2004. *Planning and administering early childhood programs* (8th ed.). Upper Saddle River, NJ: Pearson Merrill Prentice Hall.

Epstein, A.S. 2007. *The intentional teacher: Choosing the best strategies for young children's learning.* Washington, DC: National Association for the Education of Young Children.

Goleman, D. 1997. *Emotional intelligence.* New York: Simon and Schuster.

Gonzalez-Mena, J. 2008. *Foundations of early childhood education* (4th ed.). New York: McGraw-Hill.

Greenman, J. 2005. *Caring places: Learning spaces* (Revised ed.). Redmond, WA: Exchange Press.

Greenman, J. 2001. *What happened to our world? Helping children cope in turbulent times.* South Watertown, MA: Bright Horizons Family Solutions.

Hannaford, C. 2002. *Awakening the child heart.* Captain Cook, HI: Jamilla Nurr Publishing.

Harms, T., R. Clifford, and D. Cryer. 2005. *Early childhood environmental rating scale* (Revised ed.). New York: Teachers College Press.

Hemingway, E. 1925. "A clean, well-lighted place" in *The short stories of Ernest Hemingway.* New York: Charles Scribner's Sons.

Robertson, M. 2005. Using the environment rating scales for quality improvement projects. *Exchange* (September–October): 23–26.

Web Resources

Food Guide Pyramid
http://www.mypyramid.gov/
Occupational Safety & Health Administration (OSHA)
http://www.osha.gov/
National Association of Child Care Professionals (NACCP) Accreditation Standards
http://www.naccp.org/displaycommon.cfm?an=1&subarticlenbr=237
National Association for the Education of Young Children (NAEYC) Early Childhood Program Standards
http://www.naeyc.org/academy/standards/
Sample Early Childcare Forms: New York State Office of Children & Family Services
http://www.ocfs.state.ny.us/main/becs/becs_forms.asp

Curriculum Choices: Roots and Wings

Learning Goals

As you study this chapter, you can look forward to reaching these learning goals:

1. Trace the roots of early childhood learning theory.
2. Discuss the impact of brain development research on early learning theory.
3. Explain the connection between learning and relationships.
4. Name a variety of teaching strategies.
5. Summarize how to create indoor and outdoor learning spaces.
6. Gain background on the debate over "teaching to the test" versus learning through play.
7. Identify principles of social intelligence active in learning organizations.

What nourishes the imagination? Probably more than anything else, loving adults who encourage the imaginative play of children's own making.

—*Fred Rogers*

To be nobody but yourself—in a world which is doing its best, night and day, to make you everybody else—means to fight the hardest battle which any human being can fight, and never stop fighting.

— *E.E. Cummings*

Case Study: A Mother's Dream for Her Son

Marco's Mom, Marisol, wants her son to "have all the breaks in life" she never had. She plans to use her hard-earned savings to send Marco to private school when he turns five. Marisol supported your program's individualized curriculum when Marco was an infant and toddler. "That was then," she insists, "now Marco needs to learn reading, writing, math. I use flash card drills at home. Show me how you are preparing Marco to get top grades on Whitestone Preparatory School's admission test." Marco thrives on outdoor play and hates sitting still. How do you partner with Marco's Mom to help Marco?

Early childhood leaders have the honor of creating and maintaining wondrous environments for learning, for both children and adults. Early childhood teachers understand the function of "emergent curriculum," and the value of both play and structure in a child's development. Families and school systems may prefer traditional classroom teaching. In the chapter case study, Marco's Mom uses flash card drills at home and wants her son's preschool teachers to do the same. As a leader, you are likely to engage with families in the debate over what is best for their children.

The pendulum swings left to right, right to left, whether we nudge it or not. One day, parents applaud their child's free-form finger painting. The next day, parents demand children learn "basics": the 3 R's (reading, 'riting, and 'rithmetic). One decade, architects design windowless schools to focus students away from distractions. The next decade, architects design open classrooms that invite children's imaginations to soar indoors and out. One year, legislators fund early childhood programs. The next year, early childhood programs scrape to survive.

Watching the pendulum swing is akin to sitting at a ping-pong match. Our necks grow weary! Where in this bouncing back-and-forth and up-and-down movement is something steady, predictable, and enduring about how children learn?

In this chapter, we will explore spaces, places, and approaches to learning that help children develop fully, regardless of today's trend or yesterday's expectation. As the saying goes: "There are only two lasting things we can leave our children: One is roots, the other is wings."

We Stand on Their Shoulders: Roots of Early Childhood Learning Theory

Before early childhood administrators and teachers can design curriculum or spaces, they need to understand how children learn. To reach an informed conclusion about this, let's look at innovators in early childhood education theory and practice.

Froebel, Dewey, Montessori, Piaget, Erikson, Vygotsky, Pikler and Gerber, Gardner and Rogers spun golden, crimson, and purple threads of child development theory that catch our eye today. Chances are, you have studied these theorists. Building on your knowledge, I aim to capture each educational seer's gift to us. In particular, we will examine how each theorist connects human relationships with learning.

Play is the highest level of child development. . . . It gives . . . joy, freedom, contentment, inner and outer rest, peace with the world . . . The plays of childhood are the germinal leaves of all later life.

—Froebel

Friedrich Froebel

Friedrich Froebel (1782–1852) was born in Oberweissbach, Germany. Froebel believed children grow and learn as they play, and he created the kindergarten or "children's garden." He pictured school as a garden for "growing" children. Froebel famously said,

"Children are like tiny flowers; they are varied and need care, but each is beautiful alone and glorious when seen in the community of peers." Teachers tend the garden, nourishing and supporting seeds as they grow into saplings. Children, like flowers, grow strong in sunlight, fresh air, and ample nourishment, surrounded by loving support. Froebel's gift to us is this: Children blossom through play and being well cared for by adults.

John Dewey

John Dewey (1884–1952) was born in Burlington, Vermont. Dewey's message, above all, is to respect the child. A child's education must be alive, active, and interactive. "Education," he said, "therefore is a process of living and not preparation for future living." Dewey believed education for children involves and integrates the child's community and social world. Curriculum should grow organically from a child's world, her home, her backyard, her friendships, her skipping and tumbling. A teacher's work is to help the child make sense of her world. Dewey's gift to us is this: Create child-centered or "integrated" curriculum.

> The child's own instinct and powers furnish the material and give the starting point for all education.
>
> **—John Dewey**

Maria Montessori

Maria Montessori (1870–1952) was born in Chiaravalle, Italy. Montessori, the story goes, was admitted to medical school (at a time when only men were permitted to study medicine) by writing her name "M. Montessori" on the application. Montessori observed children with new eyes in order to develop theories on how children learn. To Dr. Montessori, children are passionate treasures full of unfolding fascination and competency. Environments for learning must honor children. For example, chairs cannot leave children's legs dangling, and saws and knives must be sharp enough to use.

Children, Montessori observed, are innately capable. The teacher's job is to:

- Observe and listen for the child's natural curiosity.
- Support the child as she fulfills her quest to learn.
- Step to the side, ready to observe the child's next burst of curiosity.

Dr. Montessori favored "cheerful" environments full of sensory tools for children to discover and where teachers "teach little and observe much." Montessori's gift to us is this: Support the child's learning by trusting and supporting the child's innate curiosity and ability with appropriate tools.

> It is necessary for the teacher to guide the child without letting him feel her presence too much, so that she may always be ready to supply the desired help, but may never be the obstacle between the child and his experience.
>
> **—Maria Montessori**

> The greatest sign of success for a teacher is to be able to say, "The children are now working as if I did not exist."
>
> **—Maria Montessori**

Erik Erikson

Erik Erikson (1902–1994) was born in Frankfurt, Germany, and he identified stages of children's emotional and social development. At every stage, children need the loving support of adults. From the beginning (birth to age one) children learn to trust through a caregiver's warmth and fulfillment of needs. With trust, a child is free to explore and grow. Toddlers, ages two to three, learn autonomy, if they are not condescended to or shamed. Between ages four and five, a child gains a sense of purpose, as we support her initiative instead of "guilting" her.

In some ways, Erikson foresaw the future of neuroscientific studies by paying attention to the importance of relationships at every stage of a child's development. Without relational kindness, children grow into struggling adults who ask, "Can I trust? Am I confident enough to dream and follow my dream? Will self-doubt and distrust nip at my heels all the days of my life?"

> There is in every child at every stage a new miracle of vigorous unfolding, which constitutes a new hope and a new responsibility for all.
>
> **—Erik Erikson**

Although Erikson's rather lock-step views on child development have been criticized, his gift is this: Children's emotional well-being is closely linked with their ability to learn.

Jean Piaget

> The principle goal of education in the schools should be creating men and women who are capable of doing new things, not simply repeating what other generations have done.
>
> **—Jean Piaget**

Jean Piaget (1896–1980) was born in Neuchatel, Switzerland. As an epistemologist, Piaget studied knowledge, its origin and definitions. Educators, he observed, need to understand how a child's mind works. In particular, how does a child gain knowledge? Piaget's answer to this question is that children learn by living.

The educator's job is to encourage inquiry and support the child's natural quest for knowledge. Piaget believed that "construction is superior to instruction." Children are not empty vessels waiting to be filled with information. Some of Piaget's research is now questioned because of his research methods, such as using a small, homogeneous sampling. Piaget nonetheless left us with this gift: Children are born to find answers with our support.

Lev Vygotsky

> Every function in the child's cultural development appears twice: first, between people (interpsychological) and, then, inside the child (intrapsychological). This applies equally to voluntary attention, to logical memory, and to the formation of ideas. All the higher functions originate as actual relationships between individuals.
>
> **—Lev Vygotsky**

Lev Vygotsky (1896–1934) was born in Orsha, Russia. Early on, Vygotsky saw the inadequacy of intelligence tests in identifying a child's gifts and recognized the importance of social relationships and cultural contributions within a person's development. With proper "scaffolding," or support within constructive relationships, children learn, grow, and develop their gifts. In addition to scaffolding, Vygotsky developed the concept of a person's "zone of proximal development" (ZPD). In the ZPD, teachers observe, anticipate, and stand ready to support a child in her stretch to learn the next important life lesson. Vygotsky's gift to us is this: Relationships are crucial to a child's learning.

Howard Gardner

> We must figure out how intelligence and morality can work together to create a world in which a great variety of people will want to live.
>
> **—Howard Gardner**

Howard Gardner (1943–) was born in Scranton, Pennsylvania, and is noted for his concept of "multiple intelligences." Like Vygotsky, Gardner was disenchanted with the idea that one test, the IQ test, could define intelligence. After observing young children's differing talents, interests, and capabilities, Gardner named at least nine intelligences. Along with kinesthetic, musical, and spatial intelligence, Gardner identified social and emotional intelligences.

Gardner's gift to us is his acknowledgment of the value of differing intelligences and his gift for seeing both children and adults as diversely able and talented.

Fred Rogers

> As children grow, it's important for children to love the person who they are, so they will continue to want to learn and succeed in life.
>
> **—Fred Rogers**

Fred Rogers (1928–2003) was born in Latrobe, Pennsylvania. Neither researcher nor scientist, Rogers was a creator and a communicator. After over twenty-five years with public television, "Mr. Rogers" left a visual and written compendium of emotional and social EQ insights. Children need to feel safe, valued, listened to, and encouraged to express their feelings.

> Children are not merely vessels into which facts are poured one week and then when it comes time for exams, they turn themselves upside down and let the facts run out. Children bring all of themselves, their feelings and their experiences to the learning (Fred Rogers 1994, 87).

Fred Rogers taught through relationships. He looked through the television camera lens into the eyes of each child watching. For Mr. Rogers, the relationship is the message. This understanding, that relationships are at the heart of learning, is only one of Fred Rogers' many gifts to us.

Emmi Pikler

Emmi Pikler (1902–1984) was born in Budapest, Hungary. In 1946, the Hungarian government invited pediatrician Emmi Pikler to establish residential programs for children whose families were unable to care for them after the war. Pikler accepted the challenge. Impersonal orphanages, which institutionalized children, were far from what Pikler envisioned. Instead, she created nurseries wherein:

1. Caregivers were specially prepared to build a trusting, respectful relationship with each child; and,
2. Children (babies and toddlers, in particular) were supported as they initiated their own learning.

Children raised in Pikler programs grow confident while being trusted to know what and when to learn. Pikler observed, "As a matter of principle, we refrain from teaching skills and activities which under suitable conditions will evolve through the child's own initiative and independent activity." With few manufactured toys and unencumbered settings, Pikler children have far fewer accidents than children not raised in Pikler environments.

> While learning . . . to turn on the belly, to roll, creep, sit, stand and walk [the baby] is not only learning those movements but also how to learn. He learns to do something on his own, to be interested, to try out, to experiment. He learns to overcome difficulties. He comes to know the joy and satisfaction, which is derived from this success, the result of his patience and persistence.
>
> —Emmi Pikler

The focus is on what children can do, not on what we expect they will do according to our preconceived notions of ages and stages. Dr. Pikler left us with this gift: Respect the child to "know" when she is ready to transition in her development.

Magda Gerber, also from Hungary, continued the work of Emmi Pikler and leaves us with this gift: "In time, not on time." Pikler and Gerber believed children are motivated to learn when they need to learn. Children do not develop on someone else's timetable. In response to Janet Gonzalez-Mena's question, "What is one piece of advice you have for those of us who work with infants and toddlers?" Gerber responded, "Slow down."

The Wisdom of the Elders of Many Cultures

You may have noticed that the innovators discussed in the previous section, as Janet Gonzalez-Mena points out, are of the European tradition. The early childhood field does not yet fully study or incorporate the wisdom of Asian, African, South and Central American, Middle Eastern, American tribes, or island cultures. When it does, we are sure to find emotional and social intelligence theories and practices enlightening for everyone.

> By observing different cultures, we see that there are many ways to go about caring for and educating children. There's no one right way.
>
> —Janet Gonzalez-Mena

Leaders of NBCDI (National Black Child Development Institute) have created a helpful guide entitled *School Readiness and Social Emotional Development: Perspectives in Cultural Diversity* (2006). Edited by Barbara Bowman of Chicago's Erikson Institute and Evelyn K. Moore, NBCDI president, this book is full of information on helping young children be successful from the start. In Dr. Bowman's words, risk to African-American and Latino children can be alleviated if early childcare administrators and teachers:

> Help teachers understand that teaching is not just about the transmission of academic knowledge and skills but also about motivation and dispositions, which stem from satisfying adult-child relationships. This means teachers understand and relate to culturally diverse children, their families, and communities in positive ways.
>
> —Bowman and Moore

1. Understand cultural differences. Classroom teachers need to know about the culture of the children in their classrooms and how to bridge between what the children know and what they want them to learn.

2. *Identify and treat children with special needs.* Children who are highly stressed, with a disabling condition, or whose development is atypical need a working system for diagnosis and treatment.

3. *Recognize the importance of relationships.*

To read more about Latino insights into early childhood development, see *Connections and Commitments: A Latino-Based Framework for Early Childhood Educators* by Constanza Eggers-Pierola (2005). Close, loving family-like relationships are seen as key to a child's development. For a helpful bibliography of resources on learning theories and practices from various cultural perspectives, see Appendix C.

❈ Brain Development Research and Learning Theory

> The amount and quality of love a child receives have long lasting neural consequences. . . . An emotional void often proves fatal to babies. Neglect produces children whose head circumferences are measurably smaller, whose brains on magnetic resonance scanning evidence shrinkage from the loss of billions of cells. Twenty years of longitudinal data have proven that responsive parenting confers apparently permanent personality strengths.
>
> **—T. Lewis et al.,** *General Theory of Love*

Looking back on the message of each of these early childhood innovators, I see two principles emerging. First, respectful, loving relationships are essential to learning. Second, each child innately (spontaneously from within) seeks to know her world. The early childhood leader's job is to scaffold the child's learning with supportive teaching strategies and curriculum that can adapt and evolve to meet children's needs. How do these principles and concepts line up with neuroscientific research on children's learning?

From Neurons to Neighborhoods: The Science of Early Childhood Development has become the seminal book on the science of children's brain development. Brain development research findings have been spilling out like lava since the early 1990s.

Findings to date include these principles:

1. Brain pathways, established in early childhood, most often remain with us the rest of our lives.
2. We learn though relationships, by our interconnectedness with others.
3. The more respectfully loving the relationship, the healthier the child.
4. Our cells imitate (mirror neurons in particular) the neurons of our closest caregivers early in our life (from birth to age three).
5. Experiences destructive to healthy brain development can be countered or reversed through loving relationships that a child experiences in her early years.
6. Our brains have "plasticity," flexibility to adapt, change, and learn throughout our lifetime.

Healthy and respectful relationships are essential for children to learn. The early childhood professional's job is to facilitate the child's unfolding, not to dump in facts and figures while destroying the child's desire to learn. Brain research and early childhood learning theorists agree at heart: rooted in the secure arms of trusting relationships, a child can spread her wings to soar into the world of curiosity and wonder.

❈ Relationships Are at the Heart of Learning

With these gifts from early childhood theorists, how does a director go about creating environments where children can learn? Five keys to keep in mind when contemplating curriculum and space design for children:

1. The child is the curriculum.
2. Environment is the teacher.
3. Teachers facilitate learning by supporting a child's natural curiosity.
4. Relationships provide a secure base for and much of the substance of a child's early education.
5. Boundaries, alternative teaching strategies, and structure scaffold a child's learning.

In respectful, supportive relationships children naturally explore their environment, ready to grow and learn. *The relationship itself is a teacher.* Let's examine these keys one at a time.

Child as Curriculum

Imagine a seasoned director, Chris, whose mission statement announces: "The child is the curriculum." Chris's challenge is to help teachers hone observation skills and expand their horizon of emergent learning experiences for children. Does Chris use a written curriculum? "Yes," she responds, "but as a resource, not a determinant."

The planned curriculum might focus on "families." But what if the children, instead, are curious about why and how shells wash up on the seashore? Chris's teachers can follow and anticipate ways children find answers to their question, "Why and how do seashells wash up on shore?" With Chris's support, teachers can set up a center with hands-on activities about ocean currents and seashells. Teachers can incorporate the children's interests into the planned curriculum by discussing "families in the sea."

A teacher's artistry is demonstrated through his ability to fan the curiosity of all his students. He will use a variety of creative teaching tools to connect with each student and different groups of students with different needs. A field trip to the beach may not have been planned, but the teacher will find ways to engage all the students in preparing enthusiastically for the visit.

When you recall the list of early childhood learning theorists, which pioneer(s) does Chris's approach illustrate best?

Environment as Teacher: Creating Learning Spaces Indoors and Out

"Same old, same old" classrooms put children, and many adults, to sleep. Instead, inviting places inspire children to wonder, wander, and explore. Children need safe spaces with quiet places for calm and reflection. Children equally need adventuresome areas to let out energy, refine gross motor skills, and make their way in the world. Children learn in environments rich in resources to connect them to information. For these reasons, the environment becomes the curriculum.

From birth, and most likely before, babies are intensely aware of their environments. They watch and taste, touch and rattle, roll and toss, squirm and wiggle their way to learning. Children learn about life primarily through relationships with others. Children also learn by observing and interacting with their environments. Early childhood leaders can create spaces and places that honor and engage children's quest to learn by interacting with their surroundings.

Author Margie Carter (2007) refers to the Reggio Emilia concept of seeing the environment as the "third teacher." Carter encourages us to ask what values and messages our environments communicate to children and their families.

My understanding on learning environments is this: Use your imagination and skill to help children grow their imaginations and skills. In this way, each learning space will be fresh and inviting, rather than "fungible" (like malls or pinto beans—just the same).

In Chapter 11 we examined the hefty list of requirements for safe and healthy environments. Compliance with these requirements is necessary for everyone's well-being. However, compliance can have an unintended and sometimes unfortunate side effect. Early childhood spaces can often look alike. Equipped with safety-tested furniture and toys from well-known companies, and arranged in acceptable room and playground

Creating an engaging, inspiring environment is not just interior decorating.

—Margie Carter

In many centers or play areas of family child care homes, you have to look hard to find anything of beauty. Childcare and aesthetics do not necessarily go together. Perhaps the lack of aesthetics is a sign of the times—a sign that other considerations take priority over beauty.

—Janet Gonzalez-Mena

configurations, our programs are safe but not unique. Figure 12.1 shows an example of typical infant, toddler, and preschool room arrangements:

Imagine how you might transform this typical classroom into a lively, unique, and culturally aware learning environment.

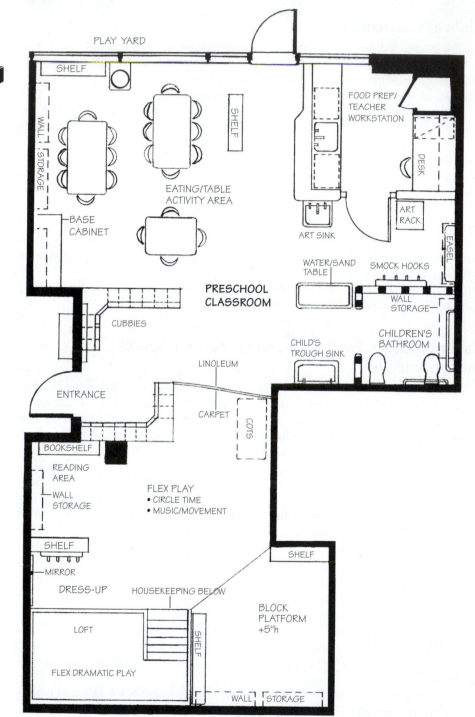

FIGURE 12.1 *Preschool Classroom Layout*

Source: From Gonzalez-Mena 2008, 228–230.

Of late, practitioners have been breaking out of the sameness mold. As you read about four diverse approaches to learning, consider how a director might call upon her staff and her own unique values and vision to create wondrous and one-of-a-kind learning spaces.

1. *Nature Action Collaborative for Children,* an international organization, unites landscape architects, health care professionals, early childhood educators, and environment groups, such as Jane Goodall's "Roots and Shoots." You can join at no cost and go online at *www.rootsandshoots.org* to share and gain information and ideas on new ways to reconnect children with nature.

2. *Music and movement in the outdoor classroom.* "Because an outdoor classroom can usually offer more space for large motor skill movements than an indoor classroom, children are able to freely experiment with multiple locomotor and non-locomotor activities. And, because sounds are absorbed in the outdoors in a way that's impossible inside, children can create their own music without disturbing others" (Van Gilder et al. 2007, 53–56). The authors note that music in the out-of-doors can offer special needs children more ease in making neurological connections. Ideas include:
   - Act like a tree to make its leaves "dance."
   - Move like creatures you see (squirrels, robins, inch worms).
   - Sing songs about what you notice.
   - Be free to play "big" outdoors in ways you cannot indoors.

3. *Living willow huts.* Can you imagine creating an outdoor hut for children that bursts into life in the spring? Rusty Keeler (2008) provides us with step-by-step instructions and drawings about how teachers and children can plant willow rods or shoots to make living willow huts. The plants sprout into tunnels, fences, huts, or anything else a child and teacher can envision.

4. *Consider the walls.* "I am encouraging teachers to step back and critically examine the quality and quantity of commercial materials on their walls to determine whether they actually contribute to children's learning or whether they ultimately silence children" (Tarr 2004, 92). Professor Tarr suggests that as children create both design and content of classroom displays, they learn more than they would from looking at a poster or commercially made snowflakes and shamrocks.

Teachers Facilitate Learning by Supporting Curiosity

Vygotsky gave us the term "scaffolding" to describe the teacher's purpose in a child's education. The teacher scaffolds the child's environment with layer upon layer of inviting learning opportunities. As Fred Rogers reminds us, a teacher does not download information and, with a click, impart that information to a child's waiting brain. He uses his passion, creativity, and authenticity in dancing with each child's curiosity. Teaching is an art we develop over a lifetime.

Effective teachers (Copple & Bredekamp, 2006):

- Get to know each child's personality, abilities, and ways of learning;
- Make sure that all children get the support they need to develop relationships with others and feel part of the group;
- Work to build a strong sense of group identity among the children to develop what is called "the circle of we";
- Create an environment that is organized, orderly, and comfortable for children;

Characteristics of effective early childhood teachers:

- Passion
- Perseverance
- Willingness to take risks
- Pragmatism
- Patience
- Flexibility
- Respect
- Creativity
- Authenticity
- Love of learning
- High energy
- Sense of humor

—**Laura J. Colker,** "Twelve Characteristics of Early Childhood Teachers"

- Plan ways for children to work and play together collaboratively;
- Bring each child's home culture and language into the shared culture of the class; and,
- Discourage tattling, teasing, scapegoating, and other practices that undermine a sense of community and make some children feel like outsiders.

Seasoned teachers are continuously learning new ways to touch children's lives and spark their curiosity. These teachers are the mature professionals (Chapter 9) that are a director's delight. Mature professional teachers inspire other teachers to keep learning and growing along with the children. Each director's job is to help teachers share their gifts while continuously learning new approaches to teaching.

Relationships Are Everything

What I have heard from creative people over the years is that their early urges toward unique self-expression were respected and supported by some loving adult in their lives—someone who would even let them paint a tree blue if that's what they felt like doing. When a friend of mine was a little boy, he liked to draw and paint a lot. One time he drew a tree and colored it blue, and some grownup said to him: "Why did you color a tree blue. Trees aren't blue!" My friend didn't draw a tree again for years . . . not until one of his teachers told him that artists can make things any shape and color they want.

—Fred Rogers, *You are Special*

Fish need water. Humans need air. Children need love. Things don't get much simpler than that.

Studies on "failure to thrive" babies sadly demonstrate the lifetime pain and suffering of unloved children. Loved children learn with confidence. Relationship is everything. "Infants at just a few days old can distinguish between emotional expressions," note psychiatrists Lewis, Amini, and Lannon (2000, 61). "Mothers use the universal signals of emotion to teach their babies about the world . . . emotion gives the two of them a common language years before the infant will acquire speech."

The work of an early childhood leader is, above all, to facilitate the sharing of unconditional human regard, or love. With love at the core, everything else flows. Author Frances Carlson (2006) documents the lasting benefits of the respectful, loving physical touch teachers give children. Even children with PTSD (posttraumatic stress disorder) can be loved out of terror into hope and confidence. The pathways (ganglia) of their neurons, stunted by trauma, stretch out and grow into healing connections. So too of adults: in accepting, loving relationships, adults, abused as children, learn to trust and thrive. Make no mistake: Leading on purpose is leading with a wise and loving heart.

Boundaries, Alternative Teaching Strategies, and Structure Scaffold a Child's Learning

NAEYC accreditation standards and many state licensing regulations require programs to use a written curriculum. Leaders can choose from a number of prepared curriculum packages that meet these requirements. *The Creative Curriculum® for Infants, Toddlers & Twos* and *The Creative Curriculum® for Preschool* are well-known purchasable curricula. Written curriculum guides with topical units, lesson plans, and a variety of teaching strategies provide structure and boundaries to a teacher's approach to learning. Any prepared curriculum, however, does not dictate a teacher's actions. Instead, the curriculum provides teachers with options within its framework.

Instructional strategies teachers can use to support children's learning include:

- Encouraging,
- Modeling,
- Demonstrating,
- Acknowledging,
- Creating or adding challenge,
- Providing information, and
- Offering cues or hints to help a child step up to her next level of competency.
  (Bowman, Donovan & Burns 2000, as related by Copple & Bredekamp 2006, 32–33)

Children respond to a wide range of teaching strategies like these. Facilitation, which we have focused primarily on, is one of a number of strategies on Bredekamp's continuum. A significant part of a director's supervisory time with her teachers focuses on helping teachers become artists in the classroom, adding more and more vibrant colors to their palettes.

"Intentional teaching" (Epstein 2006) involves being both aware of and selective about alternative teaching strategies to meet children's differing needs. The intentional teacher is focused on her goals for the children and well-versed in developmentally appropriate practice (DAP). Teachers guide children's learning by intentionally choosing approaches that will work best for the child and the age group. A teacher can encourage children to work in pairs, small teams, or explore as a whole group depending on children's learning needs and developmental levels.

Teachers in many ways are magicians, prepared and ready to pull out their toolkit of strategies to reach each class and child. Written curricula provide a context for teaching creativity to occur. A written curriculum, however, does not tie a teacher's hands or dictate that she walk a narrow path. Teachers are invited to create within the curriculum, adapting to children's curiosity and changing events in their lives.

Play is the child's pathway to learning. Play is the work of the child. Through play, the child learns lifelong skills of inquiry, exploration, and understanding. The child also learns to negotiate, share, and cooperate. Gross motor skills are developed and physical challenges present opportunities to enhance a child's self-esteem and determination. Through relationships formed during play, children develop social and emotional intelligence that will put them in good stead for the rest of their lives. When families fear their children will not do well on academic tests, families can become less willing to support their children's learning through play.

> Science has discovered emotionality's deeper purpose: the timeworn mechanisms of emotion allow two human beings to receive the contents of each other's minds. Emotion is the messenger of love; it is the vehicle that carries every signal from one brimming heart to another. For human beings, feeling deeply is synonymous with being alive.
>
> —T. Lewis et al., *General Theory of Love*

❧ Unrest and the Best of "Teaching to the Test"

Childcare Exchange, for the last fifteen years, has conducted "Insta-poll" surveys on this question: "What do you perceive to be the most serious threats to your organization?"

Early childhood professionals who responded to the poll listed these perceived threats:

1. Shortages of qualified teachers.
2. State of the economy.
3. Competition from the public schools.
4. Decreases in public subsidies.
5. Pressure from parents to teach more academics.

Consider how the fifth threat, "Pressure from parents to teach more academics," relates to Marco and his Mom in the chapter case study. Marco appears to have thrived and learned through play and exploration. Marco's Mom now has a different goal. She wants Marco to perform well on traditional pencil-and-paper testing. She is no longer satisfied with what she perceives to be a play-every-day approach to learning. If you were Marco's teacher, how would you explore this issue with his Mom? What assumptions are being made about what is "good" for Marco, both by his Mom and by you?

As reflected in the Insta-poll, Marco's story is becoming more and more common. Parents insist that their children be readily able to display knowledge of letters and words, numbers, colors, facts. Social-emotional development takes a back seat when traditional teaching methods are valued. When curriculum becomes an either/or topic, either "sit still and memorize" or "learn through play," the child stands to lose. Lillian Katz (2008) reminds us that when curriculum is viewed as either "spontaneous play or formal academic instruction," the emphasis may be off the mark.

Katz explains: "I suggest that when young children engage in projects in which they conduct investigations of significant objects and events around them and for which they have developed the research questions to find out things like how things work, what things are made, or what people around them do to contribute to their well-being, and so forth, their minds are fully engaged. Furthermore, the usefulness and importance of being able to read, write, measure, and count gradually becomes self-evident" (Katz 2008).

Effective Assessment of Young Children

Leaders will be challenged with finding a balance that is best for children and their families. Measurable learning outcomes for young children are becoming commonplace. The following are just a few examples:

In Language and Literacy

- Predicts what will happen next in a story (Colorado).
- Identifies words that rhyme (Ohio).

In Mathematics

- Determines "how many" in sets of five or fewer objects (South Carolina).
- Matches and sorts shapes (Washington State).

In Social-Emotional Development

- Shows increasing abilities to use compromise and discussion in working, playing, and resolving conflicts with peers (Head Start Child Care Framework).

Measurable learning outcomes and developmentally appropriate practices (DAP) are also interconnected with cultural beliefs and practices. Depending on a culture's values, standardized outcomes may or may not be appropriate. For example, in an Asian culture where overt conflict is to be avoided, requiring a child to use discussion when resolving conflicts may not be considered respectful. In collective cultures where being part of a group is valued over individual accomplishment, children may shy away from "standing out" within the group context.

Early childhood leaders often find themselves, both by individual preference and according to prevailing curriculum standards, balancing two curricular goals: loving relationships with measurable outcome testing.

"Take a sounding" (a nautical term for determining the depth of the water) on your preferred approach to curriculum. Do you focus more on the interpersonal relationship between teacher and child? Do you favor being able to measure a child's skills and competencies? Have you already found ways to balance the interpersonal with the objective measure?

Experts generally agree that the assessment of young children has four purposes:

- To plan instruction for individuals and groups.
- To effectively communicate with parents.
- To identify children who may require specialized programs and interventions.
- To provide information for program improvement and accountability. (NAEYC & NAECS/SDE 1991; NEGP 1998, as referenced in Council of Chief State School Officers 2008)

Close early relationships instill a permanent resilience to the degenerative influence of stress, while neglect sensitizes children to those effects.

—**T. Lewis et al.,** *General Theory of Love*

Effective assessment of young children:

- Provides information about child development over time in naturalistic settings.
- Considers development in multiple domains, including health, social, emotional, cognitive, motor, language, literacy, and math.
- Focuses on individual strengths and uniqueness.
- Recognizes and supports different intelligences and learning styles.
- Recognizes that early childhood is a time of the most rapid developmental changes in a person's life.
- Aligns with appropriate early learning standards.
- Is performance, process, and product based.
- Is <u>never</u> used to rank, sort, or penalize children. (Council of Chief State School Officers 2007; SECA 2000)

When considering assessments for young children, realize that assessment is already occurring every day. Examples of appropriate assessment for young children include work samples, teacher observations, checklists and inventories, and parent conferences (SECA 2000). Collected over time, a child's work samples reveal a natural progression of interests and skills. Ongoing written notes about a child's behavior becomes an informal assessment. Assessment for young children is active, ongoing, and dynamic.

You will have ongoing opportunities during your early childhood career to work toward balancing interpersonal with objective measures. Your knowledge as a leader of early childhood growth and development and the curricula that supports that growth will continue to be invaluable.

✳ Learning Organizations

When I walk into lively childcare programs, bustling with enthusiastic children and adults, I join right in on the happiness. When I walk into an early childhood center bogged down with unhappy adults, I fear for the children. We know moods, like colds, are catching. How can negative adults uplift children? In Chapter 8, we looked at many ways in which a leader can promote group well-being and optimism.

Now, we will, in the words of American celebrity chef Emeril Lagasse, "Kick it up a notch!" Massachusetts Institute of Technology professor Dr. Peter Senge (1990) writes about "learning organizations" in his book, *The Fifth Discipline*. In a learning organization or community, everyone grows. No one stops learning just because of status or title. Learning organizations welcome and promote experimentation and innovation.

In the early childcare field, administrators and teachers often think of maximizing children's opportunity for growth and development. What if administrators viewed adult growth and development as equally important? We know children learn more by observing and interacting with their teachers and environments than they can from any lesson plan, no matter how brilliantly conceived that plan might be. Similarly, adults need challenging opportunities and support to grow.

Emotional and social EQ support and maximize everyone's opportunity to learn. How about parents, brothers and sisters, aunts, uncles, and grandparents who accompany their children along the path of growth and development? Might the cooks and maintenance staff members in early childhood programs want to grow, along with vendors and board members?

This is all possible, according to Senge (1990, 4): "[in] organizations where people continually expand their capacity to create the results they truly desire, where new and expansive patterns of thinking are nurtured, where collective aspiration is set free, and where people are continually learning to see the whole together." Learning organizations help us "discover how to tap people's commitment and capacity to learn at *all* levels."

How can you as a leader cocreate a learning organization? To "cocreate" you involve all members of your organization, both internal and external customers (Chapter 15). These five "disciplines" that set learning organizations apart provide pathways:

1. Systems thinking.
2. Personal mastery.
3. Mental models.
4. Building shared vision.
5. Team learning.

Each discipline is "concerned with a shift of mind from seeing parts to seeing wholes, from seeing people as helpless reactors to seeing them as active participants in shaping their reality, from reacting to the present to creating the future" (Senge 1990, 69). I have yet to see a bored child in the presence of actively inquisitive adults.

> When you ask people about what it is like being part of a great team, what is most striking is the meaningfulness of the experience. People talk about being part of something larger than themselves, of being connected, of being generative. It becomes quite clear that, for many, their experiences as part of truly great teams stand out as singular periods of life lived to the fullest. Some spend the rest of their lives looking for ways to recapture that spirit.
>
> **—Peter Senge,** *The Fifth Discipline*

⚒ Director as Environment and Curriculum

What an idea! Picture this: as directors and staff learn and grow, so does the program. When leaders "make it OK" to make mistakes, everyone gets permission to take risks. When administrators scaffold the growth of every child, family, and staff member, they support their own learning. Talk about modeling! Leaders of early childhood programs continuously create curricula and strategies for both adult and child development.

Let the pendulum swing as it may. Some things are timeless. Building relational environments that celebrate growth and learning will never go out of style.

Reflection Questions

1. Reread the case study about Marco and his Mom on page 188. This case raises the challenge of honoring parents' desires ("teaching to the test") and at the same time being true to early childhood theory (supporting a child's natural curiosity). Reflect on the parent's position: what are all the reasons Mom wants Marco to "pass the tests." Now reflect on Marco's learning through play and his love of the out-of-doors. Write a dialogue between Marco's Mom and the program director or lead teacher on how they would work together on this topic.

2. Reflect on your favorite places and spaces when you were little. What were those places like for you? How did they enchant or enrich you? Did you feel safe there? In what way did those places contribute to your learning? Design a model and/or describe an early childhood program space (indoors or out) that re-creates the best of those environments you experienced as a child.

3. Take a look at the list of innovators in early childhood theory, pp. 188–191. Choose the person whose theories most appeal to you. Investigate more about this person, his or her life, and teachings. See if you can find out more about the culture and times in which this innovator lived. Choose three to five aspects of this person's life, times, and theories that fascinate you most. Write a profile (description) introducing this person to your class.

Team Projects

1. Return to Jamilah's story in Chapter 3 (page 28). Discuss and identify the barriers Jamilah faces as well as how she might achieve her vision. Using your emotional and social EQ, develop strategies for Jamilah to use with each of the barriers she faces. Present these strategies to your class.

2. Go on a treasure hunt of early childhood programs in your locale to discover classroom and/or playground designs that are imaginative, unique, and inspire children to wonder, grow, and learn. With permission, take photographs and interview staff about how children and teachers use the space. Identify the underlying reasons that these designs "work" for children. Prepare and present a visual report on the treasures you discovered.

3. Many curriculum packages, like the Creative Curriculum, are available for programs to purchase, adopt, and use. Explore at least three of these options: what is available and how do *users* feel about the curriculum? Present to your class samples of different curricula, while leading a discussion about the pros and cons of curriculum packages.

Bibliography

Bowman, B., and E.K. Moore, eds. 2006. *School readiness and social emotional development: Perspectives in cultural diversity.* Washington, DC: National Black Child Development Institute.

Carlson, F.M. 2006. *Essential touch: Meeting the needs of young children.* Washington, DC: NAEYC.

Carter, M. 2007. Making your environment "the third teacher."*Exchange* (July–August): 22–26.

Ceppi, G., and M. Zini, eds. 1998. *Children, spaces, relations: Metaproject for an environment for young children.* Reggio, Emilia, Italy: Reggio Children.

Copple, C., and S. Bredekamp. 2006. *Basics of developmentally appropriate practice: An introduction for teachers of children 3 to 6 .* Washington, DC: NAEYC.

Council of Chief State School Officers. 2008. *Building an assessment system to support successful early learners: Assessing child learning and developmental outcomes.* Washington DC: CCSSO. http://www.ccsso.org/projects/scass/projects/early_childhood_education_assessment_consortium/publications_and_products/3002.cfm.

Curtis, D., and M. Carter. 2003. *Designs for living and learning: Transforming early childhood environments.* St Paul, MN: Redleaf Press.

Day, M., and R. Parlakian. 2004. *How culture shapes social-emotional development: Implications for practice in infant-family programs.* Washington, DC: Zero to Three.

Eggers-Pierola, C. 2005. *Connections and commitments: A Latino-based framework for early childhood education.* Portsmouth, NH: Heinemann.

Elliott, S., ed. 2008. *The outdoor playspace naturally: For children birth to five years.* Sydney, Australia: Pademelon Press.

Epstein, A. 2006. *The intentional teacher: Choosing the best strategies for young children's learning.* Washington, DC: National Association for the Education of Young Children.

Gonzalez-Mena, J. 2008. *Foundations of early childhood: Teaching children in a diverse society* (4th ed.). New York: McGraw-Hill.

Greenman, J. 2006. *Caring places, learning spaces.* Redmond, WA: Exchange Press.

Katz, Lilian. 2008. Another look at what young children should be learning. *Exchange* (March): 53–56.

Keeler, R. 2008. Living willow huts—Part 2: Constructing a living willow hut. *Exchange* (January–February): 78–80.

Koralek, D., ed. 2005. Environments. *Young Children* (May).

Lewis, T., F. Amini, and R. Lannon. 2000. *General theory of love.* New York: Vintage.

Mooney, C.G. 2000. *Theories of childhood*. St. Paul, MN: Redleaf Press.

Raffanello, D. 2005. Tending the garden: What gardening can tell us about running our centers. *Exchange* (March–April): 12–14.

Rogers, F. 1994. *You are special: Words of wisdom from America's most beloved neighbor*. New York: Viking Adult.

Senge, P. 1990. *The fifth discipline.* New York: Doubleday.

Southern Early Childhood Association. 2000. *Assessing development and learning in young children.* Little Rock, AR: SECA. http.//www.southernearlychildhood.org/position_assessment.html.

Stoecklin, V.L. 2005. Creating outdoor spaces kids love. *Professional Connections* 8 (42): 1–5.

Tarr, P. 2004. Consider the walls. *Young Children* (May): 88–92.

Thomas, J. 2007. Early connections with nature support children's development of science understanding. *Exchange* (November–December): 57–60.

VanGilder, P., A.Wike, and S. Murphy. 2007. Early foundations: Music and movement in the outdoor classroom. *Exchange* (November–December): 53–56.

Web Resources

About Learning: 12 Theories of Education
www.funderstanding.com/about_learning.cfm
Center for Creative Play
www.cfcp.org/
National Program for Playground Safety
www.playgroundsafety.org
NAEYC: "Yeah, But's" That Keep Teachers from Embracing an Active Curriculum
www.journal.naeyc.org/btj/200507/03Geist.asp
Reggio Emilia Approach: Environment-as-Teacher
www.brainy-child.com/article/reggioemilia.html

Marketing and Development: If You Build It They Will Come

Learning Goals

As you study this chapter, you can look forward to reaching these learning goals:

1. Discuss the value of making a program attractive "from the outside in."

2. Determine what marketing is in early childhood education.

3. Identify procedures to assess your market.

4. Summarize how to form and support a multicultural workforce.

5. Plan ways to increase staff retention.

6. Develop effective fund-raising methods and activities.

If I were looking for a childcare provider, I'd start with a short tryout. Then I'd listen to what he or she could tell me about my child. Does the account of their time together suggest alertness, interest, and those all-important 3C's: caring, confidence and common sense?

—**Fred Rogers**

Even the highest towers begin from the ground.

—**Chinese proverb**

Case Study: Can Director Milagros Work Miracles?

Milagros has just been named director of a Head Start program, housed in an old brick mill building where shoes were once made. Her program is one of ten social service agencies in the building. The building itself sorely needs a makeover. Cold as a fortress, the old mill looks harsh and impersonal. Milagros wants to welcome and honor the diverse families who come to her center.

What steps can she take to change the dour impression people get when they see the old mill?

Have you said to yourself, "That will never happen" or "That person will never change" or "Over my dead body!"? I have.

When I was younger, I boarded an underground train from West to East Berlin, beneath the foreboding barrier of the Berlin Wall. I eyed somber Soviet soldiers standing guard with bazooka guns at abandoned subway stops along the way, as my palms sweated and my heart leapt into my throat. The customs inspectors, also underground, took what felt like a day and a night to allow us entry.

When at last I climbed into the East Berlin daylight, my vision was darkened again by destruction in every street block. Bullet and mortar holes stung buildings. Piles of rock and rubble crowded alleyways. Soldiers' heels clicked sharply on cobblestone streets. Only during a quiet respite in the one café open to Westerners could I shake the weight of the wall. On that day, I could not imagine the Berlin Wall could fall.

A few years later, the unimaginable happened. Piece by piece, the wall fell, peacefully. As I watched televised scenes of long-separated family members from both sides embracing, I promised myself I would expect miracles. If that wall could fall, others can too.

Examples of falling walls abound all around us. Walt Disney's larger-than-life dream became a reality because of his deep beliefs. "If you can dream it, you can do it," Disney famously said. "Always remember that this whole thing was started with a dream and a mouse." The actor Kevin Costner dreamed of transforming his cornfield into a baseball diamond in the movie *Field of Dreams* (1989). Against considerable odds, he built the field. Players came, fulfilling the movie's premise: "If you build it, they will come."

In this chapter, we will confront "stuck" beliefs in our field and figure out creative ways to help obstacles crumble and dreams come true.

✳ Getting "Unstuck"

Stuck beliefs are myths, with a shard of truth, that hold us back, for example:

- We should never brag about our program's strengths.
- We don't have money to improve our buildings and grounds.
- We've tried, but we can't attract diverse staff or families.
- Retaining staff is impossible. We'll lose our best staff to the public schools.
- Who has time for fund-raising!

Not every director believes these myths. On "bad hair days" (those "shadow" times, according to Carl Jung, Chapter 3), however, worries can bring even the most positive director down. Rather than let debilitating myths sneak up on a down day, directors can face these myths down in advance. Every myth contains just enough truth to be

> My great concern is not whether you have failed, but whether you are content with your failure.
>
> **—Abraham Lincoln**

convincing. For example, bragging offends many people. Sharing good news differs from bragging, especially when that news applauds families and staff.

Picture the outside of the building you are in now. What do you recall about the building? What impression did the building give you? Did you feel welcomed or put off even before you entered the building? What would you change about the outside of the building to make it more welcoming? If you need to, step outside the building for a second look.

The power of optimism plays out neurologically and spiritually. Studies show optimists possess better memory, envision more possibilities, are more competent at problem solving, and live longer, happier lives than pessimists. Optimists, willing to take risks for the better, forge new connections between brain cells. A sense of humor and perspective about failure are an optimistic leader's tools.

When we shut down possibilities, we squash hope. The only way to see what's on the horizon is to look up. The saying "One door closes so another can open" is a useful management mantra. Are you ready to discover possibilities, build new brain pathways and knock down moldy brick walls?

Myth #1: "Blowing Your Own Horn" Is Unnecessary in Early Childhood Education

First impressions count. Our ever-vigilant spindle cells sum up new situations in a snap. "I like it" or "I'm out of here," they tell us. Although spindle cells rush to judgment more rapidly about people than about things, human neurons snap to all judgments in less than a second. That is barely enough time for our professional perspective to click in.

The moment a family first spies the outside of an early childcare program, that family member, every adult and child, forms a judgment for better or worse about what they will find inside. The *curb appeal*, or sensory first impression a program exudes, inspires potential clients to drive in or drive by. A director and her team can choose ways to showcase a program as beautiful on both the outside and the inside.

Directors have told me, "We don't have money to invest in unnecessary items like landscaping or a new sign out front, when we are dedicating our funds to quality care within our walls." Other directors have said, "We don't own our building. We have to accept what the landlord dictates." Let's explode these myths.

Imagine all the ways in which you could "make over" the front of an early childhood building with less than $100.

Myth #2: We Don't Have Enough Money to Improve Our Grounds

The curb appeal of a program communicates more about what goes on inside the program than you might think. For that reason, paying attention to how the program is presented, even before a person enters the building, is important. Anyone who crosses the threshold should do so with pride. Makeovers are popular these days. When you think about making over the outside of a childcare center, imagine:

- With children, planting marigolds, sunflowers, morning glories, and snapdragons at the base of the program's sign. All of these flowers grow easily from inexpensive packs of seeds.
- Inviting a local landscaping company to make over the front yard. Post a sign thanking them for their expertise and generosity.
- Sponsoring a grounds "beautification day" with clean-up activities and prizes for families.
- Enlisting discount stores that sell outdoor plants to contribute new plants each season.

- Holding a competition among staff and/or families for creative and inexpensive makeover ideas. Choose, use, and reward the best.
- Erecting a standing bulletin board protected by an acrylic plastic sheet to display children's artwork for passersby to admire.
- Tying brightly colored balloons and banners to the outdoor sign to welcome new families or celebrate children's birthdays.

Try this: Add more creative and inexpensive ideas to the list. Notice the "bang for the buck." Little money but big hearts make for great innovations.

Marketing Isn't Just for New Cars

Marketing is paying attention to the needs of the people being served and how directors can distinguish their program in the marketplace. Marketing is presenting a program to families in an inviting, welcoming manner that indicates how they will be treated. Effective marketing also shows that families can entrust their children to a program. Curb appeal is part of a program's marketing strategy. Even before they walk through the door, families want to anticipate good things.

Marketing in early childhood education is not a glitzy, cosmetic, or shallow affair. Marketing communicates, with and without words, a program's uniqueness. The marketing adage "Distinguish yourself in the marketplace" urges directors to share their program's special strengths with the world. Even if a program has a waiting list from here to the Galapagos Islands, the program still needs marketing. Sharing the good news about a program uplifts everyone. Everyone can point with pride to the building, grounds, and what lies within.

Write three ways in which you want your program to be special. Think of what you might offer that not every other program offers.

Marketing is a creative opportunity to invoke one's emotional and social intelligence. Have you ever felt uncomfortable when someone picked you out of a crowd, presented you with an award, or asked you to be the center of attention? If so, you are not alone. Introverts, 51 percent of us (see Chapter 3), aren't the only ones who avoid being put on the spot.

Many of us were taught that drawing attention to ourselves is inappropriate. Often, I proudly watch early childhood professionals receive awards. They run like gazelles off the stage, saying, "I didn't do anything special," or "The team deserves this, not me."

Whatever your personal beliefs are about modesty and "not blowing your own horn," ask yourself, "How can we communicate our program's specialness to others?" Your community (families, children, staff, neighborhood, town, or city) benefit from the message: our program is a great place for children. I invite you to let go of the myth that promoting programs is unnecessary and immodest. Consider marketing not as blowing your own horn, but as a functional business strategy for the vitality of a program.

❧ Marketing 101: It's a Plan

Marketing strategy is formulating a plan to present a program's uniqueness and strengths to others. "Distinguishing ourselves" is setting a program apart by communicating our special vision, core values, purpose, and offerings. Distinguishing ourselves tells others what unique qualities, programs, clientele, and/or staffing make the program "one of a kind." All early childhood programs offer care and education to young children. In what original ways will your program provide quality care? Communicating this message can make or break a program's financial security.

> Most executives cannot articulate the objective, scope, and advantage of their business in a simple statement. If they can't, neither can anyone else.
>
> —David J. Collins and Michael G. Rukstad

> I am finding more and more of my calls originate from the Web. Do you have a website? If so list it everywhere you can. Even if you don't have a website . . . do a Google search for "free childcare advertising" and list your name everywhere you can.
>
> —Sherrie Silverman

> Clarity about what makes the firm distinctive is what most helps employees understand how they can contribute.
>
> —David J. Collins and Michael G. Rukstad

A marketing strategy is creating a plan to share your good news with people who need to hear it. Harrington and Tjan (2008) offer these three components of effective marketing plans:

1. *Map out your real market.*
2. *Understand your customers' objectives and work flow.*
3. *Develop products that provide users with what they value most.*

Here's how this business terminology translates to the business of early childhood.

> Marketing creates a targeted message to a particular audience who wants to hear that message.
>
> **—Larry Thorner,** director

Map Out Your Real Market

To map out a program's real market, directors must take an objective look at the families they serve and envision those they might serve. Start by studying the families already enrolled. Your goal is to discover who currently finds the program attractive. Software applications, such as Microsoft Word or Excel, offer useful tools for this kind of study.

Consider current family demographics. Demographics include income level, employment, location in the community, community involvements, ethnicity, size of family, and modes of transportation. Directors can make it easy to tally this data by creating a chart or a spreadsheet (a page broad enough to easily pick out important data) with several categories, such as the ones listed in Table 13.1. Next, fill in the chart with information about each family.

As directors tally this information, they will notice commonalities. For example, are most wage earners employed at the same or similar businesses? Are only certain neighborhoods represented? What percentage of families uses their own vehicles instead of public transportation? From this data, a program's "typical family" will emerge.

A similar market analysis of a program's employees, particularly the teaching staff, produces valuable information. This time, create a second spreadsheet and tally data about employees by using the questions in Table 13.2.

This time, data about the "typical staff" member will emerge. This is the employee who chose your program, perhaps over others. This profile of current employees can alert leaders to markets they tapped into for hiring that may still not be fully tapped. Look for trends (indications of possible directions you can go with this information).

TABLE 13.1

Family Demographics

- Where do our families live in our community?
- How far do they travel to our program?
- What transportation do they use? What transportation options are available to them?
- What is their income level?
- How many children are in each family, and what is the likelihood of each having additional children?
- Where do the wage earners work?
- What jobs do the wage earners perform?
- How did the families hear about your program?
- What other community organizations are families involved with (religious, civic, etc.)?

TABLE 13.2

Staff Demographics

- What neighborhoods do these staff members represent?
- What transportation do they use?
- In what other community organizations are they active members?
- How many children do staff have, and are likely to have?
- How did they hear about your program?
- What factors led them to accept employment with you?
- Who composes their family?
- What is the income level of the family overall?
- What ethnicities and/or cultures are represented in your staff?

Now that the director has valuable marketing information about future families and employees, she needs to locate people who fit the description of the typical family and employee. Employees are often a program's best recruiters. As a director, you may want to offer incentives to current employees who refer new hires who stay with you for six months or more. Word-of-mouth is a highly effective mode of advertising. Sharing with families and staff that you expect to have openings, and would like their recommendations, can be an effective marketing tool.

Note that leaders are not "stuck" with only one group of families or one source of staff members. Marketing surveys point the way to new markets, as well as identifying your current market. You will have options. Who else could you reach out to, and who else might add depth and variety to the program?

Understand Your Customers' Objectives and Work Flow

Stepping back to see the big picture is valuable. In the business of early childhood, "understand your customers' objectives and work flow" translates to "understand your families' needs and the demands upon them." Marketing information, when tallied, may surprise directors. Or, directors may know the program's families and employees well, and the data reinforces their expectations. Completing this marketing survey exercise with board members enlarges the circle of information and involvement.

Imagine you are a director and have gathered valuable marketing information from your surveys. You have identified your current "real market," those people who have selected you and your services. Knowing the profile of your typical family and employee tells you your "current market niche." That niche is the segment of families and staff members to whom your program appeals. With this information, you can target similar families and potential employees. The likelihood is good that you will find a match if you advertise to people who are similar to your current market niche.

Regularly ask families:
- How do you feel about our current services?
- What else do you need?

Effective program leaders monitor how well they are meeting the needs of current families. They routinely ask, "How're we doing?" They hold exit interviews with families who age out of the program or otherwise choose to leave. Directors ask clients how they feel about the services, what worked best and what they would change or add. Highly valuable marketing information is gained from exit interviews.

Leaders don't need to wait for an exit interview, however, to gather this important information. They can survey families often—formally, by written questionnaires, and informally, as families are greeted each day. They can also provide a suggestion box, check it daily, and make every effort to respond within a day to each person who made a suggestion. If you do this, word will get out that you take suggestions seriously.

Once a director has identified her program's typical family and staff profiles, she also has identified potential or target markets. Target markets fall into two categories:

1. Expanding a program's customer base to additional clients who fit your typical family and typical staff profiles; and,
2. Reaching out to people and groups you would like to serve who differ from your current typical profiles.

Should a director wish to diversify her program or reach out to additional families and staff, the marketing data will reveal who is not receiving services. If a program's families and staff are all of one ethnicity, cultural group, or locality, reaching out to other groups might become the new marketing "target." Directors and staff can devise innovative ways to connect with different communities they would like to serve.

Develop Products That Provide Users What They Value Most

Continuously asking current customers (both families and staff) to give feedback helps directors understand what customers value most. Administrators can ask, "What do you like best about our program?" and "What else might we offer that would matter to you?" In Chapter 14, we will look at family-friendly practices. Family-friendly practices include efforts to make life easier for families, such as parents' date night; sleepovers for children; providing nutritious, affordable meals-to-go; hair cutting services; and connections to "sick child" care family providers.

When a leader asks families what they need, she must be open to all suggestions. By the same token, she does not want to represent that she takes orders like a waitress. Effective directors let people know they plan to improve services whenever feasible, but for financial or staffing reasons, or because an idea discriminates against certain groups, not every suggestion can be implemented. Setting realistic expectations pays off later.

Directors can also anticipate the customers' needs, a total quality management (TQM) principle (more about this in Chapter 15). Anticipating the customers' needs is thinking of something helpful to the customer even before the customer thinks of it. For example, imagine a director who provides one pickup time a month when the program's cook demonstrates how to make yummy, nutritious snacks for children. Families will welcome this instruction, especially when the cook offers samples to taste and take home. Leaders know immediately if an innovation meets parents' needs: contented sighs will echo down the hallways.

Let's consider what to do if your marketing strategy targets diversifying your staff and your clients, and you are scratching your head on how to do that.

✄ Developing Your Staff

Myth #3: We'll Never Be Able to Diversify Our Staff

Dr. Debra Sullivan (2003), author of *Learning to Lead*, walks the talk. When she and her management team decided to learn Spanish to serve families better, she arranged lunchtime Spanish language classes. When employees felt their cultural practices weren't fully heard or valued, Dr. Sullivan made sure everyone's approaches were honored. For example, when Asian staff members viewed direct problem-solving methods as uncomfortably

We all have misinformation about people different and like ourselves, and we're all exposed to stereotypes. Prejudice is like smog: no one says, "I'm a smog-breather," but if you live in a smoggy place, it's hard to avoid breathing it. When I hear someone say, "There's not a prejudiced bone in my body," I say, look again. Because there are bones in there that you may not want, but they're there.

—**Beverly Daniel Tatum**

aggressive, she took time to work through subtler, less confrontational approaches. When men grew tired of women's need to "over-process and debrief everything," Dr. Sullivan, with humor, amended her ways. She is clear we model our vision. Her program was and is richly diverse. The message got out: Working here is a great place for everyone of every culture.

The director's ethnicity and cultural mores can establish her program's climate. Author Beverly Tatum Daniel (1997) reminds us that in powerful ways, stated and unstated, we communicate what culture is dominant (*Why Are All the Black Kids Sitting Together in the Cafeteria?*). Just as moods are catching in organizations, so too are messages about how to act and what to value.

The ethnicity or culture powerful enough to set the standard for behavior in the organization is the "dominant" one. For example, many black early childhood professionals indicate respect by addressing adults as Ms. or Mr. I learned while working with early childhood professionals of the Creek and Cherokee tribes that the term "Indian" can be preferable to "Native American." In a predominantly Anglo organization, staff members may be expected to send thank-you notes for any gift received. In Mexican American early childhood organizations, looking directly into another person's eyes may indicate disrespect. Paying attention to indicators of respect makes a difference, especially if the dominant organizational ways differ from your own.

The problem with a dominant organizational culture is that people of other heritages and practices can feel invisible, underappreciated, or rejected. Homogeneous organizations in which everyone looks the same are the result. This leads some directors to throw up their hands and say, "How can I attract staff of other cultures if they don't see anyone who looks like them here?"

We know early childhood professionals are uncomfortable with conflict. Tatum (1997, 193) takes this issue on by saying, "Some people say there is too much talk about race and racism in the United States. I say that there is not enough . . . We need to continually break the silence about racism whenever we can. We need to talk about it at home, at school, in our houses of worship, in our workplaces, in our community groups . . . It means meaningful, product dialogue to raise consciousness and lead to effective action and social change." If teachers can have these important conversations with children, adults in our programs can have these conversations with each other.

A director can do a great deal to foster a multicultural environment that attracts new families and staff.

Step 1 is to tell the truth: "Houston, we have a problem." If marketing assessments show that staff and families are homogeneous, this issue can be addressed with the board, staff, and, as appropriate, with families. Everyone benefits from a richly diverse environment. Children especially, who will inhabit a world far more ethnically diverse than California is today, need to get to know their neighbors, regardless of whether they live across town in the *barrio*, the penthouse, or "the hood."

Step 2 is to work together to investigate ways to diversify programs in far more than a cosmetic way. Leaders can devote some staff meeting time to brainstorming possibilities. They can bring in professional advisors or community experts to share ideas. Each staff member can be asked to take responsibility for finding at least one effective way to bring more diversity into the program. A director's passion for multiculturalism makes a significant impact on program diversity.

Recall how Dr. Sullivan and her staff learned Spanish to meet the needs of their program's children. Her team made the commitment *together* to become Spanish speakers. Imagine the difference this makes to families for whom Spanish is their mother tongue.

With your classmates or colleagues, make a plan for how to diversify programs. What steps will you need to take? Leaders often go through this same type of process

All of us know how important it is to fight social injustice, and all of us know just how difficult it is to gather the courage and strength to make personal sacrifices in order to make the world better for someone else. But all people have that courage and strength if they look deep within themselves.

—Valora Washington

Different groups have different needs, and people of color have a strong need for connection and empowerment. What you see in the cafeterias are affinity groups: separate "spaces" that facilitate positive identity exploration, where people can pose questions and process issues.

—Beverly Daniel Tatum

TABLE 13.3

Percentage of Prekindergarten Children Ages 3–5 Who Were Enrolled in Center-Based Early Childhood Care and Education Programs, by Child and Family Characteristics: Selected Years, 1991–2005

Characteristic	1991	1993	1995	1996	1999	2001	2005
Total	53	53	55	55	60	56	57
Poverty status[1]							
Poor	44	43	45	44	51	47	47
Non-poor	56	56	59	59	62	59	60
Race/ethnicity[2]							
White	54	54	57	57	60	59	59
Black	58	57	60	65	73	64	66
Hispanic	39	43	37	39	44	40	43
Mother's education							
Less than high school	32	33	35	37	40	38	35
High school diploma or equivalent	46	43	48	49	52	47	49
Some college, including vocational/ technical	60	60	57	58	63	62	56
Bachelor's degree or higher	72	73	75	73	74	70	73

U.S. Department of Education, National Center for Education Statistics. 2007. *The Condition of Eduction 2007* (NCES 2007-064), Indicator 2 [**http://nces.ed.gov/programs/coe/2007/section1/table/asp?tableID=662**].

with their boards and family advisory teams. If, in the end, only one effective change is made, a program has still begun to change in a meaningful way.

According to the U.S. Department of Education, National Center for Education Statistics (2007), the children in early childhood programs are already more representative of future ethnic diversity than our employees. (See Table 13.3.)

Over the years, I have learned not to expect people who differ from me to come to me. I must go to them, and go willing to learn and grow in ways that are not always comfortable. I listen and when I "get it wrong," I immediately apologize, ready to listen more deeply. At first, I may well hear anger and rage. Anyone who has been held down, unseen, and spat on has every right to his or her feelings.

Remember that the majority of individuals take things personally? As I listen, I remind myself of the Q-TIP principle, "Quit taking it personally" and listen from the heart. This is a spiritual process, wherein I rely upon the support of a power greater than myself to keep the faith. As Dr. Maureen Walker said (2001, 8):

> The path to relational healing leads us on a journey fraught with risk and imbued with promise. It is a journey of courage and faith: the courage to be mindful and to grieve, to risk letting go of old relational images that function to *contain* our anxieties, in hopes of discovering and enlarging our capacity for richer authenticity. The path to relational healing invites us to enter into conflict with faith in our human possibilities and with desire for the emergence of something new.

Along the way, by listening and asking honest questions, I hear about the individual's experience, while learning about her cultural experience. For me, this is a lifelong passion and process. The moral of my story is this: Step outside your comfort zone. Go on a treasure hunt.

The classroom—not the trench—is the frontier of freedom, now and forevermore.

—Lyndon Baines Johnson

When leaders grow a multicultural organization, they need to do everything they can to "run interference" (deal with bias in advance) before a new team member arrives. Being the only one of a particular ethnicity in an organization can be overwhelming. Each new employee can be assigned a "buddy," someone who is open-minded, empathetic, and demonstrates ample EQ and social EQ. Directors can prepare staff in advance by educating them on essentials about the new staff member's culture. Leaders cocreate an environment of trustful risk taking, wherein staff are encouraged to share their fears and hopes while working together to create a welcoming environment.

As a director, your first effort may be the hardest. With each subsequent effort to diversify, you will build upon your experience. If your team pulls together in support of growth, your new staff members will put the word out that your program is a haven for teachers and families. In the end, you and your staff have walked the talk right down the path toward understanding.

Practical Ways to Grow a Multicultural Staff

Many national groups offer tips for diversifying your staff. For example, the National Education Association (NEA) recommends:

1. *Recruit teachers from support staff.* Research has found that programs that help paraeducators become teachers offer a tremendous opportunity to increase the supply of ethnic minority teachers. This pool of school employees (teaching assistants, clerks, and others with or without baccalaureate degrees) are largely minorities. They are generally committed to education and tend to stay for long periods in the profession. Many are more mature individuals with extensive classroom experience, have roots in their communities, and are accustomed to working with challenging students.
2. *Look to high school students.* Early recruiting, getting high school students interested in teaching, is another suggestion. The NEA recommends identifying students through career surveys, counseling, motivational workshops, summer college preparatory courses, and the promise of financial aid.
3. *Use programs offering support* on increasing staff diversity including (Gloria Chaika 2004):
   • The *Hispanic Association of Colleges and Universities,* which represents 275 colleges and universities with high Hispanic enrollments, offers advice to school districts interested in recruiting Hispanic graduates.
   • The *National Alliance of Black School Educators* and *Historically Black Colleges and Universities* do the same for the African-American community.
4. *Work with what you have,* especially if your staff is homogeneous, all from the same background or culture. Louise Dermond-Sparks (2005), advocate for multicultural and anti-bias in early childhood education, has recently taken on the challenge of working with all-white groups. Here is one of her practical tips that helps children and adults in homogeneous settings:

   Invite individuals from various racial/ethnic groups in your community to interact with children on a regular basis. Ongoing face-to-face contact is the best way to break down barriers, recognize similarities, and see differences as enriching rather than as uncomfortable or strange (20).

Myth #4: Staff Retention Is Impossible

Staff retention is not only essential, but also a pleasure. We yearn to be part of a loving community. Early childhood programs can be the most loving of learning communities.

If each staff member knows how important she is to the team, she feels valued. Employees who help create the program's mission are personally dedicated to making that mission come true. As a leader, exercise every bit of your EQ and social EQ to learn about your staff, anticipate their needs, support their growth, and build a lasting team.

Remember the research about staff motivation? Money isn't the answer. Working "on purpose" is. If a teacher is passionate about what her center stands for, she will stay for years. If a teacher feels the director's respect, support, and appreciation, she will not leave. If a teacher can fulfill her own professional purpose while furthering the program's mission, she will stay. She will also inspire others to join the team.

The relationship that directors build with each staff member determines a staff member's longevity. The dedication a leader invests into building a team determines the loyalty of the team. Coming back on an Amtrak train after working near New York City, I engaged in a spirited conversation with two men in my compartment, one a health care executive and the other a well-known New England businessman and television personality. I asked them, "What's the secret to keeping your best employees?" The men responded in a heartbeat, "Trust your people, respect them, and be loyal to them. They, in turn, will be loyal to you."

Established practices of staff retention include (J.M. Klinkner, D. Riley, & M.A. Roach 2005, 95):

1. Staff who have a strong personal commitment to children and families are more likely to stay in a program.
2. A distinct, well-defined program philosophy and goals encourage professional commitment, especially when joint staff effort is involved in their development.
3. Opportunities to share ideas and support each other personally and professionally—formally through mentor teams and staff meetings and informally through social events and places to gather/relax—strengthen staff relationships.
4. Effective communication among staff and between staff, management, and families is critical.
5. Meaningful involvement in decision making improves staff morale, job satisfaction, and commitment.
6. Where staff regularly feel respect and appreciation and experience communication of both, healthy climates thrive.

Let me tell you about Director Marge from Connecticut. An active community member, she volunteered in soup kitchens, built Habitat for Humanity homes, and taught Sunday school. Everyone liked Marge and her preschool. She hired parents as teachers' aides and supported them as they completed their early childhood degrees. Marge held an annual staff retreat where community members volunteered services like massages and pedicures, and with meals cooked by center families. People sang, laughed, shared stories, and looked forward to having fun together. Over the years, "children" who had long since "graduated" from Marge's program asked if they could come back and work there. Marge never had much money. She had enough EQ and social EQ to stretch from here to the North Pole. Marge's program is a model for staff retention.

It's not the big things that kill us; it's the little things. Little things we do every day make all the difference. Directors can be endlessly creative about ways to recognize and thank teachers. Surprises like "gotcha" notes (caught you doing something great) in a teacher's box, creamy lotions and spicy gels in the staff bathroom, and handing out donated gift certificates at staff meetings all cheer a teacher's day.

Surprises work best. Directors do well to remember that a surprise can't be repeated. A director in Virginia called me, frantic that her staff expected a bigger and

The most productive form of director feedback to staff is immediate acknowledgment of a job well done

—Joan M. Klinkner, Dave Riley, and Mary A. Roach

TABLE 13.4

Little Gifts for Teachers

For more ways to reward teachers and other team members, consider these inexpensive, personal ideas (Thoughtful gifts for teachers 2008):

- A night at the movies: video store certificate, microwave popcorn, bottle of lemonade or favorite soft drinks, wrapped in the film section of the newspaper.
- Pasta dinner: a basket of specially shaped pasta, pasta sauce, fresh Italian bread, and a small chunk of Parmesan cheese with a simple grater.
- Homemade mix: all the ingredients for the teacher's favorite cookies (sprinkles, chocolate chips, icing) or pancakes (dry mix and small bottle of syrup), along with a pretty mixing bowl and spoon from a local discount store.
- Gift basket for the classroom pet (if the teacher is using her own money for pet supplies), including food, treats, toys, shavings.
- Make note cards using rubber stamps. Attach a special pen.
- Gift certificates to craft stores and other shops the teacher frequents for special supplies.
- Disposable camera with a frame for the pictures.
- Afternoon-off certificate when you or a floater will cover the classroom.
- Aprons or smocks to wear for messy activities, with teacher's name stenciled on.
- Flower bulbs (narcissus, amaryllis, hyacinth), glass "stones," and a pretty pot in which to grow the bulbs.
- A floater for the classroom at pick up time to allow teachers to have more in-depth conversation time with families.

bigger holiday banquet each year: What could she do this year to top last year! Keep your surprises fresh to avoid building unrealistic expectations of entitlement.

Make no mistake about it: being an advocate for excellent salary and benefit packages for early childhood professionals is also important. Director Lucinda e-mailed me about the "fantastic" benefits package she negotiated for her staff, after getting the staff's input. The staff didn't get everything on their wish list, but knowing that Lucinda was "going to bat for them" made a difference.

Staff retention in a word is social EQ. Relationships are golden. Keeping each relationship revitalized and dynamic is the greatest predictor of staff retention (Table 13.4). As a leader, strive for the long view, step up to the balcony for perspective, pick your battles, and maintain an "attitude of gratitude." Leaders exercise courage when they hold staff accountable for unprofessional behavior. They use EQ when they say good-bye to nonproductive team members. Your team will notice each battle you fight for quality, both outside and inside of yourself.

Case Study: Pessimistic Annie

Annie is discouraged she will never find enough qualified staff. She fears her best teachers will accept offers with better pay from the public schools. Annie admits she is behind the times when it comes to advertising online to fill teaching positions. How would you use your EQ to help Annie work on her attitude and her competencies?

✇ Developing Your Clients

Myth #5: We Need to Hire a Professional Fund-Raiser

Roger Neugebauer, founding editor of *Child Care Exchange,* surveyed over 100 early childhood programs to find out what makes fund-raising efforts successful or unsuccessful. When the surveys were assessed, Roger created "Keys to Fundraising Success" (2007, 104–106):

1. *Define your purpose:* Be clear on your intention for the fund-raiser. Let that intention motivate volunteers.
2. *Set a goal:* A specific dollar amount sets a measurable standard that people can rally around.
3. *Know the audience:* Are you likely to have individual donors? Will you need to approach organizations and businesses or both? Know the financial means of your audience and their history of giving.
4. *Make it fun:* Choose an activity that people will look forward to and get excited about, something that will take them out of their ordinary day and bring some laughter and good times.
5. *Build on strengths:* Capitalize on the skills and talents of your staff and volunteers.
6. *Look for repeaters:* When a project has been successful the first time, repeat it and you won't have to worry about "reinventing the wheel" each time.
7. *Be cost effective:* The return on time invested equals expense incurred subtracted from total income divided by the total number of hours spent by staff and volunteers on the project.
8. *Publicize aggressively:* Start with being clear on what your "product" is (what you are selling/offering), whether it is a chance to win something or support outright for your program. Get the "right message to the right people."
9. *Maximize publicity:* Use the fund-raiser to inform people about your program and how special it is. Include bulleted information on your program in the publicity.
10. *Thank contributors:* Contact everyone who helped. Let them know how much you raised and how their contribution will make a difference. Written notices on stationery unique to your program work best.

To these keys, Kathy Hines recommends that directors ask donors to say why they decided to contribute (2007, 109). Identifying what motivates each donor is valuable. Is she particularly invested in helping special needs children? Does the donor want to improve business in the area by ensuring quality childcare? By paying attention and showing sensitivity to the donor's motivation, you honor the donor and build an ongoing relationship.

> Failure? I never encountered it. All I encountered were temporary setbacks.
>
> **—Dottie Walters**

✇ Say No Way to "No Way"

If these five common myths in our profession can be faced down, how many other myths are we ready to challenge? Perhaps you have heard that "we can't find enough qualified staff" or "we're in a hiring crisis." Remember that in every myth is that shard of reality. Hiring and retaining qualified teachers is a challenge for directors. The director who says "I'll never find enough qualified staff" will find her prediction comes true.

A "self-fulfilling prophecy" like this means our future takes the shape we expect it to take. Self-fulfilling prophecies in neuroscience terms add up to brain pathways that are stuck in place. If I expect the worst, I will get the worst. If I am willing to challenge the myth, I have a fighting chance of getting different results. Every director I know who believes she can find and retain qualified staff hires and keeps her staff.

You will have scads of opportunities to accept negative beliefs or to challenge negative beliefs. I invite you to challenge any negative you are told. Someone believed the Berlin Wall could fall. You can be that someone.

Reflection Questions

1. Can you remember a time you accomplished something you never thought you could? Can you recall a belief of yours that you no longer hold dear? Have you observed changes in the world that make your life different than when you were little? Choose the most powerful of your recollections or observations about the "Berlin Walls" that have fallen in your lifetime. Record an oral reflection (or write one) or a video/DVD on "the way it was," the way it is now, and what brought about the change.

2. Imagine you are placed in charge of raising money for a childcare program. Where would you start? What resources can you find to help? What are some of your options for raising money? Investigate examples of successful early childhood fund-raising activities: Call programs in your area and select your favorite fund-raising idea. Put together a plan with your goal, measurable objectives, and publicity activities. Check your plan against Roger Neugebauer's checklist on page 215.

3. How much experience and exposure do you have to people of cultures and ethnicities other than your own? Would you like to change this experience and exposure in any way? Take a look at the steps Dr. Debra Sullivan took and the recommendations by Sparks and Ramsey. Describe how you would like to expand or alter your exposure to other cultures. Research in your community and online. Share with your class at least five steps you will take to broaden your horizons in diversity.

Team Projects

1. Recognizing and honoring teachers for their accomplishments and their EQ and social EQ competencies can take many shapes. Brainstorm as a team ideas on teacher or staff recognition. From this list, each of you will select an approach or idea you find especially inspiring. Research the idea to "round it out" with concrete examples and, if possible, real-life examples of how this idea has been used in early childhood programs. As a team, compile a list of recommendations for teacher recognition. Present this list to your classmates and lead a discussion on "what do teachers want?"

2. With rapid changes to technology, marketing strategies must change too. Share with your team all the ways in which "word can get out" to potential new teachers and directors. Go online to find the best examples of how technology can further our recruiting processes. Discuss how you might use technology to reach out to potential hires in emotionally and socially intelligent ways. Write and present a

brief guide to using technology when recruiting staff members. Share this guide with your classmates.

3. Curb appeal can influence a potential customer "to drive by or drive in." Together, create a checklist of customer friendly characteristics you would like to see on the outside of early childhood centers. Tour early childhood programs in your area to assess their curb appeal. Take your cameras with you. Prepare and present a PowerPoint presentation for your class on the best and worst curb appeal practices.

Bibliography

Chaika, Gloria. 2004. Recruiting and retaining minority teachers: Programs that work! *Education World.* *http://www.educationworld.com/a_admin/admin/admin213.shtml.2004.*

Collins, David J., and M.G. Rukstad. 2008. Can you say what your strategy is? *Harvard Business Review* (April): 82–90.

Finegan-Stoll, C. 1999. The goal of diversity training: To "teach tolerance" or model acceptance? *Leadership Quest* (Spring): 10–12.

Goffin, S., and V. Washington. 2007. *Ready or not: Leadership choices in early childhood education.* New York: Columbia Teachers Press.

Gonzalez-Mena, J. 2005. *Diversity in early care and education: Honoring differences* (4th ed.). New York: McGraw-Hill.

Harrington, R.J., and A.K. Tjan. 2008. Transforming strategy, one customer at a time. *Harvard Business Review* (March): 62–72.

Hines, K. 2007. Circles of support. *Managing Money:* 109.

Kagan, S.L., and B.T. Bowman. 1997. *Leadership in early care and education.* Washington, DC: NAEYC.

Klinkner, J., D. Riley, and Mary Roach. 2005. Organizational climate as a tool for staff retention. *Young Children* (November).

Koralek, D., ed. 2005. "Diversity" issue of *Young Children* (November).

Koralek, Derry, ed. 2005. "Leadership" issue of *Young Children* (January).

Neugebauer, R., ed. 2007. *Managing money: A center director's guidebook.* Redmond, WA: Exchange Press.

Sparks, L.D., and P. Ramsey. 2006. *What if all the children in my class are white? Historical and research background.* New York: Teachers College Press.

Sparks, L.D., and P. Ramsey. 2005. What if all the children in my class are white? Anti-bias/multicultural education with white children. *Young Children* (November): 20–27.

Sullivan, D.R. 2003. *Learning to lead: Effective leadership skills for teachers of young children.* St. Paul, MN: Redleaf Press.

Tatum, B.D. 1997. *Why are all the black kids sitting together in the cafeteria?* New York: Basic Books.

Thoughtful gifts for teachers. 2008. *The Dollar Stretcher. http://www.stretcher.com/stories/03/03dec01a.cfm.*

Torres, J., J. Santos, N.L. Peck, and L. Cortes. 2004. *Minority teacher recruitment, development, and retention.* Providence, RI: Education Alliance at Brown University.

U.S. Department of Education, National Center for Education Statistics. 2007. *The condition of education* 2007(NCES 2007–064).

Walker, M. 2001. When racism gets personal: Toward relational healing. Wellesley, MA: Wellesley College, Stone Center.

Web Resources

Department of Education equity assistance grants.
www.ed.gov/equitycenters/index.html
Interview with author Beverly Tatum Daniel.
www.familyeducation.com/race/parenting/36247.html
National Center for Education Statistics collects and analyzes data relating to education and publishes a variety of reports.
nces.ed.gov
Tips on gifts for teachers.
http://www.stretcher.com/stories/03/03dec01a.cfm
Valora Washington address on social justice.
http://www.uuca.org/sermon.php?id=68
Department of Education clearinghouse collects studies of educational interventions.
www.whatworks.ed.gov/

Performing

Putting Principles into Practice

PART IV

Every Child's Family: Building Partnerships

Learning Goals

As you study this chapter, you can look forward to reaching these learning goals:

1. Define family.
2. Identify ways to appreciate and learn about families who differ from your own.
3. Examine the legal status of families, and know who qualifies for legal protection and who does not.
4. Describe how to strengthen families and avoid labels such as "at risk."
5. Use the "ask and listen" process for building partnerships with families.
6. Explain how to serve families with special needs children.
7. Recognize the signs of traumatized children.
8. Discuss the value of "family-friendly" practices.

For child care to be a healthy part of children's growth, parents and childcare providers have to work together closely. The most important thing is that both parents and providers work together as partners to keep the child-parent relationship as strong as it can be.

—*Fred Rogers*

Call it a clan, call it a network, call it a tribe, call it a family: Whatever you call it, whoever you are, you need one.

—*Jane Howard*

Case Study: Honoring Differences: How Far Can the Willow Bend?

A visitor knocks at your door:
  Mr. Khan wants to enroll his children, Amin, 4, and Roshon, 20 months, in your program. Mr. Khan has read your mission and vision statements. He is attracted to your school's emphasis on respecting cultural diversity. Mr. Khan advises you that Amin, born a prince, will grow up to assume leadership responsibilities back home. Mr. Khan expects you to treat Amin as the prince he is and will become. Roshon was betrothed at birth. Her intended husband, back home, now 22, lives with his three wives. Mr. Khan expects you to teach Roshon to become an obedient wife and mother.

- What are your feelings about Mr. Khan and his requests?
- What assumptions do you bring to this conversation?
- How might you honor his wishes?
- Do you want to honor his wishes?

We all know what family is.

We instinctively "know" based on our firsthand experience as a member of a family (or not having been part of a family). Our experience often predicts what we think a family is and should be. Early experiences imprint upon us a powerful sense of family. Before we had words, we had family. Before we started school, we had family. Before we made life choices, we had family. Before we knew what a family was, we had family.

That knowledge is both the good news and the problem. Feelings about family run so deep that questioning our assumptions about family can be awkward and unwelcome. In this chapter, we will explore ways to learn about, appreciate, and partner with the richly diverse families in early childhood programs.

> If the doors of perception were cleansed, everything would appear to man as it is, infinite.
>
> **—William Blake**

✤ We Are Family

Children believe the world is as they experience it. If Mousadi has a mom and a dad, Mousadi believes a mom, dad, and son are family. Rico's foster family is Rico's family. Wentworth and his two dads are Wentworth's family. Tsu and her mom are a family. So interwoven is our personal experience into our definition of family that we develop deep feelings about what families should be like. No wonder when I ask early childhood professionals about their core values, many simply state: family.

Our feelings about family are so preconsciously deep that stepping back to get perspective may be difficult. Institutions that "just are," can be tricky to question. Have you ever found yourself "acting just like your mom" when you swore you never would? This deep, unspoken family connection can be explained in a neurological way (Lewis, Amini, and Lannon 2001).

As infants, our neurons line up with the neurons of our primary caregiver, like iron filings to a magnet. Through this alignment process we learn what love is from that caregiver. If we are fortunate to be raised by a loving family, we are set for life to look for other loving people. Our neurons will line up in healthy ways. If we are not so fortunate, we can end up "looking for love in all the wrong places." Like those iron filings, our neurons will home in on empty places.

In this chapter, I invite you to examine the meanings and varieties of family. I also invite you to identify those traits in families that "rub you the wrong way." Is it the "high maintenance" mom or the family who sends the nanny for the children? Can we find a

> Home is the place, when you have to go there, they have to take you in.
>
> **—Robert Frost,** "Death of the Hired Man"

connection on which to build a partnership for the sake of the children, especially when we don't share the same philosophy or practices?

Marveling at diversity among children can be a delight. Marveling at diversity in adults can be a challenge. When another adult embodies values, practices, and perspectives far different from ours, we can feel out of sorts. Each family we greet offers an opportunity for us to grow professionally as we examine our attitudes and biases about differences.

Children and families come to expect their future academic experiences will be like their early childhood experiences. The quality of experience a leader and her program provide to a family can contribute to or harm the family's trust in all future educational experiences. If a teacher or director decides a family's values or practices are not acceptable, that judgment can take away the family's desire to keep their children in the program. What precedent for all future learning do we want to set for families?

✄ EQ and Understanding Families

Consider the chapter case study, in which meeting with Mr. Khan calls for emotional and social intelligence. Step back. Imagine you are sitting with Mr. Khan. Check in with yourself on how you feel about his requests. What information does your physical response offer you? Using EQ, walk yourself through the following process:

1. *Physical Response?* Acknowledge your physical and psychological response to the situation.
2. *Feelings?* Identify the feelings associated with your response (anger, sadness, fear, shame, guilt, joy, etc.).
3. *Assumptions.* Ask what information your feelings are giving you. Reflect on what assumptions you are making. Do your assumptions and/or values match the family's?
4. *Professional Perspective?* Use this information to act wisely in the moment. How can you respond respectfully and professionally?

A common knee-jerk response to Mr. Khan's attitude has been: "Who does he think he is?" Like a Halloween cat, some of us may have "gotten our backs up."

People who make a snap judgment like this tend to answer the four EQ questions in the following or similar way:

1. *Physical Response?* My jaw is set. My face is heating up.
2. *Feelings?* I am offended to be asked to treat his son differently than his daughter. I am angry.
3. *Assumptions?* That man is wrong!
   I am ready to make Mr. Khan the "bad guy."
   Stepping back, I begin to see I am affronted because my core values (gender equality, individual freedom) are challenged. I assume each child deserves choices about her future.
4. *Professional Perspective?* My amygdala is hijacking my professionalism. Adrenalin has robbed me of perspective.

How might we be more curious about and open to hearing about Mr. Khan's cultural heritage and beliefs?

Later in this chapter, I will tell you what I learned from the seasoned midwestern director who actually had Mr. Khan knock on her door. Family members like Mr. Khan can challenge our assumptions about what is right for families.

We are not our feelings. Emotional intelligence theory reminds us that feelings are part of us, but need not control us. Although a teacher may feel angry at Mr. Khan's

We don't see things as they are. We see them as we are.

—Anais Nin

Families are of primary importance in children's development. Because the family and the early childhood practitioner have a common interest in the child's well-being, we acknowledge a primary responsibility to bring about communication, cooperation, and collaboration between the home and early childhood program in ways that enhance the child's development.

—NAEYC Code of Ethical Conduct, Section II: Ethical Responsibilities to Families

statements, the teacher is more than her anger. The teacher's biased emotional reaction to Mr. Khan does not have to dominate her relationship with him. Stepping up to the balcony of perspective allows her to use the *NAEYC Code of Ethical Conduct*, rather than be blinded by her own bias.

Since we all bring our own assumptions about the way families "should" be, we might find it worth our time to find out what other people's assumptions are.

✣ Family: It's Not What We Think It Is

Exploring Glasgow, Scotland, on a quest to learn more about my mother's family, I stepped through the gates of the St. Mungo Museum of Religious Life and Art and was enchanted. The St. Mungo explores the world's six main religions as well as all the cultures, ethnicities, and religions embodied by the people of Glasgow. In an effort to promote greater understanding and respect the museum showcases how families in each group deal with life's passages.

The first room I visited focused on birth. Our entry into the world is marked in many unique ways. One group plunges an infant into a pool of water in the ritual of baptism. Another group celebrates the "bris," traditional circumcision of male babies by a *mohel* (pronounced "moy'l"). A third group welcomes a newborn into the clan with a "naming ceremony."

In a nearby room, I discovered initiation rites. Diverse "coming of age" family practices are lavishly pictured. Jewish thirteen-year-olds, with deliberate concentration, read from the sacred book, the *Torah*, in the original Hebrew. The bar or bat mitzvah of Judaism is pictured beside a procession of Catholic girls in frilly white dresses, hands devotedly pressed in a steeple of prayer. Every Catholic boy and girl chooses a saint's name as a confirmation name. Turkish tradition crowns thirteen-year-old boys while cloaking them in the robes of royalty just before group circumcision initiates the boys into adulthood. At age fifteen, a Latina girl celebrates *la quinceañera,* the equivalent of a "sweet sixteen" ritual. Families work for months to ensure their daughters' *la quinceañera* memories will be treasured for a lifetime.

Other rooms display rituals and passages of marriage, growing into old age, and death. The diverse rituals of each group fascinated me. The universal acknowledgment of life's passages equally fascinated me. I stood for a moment, grateful for the gift the museum had given me: a glimpse into the meaning of family in all of its embodiments. I had never seen such an intriguing portrayal of family diversity.

Defining "Family"

Since my time in Glasgow, I have asked students: How do you define family? What is the meaning of family values?

Over the years, my students have come to define family as "two or more people who share similar values and goals." Does that definition cover your family? Does the definition leave anyone out? Might that be too inclusive? Are team teachers a family? Are devotees of salsa dancing family? Pinning words on an ever-changing, yet constant, reality can be like catching fireflies on a July night.

Given the diversity of families, what can family values mean? If a politician says she or he stands for family values, whose family values does that person promote? Family values most often mean the desire to return to the good old days when dad and mom were happily married, children were obedient and loyal, and everyone was of one ethnicity. Did such a family ever exist?

Definitions of family:

1. A group of individuals living under one roof and usually under one head.
2. A group of individuals of common ancestry.
3. A group of individuals united by certain convictions or a common affiliation.

—*Webster's Dictionary*

The History of the American Family

Dr. Stephanie Coontz (2000) probed statistics on the American family since our country began. She scoured the data on a quest to discover if there ever has been an "all-American family."

Can you imagine what Dr. Coontz discovered? At no time other than during the 1950s was the nuclear family (dad, mom, 1.5 children, and a cocker spaniel named Checkers) ever the norm. "Not only was the 1950s family a new invention, it was also a historical fluke" (Coontz 2000, 28). Like Glaswegian families, American families have always been diverse: one-family households, older children or grandparents raising children, foster families, adoptive families, extended families, same-sex families, and religious communities. "Our recurring search for a traditional American family model denies the diversity of family life, both past and present" (Coontz 2000, 14). When we look to the past for family values, we discover, as Dr. Coontz discovered, that no one type of family values prevailed. *What would politicians make of this information?*

Labeling Families

Have you ever walked into the teachers' lounge only to be barraged by complaints about certain families, often referred to as "those people"? As a bright-eyed and bushy-tailed first-year teacher, I soon learned that negativity about families could rain on my enthusiasm. After a while, I stayed away from complaints about how disgusting Tommy's father was, or how Tommy was just as hopeless as his father. Labeling a family negatively or gossiping about that family's foibles robs the family and us of dignity.

With the knowledge that families are naturally diverse, and that no one type of family is superior to another, let's consider how to partner with every family we meet.

Labeling families as "at risk" for abuse or neglect has been common practice. If you or your family were labeled at risk, how would you feel? A stigmatizing or ghettoization of at risk families often begins. Once labeled, that family might be pitied or shunned, categorized for likely failure.

The following exercise (along with Figure 14.1), from the Cornell Family Development Press, illustrates another way of thinking about families.

❧ Preventing and Countering Family Abuse and Neglect

The Center for the Study of Social Policy (CSSP) invites us to take the approach for preventing child abuse proposed in *Protecting Children by Strengthening Families: A Guidebook for Early Childhood Programs* (2004). Reading that guide, I was heartened to learn that 70 percent of individuals who were abused as children do not abuse their own children. I was heartbroken, however, to discover that the leading cause of death in the first year of a child's life is homicide (CSSP 2004, 23).

Isolation predicts whether a family will nurture or abuse. As noted in the CSSP study (2004, 16), "The single factor most commonly identified in the child abuse and neglect prevention literature is development of empathy for the self and others through caring relationships with friends, intimate partners, family members or professional therapists or counselors" (Steele 1997; Higgins 1994). Of all the institutions studied by the CSSP, early childhood programs were determined to play the greatest role in potentially reversing abuse and neglect by strengthening family resilience.

There are two ways of exerting one's strength; one is pushing down, the other is pulling up.

—Booker T. Washington

Of the 825,000 substantiated cases of child abuse or neglect in the United States in 1999, 14 percent represented children under the age of one year; 24 percent represented children from ages 2 to 5.

—The Center for the Study of Social Policy

 One helpful way that early childhood professionals can help families build on their strengths is through "peripheral vision": the ability to see a wider view of a family's strengths despite the reality of their struggles. Sometimes a family's problems seem so overwhelming that it is hard to see their strengths, and even harder to reflect them back to the family.

This drawing may represent a family that your program is working with. For the next minute, look at the drawing using peripheral vision and identify the strengths you see in this family. List the strengths on a sheet of paper if you like.

As an early childhood leader, you often help the most distressed and vulnerable families in a community. It can be challenging to look for strengths while you also see the reality of struggles. Families can be overwhelmed by their daily challenges as well. They may be so accustomed to seeing deficits that they might not believe you when you reflect a strength back to them.

How has a struggle in your own life helped you ultimately find a hidden strength you didn't know you had? How can we help families look for and find the hidden strengths in their struggles? When leaders believe in a family's strengths, this becomes a powerful tool to help families believe in themselves and their ability to set and reach their goals.

"Finding Strengths" exercise (including illustration by Camille Doucet) originally appeared in Empowerment Skills for Family Workers: Instructors Manual, by Katie Palmer-House and Claire Forest, Cornell Family Development Press, © 2003. Used by permission. Order info:www.human.cornell.edu/HD/FDC.

FIGURE 14.1   *Family at Risk*

Instead of looking only at a family's weaknesses, CSSP encourages us to seek and build upon families' "protective factors," or positive attributes (see Table 14.1). Protective factors include characteristics like creativity, initiative, humor, intelligence, and access to good health care and a support system (*Acts of Omission: An Overview of Child Neglect*, Washington, DC: National Clearinghouse on Child Abuse and Neglect 2001, as cited in the CSSP report 2004, 12).

TABLE 14.1

Protective Factors

- Parental resilience
- An array of social connections
- Adequate knowledge of parenting and child development
- Concrete support in times of need, including access to necessary services, such as mental health, and
- Healthy social and emotional development for children.

Source: CSSP 2004, 13.

As professionals, we can build on these family strengths. Connecting with a parent's sense of humor, her initiative to want more for her children, honors the parent. From that starting point of respect, we begin to build a relationship that could lead to a partnership for the good of the whole family, especially the children.

The following questions can help you provide support when strengthening protective factors with families (Bruno 2007, 22–29):

1. What are you having difficulty with as parents?
2. Can our staff help you deal with these challenges in any way?
3. Our program wants to be a welcoming place for families—where parents feel comfortable asking for help. What are some of your ideas on how we might do that?
4. We are particularly concerned when parents seem stressed, isolated, or overwhelmed. How might we reach out better to parents in times of stress?
5. We want to make it easy for families to communicate directly with each other. How can we do that?

These questions can lead to rich discussions with many parents, not just the parents who may concern you. Sometimes the families who look the best on the outside are the families who are struggling most at home. A family's economic background does not predict a family's stability. Strategies for early childhood programs to promote healthy families include (Bruno 2007, 29):

- Devote time to building honest, trusting relationships with the child's family.
- Invite parents to play with and observe their children in the classroom. Together, identify the child's strengths and needs.
- Cocreate a classroom parent support team and a parent advisory group.
- Offer speakers and workshops on topics requested by parents, and include parents in the planning.
- Find ways for families to communicate and share resources directly with each other, for example, through a parent bulletin board.
- Pay attention to even the subtlest of indicators that a child is under undue stress.

> Nostalgia for a more placid past fosters historical amnesia.
>
> **—Stephanie Coontz**

Building bridges and capitalizing on family strengths is a worthy goal. In cases, however, where abuse or neglect is suspected or likely, our responsibility as mandated reporters takes precedence. If we believe a child is in danger, we need to work with other professionals who can step in to prevent abuse and neglect.

Abuse and neglect are unfortunately very common. During 2006, according to statistics from the U.S. Department of Health and Human Services, over 900,000 children were determined to be victims of abuse or neglect. More than 60 percent of the children experienced neglect, 16 percent suffered physical abuse, and nearly 9 percent suffered sexual abuse. These "official" reports of abusive behaviors are estimated to be far lower than actual incidents of abuse, however. According to a 1995 Gallup Poll, almost 25 percent of surveyed adults reported that they had been victims of sexual abuse as a child (English 1998).

As a survivor of abuse and neglect, I would like to believe that families, with help, can break the cycle. However, I know through experience that not every family is open to change. In those cases, protecting the children becomes our greater priority.

"Ask and Listen" Process

The ask and listen process is common sense but not common practice. At heart, this practice requires us to "step aside" from our assumptions and judgments to open our hearts to learning more about each family. This process works especially well when we find our "buttons get pushed" by a family member like Mr. Khan.

The ask and listen process has three components:

1. Bring a curious, receptive, generous attitude to the conversation.
2. Listen without judging, as if you were on a treasure hunt.
3. Acknowledge your bias, and then place it to the side, in order to fully hear the other person.

Have you been pulled over for speeding by a police officer? If so, you were probably asked, "Do you know how fast you were going?" Does that question feel open-ended to you? Most likely, it does not. The officer already knows the answer. His radar gave him all the data he needed. Rather than asking a question, the officer made an indirect statement, "I know exactly how fast you were going. You were speeding." Although he is likely right, his approach, along with the ticket, can send drivers into a tizzy.

The "open" end of an *open-ended question* is an invitation to the other person. Curious people who want to learn something by asking open-ended questions. "Can you tell me about your child?" opens the door for a parent. A *redundant question* is a statement with a question mark at the end. "Will you ever get here on time?" sounds like "You are always late." Redundant questions slam doors to further sharing. The police officer in the previous example was not interested in the driver's response. Most drivers get the message.

> We respond with openness to an open-ended question. We feel the negative judgment in a "redundant" question. We tend to avoid people who judge us negatively.

Our EQ tells us that consistency between the words we use and our nonverbal behavior is an indicator of honesty. Redundant questions rarely fool the listener. A scowling face is not an openly questioning face. The redundant questioner will be perceived as not being fully honest with the listener. Simple as that may sound, according to Myers-Briggs statistics, 55 percent of us have difficulty asking open-ended questions.

Most of us want to be respected and accepted for who we are. We already know our imperfections, and being reminded of them can be painful. A parent, when asked a redundant question, shuts down. She not only distances herself, but also may feel resentful or angry. A parent who is listened to carefully is much more likely to become a partner. When leaders "ask and listen," they invite the best from themselves and others. Effective administrators put aside being judge and jury and wholeheartedly connect with the parent. When we listen with honest curiosity, we are on the path to learning about family diversity.

Suspending Judgment to Make Room for Wonderment

Dr. Malcolm Gladwell (2005) confirmed that, whether we want to or not, we make judgments of others "in the blink of an eye." Recall Mr. Kahn's request in the case study. Even if you want to be open to Mr. Khan, you may have initial biased reactions. Our early experiences lead to expectations for behavior.

TABLE 14.2

Ask and Listen Steps

- *Acknowledge the assumptions* you bring to the conversation.
- *Set the assumptions to the side.* This does not require you to let go of your assumptions. However, you do need to accept that, to another person, the glass may be half empty. Accept that you view the same situation differently.
- *Stay focused on serving children and families.* Choose to learn about another family's practices, values, beliefs and desires.
- *Find common ground.* Seek points of agreement, ways in which the family's uniqueness can be honored along with the program's vision.
- *Name the differences.* Level with one another about what appears to be nonnegotiable, e.g., state and federal laws and regulations.
- *Review together standards and requirements* set by laws, regulations, accreditation, and program philosophy. Together, find ways to honor the family's difference while acting "in the spirit of the law," or help the parent find another program that better fits the family's needs.

For example, I expect girls and boys to have a right to the same opportunities. I was raised when girls were shut out of career choices, and boys were not allowed to cry. Ensuring that children will have many opportunities is important to me. Mr. Khan's culture appears to afford more rights for males than females. He asks if I will treat Amin as royalty, while I teach obedience to Roshon. My gut responds, "No way!" My negative judgment leaves no room for wonderment.

What if instead, I set aside my assumptions so I can *ask* and *listen* to Amin and Roshon's dad? (See Table 14.2.) Perhaps I could learn about the traditions, practices, and hopes of this man who differs from me? If I listen in wonderment, might I hear how this father loves his children? That he wants what is best for them? That he wants to prepare them for success according to the standards of his religious and cultural traditions?

The poet Samuel Taylor Coleridge suggested we take a "willing suspension of disbelief" to enter a realm of possibility. The ask and listen process opens that realm to us as early childhood leaders.

Third Space

Janet Gonzalez-Mena (2007) likes to call the relationship that develops between people the "third space." She describes third space as, "Moving from dualistic thinking to holistic thinking in the face of what seems to be a contradiction or a paradox. If I disagree with something you are doing with your child, it's possible I have a blind spot. My blind spot leads me to consider our differing views to be a problem. What do I do?"

Reframing the issue, putting it in a new "picture frame," helps us look at the same picture in a new way. For example, Gonzalez-Mena recommends we reframe this situation from, "I have a *problem* with you," to "You and I have *different views*." She credits Barrera, Corso, and MacPherson (2003, 81) for this perspective on third space: "A third space perspective does not 'solve the problem.' Rather, it changes the arena within which that problem is addressed by increasing the probability of respectful, responsive, and reciprocal interactions. In so doing, an optimal response to the situation becomes more likely."

TABLE 14.3

Ask and Listen: Open-Ended Questions

- Tell me about your child.
- What is important to you in raising your child?
- What activities does your family enjoy together?
- What soothes or comforts your child?
- I am interested in learning more about your culture. What do you recommend?
- Tell me one of your favorite early memories of your child.
- Is there anything else you would like to help me understand about you and your family?

Can I share with you now what I learned from these theories and practices about how to welcome Mr. Khan? (See Table 14.3.) Instead of advising Mr. Khan to find another program, the director said to him:

"I would like to learn more about you and your family's culture. Could you tell me, 'What does it mean to be a prince in your culture?' Mr. Khan explained that a prince was responsible, accountable, and decisive. The director said that her program encouraged children to learn those traits.

The director next asked, "Could you tell me more about Roshon's role as an obedient wife?" Mr. Khan, appearing to hold back tears, said simply: "We are in very hard times back home. The wife and mother helps us all feel safe, and that life will go on. She is the glue of the family." "What are your hopes for both of your children?" inquired the director. "Ah," Mr. Khan sighed, "I just want them to be happy."

Did the director enroll Amin and Roshon? Yes. Did the children thrive? Yes. By asking and listening, the director and Mr. Khan found the best of possibilities in each other. A family that appeared unacceptable became part of the program's family.

That director taught me a lifetime lesson.

When the Dominant Culture Prevails

How far can the willow bend before it snaps? When might valuing family differences go too far? At times, our state, federal, and professional standards require us to enforce what is right for the majority, while abandoning the differences of the minority.

For example, every child in this country has been mandated to learn English. The necessity, as declared by the Supreme Court, for a common language means that children raised with a "minority" language must not speak their native language at school. In our profession, standardized practices prevail over individual approaches in many cases. For example, universal precautions such as hand washing and wearing plastic gloves are required. Class sizes are mandated. Child abuse and neglect are criminal offenses in this country. By law, we are mandated reporters of abuse.

Consider what you would do in this situation: New toddler teacher Jessica tells you emphatically that Ho Sook's parents must be reported for abuse. While changing Ho Sook's diaper, Jessica noticed bruises all over the toddler's bottom and lower back. Resolutely, Jessica states she must do her duty as a mandated reporter. As Jessica's director, what do you do and say?

Would you report Ho Sook's parents for abuse? Unless the child is in immediate danger, you could contact the parents first to find out what might have happened. If you ask her, Ho Sook's mom would tell you about "Mongolian spots," blue and black skin pigmentation common among Asian, African, and Latino children. These spots typically disappear by adolescence. Taking time to make the call, and preserve a moment for wonderment, can protect the child, your program, and your partnership with Ho Sook's family. Jessica might learn that "ask and listen" works.

Imagine a different scenario in which Jessica notices red streaks down young Lia's back. Now Jessica knows to ask Lia's parent before calling social services. The parent happily notes how much healthier Lia is this morning, as compared to the weekend, when Lia was "coming down with a cold." Lia's mother describes the "coining" process of quickly running hot coins in a line down a person's back to expunge illness. The parent explains that she learned coining from her mother, just as her mother learned the process from her grandmother. Jessica is now able to research coining, particularly as a Hmong practice.

In the process of learning about Lia's culture, Jessica can read Anne Fadiman's *The Spirit Catches You and You Fall Down* (1997), about a Hmong child's painful history in America. The child described in Fadiman's book was lost between the dominant (American) culture's medical practices and her own culture's traditions. According to American doctors, Lia's parents were negligent. According to Lia's parents, the American doctors were harming their baby.

When dominant and nondominant cultures clash, a decision needs to be made. Sadly, our country has a history of quashing the rights of minorities. During World War II, Japanese-Americans were herded into camps. They lost their homes, businesses, and often their self-esteem in the process. Indian tribes and African-Americans also suffered unbearably. Even today, immigrants to this country as well as the nation's poor often get second-class treatment. Early childhood programs can help our future generations diminish cultural misunderstanding and injustice.

Teacher Jessica can thank Lia's parents for explaining coining to her. She can also affirm for them how energetic Lia is this morning. Jessica and her director need to balance the desire to honor the family's practice with the expectations of the larger society. The director may point out that mandated reporters—like early childhood professionals, doctors, and nurses—are required to report signs of abuse. Not every mandated reporter will ask the origin of the red marks on Lia's back before calling authorities, however. For this reason, Lia's family may need to inform others on a "need to know" basis about the well-intended nature of the cultural practice.

Legal Status of "the Family"

Traditionally, laws have protected only those families united by marriage, meaning married couples have rights unmarried couples do not. Laws have also defined marriage as a union of a man and a woman. This definition did not extend marriage protection to unmarried couples, including same-sex partners. In 1996, Congress passed the Defense of Marriage Act to nullify legalization of gay marriage by the states.

Worldwide, the legal definition of marriage is evolving. The Netherlands made same-sex marriage legal in 2001. Canada allows gay couples to marry without a residency requirement. This applies to same-sex couples of all nationalities. Massachusetts was the first state in America to legalize same-sex marriage. Slowly, states like Vermont and New Hampshire have begun to create a "civil union" status. Civil unions carry many of the rights previously afforded only to married (heterogeneous) couples.

This changing definition of marriage and family carries over to early childhood. Do gay and lesbian families, staff, and children feel welcomed to your center? How many books in your classrooms depict all kinds of families? Is your program welcoming to transgender and transsexual families?

Where do you stand on this as a leader? Even if a leader welcomes all families, she or he may find that program families do not welcome each other. In that case, the leader, with all families, can examine together the program's mission in line with accreditation standards. In the end, families who discriminate against other families may choose to leave for more homogeneous programs.

Families of Special Needs Children

Perhaps you have read the story about the family who thought they were making a trip to sunny hill towns in Italy? When they excitedly got off the airplane, they discovered they landed in an unknown, unexpected, and unprepared-for foreign country. The story's sweet conclusion is that the family, although stunned, found many things to love about where they landed. Families of special needs children are often given a copy of this story by well-meaning professionals.

The moral of the story often holds true; each special needs child is a gift to her family. However, painful dynamics burden these families too. The divorce rate for families in general is high—approximately 50 percent for first marriages—but it is even higher for couples with children with disabilities (Marshak and Prezant 2007). Depression is also common. Guilt- and shame-filled responses like "What did I do wrong?" are natural. To say "I know how you feel" rarely is a comfort.

Case Study: Laura

Laura's Mom, Mrs. Petrozullio, believes her daughter is perfect. Every time Laura's teachers attempt to share information on Laura's troubling behaviors, Mrs. Petrozullio insists: "Laura never does that at home. You must be provoking her!" Last Friday, Laura bit Alonzo; Monday, she punched Josephina in the belly. Today, Laura, refusing to sit with others at circle time, began to pull belongings out of everyone's cubby. Laura often swears to herself, making no sense to others. She rarely, if ever, makes eye contact. Laura's teachers, becoming anxious, want Laura to be evaluated. They fear Mrs. Petrozullio's reaction. As director, what would you do?

Would the "ask and listen" process help? Absolutely. There are many times when a parent of a special needs child yearns to simply be heard by someone who also loves her child. By calling upon your EQ to listen in all ways to Mrs. Petrozullio, you also help Laura.

The Americans with Disabilities Act (ADA) ensures that all children, including those with special needs, have opportunities to grow and learn. Our challenge in early childhood is to find ways to support parents and teachers with all the extra responsibilities that attending to special needs children brings. *Protecting Children by Strengthening Families* (2004, 38) offers early childhood professionals the following guidelines for working with families of special needs children:

1. Connect families with parenting materials and websites, support groups and play groups, and community resources specific to their children's special needs.
2. Check regularly with parents about their challenging parenting issues.
3. Be sensitive to parents' frustration, protectiveness, guilt, loss, and other related feelings, and acknowledge their challenges.
4. Support parents in developing appropriate developmental expectations for their special needs children.
5. Check in with parents about the impact their children's special needs are having on family dynamics and parental stress.
6. Be especially supportive at the time that special needs are initially identified.
7. Provide speakers and resources on topics of interest and concern.
8. Ensure that parent-child activities are appropriate for families with special needs children.

I offer you this additional list of recommendations for working with families of special needs children based on my own experiences and research:

1. Ask parents to describe their child. What delights, soothes, inspires, engages the child?
2. Provide factual feedback daily.
3. Share the "good news" along with the difficult news.
4. Invite parents to the classroom, to play with and observe their child.
5. Ask parents what they do at home that helps the child. Learn from their experiences. Tell parents when their advice has been useful. Give concrete examples.
6. Together, look back over the child's progress and identify patterns of behavior that may require additional help.
7. Have resources available (DVDs, websites, articles) as well as contact information (professionals, support groups, other parents willing to share their experience).
8. Instead of saying "I know how you feel," consider saying "I can only imagine what this is like for you. I am interested in hearing whatever you want to share so we can work together. We both love your child."

Early childhood professionals can be an invaluable source of support and comfort to families with special needs children.

"Perfect" Families

Have you known anyone who grew up in the "perfect" family? Were you so fortunate? If I asked you to describe the perfect family, what might you say? One possible answer is, "I envision a family where children and the adults who care for them are treasured, safe, nurtured, challenged to become the best they can, and, above all, loved unconditionally."

No one grows up in the perfect family, although the family may appear to be perfect on the outside. Dark secrets of violence, abuse, and neglect can lurk inside seemingly perfect homes. Be aware that children from seemingly perfect families may also be in need. As a leader, you can support your staff in learning more about how to recognize indicators of possible abuse and neglect (Bruno 2007, 24):

- *Abnormal startle responses:* Children respond to unexpected noises or movements with an instantaneous, fearful, and magnified reaction.
- *Memory and concentration problems:* When asked a seemingly simple question, abused children may look like little adults, frowning in concentration, as if their lives depended on getting the answer right.
- *Feeling worse when reminded of the trauma:* Children who have been abused often tense up in discomfort upon seeing an adult enter the room, such as when a relative comes to pick up the children.
- *Avoidance:* Neglected children, who fear revealing family secrets, may avoid situations where they could "slip" and reveal something they were told never to tell. This reluctance can show up as resistance to new things, or even to playing freely.
- *Hypervigilance and hyperarousal:* Children with PTSD (posttraumatic stress disorder) are on the lookout for danger. They may fret and worry greatly about situations in which they have little or no control. Relaxing at naptime may not be possible for the hypervigilant young child.

For helpful information on what teachers can do to help traumatized children, go to *www.fema/gov/kids* and *www.nmha.org/reassurance/children.cfm*.

Something I learned as a student in an early childhood class in 1967 stuck in my mind. "Your client is not the child, but the family." The teacher of that class, Lillian Katz, University of Illinois professor and a pioneer in the field, is the one who made that statement. I have never forgotten what she said, but it has taken many years for the field as a whole to begin to understand and embrace that concept.

—Janet Gonzalez-Mena

Parents Out-Needing Children: High Maintenance Family Members

Can you name a family who is not under stress? I cannot think of one. Every family faces challenges and stressors. Stressed family members can spill their anxieties over onto us.

Do you know a "high maintenance" family member who needs or demands so much of your time that you feel in danger of neglecting your other responsibilities? High maintenance people are often needy. They need attention and care and, often, useful information. Use your emotional intelligence to listen beneath the words. Ask, "What does this person really need from me?"

As you work with needy family members, this process, taken a step at a time, will help both the parent and the program:

1. Give the parent your total attention for a specific, reasonable, and limited amount of time.
2. If advisable, set up a regular time to talk with the parent.
3. Assist the parent in meeting other parents with similar questions and concerns.
4. Help the parent find and connect with community resources.
5. Enlist the parent in using her strengths and skills to help in the classroom or the program.
6. If the parents' demands on you become overwhelming, help the parent find another program that might offer her more individual attention.

In the best-case scenario, the high maintenance family members will evolve into your program's most energetic supporters. In the worst-case scenario, the family member may benefit from your assistance in finding another program that better fits her needs.

✕ Family-Friendly Practices

Being "family friendly" means placing the needs of the family first, by offering services to reduce stressors and make it possible for families to enjoy quality time.

Family-friendly programs might offer haircuts for children; dry cleaning drop-off and pickup; freshly cooked, nutritious meals-to-go; and sleepovers for children, all to reduce family stress. When you read Chapter 15 about quality, you will see how total quality management (TQM) principles set the standard for anticipating your client's needs.

Gwen Morgan, early childcare leader, discovered that a defense company in the northwest had pioneered early childhood family-friendly practices during the intensity of World War II. This company, Kaiser Corporation, hired the most qualified teachers from around the country, paid them generously, and covered their moving expenses and housing. Teachers were treated as invaluable professionals, with management listening to and implementing their ideas for improvement.

Kaiser Corporation provided 24-hour childcare. A special care unit staffed by a medical team served children who were ill. Children and their families received free medical and dental care on site. A family's every possible need, right down to an extra shoelace or spare button, was taken care of in advance. One poignant image sticks in my memory: specially designed bathtubs, raised to the level of the teachers, were designed to reduce stress on teachers' backs.

The funding that empowered Kaiser to be so family-friendly flowed from the United States government War Office. Company employees built naval war ships on site. No cost was spared to serve the war effort.

Today, military funding is dedicated to other efforts. Nonetheless, Kaiser's family-friendly methods can still be practiced. Using our EQ resourcefulness, we can engage

---

T A B L E   1 4 . 4

Top Ten Family-Friendly Practices

1. *Form parent advisory groups* to allow parents to share new ideas and common concerns. Parent advisories can also advise the director on questions about how the program is doing.
2. *Invite speakers to share topics of interest to parents.* Popular topics include discipline, ADHD, toileting, what to expect at different stages of development, and activities to do with children at home.
3. *Post colorful bulletin boards* for families to share information with one another.
4. *Provide opportunities for parents to use their strengths* to assist the program. Reading stories, raising money, and participating in clean-up days are all activities that contribute to program quality.
5. *Offer "Parents' Night Out" events,* in which programs stay open late on Friday evenings to allow parents time together without the children.
6. *Feature yoga and exercise classes* on site for parents and children.
7. *Provide spa treatments,* offered without cost by local massage therapists and cosmetologists, to rejuvenate and alleviate parental stress.
8. *Provide a family lending library* of DVDs, books, games, and resource materials.
9. *Provide additional staffing for the end of the day* to enable families and teachers to talk, while the additional staff members care for the children.
10. *Plan family recognition dinners and events,* with food, transportation, and childcare provided to celebrate the families in the program.

---

parents and meet their needs without huge additional funding. Consider the family-friendly practices in Table 14.4.

Family as Teacher, ECE Professional as Learner

> To listen to families, acknowledge and build upon their strengths, and learn from families as we support them in their task of nurturing children.
>
> **—NAEYC** *Code of Ethical Conduct,* **Section II, I-2.4**

In the end, as at the beginning, we have choices. Today, a parent like Mr. Khan may walk through your door. Tomorrow, a twelve-year-old mother may seek your services. She may want to put her friends on the list of people authorized to pick up the baby. Each person we encounter will offer an opportunity to learn more about "family" in all its meanings. Families who feel our respect and appreciation will readily become our partners in helping each child become her best. Barriers we put up to keep others out become cages for ourselves. Each child and her family is a gift, if we choose to open our hearts to the possibility. We just need to ask and, then, listen.

Directors have the opportunity to create, with their staff, environments where every child's family is welcomed. Consider how you, as a leader, would build bridges with the two families described below.

Case Study: Baby Emmaline Rae

Baby Emmaline Rae's father, Wilbur, tells her teacher, Luis, that Luis cannot change Emma's diaper. "If any man sees my daughter unclothed, she will be shamed," Wilbur warns. Wilbur and his family are dedicated members of their evangelical church. The church requires modesty, especially between the sexes. Wilbur has never given his daughter a bath, changed her diaper, or seen her unclothed. He relies on his wife and female church members, all of whom are strongly supportive. Luis is your best infant teacher. You are often understaffed.

What is your feeling response to Wilbur's demand?

What assumptions do you bring to the conversation?

How can you apply the "ask and listen" process?

What solutions might you develop together?

Case Study: Scooter

School-aged Scooter enjoys being in your summer camp and after-school programs. A theatrical child, he will try on anything from a frothy wedding dress to a Darth Vader mask. He likes to wrap long, bright scarves around his neck and pretend he is flying like the Red Baron or dancing like Isadora Duncan. Scooter's dad, Ramon, is fiercely supportive of Scooter's individuality. His other dad, Timothy, instructs you "to make Scooter fit in better and act like a boy." Timothy and Ramon, at pickup time, find their son playing dress-up with girls, while most of the boys are outside playing soccer. Timothy demands that you "tell Scooter in no uncertain terms never to play dress-up again."

How do you feel about Timothy's instructions to you? Have you felt "caught in the middle" like this before? What guidance does the NAEYC *Code of Ethical Conduct* offer? What is your professional challenge with this family? What steps would you take?

Reflection Questions

1. One hundred or five hundred years into the future, in what ways do you predict families will have evolved? What, if anything, is "timeless" or enduring about families? What is most likely to change, or even become extinct, about the family as we know it today? Consider this: In 1977, sociologist Amitai Etzioni predicted marriage would be extinct by the 1990s. Prepare a representation (collage, drawing, poem, song, paper) that conveys your prediction.

2. Investigate the evolution of the family. Since the beginning of time, what has changed and what has endured? Choose a particular ethnic group or culture. Research ways in which that group's family traditions, practices, values, and beliefs have evolved. Write a paper on your findings.

3. Identify at least two types of families that differ from your own family of origin or your chosen family. Consider families that differ from yours in ethnicity, culture, religion, and gender orientation. List what you would like to learn about these families. Interview a member of each of those types of families, using the "ask and listen" process. Summarize in writing the insights you gain.

4. Brainstorm as many family-friendly practices as you can. Identify what your own program is presently doing to be family-friendly. Visit other programs or interview other directors to get additional ideas. Make a list of at least ten family-friendly practices that could be put into effect today. Estimate the cost (if any) of each practice. Present to your class.

Team Projects

1. As individuals, write your definition of family and list your family values. As a team, share your definitions and lists. What do you have in common and what is different? Research definitions of family and family values (online, through journal

and other articles, books, and/or interviews). Present a report on the meaning of family and family values from at least three different viewpoints.

2. Research and discuss the benefits and challenges of working with families as partners. Identify situations in which you have both enjoyed and felt challenged in your relationships with families. Prepare three case studies of challenging situations with client families. Using resources such as *Young Children* and/or *Childcare Exchange*, find at least five pointers apiece on how to partner better with families. Lead a class discussion on your case studies; present the pointers you found.

3. Brainstorm a list of all the possible varieties of families (e.g., foster families, same-sex parents, nuclear, entire village). Research the history of at least three types of families in American history. What legal recognition has that (type of) family enjoyed? What discrimination has that group faced? Present your findings to the class. Invite your classmates to speculate on what family variety will be the most popular in the future, and what type will be most protected by law.

4. Many early childhood programs are homogeneous, representing families that have a great deal in common. How diverse is your own program, and how diverse would you like it to be? Identify programs with genuinely diverse families. Interview the directors of those programs to discover the factors and/or efforts that led to that program's heterogeneity. Prepare a list of steps early childhood programs can take to promote and ensure family diversity.

Bibliography

Barrera, I., R.M. Corso, and D. MacPherson. 2003. *Skilled dialogue: Strategies for responding to cultural diversity in early childhood.* Baltimore: Paul Brookes.

Bloom, P.J., and E. Eisenberg. 2003. Reshaping early childhood programs to be more family responsive. *America's Family Support Magazine*, pp. 36–38.

Bowman, Barbara, and Evelyn K. Moore, editors. 2006. *School readiness and social emotional development: Perspectives in cultural diversity.* Washington, DC: National Black Child Development Institute.

Bruno, Holly Elissa. 2003. Hearing parents in every language: An invitation to ECE professionals. *Child Care Exchange*, September–October, pp. 58–60.

Bruno, Holly Elissa. 2007. Teachers may never know: Using emotional intelligence to prevent and counter child neglect and abuse. *Dimensions in Early Childhood* 35(3): 22–29.

Christian, L.G. 2006. Understanding families: Applying family systems theory to early childhood practice. *Young Children* 61(2): 12–20.

Coontz, Stephanie. 1992, 2000. *The way we never were: The American family and the nostalgia trap.* New York: Basic Books.

Coontz, Stephanie. 1997. *The way we really are: Coming to terms with America's changing family.* New York: Perseus Books.

Crittenden, Danielle. 1999. *What our mothers didn't tell us.* New York: Simon & Schuster.

English, D. 1998. The extent and consequences of child maltreatment. *The Future of Children* 8 (Spring): 39–53.

Fadiman, Anne. 1997. *The spirit catches you and you fall down: A Hmong child, her doctors, and the collision of two cultures.* New York: Farrell, Straus & Giroux.

Gladwell, Malcolm. 2005. *Blink: The power of thinking without thinking.* New York: Little, Brown and Company.

Goleman, Daniel. 2006. *Social intelligence: The new science of human relationships.* New York: Bantam Books.

Gonzalez-Mena, Janet. 2007. What is third space and how do we get there? Unpublished paper presented at NAEYC annual conference, November 6.

Gonzalez-Mena. 2009. *Child, family and community: Family centered care and education,* 5th edition. Upper Saddle River, NJ and Columbus, OH: Pearson/Merrill/Prentice Hall.

Im, J.P., R. Parlakian, and S. Sanchez. 2007. Rocking and rolling: Supporting infants, toddlers, and their families. *Young Children* 62(5): 65–67.

Katz, Johnathan. 1995. *The invention of heterosexuality.* New York: Dutton.

Keyser, J. 2006. *Building a family centered early childhood program.* Washington, DC: NAEYC.

Lewis, T., F. Amini, and R. Lannon. 2001. *A general theory of love.* New York: Vintage.

Marshak, L.E., and F. Prezant. 2007. *Married with special-needs children.* New York: Woodbine House.

Meyerowitz, Jo Ann. 1994. *Not June Cleaver: Women and God in post-war America, 1945–1960.* Philadephia: Temple University Press.

Powell, D.R. 1998. Research in review: Reweaving parents into the fabric of early childhood programs. *Young Children* 53(5): 60–67.

Protecting children by strengthening families: A guidebook for early childhood programs. 2004. Washington, DC: Center for the Study of Social Policy. April. Online: *www.cssp.org.*

Sugarman, Steve, Mary Ann Mason, and Arlene Skolnick, eds. 1998. *All our families: New policies for the new century.* New York: Oxford University Press.

Ury, William. 1999. *Getting to peace: Transforming conflict at home, at work and in the world.* New York: Penguin Group.

U.S. Department of Health & Human Services. 2006. *Child maltreatment 2006: summary.* Washington, DC: Administration for Children and Families. *http://www.acf.hhs.gov/programs/cb/pubs/cm06/summary.htm.*

Web Resources

Family-Centered Practice
http://www.childwelfare.gov/famcentered/

Harvard Family Research Project
http://www.gse.harvard.edu/hfrp/

Partnering with Families and Communities
http://pdonline.ascd.org/pd_online/success_di/el200405_epstein.html

Recognizing Child Abuse and Neglect: Signs and Symptoms
http://www.childwelfare.gov/pubs/factsheets/signs.cfm

Supporting Families of Children with Disabilities in Inclusive Programs
http://journal.naeyc.org/btj/200601/KaczmarekBTJ.asp

Quest for Quality: Licensing, Accreditation, Codes of Ethical Conduct, Professionalism

Learning Goals

As you study this chapter, you can look forward to reaching these learning goals:

1. Understand the challenge of defining quality.
2. Identify who contributes to the definition of quality for early childhood educators.
3. Craft an evolving definition of professionalism that embraces emotional and social intelligence.
4. Discuss and apply total quality management (TQM) principles.
5. Utilize codes of ethical responsibility.
6. Explain how accreditation standards relate to quality improvement.
7. Name various types of quality rating scales.
8. Practice how to stand for quality and professionalism while under stress.

Please think of the children first. If you ever have anything to do with their entertainment, their food, their toys, their custody, their childcare, their health care, their education—listen to the children, learn about them, learn from them. Think of the children first.

—*Fred Rogers*

The noblest moral law is that we should unremittingly work for the good of mankind.

—*Mahatma Gandhi*

Case Study: Advocating for Quality

Mohammed, new director of Kids Come First Academy, has taken the "outside pathway" to leadership. He was selected over several internal candidates, all of whom are female. The Academy's board of directors expects Mohammed to "take charge over unruly teachers and turn the school around" to meet new accreditation standards. Board chair Reginald lets Mohammed know that prior director Pam was fired for failing to motivate teachers to develop the necessary classroom portfolios.

Mohammed was attracted to the position because the school looks like the United Nations in terms of family diversity. As Mohammed prepares for his first all-staff meeting, he wonders, "What can I do to motivate teachers, many of whom resent me already, to dedicate themselves to the accreditation process?" Mohammed picks up his cell and calls you for advice. Mohammed tells you he has never been the only male in any of his prior positions. "What should I do?" he asks.

Mohammed's dilemma, in the chapter case study, is not unusual. With evolving accreditation standards, as with any change, many staff members resist: "Who has time, with our already demanding jobs, to work on all those classroom portfolio details?" Directors who aim to improve program quality, while hoping to make everyone happy, find themselves facing the same problem as Sisyphus, a Greek mythology character.

Sisyphus's responsibility was to push a large, round rock up to the top of a mountain. He fortified himself, took a deep breath, and got to work coaxing the rock up the steep incline. Each day, Sisyphus toiled and sweated. Each day, he pushed the rock a little farther up the mountain. Regardless of how hard Sisyphus pushed, or how high he aimed, the heavy rock rolled right back to the bottom of the mountain at the end of the day.

Leaders, like Sisyphus, often feel alone in their push to the mountaintop of quality. To roll the rock to the top and keep it there requires a team dedicated to the same goal. Persuading teachers to take a stand for quality, especially when that stand requires additional rigorous work, calls upon every bit of EQ the leader has painstakingly developed. In this chapter, we will team up to help Sisyphus roll the stone to the top.

❖ Functional versus Dysfunctional Teams

As we take on this challenge, let's keep in mind the characteristics of functional versus dysfunctional teams. Author Patrick Lencioni (2002) spells this out for us in Table 15.1.

Mohammed's staff appear to be lacking trust, commitment, and focus on achieving the collective result of meeting accreditation standards for a quality program.

TABLE 15.1

Functional versus Dysfunctional Teams

Dysfunctional Team	Functional Team
Absence of trust	They trust one another.
Fear of conflict	They engage in unfiltered conflict around ideas.
Lack of commitment	They commit to decisions and plans of action.
Avoidance of accountability	They hold one another accountable for delivering against those plans.
Inattention to results	They focus on the achievement of collective results.

Lencioni advises, "A little structure goes a long way toward helping people take action that they may not otherwise be inclined to do." Good news! Accreditation processes provide more structure than the frame of a skyscraper. Charts and check-off lists abound.

"One of the most difficult challenges for a leader who wants to instill accountability on a team is to encourage and allow the team to serve as the first and primary accountability mechanism" (Lencioni 2002, 188–190).

⚔ Quest for Quality:
Who Defines Quality in Our Profession?

Agreeing on indicators and a definition of quality is a leadership issue that can be as difficult as herding cats. For help with defining quality, most professions turn to a central authority for the answer.

For attorneys and doctors, one authorized group defines quality. Lawyers turn to the American Bar Association. Doctors rely upon the American Medical Association. In early childhood, naming a central authorized organization is not easy. Our authorities on quality are professional organizations like NAEYC, NBCDI, or NACCP, state licensing authorities, federal regulators and/or private organizations, or some combination thereof. Each of these entities offers valuable contributions, but none has the ultimate authority to define quality for early childhood. This ambiguity contributes to the complexity of understanding quality in early childhood.

Written Standards for Quality

In the midst of these questions, drafting standards for quality is not an easy task. Objective criteria for quality and professionalism can display the dry elegance of a captured butterfly pinned to a scientist's display board. Instead of a fluttering and dancing creature, the butterfly is stuck as an inert specimen. Opalescent and delicate as this butterfly is, the butterfly no longer flies.

The point is this: In early childhood, professionalism and quality do not hold still. They grow and change as the field evolves and changes. *Given the dynamic nature of our profession, can we isolate standards for quality that are timeless and enduring?* Can those standards embrace emotional and social intelligence, to complement rational analysis?

Quality Definitions That Honor Cultural Diversity

"Top quality," "the highest standard of quality," and "first-rate performance" all aim to describe the best of the best. How does a director know her program is a quality program? In the highly interpersonal, culturally diverse field of early childhood, can external, across-the-board standards reflect the quality of different communities? When is one's "personal best" good enough? Must we be perfect to be professional?

Defining quality is akin to choosing a political party. So much depends upon our own view of the world. Stephanie Feeney and Nancy Freeman (2000, 17), authors of *Teaching the NAEYC Code of Ethical conduct*, note, "To a large extent, professional values and ethics are an extension of personal values and morality, so we begin with those topics."

Personal values predict our definition of quality. One director may see quality as treating each person who comes through her door as a special, unique individual. Another director may understand quality as "crossing all the t's and dotting all the i's" on

---

Sit down before fact as a little child, be prepared to give up every preconceived notion, follow humbly wherever or whatever abysses nature leads, or you will learn nothing.

—Aldous Huxley

Be glad of life, because it gives you the chance to look up at the stars.

—Henry Van Dyke

accreditation checklists. Incorporating Reggio Emilia observation and documentation techniques may be another director's vision for quality.

Most professions, as noted, like law, medicine, and dentistry, rely on external, objective standards for quality, for example, passing a rigorous test like the bar exam or national medical boards. Relying on external standards ensures consistency. This approach also brings drawbacks.

If a person is not a good test taker, should he be excluded from a profession? Picture a highly competent infant teacher whose learning disabilities prevent her from wrapping her mind around university courses. Does a director further or lessen quality by letting her go? Courage, caring, and integrity are key to early childhood professionalism and quality. No standardized test today accurately measures these qualities.

External standards bring consistency: everyone is required to comply. My colleague Dr. Luis Vicente Reyes recalls getting poor marks as an infant teacher from external evaluators. Luis maintains his more physical, "roughhousing" ways are gender-based and particularly appealing to active, energetic children in his care. He felt the external evaluators unfairly held him to a female standard for care. Early childhood education needs a quality measurement system that honors and embraces cultural and gender diversity.

> A foolish consistency is the hobgoblin of little souls.
>
> **—Henry David Thoreau**

> Mark Twain, author of *Huckleberry Finn*, noted that if we try to define humor, the patient dies on the dissecting table. If you have ever been asked to explain a joke, you know the magic moment of laughter has been lost. Attempting to put the intangibles about quality into words can meet the same fate.

Nursing Profession's Quest to Redefine Quality

To gain perspective, let's consider another service profession's quest to define quality. During the 1980s, I served as vice president for Academic Affairs at a University of Maine campus. The head of the nursing faculty was one of my direct reports, and our shared goal was to provide the best possible nursing education for our students and the communities they served.

Our campus had traditionally offered an associate's degree in nursing, but change was in the air. I found myself on the bumpy road of shifting standards. For years, nurses had been educated in hospitals through hands-on experience with patients. Hospitals granted students professional titles like RN (registered nurse) and LPN (licensed professional nurse). Missing from most hospital training programs, however, were courses that broadened the nurse's understanding, such as Social Determinants of Health (University of Washington School of Nursing). While nursing students could give shots and take blood pressure, they were not consistently exposed to the research and rationale behind the processes.

Quality varied from one hospital's training program to another. As a result, nurses were paid little. The status of the nursing profession was low, despite how hard nurses worked and how valuable their services were.

Low status and inadequate pay for hard, invaluable work—do these sound familiar? The nursing profession's quest for quality provides clues for early childhood to examine.

Nationwide, nursing educators devised a plan to break the profession out of the low status and low pay morass. Their vision was to professionalize nursing so that no one could challenge the importance of a nurse's work or the value of her education. As the professional organization set standards to require baccalaureate degrees for nurses, associate degree RN and LPN programs were targeted for extinction. A rigorous curriculum was put into place that ensured exposure to the "why's" and not just the "how-to's" of nursing practices.

> Not everything that is faced can be changed, but nothing can be changed until it is faced.
>
> **—James Baldwin**

Consider the nursing profession today. Notice the high demand for nurses, their salary increase, and rigorous educational requirements. These victories were hard won. In the process, however, a number of "practical" nurses who could not transition into the new educational requirements were left behind.

NAEYC's rigorous accreditation standards that went into effect in 2006 are reminiscent of the efforts made by nursing educators to uplift the profession's standing. What was gained and what was lost in this process of standardizing quality and defining professionalism through consistent, objective, and, at times, impersonal standards?

As the early childhood field increasingly values emotional and social intelligence, its professional standards must encompass this knowledge. Note the difference in these two statements:

1. Revised standards clarify how we understand quality; and,
2. As we clarify how we understand quality, our professional standards change.

This is the chicken and egg of defining quality, outside in or inside out.

An Evolving Definition of Professionalism

Should early childhood follow suit with the nursing profession? What can we learn from their experience? Understanding the value of emotional and social intelligence holds a key to the answer. Our "bedside manner" is our ability to read people as well as we read books and to intuit what to do with that information. Early childhood practitioners may have PhDs in life skills but only a few college courses toward an associate's degree.

 The definition for early childhood professionalism must embrace nonverbal, often difficult to measure, but invaluable interpersonal expertise. Capturing the quality of a caregiver's smile is like pinning a butterfly to a display board.

Remember the leader's challenge of holding two opposing values, one in each hand? The medical profession is taking note of two things:

1. The high value patients place on a doctor's bedside manner; and,
2. Medical students' lack of training in this area.

To remedy this disparity, the medical field is increasingly including EQ in its evolving definition of quality. This quest for quality is similar to changes occurring in early childhood. The field recognizes the need for professional standards that combine core competencies and interpersonal skills. Professionalism and quality are closely knit, so understanding professionalism can clear some fog.

In her forthcoming paper *Is Profession a Noun?* Gwen Morgan takes on the challenge of defining professionalism. Gwen "tells it like it is" in saying, "We encounter turbulence and discomfort when we try to give it a definition." After painstakingly outlining the history and evolution of professionalism, Gwen concludes, "We need to make our meaning clear, especially in our own minds. To do this, we need to develop our "only ifs," such as the following.

Professionalism (in early childhood education) is a noun, but only if:

- Our knowledge base is free of gender bias and encompasses a valuing of caring as essential.
- Our professional education can enable us to relate to other helping professions and collaborate well with a focus on families.
- The recognized knowledge base meets all the needs for those in the field, including infant/toddler teachers, special needs, school-age programs, directors, family childcare.
- Our concept is one of lifelong learning at all degree levels, and beyond, with opportunity to gain in status and salary for individuals within the field through more learning.

- There is not permanent social class distinction between newcomers entering the field in assisting roles, only if they will be given opportunities to move into more complex roles.
- We can define a parent/professional relationship that does not rely on a status inequity, that primarily negotiates and exchanges information, rather than imposing expertise.
- Our higher education system can offer access to many more low income and minority group members, most of whom will be employed while learning.
- Our fields would attract generalists who care about working with children, families and community, would offer supports to enhance their work, income, and self-esteem.
- We would welcome diversity of cultures, races, life-styles, for both men and women. It would welcome not exclude: emphasize cooperation not competition.
- The content of educational opportunities is both challenging and suited to the work performed.
- Our profession would develop leaders to speak out for our principles: valuing the uniqueness of each child, creating an intimate safe and healthy environment for small numbers of children.
- We would view parents as colleagues (rather than clients, patients or customers) in the task for raising a generation of active, healthy, involved citizens." (2009, draft of paper in progress)

Given the evolving nature of our profession, let's look to the business field to see if their understanding of quality might help us.

⚔ Total Quality Management (TQM)

Every time you are asked to complete an evaluation form, you benefit from TQM standards. When you find fresh fruit at a hotel registration desk and chocolates on your turned-down bed, you benefit from TQM. When you read Paula Jorde Bloom's *Blueprint for Action: Achieving Center-Based Change through Staff Development*, you will find TQM principles applied to the early childhood education field. When you review NAEYC standards for classroom and program portfolios, you also will see TQM in action.

TQM views quality as a start-to-finish process of creating a product or providing a service that will be just what the customer needs. Total quality management practice shifts the focus from the provider's needs to the client's.

This may be hard to picture, but prior to TQM, customers' opinions were not considered important. Manufacturers virtually held buyers hostage. When Henry Ford proclaimed, "They can have any color Ford they want, as long as it is black," he spoke for his times.

Competition pushed manufacturers and service providers to scurry for ways to distinguish themselves in the market place. Suddenly, a black automobile was not enough. The company that provided variety was the company customers preferred.

Three flavors of ice cream—vanilla, chocolate, and strawberry—no longer attracted customers. Baskin-Robbins became a household name when it distinguished itself by offering thirty-one flavors of ice cream in 1953. Does anyone recall a day when automobile companies did not introduce a new model every year? Shifting the focus to customers' needs and wants changed everything. TQM drove this revolution.

Total quality management, the brainchild of L. Edwards Deming, emerged after World War II. Deming viewed TQM as meeting and exceeding the needs of the customer

Total quality management (TQM), in theory and practice, provides clues to quality.

by providing excellence in service and product. Given Henry Ford's attitude, Deming's idea of shifting the focus from the manufacturer's needs to the customer's needs was a radical notion.

Deming's ideas on quality, so readily accepted and practiced today, were not immediately embraced in America. Sent by the United States government to assist in revitalizing the Japanese economy, Deming took his ideas with him to Japan. The rest is history. Japanese manufacturers embraced TQM. In a short space of time, Japanese products became synonymous with quality. Sony and Mitsubishi dominated the electronics market. "Made in Japan" came to mean a better product.

American manufacturers took notice when their customers purchased a Toyota Camry or a Honda Accord over Lincoln town cars and Pontiacs. Toyota not only rivaled American car companies, but outpaced all-American favorites like American Motors. Henry Ford would be eating his words.

This shift to focusing on customers is significant for early childhood programs. Customers, thanks to TQM, have come to expect not only quality workmanship and products, but quality service as well. As service providers, early childhood professionals function in a world of TQM expectations.

What are those *TQM expectations and standards?* In a nutshell, providers need to practice these principles:

1. The customer is always right.
2. Anticipate the customer's needs.
3. Not only meet but exceed the customer's expectations.
4. Serve both "internal" and "external" customers.
5. Empower employees to make appropriate decisions.
6. "Benchmark," or regularly evaluate yourself, your service, and/or product.
7. Practice "continuous improvement."

Let's take these principles of quality one at a time to see what they tell us about quality in early childhood.

The Customer Is Always Right

When Mrs. Petrozullio declares that her daughter, Laura, is perfect and accuses you of provoking Laura's disruptive behavior, is Mrs. Petrozullio right? When Tedy's grandmother insists she has paid her bills, but you have no record of her payments, is Tedy's grandmother right? How about toddler teacher Missy, who calls in sick every Friday and Monday, and you discover she is cavorting at the beach over her long weekends. Is Missy right? What could Deming have meant? How can someone who is just plain wrong be "right"?

With the help of emotional intelligence, we can find a deeper answer. What is the basic need of each family and child? Respect. Each person who walks through the door is worthy of respect. In this way, the customer is always right. That is, each customer has the right to our respectful attention.

Recently, I asked a group of customer service professionals, "Is the customer always right?" A young man shouted *"no way!"* He was unwavering and certain that one family he had worked with was wrong. He felt his duty was to show the family how wrong they were. The customer service provider may have won the battle, but he lost the war. Had the family felt respected, they may have been much more open to entertaining other viewpoints. Admitting a mistake to a judgmental person is next to impossible.

Mrs. Petrozullio, Tedy's grandmom, and Missy's stories differed greatly from their director's understanding of the situation. Nonetheless, by giving each person the benefit of the doubt, the director respectfully moved from a "gotcha" attitude to a problem-solving mode.

This does not mean Missy's absenteeism was acceptable, nor was delinquent bill paying. However, by using social EQ and due process (Chapters 2 and 4), a director can identify the underlying issues and assess if those issues could be mutually and respectfully resolved.

Anticipate the Customer's Needs

There is magic in this principle: Anticipate and act on the customer's needs. If an early childhood education program can provide families with something they need, but have not yet dreamt of, a director brings magic to the moment.

Director Johanna in New Hampshire provides "sleepovers" for children when the stressors in their parents' lives overwhelm them. Johanna believes her job is to "make things easier for families to enjoy being with their children."

Have you ever received a gift you adored, but never knew you wanted? For my sixtieth birthday, I invited friends to "surprise me" in any way they wished. Throughout that year, I received phone calls, cards, and gifts I never anticipated.

My favorite gift arrived via UPS from my sunny Miami colleague Luis Hernandez. Luis graduated from college in chilly western Massachusetts and recalled New England winters with a shiver. His gift to me was a multicolored, transparent, 14-foot banner of tropical fish. You bet, in a heartbeat I unfurled those fish to dart across my ceiling. Every time I looked up, I smiled. Luis had anticipated my need: the warmth of the tropics in the ice of Massachusetts!

Early childhood programs have opportunities daily to anticipate and meet families' needs (Chapter 14). Here are some examples directors have shared with me:

- Offer steaming cups of freshly brewed coffee or herbal tea to parents, sending them on their way with a smile after they drop off their children.
- Bake healthy oatmeal cookies or other snacks with the children. Send a bag of these treats home with the children.
- Create a cozy drop-off space for families with overstuffed chairs and couches.
- Surprise parents with a special photograph of their child, with a "frame" decorated by the child.
- Schedule family nights with fun intergenerational activities.
- Organize trips for families to the child's next school to meet teachers, view the facility, and begin relationships to smooth the transition from your program.

In our service profession, respecting customers and anticipating their needs are two indicators of total quality. Consider how you may have anticipated another person's needs. Have you, like Luis, given a gift that was longed for but not requested? What additional ways can directors "surprise" families by meeting their needs and unspoken desires?

Not Only Meet, but Exceed, the Customer's Expectations

Every family has the right to expect a childcare program that meets state licensing requirements. Clean surfaces, safe spaces, and a beneficial teacher-student ratio are some of the expectations families have that licensing standards require.

Licensing standards set the basic standard, not the optimal standard. States vary on what that basic standard is. As a program leader, you will have the right to go far beyond the basics. Classrooms that are colorful and intriguing for children, with spaces for different activities, meet and exceed licensing requirements. Teachers who have studied early childhood and are richly experienced in and passionate about the field meet and exceed licensing standards. Offering chair massages to overwhelmed parents is not mentioned in any licensing standard I have read.

FIGURE 15.1   *Stairway to Quality*

The *"stairway to quality"* (Figure 15.1) helps us picture how to not only meet customer expectations, but exceed those expectations. Accrediting agencies' standards are full of examples that show how to create quality services far beyond basic licensing requirements. Go to *naeyc.org* to compare accreditation standards with your state's licensing requirements.

Serve Both Internal and External Customers

External Customers

Internal customers are members of an organization. Internal customers serve external customers.

To provide quality, service providers must intimately know their customers. Who are these customers? Yes, early childhood programs serve children. As Fred Rogers reminds us, "Think of the children first." Our contracts for service, however, are not with the children but with the family.

According to TQM principles, "external customers" are customers who pay for services. External customers come to programs "from the outside." Your job as a leader will be to serve families while they are with you, in a way that supports and improves the quality of life when they are not with you. Picturing a program's external customers is not difficult. Finding customers who are not families, however, may be like a "Where's Waldo?" puzzle.

TQM theory expands the definition of customer. Not only do early childhood programs serve external customers, but they serve "internal customers" as well. Who could this be? In addition to families, who else depends upon a program's services? To answer these questions, picture others who need a director's attention and care.

Internal Customers

As you may imagine, internal customers come "from within" an organization. Internal customers do the work of the organization. Teachers, custodians, part-time staff, cooks, administrators, consultants, board members, and other staff are internal customers. All of these individuals have needs. Internal customers may not always be clear on expressing these needs. Although directors are not mind readers, they may feel like they need this skill! If a director fails to anticipate, meet, and exceed her internal customers' needs, she can find herself in an unhappy organization.

The "stairway to quality" applies to internal customers, too. A teacher's basic need is a regular paycheck, steady job, and a furnished classroom. She also needs effective supervision, feedback on her performance, and interconnectedness with colleagues. She needs recognition for her contributions and rewards for going above and beyond what is expected. Beloved directors anticipate and exceed employees' needs.

No pressure, no diamonds.

—Mary Case

Examples of meeting and anticipating internal customers' needs include:

- Hold annual staff retreats in alluring settings.
- Provide enjoyable team building activities.
- Bring in inspirational trainers on desired topics (e.g., classroom management).
- Give out gift certificates to acknowledge special contributions.
- Pay for staff to travel and attend early childhood conferences.
- Mentor staff individually to help them realize their worth.
- Create a staff lounge, as comfy and welcoming as home.

What Motivates Internal Customers the Most?

Employees leave their jobs when one or more of the following needs are not being met: trust, hope, sense of worth, and competence (Branham 2005, 19–20). How do directors help staff remain motivated when career choices are somewhat limited within early childhood programs?

Research (Butler & Waldroop 1999) from Harvard Business School offers guidance. Financial rewards do not sustain staff motivation. Although making a reasonable wage is crucial, being paid well is not the major motivator for most staff. Nor is being competent in a particular line of work. In other words, an employee may be competent at number crunching but not enjoy working with figures. Doing what we do well also does not necessarily motivate us.

Employees are most highly motivated when they are doing work aligned with their "deeply embedded life interests" (DELIs). DELIs include:

1. *Mentoring and Counseling*: Helping others grow professionally.
2. *Managing People*: Motivating others to achieve success.
3. *Managing Projects/Enterprises:* Taking the lead on an endeavor.
4. *Translating Technology*: Applying computer expertise to ECE settings.
5. *Theorizing*: Leadership in envisioning "big picture" innovations in the field.
6. *Number Crunching*: Figuring out accurate and streamlined budgets/finances.
7. *Artistic Expression*: Creating an original way to do the work.
8. *Teaching*: Delighting in contributing to growth and knowledge.

Identifying your DELIs is an important first step in being highly motivated as an administrator. Likewise, helping staff members to uncover their DELIs will revitalize them (Bruno & Copeland 2000). The closer our daily work aligns with our deeply embedded life interest, the more content we are professionally.

The greatest good you can do for another is not just share your riches, but to reveal to them their own.

—Benjamin Disraeli

Do you know a director who yearns for the classroom? Her DELI may be teaching, not mentoring, leading people, and managing projects. Her excellence in the classroom may have propelled her into administration. She left her passion in the classroom with her students. Only in the classroom with the children does she feel renewed and uplifted.

Do you work with a teacher who enjoys helping new teachers develop? That teacher's DELI may be mentoring and counseling. A wise director will find ways for the teacher to mentor others. Do you know a staff member whose clothing and jewelry are "wearable art," and whose classroom vibrates with learning experiences? Her DELI may be artistic expression. Intuitive directors will invite that staff member to beautify shared center spaces.

Honoring staff members as internal customers is a clue to staff retention as well as to quality. One director, with no extra funding, created titles to capture the DELI of each of her staff members. She dubbed one teacher "Creator of special moments," another "Family comforting specialist," and another "Bulletin board expert." Internal customer satisfaction directly influences external customer satisfaction.

Was anyone excluded from the internal customer list? Unless the director's needs are anticipated and met, the pivotal internal customer will be hurting. Self-care for directors, including participation in directors' support groups and leadership courses, travel to inspiring conferences, and vacation time away from the program, is invaluable for the number 1 internal customer: you. Quality begins with you. Add the director's name to the top of the list! For a director to lead on purpose, she needs to take care of herself, especially when demands on her are the most frantic.

Empower Employees to Make Appropriate Decisions

One morning, a janitor in a Richmond, Virginia, early childhood center welcomed a new family when no one else was available. Nothing in the janitor's job description told him to welcome visitors and put them at ease. Nevertheless, the janitor took time away from his assigned duties to greet the family and show them around the center. The janitor did what the program needed. He felt empowered to make the decision to help. Effective leaders create working environments in which employees feel empowered to put TQM into action.

An empowered employee is at ease making decisions in the moment to be customer-friendly. Most job descriptions include boilerplate, generalized phrases such as "be a team player" and "perform any additional tasks assigned by the director." Nonetheless, some employees take the stance that they will not do anything if it is not literally stated in their job descriptions. With TQM, employees know quality begins with them. TQM furthers the supervision principle: Expect employees to take responsibility for their own professionalism.

Benchmark or Regularly Evaluate All Aspects of Your Program

The term *"benchmarking"* literally derived from the marks a worker carved onto a bench with a knife each time a product or process was successfully completed. Back in the day before calculators and computers, those benchmarks served as record keepers. Henry Ford's Model T assembly-line men used benchmarks to guage the history of their productivity.

I often picture myself carving a notch in a bench when I complete a challenging task. On my office whiteboard, I mark off each chapter of this book as I complete it, and again as I revise each chapter. Seeing each tangible mark keeps me motivated. Celebrations of accomplishments are another form of benchmarking.

My administration class visited Director Nicole St. Victor at the Yawkey Center in Dorchester, Massachusetts, on the first day NAEYC external evaluators were scheduled to review her program. Nicole wheeled out her program's portfolio in an impressive set of hanging files. Each of the ten NAEYC standards was sectioned off in order. Within

TABLE 15.2

NAEYC Program Standards Benchmarks

1. *Relationships:* promotion of positive relationships with all children and adults;
2. *Curriculum:* leads to social, emotional, physical, language, and cognitive development;
3. *Teaching:* developmentally, culturally, and linguistically appropriate and effective;
4. *Assessment of child progress:* ongoing, systemic, formal and informal, and shared with families;
5. *Health:* nutrition and health standards to protect children and staff;
6. *Teachers:* qualified, knowledgeable and dedicated;
7. *Families:* collaborative, culturally respectful relationships with families;
8. *Community relationships:* interconnectedness and support for communities served;
9. *Physical environment:* safe, healthful, well maintained indoors and outside;
10. *Leadership and management:* policies, procedures, systems implemented by qualified administrators.

each section, Nicole had placed file after file of documentation on how each standard was met (see Table 15.2). Despite her in-depth, first-rate benchmarking, Nicole was still apprehensive about the evaluation. The prospect of our quality being judged as "passing" or "failing" activates sweaty palms for many of us.

Portfolios benchmark whether early childhood measurement standards are met. For a program to be accredited, the director must submit both an overall program portfolio and one portfolio for each classroom. A portfolio is a transportable collection of documented materials such as papers, photographs, and CDs. A portfolio consists of all the ways a director or teacher "benchmarks" or keeps track of a program's progress toward established goals.

Consider this example. NAEYC holds teachers to the standard of effectively involving families: "The program establishes and maintains collaborative relationships with the child's family to foster children's development in all settings. These relationships are sensitive to family composition, language, and culture."

A teacher's classroom portfolio would document in detail what she has done to meet that standard, such as:

1. The *teacher's written description* of her professional philosophy and steps she has taken to involve families;
2. *Photographs* of parents interacting with children in the classroom;
3. *Fliers* inviting families to program-sponsored family activities;
4. *Classroom newsletters* created by teachers with helpful information;
5. *Evaluation forms* for parents to complete on classroom quality;
6. *Lists* of classroom parents who serve on the Parent Advisory Board;
7. *Comments written by families,* including completed evaluation forms.

In these ways, a teacher's classroom portfolio benchmarks progress on effective family involvement.

Select a different NAEYC standard (see *naeyc.org/*). Develop your own list of portfolio activities that would show the degree to which a teacher has met the standard.

Benchmarking comes more naturally to individuals who enjoy details and order. Professionals with Sensing and Judging as MBTI preferences find documentation comes naturally. Benchmarking can stress teachers who prefer interaction to record keeping. MBTI Perceivers often prefer to "live in the moment" rather than hold still to record detail after detail. Supervisors, who know each teacher's strengths and shortcomings, can help staff build on strengths to benchmark their successes.

Continuous Improvement

There will come a time when you believe everything is finished. That will be the beginning.

—Louis L'Amour

"Resting on our laurels" is not part of the TQM quality equation. Deming's theory, instead, exhorts us to find ways to better ourselves, especially when we are at our best. How can the best get better? Don't we deserve a break from the rigors of improvement? When we hear from NAEYC that we have been reaccredited, we can take a rest, right?

Practically, yes, we can celebrate and enjoy our hard-earned success. We also can call upon our uplifted spirits to help us take a fresh look at our mission and vision. What is that next step toward our dream? Continuously improving and enjoying our successes need not be mutually exclusive.

Continuous improvement is always looking for and finding ways to grow and change for the better. Leaders who are not only open to but actively seek feedback receive the highest evaluations from their employees. This asking and listening is ongoing.

New York City Mayor Ed Koch walked through the neighborhoods of his city asking, "How am I doing?" Koch's legacy is his affable willingness to ask for feedback from his constituents.

Imagine a toddler classroom that receives great praise for its innovative curriculum. The teachers in the classroom, however, think that families could be more involved. Continuous improvement for these teachers means building on the strength of their innovative curriculum to find more ways to involve families. Continuous improvement brings a dynamic of renewal to the classroom.

✖ Quality and Professionalism: Doing the Right Thing While Reaching for the Stars

Has a definition of quality or professionalism surfaced yet? At least we have clues. Quality is doing our best, within the context of standards that call us to reach for the stars. Professionalism is continuously making choices to do the right thing. How do directors know what the right thing is, especially when values and cultures differ?

Codes of Ethical Conduct as Pathways to Quality

Another indicator of quality is the profession's code of ethics. That code stands as a guide to how a professional acts. Codes exist, in part, so directors can turn to them when faced with prickly dilemmas. One such code is the National Association for Child Care Professionals (NACCP) Code of Ethics (see Table 15.3).

Unlike the butterfly pinned to the display board, a code of ethics needs to be a "living" document. Living documents are timeless and enduring, able to withstand crises and change. Leaders and staff alike depend on such codes of conduct to guide them through current and future issues.

Codes are also "touchstones." A touchstone is that rocklike object we can hold and feel. Touching something cool like a stone can bring us to our senses and back to reality. Another word for touchstone is a talisman. Some people wear religious symbols on necklaces as a talisman of what matters most deeply to them. A leader's code of ethics is her touchstone for quality.

In Chapter 3, "Leading on Purpose," you listed your core values. Revisit those core values in order to revise them into your professional core values. For example, if respect is your core value, you might list "Respect for the cultural differences of families, staff members, and our communities" as your professional core value. Once you have drafted your own professional core values, compare them with NAEYC's core values in Table 15.4.

T A B L E   1 5 . 3

National Association for Child Care Professionals (NACCP) Code of Ethics

The National Association of Child Care Professionals is an association of people who are leaders in the field of early care and education. As an association, we believe that child care is a profession and that it is our responsibility as professional women and men to lead our centers in an ethical manner. Recognizing that the association is a vital link in this process, we determine to govern our individual centers as follows:

1. To maintain the ethical standards of the National Association of Child Care Professionals to more effectively serve our children, their parents, and the field.
2. To continually remember that ours is a service industry. We are committed to providing quality child care to our children and their families, and we place this service above personal gain.
3. To conduct our business in a way that will both maintain goodwill within the field and build the confidence of parents, the community, and fellow professionals.
4. To cooperatively work with parents and faithfully deliver the kind of service promised to them, whether orally, in writing, or implied.
5. To charge a fair tuition that will enable us to pay a fair living wage to the director and staff at our centers.
6. To maintain the appropriate child-to-staff ratios that will ensure provision of quality service to our children and their families.
7. To hire qualified individuals and to train them to work within the guidelines of this code of ethics.
8. To avoid sowing discontent among the employees of competitors with the purpose of embarrassing or hindering their business.
9. To avoid possible damage to a competitor's image by purposefully misleading parents, members of the community, or fellow professionals.
10. To support the policies and programs of our association and to participate in its regional and national activities.
11. To conduct ourselves at all times in a way that will bring credit to our association and the child care field.

Core Values of NAEYC

Shared core values set a standard for quality in our profession. Nonetheless, given our different backgrounds and beliefs, we will not all have the "same take" on what standard or value matters most. The "right answer" may depend on who is interpreting the standards. When disagreements of this sort pop up like mushrooms after steady rain, leaders have ethical dilemmas. NAEYC advises, "When we face a dilemma, it is our professional responsibility to consult the Code and all relevant parties to find the most ethical solution." Shared core values will help directors and staff come to a solution.

Over the years, I have come up with a one-word code of ethics: *respect.* When I act with respect for children, peers, families, early childhood, and myself, I act ethically. I remind myself of what Isaac Asimov famously said, "Never let your sense of morals get in the way of doing what's right." Sometimes an individual's personal set of values needs to take second place so that a greater good can emerge.

If you recall the difference between the "spirit of the law" and the "letter of the law," you have another insight into how to solve ethical dilemmas based on differences in values. If we go deep enough beneath the surface, we can find a place where we can agree.

TABLE 15.4

NAEYC Core Values

Standards of ethical behavior in early childhood care and education are based on commitment to the following core values that are deeply rooted in the history of the field of early childhood care and education. We have made a commitment to:

- Appreciate childhood as a unique and valuable stage of the human life cycle
- Base our work on knowledge of how children develop and learn
- Appreciate and support the bond between the child and family
- Recognize that children are best understood and supported in the context of family, culture, community, and society
- Respect the dignity, worth, and uniqueness of each individual child, family member, and colleague
- Respect diversity in children, families, and colleagues
- Recognize that children and adults achieve their full potential in the context of relationships that are based on trust and respect

Source: NAEYC *Code of Ethical Conduct*, revised April 2005, Preamble

Case Study: Doing the Right Thing

Teacher Tipitina makes every effort to do the right thing, even though her personal value might have to take second place. Tipitina is a devout Baptist. She believes food should be blessed before it is eaten. Only one family, Isaiah's, shares Tipitina's belief. As Tipitina and her aide serve the children snacks, Tipitina invites Isaiah to help serve. Tipitina and Isaiah silently bless their own food before they eat it.

Tipitina agrees that no one should be able to enforce her religious beliefs on others in an early childhood setting. Case studies that conclude this chapter will give you the opportunity to practice ethical problem solving.

When Is a Profession Professional?

Every profession works through the process of defining what professionalism means. What "value added" does our profession offer? What behaviors ensure that customers receive our best? What kind of reputation do we want to have? These are questions that each professional organization must answer. As times change, professional standards change along with them. However, some core values are timeless. Those values rarely will change, and can be said to "withstand the tests of time."

As we seek to define professionalism in early childhood, we need to know what will endure. In *Ethics and the Early Childhood Educator: Using the NAEYC Code*, Feeney, Freeman, and Moravcik (1999) spell out what a profession is. They say a profession:

- Requires practitioners to participate in *prolonged training* based on principles that involve judgment for their application, not a precise set of behaviors that apply in all cases.
- Professional training is delivered in accredited institutions. Members of the profession control rigorous *requirements for entry* to the training.
- Bases its work on a *specialized knowledge and expertise,* which is applied according to the particular needs of each case.

- Members of the profession have agreed on *standards of practice*—procedures that are appropriate to the solution of ordinary predicaments that practitioners expect to encounter in their work.
- Is characterized by *autonomy*—it makes its own decisions regarding entry to the field, training, licensing, and standards. The profession exercises internal control over the quality of services offered and regulates itself.
- Has a *commitment to serving a significant social value.* It is altruistic and service-oriented rather than profit-oriented. Its primary goal is to meet the needs of its clients. Society recognizes a profession as the only group within the community that can perform its specialized functions.
- Has a *code of ethics* that spells out its obligations to society. Because the profession may be the only group that can perform a particular function, it is important for the public to have confidence that the profession will meet its obligations and serve the public good. A code of ethics communicates the unique mission of a field and assures that services will be rendered in accordance with high standards and acceptable moral codes.

The foundations of justice are that no one be harmed, and next that the common weal (well-being) be served.

—Cicero

In early childhood, professionalism is holistic, the sum of all of its parts. "Do no harm" prevails as our underlying value. However, early childhood stands for far more. Our professionalism begins with state licensing standards, proceeds to rigorous accreditation standards, and culminates in the highest standards set by individual programs. At every level, the early childhood leader's code of ethics guides him to make ethical decisions.

Definitions of "Professional" That Embrace Emotional Intelligence

Quality has much to do with holding ourselves to a standard of conduct as we aim to improve everything we do. Professionalism is determined by a set of external but agreed upon universal guidelines for how a group of people will conduct themselves.

How does professionalism and quality, so defined by external objective standards, fit with our understanding of emotional and social intelligence? After all, EQ relies upon an individual's integrity in how she conducts herself and how she interacts with others. Can an objective standard, which can sound dangerously close to a one-sided IQ approach (thinking unencumbered by emotion), embrace and honor EQ's holistic ways?

This question is before us now. As a leader in the early childhood profession, you will significantly impact how professionalism and quality are defined. Standards for quality and professionalism must be "living." When standards are living, they embrace the heart and mind as no longer separate.

Consider the following standard of professionalism and how it explicitly incorporates EQ. In what ways does this standard connect the heart and the mind? How might a director "measure" a staff member's competency in an area such as this?

- *Teacher candidates and candidates for professional roles are knowledgeable, competent, and sensitive in working with diverse populations and in diverse settings. . . .* Diversity is fused with the development of Emotional Intelligence and Professionalism to facilitate sensitive and respectful communication in all settings. (Wright State University College of Education and Human Services, *The Conceptual Framework: Developing the Art and Science of Teaching, http://www.cehs.wright.edu/main/conceptual-framework.php,*2000).

The definition of quality in our profession will continue to evolve as our knowledge base and understanding evolve. Our task may well be to observe, enjoy, and learn more about the butterflies dancing in the meadow, rather than attempt to pin their wings.

✂ Taking a Stand for Quality and Professionalism While under Stress

Quality has many faces. One federal law, the Americans with Disabilities Act (ADA), aims to raise our ethical quality as a nation by requiring equal rights for the disabled. As we saw in Chapter 7, the ADA, as a relatively "young" law, sets a broad standard open to interpretation. Each case that involves an ADA issue furthers our understanding of ethical quality.

Use the cases that follow to apply what you have studied about quality and professional ethics in our field. How would you promote quality and what is your ethical responsibility as you approach the following cases about Bonita, Maryanne, Gracie, and Hugo?

Remember: The ADA does not require employers to hire or continue to employ a person because of his or her disability. The ADA ensures that anyone with a disability is provided what she or he needs to have an equal chance at being hired, promoted, and to perform the job.

Remember: A disability does not justify poor performance. However, employers must make "reasonable accommodations" to enable the disabled employee or applicant to interview for and/or perform the job. The key question, when hiring, is: "Can the applicant perform the functional requirements of the job?" Once an employee is hired, the key question is: "Is the employee performing the functional requirements of the job" and "Have I made reasonable accommodations to help her or him perform her job?"

Remember: Nothing in the ADA condones an employee's violation of a workplace policy or releases that employee from disciplinary processes like progressive discipline. Directors must determine:

1. Does the employee have a disability covered by the ADA?
2. Is the disability the cause of the poor performance?
3. What reasonable accommodations can we make?
4. Have I documented everything?
5. If I discipline this employee, can I show that she or he violated a workplace policy and knew the consequences for her actions?

With these points in mind, consider how you would approach the following case studies.

Case Studies

 # Bonita

Bonita, head of your school-age program and summer camp, confides she is a recovering alcoholic and member of AA. Bonita asks your permission to call her AA sponsor whenever she feels she is "slipping" into old, unhealthy behaviors like isolating herself or blaming others for her problems.

Bonita cannot predict when she will need to call her sponsor. She is clear she cannot work for you if she does not have this "pressure release valve."

1. What are your responsibilities to the program, children, parents, and Bonita?
2. Is Bonita's disease covered by the ADA?
3. If Bonita were still drinking, would she be covered by the ADA?
4. What steps would you take with Bonita?
5. How will your choices affect the quality of your program?

Maryanne

Maryanne's pungent body odor offends everyone. Children whisper "pee-you." Teachers keep their distance or gossip about Maryanne. Parents frown. When teachers complain to you, they say, "I don't want to hurt Maryanne's feelings, so I can't talk with her about this."

1. Name all the issues you see in this case.
2. What opportunity does this situation give you to enhance quality?
3. Might the ADA be involved? If so, how?
4. What steps would you take with teachers who gossip about Maryanne?
5. What do you say to parents and children who are bothered by the body odor?

Gracie

During her initial twelve years with your program, toddler teacher Gracie performed well. This year, however, the quality of Gracie's work has plummeted. Gracie complains she doesn't have patience or energy to complete "all those nitpicky" classroom portfolio tasks. She has started to call in "sick" most Fridays and Mondays. She brushes parents off instead of taking time to answer questions.

Melvin, Gracie's team teacher, is exhausted from attending to all the things Gracie neglects. Today, you found Gracie nodding off during the children's naptime. When you bring these issues to Gracie's attention, she sniffs, "I'm depressed, that's all. What's a few bad months compared to years of giving my heart and soul to the children?"

1. What are your responsibilities to the program, parents, children, yourself, and Gracie?
2. Might Gracie have a disability covered by the ADA?
3. What questions can you ask Gracie?
4. What steps would you take with Melvin?
5. What can you share, if anything, with parents or colleagues who want to know what's going on with Gracie?
6. What action will you take with Gracie?

Hugo

Hugo, recently granted U.S. citizenship after serving in Afghanistan, brings bilingual skills and a wealth of cultural competencies to share from his childhood in Guatemala. Children and families adore Hugo for his creative lesson plans, energetic playfulness, and compassion for anyone in need. Hugo is loyal, hardworking, and punctual.

Hugo appears anxious and disoriented at times. He gets red-faced, gasps for breath, forgets where he is, and panics. Hugo dismisses these incidents as "no big deal." He says his ADD helps him understand how to work with Annie and Angel, children in his class with ADHD. You know war veterans can suffer from posttraumatic stress disorder (PTSD). You are concerned for Hugo's well-being and worried he may neglect the children during one of his "panic attacks," "flashbacks," ADHD moments, or all three.

1. Name the ethical and/or legal issues in this case.
2. What are your responsibilities to everyone involved?
3. What questions can you ask Hugo?
4. If Hugo tells you he doesn't need medical help, what are your options?
5. If quality is your goal, what steps would you take?

Reflection Questions

1. Choose one experience you have had that helped you deepen your understanding of professionalism. What happened? What issues were raised? What choices could have been made? Was the action taken professional? State your definition of professionalism as you came to understand it from this experience. Consider your definition in light of Feeney and Freeman's comments (page 240). Write a paper or create a video with commentary.

2. Do definitions of quality vary from culture to culture? Interview three or more people who share your cultural background by asking questions like "What is quality to you?" and "Can you give me examples of good and bad quality in customer service?" Summarize and assess your findings. Now repeat these interviews with three people whose cultural background differs from your own. Again, summarize and assess your findings. What have you learned about perceptions of quality?

3. Read the case study about Maryanne on page 255. How do you feel about Maryanne, the other teachers, the children, and the parents? Imagine yourself as the director of the program, and as Maryanne's supervisor. To ensure quality, how would you answer the questions posed by the case?

Team Projects

1. As a team of no more than four classmates, ask your professor for a copy of the game "Is it ethical?" (*Teaching the Code of Ethical Responsibility*). Read the instructions and play one round of the game. Now, create four or more additional "situation cards" that represent ethical dilemmas envisioned/experienced by each team member. Using these additional cards, present and play the game with your class in order to raise ethical questions that concern you.

2. Each team member chooses a different profession (law, social work, veterinary medicine, physical therapy, nursing, etc.) to study. Research standards for membership in the profession. Read their code of ethics. Meet again with your team to share and compare what you learned. Select one important section from each professional code of ethics. Share your findings with the class, and lead them in a discussion of what should be in a universal professional code of ethics.

3. With your professor's approval and guidance, prepare to visit and evaluate customer service at a nearby grocery store, restaurant, hotel, or other organization. Using the "stairway to quality," create a checklist of customer service standards and a set of interview questions for customers and employees. Visit the service provider to assess the quality of its customer service. Pay attention to both external and internal customers. Upon returned from your visit, as "external evaluators," share your assessment.

4. Read the case studies on pages 254–255 aloud to each other. Choose two or three cases that interest you the most. Discuss your answers to the questions that follow each study. Use either the NAEYC or NACCP code of ethics as your guide. Write a team report on pointers for problem solving ethical dilemmas.

Bibliography

Americans with Disabilities Law of 1990, United States Public Law 101–336, 104 stat. 327, enacted 1990-07-26.

Bloom, Paula Jorde. 1991. *Blueprint for action: Achieving center based change through staff development*. Lake Forest, IL: New Horizons Press.

Branham, L. 2005. *The 7 hidden reasons employees leave: How to recognize the subtle signs and act before it's too late.* New York: AMACOM.

Bruno, Holly Elissa, and Margaret Leitch Copeland. 2000. Staff retention in childcare using an internal customer service model. *LeadershipQuest* 4(2): 5–7.

Butler, T., and J. Waldroop. 1999. Job sculpting: The art of retraining your best people. *Harvard Business Review* , September–October: 144–151.

Code of ethical conduct & statement of commitment. 2005. Washington, DC: NAEYC.

Deming, W.E. 1986. *Out of the crisis.* Cambridge, MA: Massachusetts Institute of Technology, Center for Advanced Engineering Study.

Feeney, Stephanie, Nancy Freeman, and Eva Moravcik. 1999. *Ethics and the early childhood educator: Using the NAEYC Code.* Washington, DC: NAEYC.

Feeney, Stephanie, Nancy Freeman, and Eva Moravcik. 2000. *Teaching the NAEYC Code of ethical conduct.*Washington, DC: NAEYC.

Hiam, Alexander. 1992. *Closing the quality gap: Lessons from America's leading companies.* Englewood Cliffs, NJ: Prentice Hall, Inc.

Hostetler, K.D., and B.S. Hostetler. 1997. *Ethical judgment in teaching.* Boston: Allyn and Bacon.

Hunt, V. Daniel. 1992. *Quality in America: How to implement a competitive quality program.* New York: Irwin/McGraw-Hill.

Jablonski, Joseph R.1992. *Implementing TQM: Competing in the nineties through total quality management.* 2nd ed. San Francisco, CA: Pfeiffer.

Kipnis, K. 1987. How to discuss ethics with teachers of young children. *Young Children,* 42 (4), PPS 26-30. Washington, DC: NAEYC.

Lencioni, Patrick. 2002. *Five dysfunctions of a team: A leadership fable.* San Francisco, CA: Jossey-Bass.

Martin, Justin. 2007. Do your customers love you? *Fortune Small Business, Extreme Customer Service,* October, pp. 72–82.

McManus, Kevin. 1999. Is quality dead? *IIE Solutions,* July.

Morgan, Gwen. 2008. "Is profession a noun" (draft of paper in progress).

National Association for the Education of Young Children. 2005. *Code of ethical conduct & statement of commitment.* Washington, DC: NAEYC.

Roberts, Harry V., and Bernard F. Sergesketter. 1993. *Quality is personal: A foundation for total quality management.* New York: The Free Press.

Stonehouse, Anne. 1998. *Not just nice ladies.* Castle Hill, New South Wales, Australia: Pademelon.

Strike, K.A., and P.L.Ternasky, eds. 1993. *Ethics for professionals in education: Perspectives for education and practice.* New York: Teachers College Press.

Weiss, Howard J., and Mark E. Gershon. 1989. *Production and operations management.* New York: Allyn and Bacon.

Youngless, Jay. 2000. Total quality misconception. *Quality in Manufacturing,* January.

Web Resources

Total Quality Management Background Information
www.bpir.com
History of Nursing Profession
www.nursingdegreeguide.org/articles/
Malcolm Baldrige TQM Award Criteria
www.tqe.com/baldrige.html

Reforming

Renewing, Refreshing, Dreaming of What Might Be

Leadership Principles to Take with You: Learning to Love the Questions

Learning Goals

As you study this chapter, you can look forward to reaching these learning goals:

1. Clarify what matters most in the study of early childhood leadership.
2. Compare and contrast leadership, management, and administration.
3. Explore new ways of seeing old concepts.
4. Capture leadership principles to take with you.
5. Identify your choices for the future.

It came to me ever so slowly that the best way to know the truth was to know what my inner truth was . . . and trying to share it—not right away—only after I had worked hard at trying to understand it.

—*Fred Rogers*

Be patient toward all that is unresolved in your heart, and learn to love the questions themselves.

—*Rilke*

✕ The Purpose of "Leading on Purpose"

When I wrote this book and thought about you reading the first page, I was clear in my intention: acknowledge and honor the power of emotional and social intelligence in early childhood education leadership. In this book, integrity and loving relationships deserve the same respect that IQ has commanded, if not more. My purpose is to affirm that the profession you have chosen, despite low pay and status, is one of the most important professions on earth. Emotionally intelligent leadership in early childhood is a trust, a calling, as much as it is a career, and more than it is a job.

When you "touch the life of a child, you change the world." As you help another adult bloom and share her gifts, you enrich the world. Every time you accept more of your true self, that perfect imperfectness, you heal the world. Early childhood educational leadership makes the world more welcoming for everyone, one child, one family, and one professional at a time. To make a difference, a leader needs to build trusting, respectful relationships, one person at a time, beginning with herself.

Stop for a moment to ask: What affected me most as I read this textbook? What surprised me? What information will I take away to use in my future? How have I changed my perspective, affirmed my understanding, or both?

From my viewpoint, each chapter has an essential point, or "bottom line." Your professor's perspective or yours may differ. What key point did you take away from each chapter?

. . . Scientists have worshipped the hardware of the brain and the software of the mind; the messy powers of the heart were left to the poets. But cognitive theory could simply not explain the questions we wonder about most: why some people just seem to have a gift for living well; why we like some people virtually on sight and distrust others; why some people remain buoyant in the face of troubles that would sink a less resilient soul. What qualities of the mind or spirit, in short, determine who succeeds?

—**Nancy Gibbs**

Chapter	Bottom Line
1	Know yourself, inside and out
2	Understand how relationships "work"
3	Identify your purpose, direction, and leadership style
4	You have choices about how to make choices
5	Be knowledgeable about your first steps as leader
6	Partner with change: pick your battles
7	Prevent legal and ethical problems
8	Build a team of problem solvers
9	Supervise people in a way that brings out strengths and addresses challenges
10	Be proactive and communicative in budget management
11	Create safe, healthy, inspiring environments
12	Understand how to promote learning
13	Spread the good word about early childhood programs
14	Welcome, learn from, and partner with all families
15	Quality is an ongoing quest
16	Expect the best as a lifelong learner and leader

Reflecting helps you go forth as a leader. Now let's look at the remaining principles, data, and theories to further coalesce your knowledge.

✕ Leader, Manager, or Administrator: What Is a Director?

Make a list of your daily responsibilities and functions. Are you a teacher? A student? Family member? What functions do you serve? What responsibilities must you meet?

Now, draw a circle. Look back at your list. Make a "guess-timate" of the percentage of time each day you devote to each function or responsibility. Divide and fill in the circle like a pie chart, with percentages of time you devote to each piece (function and/or responsibility) of your daily pie. For example, being a student requires what percentage of your time each day? Make that percentage a piece of your pie. (Adapted from Gwen Morgan's college course, "The Human Side of Management: The Early Childhood Organization, at Wheelock College, Boston.)

"Leader" is a term loaded with meaning. Leaders help others envision what cannot be seen. A run-down building, like the spirit of a team, can be revitalized with visionary leadership. A talented teacher with low self-confidence might discover her strengths when a leader acknowledges them. A family, isolated from others by work, language, or unpopular beliefs, can find a welcoming community. A childhood program can spring to life from a leader's dream. Leaders have power to change things.

In many cultures, as with gender expectations, standing out or identifying oneself as a leader is unacceptable. My colleague and friend Marcia Farris designs and holds successful early childhood conferences, studded with substantive workshops and inspiring presenters. Marcia rarely designates a conference, course, or even a workshop "for leaders." Not many early childhood professionals, in Marcia's experience, identify themselves as leaders.

If not leaders, what then are directors? Some authors distinguish leadership in early childhood from management or administration of early childhood. Let's take a look.

Managers are responsible for putting systems in place and making sure those systems, like supervision and budgeting, proceed effectively. A manager's focus is to run a smooth operation in line with established goals. Management differs from leadership in the amount of vision and initiative required. Managers are more responsible for the operation, and less responsible for the creation of the vision. Managers have leeway to make changes mainly in their own area. An educational or curriculum coordinator can make supervision decisions, but rarely budgetary decisions.

Administrators are implementers. An administrator attends to whatever needs to be done. She follows policies, implements procedures, and takes care of nitty-gritty tasks to keep the program on track. Focused on routine duties, administrators rarely have time or feel authorized to make long-term, substantial changes. Someone else sets the vision (the leader) and takes care of putting systems into place (the manager). The administrator orders supplies, deals with complaints, winds weary old clocks, plunges the toilet, and makes sure teachers get paychecks on time.

Leaders step back to get perspective and step up to the challenge of promoting change. Administrators take care of everyday business. Leaders determine the purpose and future of the organization. Dr. Debra Sullivan (2003), in her book *Learning to Lead: Effective Leadership Skills for Teachers of Young Children,* notes that leaders plan, while administrators carry out plans.

What do you think: Is an early childhood director a leader, manager, or administrator?

Directors report they are all of these. Directors want more time to serve as leaders and less time putting out fires. Directors long for time to plan and create new directions. This is the dilemma of early childhood leadership—choosing priorities that are true to your purpose.

When we work "on purpose," we lead. When work takes leaders off purpose, they feel as if they are just performing tasks and doing a job. Interestingly, burnout results from the loss of meaning in our work. How can a director deal effectively with all the demands on her time and still make time for "big picture" changes? Keep your eyes on the prize of what matters to you most, and learn to delegate wisely.

Stephen Covey used a ladder to illustrate the difference between leadership and management in his book *Seven Habits of Highly Effective People*. Management is concerned with getting up a ladder in the most effective and most efficient manner. Leadership is making certain the ladder is on the right wall.

—www.Leadershipjot.com

Leaders "keep their eyes on the prize." Administrators "keep their noses to the grindstone."

Remember this—very little is needed to make a joyful life. It is all in your way of thinking.

—Marcus Aurelius

Delegation, assigning a task to another and letting go of attempting to control the other person's process, requires EQ and social EQ. When a leader identifies her purpose and priorities, she exercises EQ. When she "reads" her staff well, helping them grow as professionals, she identifies who best will handle delegated tasks. Her social EQ is knowledge of staff strengths, motivation, and blind spots. Knowing what, when, and to whom to delegate is part of the art of leadership. Remember what Jeree Pawl said, "I've been doing supervision for 40 years and I am just beginning to get the hang of it."

Striving to be emotionally and socially intelligent as a leader: is that enough? Being a lifelong learner: will that attitude carry leaders through the times when they know little or nothing about a new subject?

⚔ New Ways of Seeing Old Things

Debating the Worth of Emotional and Social Intelligence

The study of emotional and social EQ sets off passionate reactions, both pro and con.

Some critics argue that EQ is unsubstantiated by rigorous scientific analysis and little more than cotton candy. They question the existence and/or value of emotional intelligence. Daniel Goleman's work, in particular, has come under criticism. Psychologist Hans Eysenck lambastes Goleman's theories in this way (2000, 109):

> [Goleman] exemplifies more clearly than most the fundamental absurdity of the tendency to class almost any type of behavior as an "intelligence" . . . the whole theory is built on quicksand; there is no sound scientific basis.

A growing body of scientific research, however, shows support in favor of EQ theory (Cherniss et al. 2006; Viadero 2007). The data shows a strong link between EQ and real-world success, for both children in the classroom and adults in the workplace. The most successful individuals aren't solo performers with a high IQ and internal drive—rather, they are team builders who stay calm under pressure and know how to get along with others. Neuroscientific studies also are exploring the neural differences between EQ and IQ behaviors and the dynamic relationship between the brain and social interaction.

As you read both support and criticism for Goleman's theory, how does it affect your view of EQ and social EQ? You will have ample opportunities as an early childhood professional to hear and participate in this ongoing debate.

Throughout this book, we have noted the leadership dilemma of holding two opposite beliefs, often-warring theories, one in each hand. You might feel, as you attempt this, that you are holding two yowling cats back from fisticuffs. On the one hand, EQ is invaluable. On the other hand, EQ is an unscientific fraud. Any new theory, fairly enough, will come under scrutiny and possible attack. Remember the percentage of individuals who welcome change?

I propose we consider both IQ and EQ as a "both . . . and" rather than an "either . . . or." Both definitions of intelligence have their merit and their place. One does not have to exclude the other. At times, a leader needs to exercise the "letter of the law" (impersonal, objective, and intellectually critical) approach to decision making. At other times, leaders need to use the "spirit of the law" in managing through relationships, accepting and working through all the unspoken, synaptic (neuron to neuron), and emotional communication modes available.

The early childhood profession works hard to earn respect. It documents, assesses, codifies, analyzes, and otherwise applies traditional "hard" scientific approaches to the field. The latest version (2006) of NAEYC accreditation standards exemplifies that desire to professionalize beyond reproach. Hard data is persuasive. Rigorous, rational

What if we paid attention to this Native American Indian proverb? "Treat the earth well. It was not given to you by your parents; it was loaned to you by your children."

Neuroscience is afraid of consciousness, so we study the brain like it's a computer. But there's no computer like this, everything is emotional.

—Don Katz

approaches earn respect. "Soft" or nonscientific approaches remain suspect. Perhaps we could take the best from both approaches, rather than use one to negate the other.

Rediscovering Traditional Ways of Communicating EQ Principles

Because emotional and social intelligence has been considered soft rather than hard scientific knowledge, EQ has flourished more outside the university than within the walls of ivy. EQ and social EQ have been the heart of ethnic leadership wisdom for centuries. When we want to "get to the heart" of a matter, we often turn to Native American elders.

Examples of this are plentiful. Black Elk knew, "Grown men can learn from very little children, for the hearts of the little children are pure. Therefore, the Great Spirit may show to them many things which older people miss." Crazy Horse spelled out this core leadership principle: "A very great vision is needed and the man who has it must follow it as the eagle seeks the deepest blue of the sky." Chief Seattle forewarned, "All things share the same breath—the beast, the tree, the man, the air shares its spirit with all the life it supports."

EQ wisdom is passed down from our elders and soothsayers (truth tellers) by oral tradition, poetry, fables, parable, and song, more than through academic textbooks. If you can sing or recite your favorite song lyrics or poem, you invoke that wisdom. "Beauty is truth, and truth, beauty. That is all ye know on earth and all ye need to know," wrote John Keats (*Ode to a Grecian Urn*, 1819). Quotations, sprinkled throughout this text, summarize in a few lyrical words the heart of emotional and social EQ.

Recall the message of your favorite children's book. What "life lessons" does that book pass on to children?

Children's book authors create in the realm of EQ and social EQ. *The Velveteen Rabbit* (1922), tattered and aged, is still heartachingly lovable. On Miss Tizzy's block (1993), everyone matters, and every one looks out for the other. *And Tango Makes Three* (2005) reminds us that love makes a family. *Where the Wild Things Are* (1988) comforts us with the message that we all have a wild side and the wild side is nothing to fear. *I Love You Stinky Face* (2003) lets a child know she will always be loved, no matter what.

"Soft" knowledge can carry us through our hardest times. We remember what touches our heart. Facts can fade, meaning remains.

Wisdom gives rise to courage. Courage gives rise to compassion. Compassion gives rise to wisdom.

—Daisaku Ikeda

Mistakes are the portals of discovery.

—James Joyce

Nonverbal, Nonneural, or Both?

Naming something for the first time changes the way we see things. To consider EQ and social EQ, we need to examine assumptions. Consider the well-established term "nonverbal." Think of what nonverbal indicates: the multitude of ways we communicate without words. Now, consider a new term: "neural." Neural or "synaptic" indicates all the ways our neurons constantly communicate before that communication turns into words.

The majority of our communication is through neural connection (65 to 90 percent), rather than verbal connection. Our most used form of communication is labeled by what it is not (nonverbal) rather than what it is (neural). What if we chisel our terminology more accurately before we "write it in stone"? The term nonverbal is, in some ways, backwards.

To be accurate, we communicate neurally and "nonneurally." Neural communication, not verbal communication, serves as our first language. We respond neurally in a split second. Since neural communication is the standard communication, other forms of communication should be described accordingly. The term "nonverbal" is not expansive enough to describe all the neural forms of communication. Nonverbal conveys what is lacking in neural communication. Neural conveys the enormity of what takes place.

Words, rich as they can be, are nonneural communication. Words are the best-known nonneural mode of communication. Words matter most when they spark synaptic connections. Otherwise, words "fall on deaf ears." To follow suit, words can be termed nonneural, or verbal communication.

This difference may sound like semantics—just more words. However, when we accurately name something, that naming communicates meaning. The next time you hear the term "nonverbal" consider the more accurate term, "neural." Changing the terms we use is like any other change: resistance is inevitable. Nonetheless, changing the way we look at things opens us to the future.

> People are like stained glass windows. They sparkle and shine when the sun is out, but when the darkness sets in, their true beauty is revealed only from the light that is within.
>
> —Elizabeth Kubler-Ross

⚹ Leadership Principles to Take with You

Make a list of the traits you feel a good leader needs to have. Which of these traits reflect your areas of strength? Which of these traits would you like to develop in yourself?

Good Boss versus Bad Boss

In light of the list you just made, see what you think of the list in Table 16.1. Effective leaders differ from ineffective leaders in these ways (Goleman 2006, 277):

TABLE 16.1

Good Boss versus Bad Boss

Good Boss	Bad Boss
Great listener	Blank wall
Encourager	Doubter
Communicator	Secretive
Courageous	Intimidating
Sense of humor	Bad temper
Shows empathy	Self-centered
Decisive	Indecisive
Takes responsibility	Blames
Humble	Arrogant
Shares authority	Mistrusts

The "good boss" list describes traits of an effective relational leader. The "bad boss" list describes a person who cannot yet bring self-knowledge or empathy into relationships. Consider the good boss traits as leadership principles.

Additional leadership principles are highlighted throughout the remainder of this chapter.

Becoming the Good Boss

Tell the Truth Lovingly

Researcher and author Antonio Damasio (1995) notes that joy, or freedom from stress and worry, opens us to learn more. Joyousness, optimism, enthusiasm are all neurological "maximal harmonious states" according to Damasio. Another researcher, L.G. Aspinal

> It doesn't hurt to be optimistic. You can always cry later.
>
> —Lucimar Santos de Lima

(1998), finds that when we are confident and upbeat, we are more able to seek out and take in information, even if the information is difficult to hear.

These principles readily apply to the leader as supervisor. Goleman notes (2006, 277): "If leaders establish such trust and safety, then when they give tough feedback, the person receiving it not only stays more open but sees benefit in getting even hard-to-take information." Much of leadership is helping others see. Telling the truth lovingly creates trust and safety for change.

Lead with Integrity

"Walking the talk," not asking others to do what you wouldn't do, and living on purpose all evidence integrity. A good boss leads with integrity. Much of what a "good (early childhood) boss" does is help others find their gifts, while outgrowing their weak points. Shaming, blaming, and threatening are ineffective. Leveling with others, by leveling with yourself first, allows you to exercise your integrity. The difference will be felt and appreciated.

Let's compare the good boss–bad boss characteristics with recent research findings (DeLong, Gabarro, & Lees 2008) on characteristics of leader as mentor. An outstanding mentor:

- *Is someone absolutely credible whose integrity transcends* the message, be it positive or negative.
- *Tells you things you may not want to hear* but leaves you feeling you have been heard.
- *Interacts with you* in a way that makes you want to become better.
- *Makes you feel secure* enough to take risks.
- *Gives you the confidence* to rise above your inner doubts and fears.
- *Supports your attempts to set stretch goals* for yourself.
- *Presents opportunities and highlights challenges* you might not have seen on your own.

Harvard Business Review (2008, 118) researchers found employees "are almost hardwired to smell the faintest trace of negative feedback." Neurons of even the thickest-skinned employees quiver from the message: "You are not getting it right."

However we slice the definition, a good leader inspires, confronts, and supports others respectfully. For the leader to be good, she does all these things in the context of relationships. Otherwise, the tree falls silently in the forest.

⚔ Leadership for the 21st Century

Seeing into the future is both impossible and magical. We cannot know what happens in the next moment, let alone the next year or decade. This doesn't stop us from imagining. Envisioning the way we want to grow as leaders clears the way to our unseeable future. What follows are both leadership principles and findings on how leadership for the 21st century is envisioned.

Build Partnerships for Growth

As I researched views on leadership for the 21st century, I found an emphasis on influencing change through respectful relationships. Rost (1991), for example, in *Leadership for the Twenty-First Century*, defines leadership as "an influence relationship among leaders and followers who intend real changes that reflect their mutual purposes" (102). To Rost, the importance of relationships and ethics has been greatly overlooked. Along with influencing through dynamic relationships, Rost foresees adaptability and self-awareness as leadership tools for this century.

The person who has never made a mistake will never make anything else.

—George Bernard Shaw

Be True to Your Core Values

Harvard Business Review (vol. 86, no. 1) is devoted to "Leadership and Strategy in the Twenty-first Century." Author Rosabeth Moss Kanter (2008, 45), in "Transforming Giants: What Kind of Company Makes the World a Better Place?" offers this insight:

> Values turn out to be the key ingredient in the most vibrant and successful of today's multinationals. I refer not to the printing of wallet cards but to the serious nurturing of values in hearts and minds. Once people agree on what they respect and aspire to, they can make decisions independently and not work at cross-purposes. When they team up on a project, they communicate and collaborate efficiently, even despite great differences in backgrounds and cultural traditions, because they have a strong sense of business purpose and company identity.

Agreed upon core values, according to Kanter, bring us together when our cultural backgrounds differ.

Foster Multicultural Communities

Kanter's observation is powerful. Leaders need insight and foresight to foster thriving multicultural organizations. Early childhood education programs need to invite and welcome a world of differences. Our effort as leaders begins within: "What are my blind spots? My biases? How do I need to grow?" As a leader grows, so grows her program. Early childhood leaders were asked: "How do you envision leadership in early childhood care and education in 2015?" ("Leaders on Leadership" 2005, 20–21)

How do you suppose these leaders responded? What would you say if you were interviewed?

Almost every leader interviewed talked without reservation about global perspective and local activism. "Leaders will require knowledge of myriad cultures and even the ability to speak another language or two," advises Scott Seigfried from Ohio. Luis Hernandez in Miami foresees that "leaders will know about various populations, languages, cultures. . . . and have broad view of the world." Davida McDonland, Washington, DC, envisions leadership in 2015 as "representative, diverse, inclusive, innovative, forward thinking, from the bottom up, not from the top down."

Be as Curious as a Child

Hearing from people outside of early childhood on learning from children is refreshing. According to engineer Paul Polak (2008, 32–35), whose dream is to end poverty by supporting struggling farmers across the world: "There is a simple and direct curiosity in childhood and a love of play that we tend to miss badly in our approach to problem-solving as adults. If you think like a child, you can quickly strip a problem down to its basic elements." Mr. Polak shares his experience of being curious as a child when taking on the challenge of designing a cost-effective industrial oven for a rural community:

> In 1996 I was in Cachoeira, an Amazon rain-forest village, trying to figure out how rubber-tappers could dry Brazil nuts at the village gathering point so they could increase their income. We had to design a village drier to replace the large industrial driers of big-city plants. When we walked through the villages, I saw that every second house had a *forno de farinha,* a two-foot high baked-clay surface with an eight-by-ten stovetop used to dry manioc flour. When I saw all these ovens . . . I realized each of them could become a Brazil nut drier. We just needed to think like children instead of engineers. (2008, 32)

Definition of stress: When your gut says "No way" and your mouth says "Sure, I'd be glad to do that."

—**Sue Baldwin**

How wonderful that nobody need wait a single moment before starting to improve the world.

—**Anne Frank**

The person who pursues revenge digs graves.

—Proverb

Instead of importing, at great expense and effort, large industrial Brazil nut driers, Polak and his local team built a drier from scratch in less than 2 hours. This "beginner's mind," the curiosity of a child, is a powerful leadership tool.

Take Care of You

Happiness may be "a by-product of an effort to make someone else happy" (Gretta Booker Palmer). Altruism, selflessly battling the world's problems while helping others, is admirable. As we discussed in Chapter 6, "Partnering with Change," directors who prevent burnout from overextension take care of themselves first. Self-care is a hard practice to learn.

"Caregivers syndrome," becoming ill from overextension, is a danger for early childhood professionals. Working 12-hour days, taking work home, and trying to "fix" other people and their problems can become habits of self-destruction. Directors need to look guilt squarely in the face and say, "Back off! I am taking time just for me." This act of boundary setting, although awkward for many of us, is essential to restoring our energy.

Let Go

The gods laugh most when people pray for perfection.

—Japanese proverb

My goal is to show my adult children that no matter what my age might be, I can always find ways and time to laugh and have fun with life. Humor is a great coping skill.

—Sue Baldwin

The other essential dynamic of self-care is learning to "let go" of worry, self-doubt, and beating yourself up for not being perfect. Choose your battles and let go of the others. Manage your energies. Thinking you can be all things to all people is a deadly myth. If you believe this myth, you hurt yourself. Lead "on purpose," take a stand for what you believe in, and let go of thinking you can "make" anyone else change. Let your actions speak for themselves.

The serenity prayer is a director's trusted friend. The one person on earth you can change is yourself. Let go of what you cannot change, other people. Wisdom and self-respect are the gifts you receive in return for letting go. This works especially with holding onto a resentment or worry. Let it go.

Ask for Help

Directors' support groups can be havens of sanity and humor. There's nothing like hearing that another director has dealt with the same problem you are facing to help you keep perspective. "I don't feel alone!" directors happily tell me once they join or establish a directors' group.

Change takes time: *Researchers have found that new neurons continue to mature for six to eight weeks after they are first generated and that the new neurons receive input from higher brain regions for up to 10 days before they can make any outputs. The other brain regions then continue to provide information to the new neurons as they integrate into existing networks.*

Back on page 93, I invited you to complete a chart with the names of people in your support system. If you were to revisit that chart today, would you change anything? Have you met someone while taking this course to add to your list? Have you removed a "high maintenance" person who was draining and not replenishing your energy?

Every time my confidence flagged as I wrote this book, I asked for help, from a friend, family member, or my spiritual source. You don't have to be religious to have a spiritual source. Spirituality is the belief that there's more to life than what we see on the surface. Every leader has access to her own deeper source of inspiration and comfort.

Find, Use, and Love Your Sense of Humor

Do you, like me, know you are in trouble when you lose your sense of humor? You may have heard about author Norman Cousins (1979) who believes he healed himself from cancer through laughter. Belly laugh after belly laugh rolled out of him, as he watched the

Marx Brothers' slapstick antics on film. Yoga, the meditation practice of breathing and stretching our bodies and spirits, includes a "laughing meditation." Laughing meditation is just that: laughing, even if nothing is funny. I was skeptical about this practice. "It's not funny and I feel silly," I protested. Silly me. I "ha-ha-ha'd" my way into an upbeat place, where I once again found the humor in things. Laughter is a way of getting to the truth.

Your Choices from Here: Learn to Love the Questions

You and I need to say good-bye. Our course is about to end. I am going to miss you. I wrote this book with you in mind and in heart. I appreciate your choice to be an early childhood professional.

As a "recovering attorney," who realized later in life how valuable the early childhood profession is, I mean what I say. Early childhood education enriches children's lives and uplifts their families. As an early childhood educator, you have an impact beyond what you ever imagined. When little ones grow up and seek you out to thank you, you will know what I mean. Perhaps you already do.

Remember the TQM (total quality management) principle of "continuous improvement"? Are you feeling ready for your next step? No one I know has all the answers. Learn to love the questions, especially the questions that challenge you most deeply. They'll keep you on your purpose.

Please take this gift with you: Fulfilling, happy, and honest relationships are the heart of growth and learning. You can choose how you relate to everyone, including yourself. Choose kindness.

Hope is the thing
with feathers
that perches in the soul
and sings the tune without words
and never stops—at all.

—Emily Dickinson

Celebrate "the beauty and allure of imperfection: the cozy familiarity of a worn-out pair of jeans, the rustic elegance of an old Italian villa, the faded splendor of well-used china handed down from your grandmother's attic."

—Taro Gold

Reflection Questions

1. Without leafing back through this textbook, reflect on and write about what you most remember learning. Jot down what you recall. Next, reflect on these questions: What do you feel will stay with you? What will be useful? What might you have liked to hear more about? What was not included that you would have liked to have had covered? When you have finished writing your reflection, open the book. Is there anything else you might want to add to your reflection? If so, add that.
2. Your instructor has offered lectures, facilitated discussions, and organized other classroom learning experiences. Select three of these learning experiences that were most helpful to you. Write a description and/or prepare a video with commentary on what you learned from these.
3. The title of this chapter, "Learning to Love the Questions," is taken from Rilke, who said: "Be patient toward all that is unresolved in your heart, and learn to love the questions themselves" (1993, 35). What does this quote mean to you? What are the unresolved questions you feel you could "learn to love," particularly about your future as an early childhood professional? Which of the leadership principles that you take with you might help you the most with these questions?

Team Projects

1. As individuals, revisit your response to the "Exercise Your EQ" exercise on page 267 when you were asked to answer the question: "How do you envision leadership in early childhood education by 2015?" Next, share your answers as individuals with your teammates. Discuss together what changes you expect will take place and what the greatest challenges will be. In particular, how do you think the eventual demographic shift, from a majority Anglo country to a majority people of color nation, will affect and be affected by changes in our field? Research other professionals' predictions on these questions. Lead a class discussion on these questions and your findings.

2. Throughout this chapter, "leadership principles to take with you" are highlighted. As individuals, make your own list of leadership principles. Compare this with your core values that you developed as you studied Chapter 3. With your team, share your core values and leadership principles. Together, create core values and leadership principles for our profession. Translate the important points of your discussion into a PowerPoint or video presentation for your class.

3. Discuss this: "Because emotional and social intelligence has been seen as 'soft' rather than 'hard' scientific knowledge, EQ has flourished more outside the university than within the walls of ivy. EQ and social EQ have been the heart of ethnic leadership wisdom for centuries. When we want to get to the heart' of a matter, we often turn to Native American elders." As students, what have you noticed about whether EQ, social EQ, and IQ are valued in university courses? Have the insights of people of color and ethnic groups been included or emphasized in your studies? As individuals, investigate and select a group of individuals whose insights have not been adequately incorporated into academic courses. Share the wisdom of this person or group with your teammates and next with your entire class. Lead a discussion with classmates.

Bibliography

Aspinal, L.G. 1998. Rethinking the role of positive affect in self-regulation. *Motivation and Emotion* 22: 1–32.

Baker, B. 2008. How tastes turn into feelings. *Boston Globe,* March 24: C2.

Cherniss, C., M. Extein, D. Goleman, and R.P. Weissberg. 2006. Emotional intelligence: What does the research really indicate? *Educational Psychologist* 41 (4): 239–245.

Cousins, N. 1979. *Anatomy of an illness as perceived by the patient.* New York: W.W. Norton. & Company, Inc.

Covey, S. 1990. *Seven habits of highly effective people.* New York: Free Press.

Damasio, A. 1995. *Descartes' error.* New York: Perennial.

DeLong, T, J.J. Gabarro, and R.J. Lees. 2008. Why mentoring matters in a hypercompetitive world. *Harvard Business Review* (January): 115–121.

Eysenck, H. 2000. *Intelligence: A new look.* Piscataway, NJ: Transaction Publishers.

Gold, T. 2004. *Living Wabi Sabi: The true beauty of your life.* Kansas City: Andrews McMeel Publishing.

Goleman, D. 2006. *Social intelligence: The new science of human relationships.* New York: Bantam Dell.

Kanter, Rosabeth Moss. 2008. Transforming giants: What kind of company makes the world a better place? *Harvard Business Review* 86(1): 45.

Leaders on leadership. 2005. *Young Children,* January, 20–21.

Lencioni, P. 2002. *The five dysfunctions of a team: A leadership fable.* San Francisco, CA: Jossey-Bass.

Polak, P. 2008. Twelve steps to practical problem solving. *Worldark: Ending hunger saving the earth.* Heifer International (March–April).

Rilke, R.M. 1993. *Letters to a young poet.* Translated by M.D. Herter Norton. New York: W.W. Norton.

Rost, J.C. 1991. *Leadership for the twenty-first century.* New York: Praeger.

Sullivan, D.R. 2003. *Learning to lead: Effective leadership skills for teachers of young children.* St. Paul, MN: Redleaf Press.

Viadero, D. 2007. Social-skills programs found to yield gains in academic subjects. *Education Week* 27 (16): 1, 15.

Wen, P. 2008. Culture gap: American doctors learning about immigrant ills. *Boston Globe.* March 24.

Bibliography of Children's Literature

Gray, L.M. 1993. *Miss TIZZY.* New York: Aladdin Paperbacks.

McCort, L., and C. Moore. 2004. 1997. *I love you stinky face.* New York: Scholastic.

Richardson, J., and P. Parnell, 2005. *And tango makes three.* New York: Simon and Schuster Books for Young Readers.

Sendak, M. 1988. *Where the wild things are.* New York: Harper Collins.

Williams, M. 1922. *The velveteen rabbit.* New York: Avon Press.

Web Resources

Caregiver Syndrome
http://www.revolutionhealth.com/blogs/michaelrabowmd/caregiver-syndrome-6572

Caregiver Syndrome: Definition, Symptoms, and Tips
http://www.squidoo.com/caregiver-syndrome

Critical Review of Daniel Goleman
http://eqi.org/gole.htm

Discussions on Leadership Topics
http://www.Leadershipjot.com

The EQ Factor: New Brain Research
http://www.time.com/time/classroom/psych/unit5_article1.html

Leadership for the 21st Century
http://www.joe.org/joe/1994june/tt3.html

New Brain Cells Listen before They Talk
http://www.eurekalert.org/pub_releases/2007-10/yu-nbc103007.php

Appendix A

Marketing Tips from http://www.wccip.org/tips.html
Wisconsin Childcare Improvement Project

Definitions

Marketing

The sum total of efforts to attract customers and the long-range plan to keep them.

External Marketing

Signs, media ads, news releases, posters, brochures, and other printed materials.

Internal Marketing

Cultivating word-of-mouth recommendations.
Retaining current customers by satisfying their needs.

Customers

People who purchase goods or services.

No marketing plan fits all childcare programs. Each program will need to develop its own mix of marketing techniques. The average consumer needs to see or hear about a product or service three times before they respond to it, so it is a good idea to use a variety of external marketing techniques to ensure the community's attention.

First impressions are very important. The first 60 seconds of contact may win you a new customer or drive one away. Over 90 percent of parents rely on recommendations from relatives, friends, and coworkers, so pleasing your current families is essential to long-term stability. A happy customer will tell three or four others; a dissatisfied customer will tell ten.

The following lists will help you consider the elements to include in developing your program's marketing plan.

Marketing

Initial Phone Contact
- Have phone located in an area with a minimum of noise.
- Answer promptly, three rings or less.

- Use an answering machine with a friendly message.
- Check for messages regularly.
- Return calls promptly.
- Maintain a phone log of inquirers.
- Follow up inquiries.

Initial Visit

- The visit begins outside; pay attention to the building's exterior and the entryway.
- Are outdoor play areas clean and appropriately staffed?
- Locate office where you can see visitors entering.
- What do parents hear when they enter?
- What do parents smell?
- What do parents see?

Greeting Parents and Children

- Greeting begins with your appearance.
- Welcome the child by bending down to eye level.
- Use visitors' names several times during the conversation.
- Listen to visitors' questions.
- On a tour, describe typical activities and point out signs of quality:

    High level of staff training.
    Accreditation certificate.
    Absence of serious noncompliance notice beside license.

- Sell your program:

    A photo album of past events.
    Collection of past newsletters.
    Letters of testimonial from other parents.

- Get information from the visitors:

    Name.
    Address.
    Phone number.
    Child's birth date.
    Schedule needed.

- Follow up with a thank-you note immediately, and a phone call later.

External Marketing

Advertising will be a significant part of your marketing plan and budget. Advertising costs can range from free to very expensive.

Child Care Resource and Referral (CCR&Rs) *www.wisconsinccrr.org*

- Serve all areas of the state: maintain databases on *all* regulated childcare in their region.
- At no cost to childcare providers, parents contacting CCR&Rs receive a list of all regulated childcare programs that meet their needs.

Printed Materials

- Business cards.
- Outdoor signs.
- Newspaper advertising.
- Imprinted T-shirts, caps, totes, and the like.
- Brochures.
- Posters/flyers.

News Media

- Radio.
- Television.
- News releases:

    Hiring of a new director or teacher.
    Staff attendance at a national seminar.
    Announcement of a new site or service.
    Special activities, unusual field trips.
    Free health screening offered at center.

Special Events

- Participate in local parades.
- Maintain a booth at a community fair.
- Volunteer for a local fund-raising marathon.

Other Marketing Ideas

- Invite elected officials to visit.
- Invite news media.
- Public speaking:

    Civic.
    Church groups.
    High school classes.

- Display children's art in the community.
- Offer your space for classes such as Lamaze, La Leche, or parenting classes.
- Partner with technical schools and other training programs.

Internal Marketing

Word-of-mouth recommendation is a powerful vehicle for attracting new clients.

Stimulating Word-of-Mouth Recommendations

- Welcome parents at all times.
- Value parents' opinions.
- Invite feedback.
- Respond positively to suggestions.
- Reward parents who recruit new families.
- Include parents in activities and field trips.
- Invite parents to lunch.
- Display photos of children at play.

- Have evening family events.
- Involve staff by helping them:

    Value parents as customers.
    Understand the importance of parent partnerships.

- Hold parent conferences regularly.
- Be sensitive to diverse family structures.
- Develop an "alumni" mailing list:

    Send an annual newsletter.
    Invite to special celebrations.

Final Words on Marketing

A successful business has as marketing plan:

    What can be done now?
    What can be done in the next six months?
    Plan for next year, for five years from now, and beyond.

Keep attuned to trends and future projections:

- CCR&R surveys of supply versus demand.
- Census Bureau data.
- School district projections based on birth rates and demographics.

Plan proactively rather than reactively for the years ahead.

Source: WCCIP • 2109 S. Stoughton Road, Madison WI 53716 • **Ph** 800.366.3556 • **Fx** 608.224.6178

These tip sheets were developed by WCCIP, March 1998, with funding from the WI Dept. of WFD, Office of Child Care, and DHFS.

Appendix B
Glossary of Budget Terms

actual expense budget   Keeps a running tab of what you pay out and take in each month, as compared to what you predicted in the projected budget.

cash flow analysis   A process you can use to find out how much money you have on hand.

cash reserve   A fund you can use on "rainy days," especially when your cash flow is weak.

depreciation   The anticipated loss of an asset's value over time.

expenses   What you pay out, for example, salaries, insurance, supplies, fees, consultant and trainer costs.

fees   Additional costs for parents, including registration, co-pay, special supplies, and special event fees.

fiscal year   The year as measured by your program's budget, usually July 1–June 30.

garnishing   Takes a percentage "off the top" of someone's income to pay unpaid bills directly to the program.

in arrears   Past due amounts; unpaid bills.

in the black   The program is making enough money to pay all its bills.

in the red   The program does not have enough income to meet its expenditures.

job sharing   Two teachers work at complementary times to do the work of one teacher.

line item   The term given to each item that needs consideration in the budget such as personnel, utilities, and supplies.

liquidity   Like cash flow, being "liquid" means you have monies on hand to use when you need them.

Medicaid   Employers are required to pay into employees' fund for future medical care.

net income   The total earned after expenditures are taken out.

one time expense   Like paying the fee for a marriage certificate, you hope you only have to pay this once.

payroll   The actual costs of salaries, including your own.

P&L   Nickname (acronym) for profits and losses report.

projected budget   Your prediction about upcoming costs over a period of time.

revenue   Incoming money usually from parent fees, childcare subsidy, and grants.

reconciliation   Process of checking your prediction on will be earned and spent against what was actually earned and spent. Reconciling is making adjustments in incoming and outgoing resources.

sliding scale   Adjustments in the amount you charge, based on a family's income or based on the number of children the family and/or teacher enrolls.

Social Security   Employers contribute to each staff member's Social Security funds, maintained by the federal government.

spending down   A phrase used to describe the process of paying out the monthly/regular expenses in a timely way. A board member may ask about your "spend down" this month.

taxes   The percentage of income the federal, state, and local government charge to provide their services.

viable   Operating "in the black" as opposed to in debt.

worker's compensation   A system regulated in state law that issues payments and provides medical care to employees who are injured or disabled during the course of their employment, regardless of fault.

Appendix C
Books and Articles That Explore Culturally Diverse Roots of Early Childhood Practices

Akbar, Na'im. *The Community of Self.* Tallahassee, FL: Mind Productions, 1985.

Allen, Paula Gunn. *Off the Reservation.* Boston: Beacon Press,1998.

Banks, James A. *Cultural Diversity and Education.* Boston, MA: Allyn and Bacon, 2001.

Bernhard, Judith K., Marlinda Freire, Fidelia Torres, and Suparna Nirdosh. "Latin Americans in a Canadian Primary School: Perspectives of Parents, Teachers, and Children on Cultural Identity and Academic Achievement." *Canadian Journal of Regional Science* (Spring, Summer, 1997): 217–237.

Bernheimer, Susan. *New Possibilities for Early Childhood Education. Stories from Our Nontraditional Students.* New York: Peter Lang, 2003.

Brody, Hugh. *The Other Side of Eden: Hunters, Farmers, and the Shaping of the World.* New York: North Point Press, 2001.

Bronfenbrenner, U. *The Ecology of Human Development: Experiments by Nature and Design.* Cambridge, MA: Harvard University Press, 2005.

Bruno, Holly Elissa. "Hearing Parents in Every Language: An Invitation to ECE Professionals." *Child Care Information Exchange,* #153 (September/October 2003): 58–60.

Cajete, Gregory. *Look to the Mountain: An Ecology of Indigenous Education.* Durango, CO: Kivaki Press, 1994.

Child Care Health Program. *Serving Biracial and Multiethnic Children and Their Families.* Berkeley, California: The Child Care Health Program, 2003.

Cleary L.M., and T. D. Peacock. *Collected Wisdom: American Indian Education.* Needham Heights MA: Allyn and Bacon, 1998.

Coll, Cynthia Garcia, Gontran Lamberty, Renee Jenkins, Harriet Pipes McAdoo, Keith Crnic, Barbara Wasik, Hanna Garcia, and Heidie Vazquez. "An Integrative Model for the Study of Developmental Competencies in Minority Children." *Child Development,* 67 (1996): 1891–1914.

Cooper, R., and E. Jones. "Enjoying Diversity." *Exchange* (October 2005): 6–9.

David, J., O. Onchonga, R. Drew, R. Grass, R. Stechuk, and M. S. Burns. "Head Start Embraces Language Diversity." *Young Children,* 60(6) (2005): 40–43.

Day, M., and R. Pariakian. *How Culture Shapes Social-Emotional Development: Implications for Practice in Infant-Family Programs.* Washington DC: Zero to Three, 2004.

DeLoache, Judy, and Alma Gottlieb. *A World of Babies: Imagined Childcare Guides for Seven Societies.* New York: Cambridge University Press, 2000.

Deloria, V., Jr., and D. R. Wildcat. *Power and Place: Indian Education in America.* Golden, CO: Fulcrum Resources, 2001.

Delpit, Lisa. *Other People's Children: Cultural Conflict in the Classroom.* New York: The New Press, 1995.

Delpit, Lisa, and Joanne Kilgour Dowdy, eds. *The Skin That We Speak.* New York: The New Press, 2002.

Eggers-Pierola, C. *Connections and Commitments: Reflecting Latino Values in Early Childhood Programs.* Portsmouth, NH: Heinemann, 2005.

Fadiman, Anne. *The Spirit Catches You and You Fall Down: A Hmong Child, Her American Doctors, and the Collision of Two Cultures.* New York: Noonday Press, 1997.

Fernea, Elizabeth Warnock. *Children in the Muslim Middle East.* Austin: University of Texas Press, 1995.

Garcia, Eugene, Barry McLaughlin, Bernard Spodek, and Olivia N. Saracho. *Meeting the Challenge of Linguistic and Cultural Diversity in Early Childhood Education.* New York: Teachers College Press, 1995.

Gonzalez, Doris. *Hablemos de Ninos.* Caguas, Puerto Rico: Impresos Taino, 2001.

Gonzalez-Mena, J. *Diversity in Early Care and Education: Honoring Differences.* New York: McGraw-Hill, 2004.

Greenfield, P. M., B. Quiroz, and C. Raeff. "Cross-cultural conflict and harmony in the social construction of the child." In *New Directions for Child and Adolescent Development,* S. Harkness, C. Raeff, and C. M. Super, eds. San Francisco: Jossey-Bass, 2000, pp. 93–108.

Grieshaber, Susan, and Gaile S. Cannella. *Embracing Identities in Early Childhood Education: Diversity and Possibilities.* New York: Teachers College Press, 2001.

Hale, Janice E. *Black Children: Their Roots, Culture and Learning Styles.* Baltimore, MD: Johns Hopkins University Press, 1986.

Hooks, Bell. *Rock My Soul, Black People and Self-Esteem.* New York: Atria, 2003.

Hsu, Francis L. K. *Americans and Chinese: Purpose and Fulfillment in Great Civilizations.* Garden City, NY: Natural History Press,1970.

Johnson, David, and Roger Johnson. "Cultural Diversity and Cooperative Learning." In *Cooperative Learning and Strategies for Inclusion,* 2nd ed., J. W. Putname, ed. Baltimore. Brookes, 1998.

Kagiticibasi, Cigdem. *Family and Human Development across Cultures.* Mahwah, NJ: Erlbaum, 1996.

Kawagley, A. Oscar. *A Yupiaz Worldview: A Pathway to Ecology and Spirit.* Prospect Heights, IL: Waveland, 1995.

Lee, Joann, *Asian Americans.* New Press, 1992.

LeVine, Robert A., Sarah LeVine, P. Herbert Leiderman, T. Berry Brazelton, Suzanne Dixon, Amy Richan, and Constant H. Keefer. *Child Care and Culture: Lessons from Africa.* Cambridge University Press,1994.

Lewis, C. C. *Educating Hearts and Minds: Reflections on Japanese Preschool and Elementary Education.* New York: Cambridge University Press, 1995.

Nee-Benham, Maenette Kape ahiokalani Padeken Ah and Joanne Elizabeth Cooper, eds. *Indigenous Educational Models for Contemporary Practice: In Our Mother's Voice.* Mahway, NJ: Erlbaum, 2000.

Neihardt, John G. *Black Elk Speaks.* New York: Pocket Books,1972.

Nsamenang, A. B. *Human Development in Cultural Context: A Third World Perspective.* Newbury Park, CA: Sage, 1992.

Payne, Ruby K. *A Framework for Understanding Poverty.* Highland TX: Aha! Process, Inc., 2003.

Pence, Alan R. "Reconceptualizing ECCD in the Majority World: One Minority World Perspective," *International Journal of Early Childhood* 30.2 (1998): 19–30.

Rael, Joseph. *Being and Vibration.* Tulsa, OK: Council Oak Books, 1993.

Ramsey, P. G. *Teaching and Learning in a Diverse World,* 3rd ed. New York: Teachers College Press, 2004.

Rogoff, B. *The Cultural Nature of Human Development.* Oxford and New York: Oxford University Press, 2003.

Ross, Allen C. (Ehanamani). *Mitakuye Oyasin: We Are All Related.* Denver: Wichoni Waste, 1989.

Siraj-Blatchford, Iram, and Priscilla Clarke. *Supporting Identity, Diversity and Language in the Early Years.* Philadelphia: Open University Press, 2000.

Some, Sobonfu. *The Spirit of Intimacy: Ancient African Teachings in the Ways of Relationships.* New York: HarperCollins/Quill, 2000.

Soto, Lourdes Diaz. *Language, Culture, and Power: Bilingual Families and the Struggle for Quality Education.* New York: State College of New York Press, 1997.

Tan, A. L. *Chinese American Children and Families: A Guide for Educators and Service Providers.* Otney, MD: Association for Childhood Education International, 2004.

Tedla, Elleni. *Sankofa: African Thought and Education.* New York: Peter Lang, 1995.

Valdes, Guadalupe. *Con Respeto: Bridging the Distances between Culturally Diverse Families and Schools.* New York: Teachers College Press, 1996.

Wolpert, E. *Start Seeing Diversity: The Basic Guide to an Anti-Bias Classroom.* St. Paul, MN: Redleaf Press, 2005.

Zepeda, M., J. Gonzalez-Mena, C. Rothstein-Fisch and E. Trumbell. *Bridging Cultures in Early Care and Education.* Mahwah, NJ: Erlbaum, 2006.

Index